CLASH OF EAGLES

CLASH OF EAGLES

American Bomber Crews and the *Luftwaffe 1942–1945*

Martin W. Bowman

Pen & Sword
AVIATION

First published in
Great Britain in 2006
by Pen & Sword Aviation
an imprint of Pen & Sword Books Ltd
47 Church Street, Barnsley
South Yorkshire, S70 2AS

ISBN 978-1-84415-413-5

Typeset by Concept, Huddersfield, West Yorkshire

Pen & Sword Books Ltd incorporates the Imprints of Pen
& Sword Aviation, Pen & Sword Maritime, Pen & Sword
Military, Wharncliffe Local History, Pen & Sword Select,
Pen & Sword Military Classics and Leo Cooper.

Contents

Laughter in the crew room
'Chutes upon the floor,
Coffee in the tankards
Hail against the door,
Telling of the hazards
That faced the bomber boys,
Searchlights feebly waving
Like phantom children's toys,
Scorning thoughts of peril
Within the hornet's nest,
Then turning like tired eagles
When coming home to rest,
Faced the common danger
A grim, determined band,
Messengers of freedom
O'er every conquered land.

'Grey Dawn', Robert S. Nielsen

Prologue

The station is dark and silent at 0105 on this June morning. A chill wind ruffles the grass, an old moon hangs low over a neighbouring wood and high in the clouded sky a nightfighter drones by on patrol. The plane guards wait watchfully within the monolithic shadows of the bombers. A wandering jeep cruises the perimeter track behind two pale blue spots of light. In Hangar 1 a night crew is changing an engine on Rain of Terror. *At the motor pool the truck crews, alerted, doze fitfully. In the station headquarters building, behind the gasproof doors, the windowless offices which house the Message Centre and the Operations Room are quiet but bright with light. In the Message Centre a sergeant and a PFC are talking shop, in Operations the Watch Officer is reading a book, and, down the hall, the Intelligence Duty Officer is writing a letter home.*

Target Germany, 1944

The Bombing Mission, by George Rubin, 486th Bomb Group

The Quonset hut is dark and cold. The two stoves, one at each end, have gone out. They need more coal or discarded bomb casings to start them up. Suddenly a light appears in the doorway of the hut. It is the Sergeant at Arms with a flashlight. He moves quickly from bed to bed, shining the light in our eyes. Splude, Jessen, Brown, Manfred, Rubin – 'Get up, rise and shine, the mission is on for today'. My watch says 4 am. I get up feeling groggy and put on my long johns over my regular underwear, woollen socks, shirt and pants and then my flying suit over all of this. I tie up the laces of my GI shoes and put on my green lined flight jacket. It is cold and windy as I step out into the night, carrying my towel and toilet kit and walk slowly over to the latrine and the water closet. Other crewmembers are already there. There is very little conversation. I make do with a fast wash up and maybe a shave. Not too close or your face will be irritated by the oxygen mask. Then back to the Quonset to get a scarf and a knit cap to wear.

It's cold and clear as I walk the quarter mile or so to the mess hall wondering where the bombing mission is going today. I enter into a long well lit and warm building filled with airmen getting their breakfast or eating it. It's hard to feel hungry. Partly it's due to the hour and also the nervous gut feeling about the mission. There is very little conversation at the table. Just drink your coffee and pick at the food. Then it's back out into the dark and the cold night. A grey light has started to fill the sky in the east. It's another long walk to the flight lockers.

I open my locker and take off my flight jacket and flying suit and put on an electrically heated suit, another pair of socks and electrically heated flying boots. I put the flight suit on over all of this and then the flight jacket goes back on. I put my electrically heated gloves in my jacket pocket and my flying helmet is either put on or carried. I mustn't forget the oxygen mask and

Polaroid flying goggles. My GI shoes I sling over a shoulder and I put on a pair of warm gloves and a scarf. My wallet and other identification I leave in the locker. I hope that if I don't return, these items will find their way home to my parents. Next door I sign out for my parachute and escape packet consisting of a compass, map, German money and phrasebook and a .45 calibre pistol.

Then it's a short walk to the briefing room: a long Quonset with rows of chairs and a covered map at one end. There is some banter by the crewmembers – unfunny jokes about what target is under the curtain, a story about the last mission and who was it who couldn't hold his breakfast down over the target or had to take a shit on the bomb run. Then a sudden call of 'Attention!' The briefing officer appears and the curtain over the map is pulled back. There are groans and curses and 'Not back there again?' There is your target. Long coloured strings show the route to and from the target, altitude, bomb load, ETA, areas of intense flak and where you can expect fighter interception and how many groups are involved in the mission. I have a sick feeling when I look at the strings going deep into Germany. This will be a long mission. There are very few questions.

We are dismissed from the briefing and leave now for the hardstand and our plane. Some walk, others bike, or ride over in a jeep. The sky is now light as dawn approaches. I arrive at *Oh! Miss Agnes*. The ground crew is at work loading the bombs. Today it will be twelve 500 lb demolition bombs. I check with the ground crew about the A-4 bomb shackles and inspect all the .50 calibre machine-guns – two in the tail, two in the waist, two in the ball turret, two in the top turret, two in the nose turret and one in the nose. All are in place and so is the ammo. I walk around the plane, silver and shiny as the sun hits it with its yellow strips over the waist and the wings and the big black square 'W' on the tail. I swing on board through the waist door hatch and deposit my parachute near the left waist gun. This is a safe place. Then I begin my pre-flight check. Oxygen-pressure full on the dial. The dial next to it shows the little lips moving up and down – oxygen is coming out. I check the emergency bottles and the large oxygen tank on top of the ball turret. They are full. I connect the intercom; I check that I can hear and that the throat mike is transmitting my voice. I check that the guns and the ammo clips are in place. Outside again the sun is up now and with the other crewmembers' help the ground crew pull the props through the usual nine times to clear out the cylinders. I take a last look around the field and re-enter through waist hatch. I watch as the rest of the crew comes aboard.

Manfred the tail gunner enters the waist and crawls back to his position. He will spend the next 6 to 7 hours on his knees. Brown goes into the radio shack area just forward of the waist and begins to check all his equipment. Splude sits down near me, with not much to do until we are airborne. Jessen goes up front behind the pilot and co-pilot seats, where he checks out his turret, all the instruments and the fuel and oil pressure. The navigator, bombardier, pilot and co-pilot swing aboard through the front hatch. Each has done a pre-flight check of their equipment and the entire plane. I sit in the waist. It is a time of tense quiet. The spell is broken by the whine of the No. 3 engine starting up.

Wiley has given the command, 'Clear. Contact!' Outside, a member of the ground crew stands next to the engine with his fire extinguisher. The prop rotates slowly, then the engine catches. Smoke comes out of the exhaust and the engine is running. This is followed by engine 4, then 1 and 2. All four are running smoothly. The pilot releases the brakes and we move off the hardstand and line up behind other planes in the squadron. Soon all thirty-six aircraft, plus a few spares, are lined up along the taxiways. We wait for the green flare from the control tower to signal that the mission is 'on' or the red flare that means the mission is 'scrubbed'.

The green flare goes off overhead. One by one we move up to take off. Brakes squealing, engines revving up and dying down. Wiley and Demerath finish their pre-flight check. We are now lined up for take-off. The green lantern blinks on the runway in front of the plane. The engines rev up, the entire aircraft shudders, the brakes are released and slowly at first we roll forward then pick up speed – 50, 60, 75, 95, 110. Slowly we rise, and the wheels come up. Great Waldingfield disappears below us. Jessen comes back to lock and check the tailwheel. We are in the clouds now. The plane bucks and I feel as if I'm on a roller coaster as the plane rises and suddenly falls. I hold on and chew away on my juicy fruit gum, hoping we are soon out of this and scared that we may hit another aircraft or crash land. We are caught in the prop wash of the planes in front of us. I hold on tight and suddenly as it started it stops and now smoothly we continue to climb to 'Nightdress', the first radio marker. We come out of the clouds into bright sunlight and begin to assemble on the lead aircraft of our squadron.

We continue to climb, circling to the next radio marker and group assembly. Above the clouds now, the group slowly forms: high squadron and lead, middle, low and the tail-end squadron. We are at 10,000 feet and the pilot tells us to go on oxygen. I check my oxygen mask and watch the little lips on the flow indicator move up and down as I breathe in the oxygen. I check the plug connection to my electric suit and turn up the rheostat to 'high', as the cold in the plane becomes more intense. The group meets the rest of the wing and over 800 aircraft head for the English coast. The long white streams of contrails from each plane fill the blue clear sky. Over the Channel the pilot checks in on the intercom and tells all positions to check guns and test-fire. I check the waist guns. Twice I charge the .50 calibre gun and fire out into space, watching the tracer bullet (every fifth shell) light up the blue sky. It's good to fire the guns. It's something I know a lot about and it gives me a sense of control during the mission. With the guns I can protect myself and the rest of the crew. I lock them in place and check the heating plate over the top of the gun, a new device that helps prevent jamming in cold temperature. It will probably be about −40 or −50 below zero soon.

The French coast appears below. It's time for Splude to enter the ball turret. I help him open the ball hatch and watch as he climbs in, and plugs in his oxygen and heated suit. I close and lock the hatch. The whine of the ball motor starts up as he checks all the different positions of his turret and then he test-fires his guns. I check in with him on the intercom. I will do this from now on for the rest of the mission.

The pilot tells us we are over Germany. Watch out now for fighters. Our 'Little Friends' protection of P-51s will soon peel off and leave us. The first flak appears off our wing: small black puffs that seem to follow us along. Soon the entire sky is filled with flak. I can hear it and feel it as the plane rises and falls due to the explosions. They sound like pebbles hitting the plane. I lay out my flak jackets on the floor as protection and also use them to cover my parachute. The group tries evasive action and I open the floor hatch and begin to throw out the chaff (small strips of tin foil that are supposed to give German radar the wrong signal and direction). The flak seems to get heavier and closer. There is a hit in the right wing behind No. 3 engine, then above my head near the door. There is nothing you can do about the flak but feel scared and alone. The waist of the B-17 can seem like a very lonely place, with the flak all around you and radio silence, so you can't yell, scream or shout out your fear to anyone. I just chew harder on my chewing gum.

Wiley tells us that we are now on the IP (Initial Point) of the bomb run. I go into the bomb bay and arm the 500 lb bomb by removing the Carter pins from the nose fuse and the tail propellers. I check each A-4 shackle to see that it's set for automatic release. In the waist again I put back the emergency oxygen bottle that I used in the bomb bay and hook up again to my oxygen and my suit rheostat. I squeeze my oxygen mask to break up any ice that has formed from condensation. Wiley hands the plane over to the bombardier. We are on the bomb run. The bomb doors open and as the bombs release, Brown in the radio shack announces that all the bombs are 'away'. He can see them from his position. I have set up the K-12 camera to take pictures of the bomb strikes. It is too overcast to get very good shots but I snap away. Having something to do eases the tension.

The plane takes a leap upward as the bombs let go. The bomb bay doors close and we make a sharp left turn and gain altitude as we start our trip home. The lead group reports, 'Bandits at 3 o'clock!' I get my guns ready. The ball turret and the upper turret also search the sky. I put my Polaroid glasses on to check out each of the waist windows. Flak begins again. We are bouncing all over the sky. There is too much going on to be scared. I would love to shoot the .50 calibre waist guns and feel that I was doing something – anything. There is so much fear and loneliness of being a sitting duck to flak and fighters.

Soon the alert for enemy fighters is called off and the flak gradually stops. We are back over Belgium and down to 10,000 feet. I take my oxygen mask off and use the relief tube for the first time. I do not like to use it at altitude, as the urine stream freezes into ice particles. I sit down for the first time in the last 4 hours. The intercom is busy with talk and how each position is doing. I help Splude out of the ball and go forward to stand behind Wiley and Demarath. Wiley has his headset over one ear. The other is red from hours of wearing it. Demarath is doing the flying. It is a time to relax. I take out my chewing gum and press it into the armour plate around my waist gun. It sits there lined up with all the others from each bombing mission. Cookies are passed around. Maurides and Stiftinger leave the nose, stretch out in the waist and chat with

Brown in the radio room. The intercom is turned to music from home. Ann Shelton and Vera Lynn singing and the Glenn Miller band.

We are over the Channel – you can see the cliffs of Dover and then Great Waldingfield. We peel off and slowly circle with wheels down. Some of those ahead of us in the landing pattern with wounded aboard send out red flares. Jessen goes back to lock the tail wheel. We touch down, brakes squeal and slowly we taxi back to our hardstand. I open the waist hatch and pile out with all my equipment. You feel a little wobbly; maybe for the hours confined in the plane or all that oxygen you have been breathing. It is 1530 hours.

The armament ground crew arrives with their truck and we dismantle all the machine-guns. The bomb bay is opened and we check all the releases. The guns go back to the shop for cleaning for the next mission, the spent cases in the waist are policed up and then it's off to the debriefing hut. Intelligence officers ask me a set series of questions. I'm asked what I saw, what damage we had, what other aircraft I saw hit or go down. After a half-hour of this it's outside again. The Red Cross gals are offering me a shot of whiskey and peanut butter sandwiches. Try it sometimes, whiskey and peanut butter on an empty stomach. Back to the lockers. I turn in my parachute and hang up my flying clothes. Then it's bike, walk or jeep back to our Quonset hut to fall into bed, too tired to think or eat or anything. Later, I will get up and check the bulletin board to see if our crew is alerted for a flight tomorrow.

Then it's time for dinner. I walk to the mess hall with Brown or Splude. It's 1800 and the sun is still high in the sky as we are on double daylight saving time. The sun will not go down until at least 2300. After dinner it's over to the NCO club to listen to some good jazz on the piano or take in a post movie. Then it's back to my bunk to put on the radio and begin a letter home. What can I write that won't be censored? 'I went on another mission today.' How can I describe my feelings? I'm tired, but the fatigue is entwined with fear and knowing that tomorrow or maybe the day after I will go through this same ritual. Each time the odds against coming home get higher and higher. Lately I have gone more often to the post hospital to visit wounded gunners from other crews. I have seen beds left empty when a crew does not return and then watched as the personal effects are removed. Will this be me next? No wonder I never make up my bed when we go out on mission. To make it means you are not coming back. I have recently been reading some of the psalms in the bible I was given when I arrived at the base, especially Psalm 139 – 'If I take the wings of the morning ...'

I wonder when this will end.

CHAPTER 1

Castles in the Air

These lines are dedicated to a man
I met in Glasgow, an American.
He was an Army officer, not old,
In the late twenties. If the truth were told
A great deal younger then he thought he was
I mention this ironically because,
After we'd had a drink or two, he said
Something so naive, so foolish, that I fled.
This was December, Nineteen Forty Two.
He said: 'We're here to win the war for you.'

Lines to An American Officer by Noël Coward

'Our arrival in Great Britain' wrote Robert S. Arbib Jr,[1] 'was marked by one of the most ignominious moments in what my friends refer to sarcastically as my Army career. It found me kneeling in the middle of a main street in Glasgow, trying to salvage the scattered contents of seven cartons of cigarettes, which were strewn in the path of the on-marching battalion. This chaotic predicament was witnessed by every member of the battalion; each had a comment as he passed. It was the source of much wonder and a certain amount of gentle raillery by the casual bystanders who had come to welcome and applaud us as we marched, the New Saviours of Mankind, from our transport. I ruined the show.

But this catastrophe was near the end of that memorable day which had found us at dawn off the Irish coast, heading down though the bright calm of the sheltered Irish Sea to Scotland. It was the 17th day of August 1942 and our ship, the *Monterey*, was a component of the largest troop convoy thus far to be transported overseas. Some 4,000 of us – unhappy, eager and excited were packed aboard this vessel which had been designed as a pleasure cruise ship for seven hundred passengers. If there had been 4,000 possible ports of debarkation, there would have been that many convictions on board as to our destination.

'I'll bet it's the tropics,' said Tommy Williams, who was surer about most things than many of us. 'They gave us yellow-fever shots, didn't they? They gave us mosquito nets and head-nets too. It's the West Coast of Africa, sure as Sin!'

But as day followed day and the weather remained stormy and cool and it was obvious in spite of our zig-zag course that we were headed generally north-east, we remembered that we were carrying all our winter equipment too – our mackinaws, overshoes, woollen clothing, heavy woollen socks. 'It's Greenland or Iceland,' ventured Tom Stinson, who would have taken his transit and level rods to Hell if the Army had ordered him there.

'Or Russia or Ireland mebbe,' added Shorty Weathers, who would have followed Tom to Hell if Tom had been ordered to survey the place for an army camp.

'I still say England,' I argued, displaying a tattered clipping from the *New York Times*, saying that 150 aerodromes for the American Air Forces were urgently needed in England and would be built by American soldiers. 'Airfields in England. That's us.' For once I was right. That was us all right – airfields in England.

It was fine to have calm seas and sunshine again and land far off on both horizons, after our twelve anxious days on the sub-infested North Atlantic. It was better yet when two silver fighters dived down from the blue and welcomed us with exuberant sportiveness. 'Spitfires!' we all shouted, for that was the only English airplane we knew by name. We came to know that graceful whistling little aeroplane quite well later and all the other British aircraft too – and those first to greet us that morning were Spitfires after all.

By then the marathon poker and dice games had ended and we had bolted our last meal in the steamy dining hall and heard the soldier-waiters urging us on for the last time with their shouts of 'Get it down now and look at it later!' We crowded the rails, looking with wonder at the strange shore as we drew nearer. Each new landmark, each more-clearly discernible point of interest drew its attention and comment. It wasn't the ice-bound coast of Greenland or the bleak rock of Iceland; it was the incredibly green and trim landscape of Scotland – the Firth of Clyde.

Ed Higinbothom and I had sneaked up unnoticed to the sun deck 'Strictly Reserved for Officers' and were standing by the rail, fascinated and bemused. The *Monterey* wound its slow way up the Clyde, past Ailsa Craig with its white frosting of gannets, past the big harbour of Gourock and then Greenock and into the narrower waters of the river that runs into the very heart of Glasgow. Everything was new, every detail was noteworthy. We were in a war zone at last! We stared at our first barrage balloons, moored to barges in the river. We saw a freighter with a gaping torpedo hole at the waterline. We noted little camouflaged naval craft and one large aircraft carrier moored in Gourock harbour.

'Looks nice,' said Ed, echoing my thoughts as we looked at the grey stone houses, the neat hedges and at the green and brown hills above.

'Seems quiet, almost empty,' I added, searching for some signs of life on the shore. Now and then a red tramcar would run along the road following the river but there were no automobiles, no people walking along the riverbank. Little trains whizzed up and down the tracks along the river, their engines hitched on backwards.

'Just like the British,' said Ed, who was a proud Maryland Irishman. 'Always doing everything hind-end-to.' 'Tiny little trains aren't they?' I answered. We walked from one side of the deck to the other, looking for new sights, absorbing hungrily what we saw – trying to peer ahead into our unknown future here and the new life that we would be leading in this strange land. We looked for traces of war and discussed the evidence of bomb damage that lay all around us. But we hadn't heard that Glasgow had ever been bombed and we were not certain that the occasional open space between buildings or gutted buildings were signs of the blitz. We soon discovered that they were indeed bomb damage but we needed further verification for this first encounter. We noticed that all the factories and workshops, chimneys and water-tanks were camouflaged in dirty shades of green paint. But the camouflage seemed old and neglected, as if it had been hastily applied during the early days of the war and then had been found useless.

As the river narrowed we moved between the great shipyards for which Glasgow was famous to us. There were many ships and landing craft there, in all stages of construction but where were the swarms of workers we expected to see? We wondered where everyone was. There was some noise and activity but the excited clamour and bustle of the waterfront was missing. It was a quiet, peaceful summer day. Whistles blew from some of the workshops as we passed and a few workers ran out to wave. Many were women and we noticed that they were somewhat grimy and muscular. They were more workers than women, in their slacks and sweaters and overalls. They seemed sincerely glad to greet us.

It was mid-afternoon when we finally made fast to our dock and we hung over the rails and out of portholes to talk with the men on the quay. British soldiers stood below and joined in the sport of jumping for apples, oranges and cigarettes that we tossed down. We didn't know that these would be the last oranges we would see for more than a year.

We were in good spirits now and we looked at the British soldiers curiously. Strange uniforms ... strange caps ... strange shoes. For a time we were silent, for we did not know what to say to them.

'Where are we?' someone called.

'Glazzga,' answered a native.

'How are the women?' someone shouted tentatively.

The soldier smiled. 'Yew'll soon find oot,' he returned, in a voice that had been dragged through a bed of thistle.

'When does the next boat sail for America?' shouted Johnny Ludwig.

'Canna taell ye thot,' replied the Scottie. 'Bu' ah can taell ye thus ... yew'll no' be on ut!'

American ground echelons en route for Great Britain came by sea across the sea lanes of the North Atlantic, which were infested with German U-boats that could and often did, sink ships of every description. Troop ships were not immune. Men like Arbib and his buddies were destined to help build airfields in East Anglia, which in 1942 was a battlefront. The RAF in the UK used over 1,000 airfields alone, so it is with some justification that Britain was referred to as 'a vast aircraft carrier anchored off the north-west coast of Europe'. East Anglia had a great preponderance of these airfields, many of which had been built during the 1930s expansion period for use by RAF Bomber, Fighter and Coastal Command squadrons in time of war. With America's entry into the conflict after the Japanese attack on Pearl Harbor on 7 December 1941 and Germany's declaration of war on the United States, some stations in once peaceful countryside were earmarked for 8th Bomber Command. Bases like Podington and Thurleigh in Bedfordshire and Molesworth, 10 miles west of Huntingdon and Grafton Underwood in Northamptonshire, would all become American bomber bases. There were transitional problems to overcome of course. Bassingbourn near Royston, Cambridgeshire, became the second home to the 91st Bomb Group who were at first based at Kimbolton, where the runways, built for fighter planes during the Battle of Britain, soon broke up under the weight of the Flying Forts. More airfields were needed for the 8th Air Force so the Air Ministry and American Engineer battalions cut a swathe through the furrowed fields of Norfolk, Suffolk and Cambridgeshire, leaving in their wake bases destined for use by bomb wings and fighter groups. At first the USAAF had only seventy-five airfields in the UK but the total eventually reached 250, costing £645 million, £40 million of which was found by the American Government. By the end of the Second World War 360,000 acres of land had been occupied by airfields and a staggering 160 million square yards of concrete and tarmac had been laid down.

In March 1942 General Ira C. Eaker, a square-jawed, tough-looking but soft-speaking Texan, finally established his headquarters in the three-storey, bomb-proof underground Daws Hill Lodge building at Wycombe Abbey on the green flanks of the rolling Buckinghamshire Chilterns, 30 miles west of London. Before the war the old white-stoned building among linden trees on a landscaped knoll just 1.5 miles south of the town of High Wycombe had been a school for girls. When Eaker had chosen 'Pinetree' to plan the future of his embryonic and untried bombing force, some of the bedrooms still displayed a prim little card that said, 'Ring twice for mistress'. Now, khaki-clad American women were assigned positions as secretaries, filing clerks and communications operators. The teletype room would soon clatter to the sound of daily mission field orders being sent out to units, while the telephone switchboard would become the largest hook-up in England. WAACs were also trained to receive the results of interrogation from operational groups and develop reconnaissance photos of strikes made on bombed targets in dark rooms. At first, Eaker had met opposition to his plans to take over the Abbey complex, which was only 4 miles from RAF Bomber Command Headquarters and could house 400 personnel, but the British authorities had finally relented. The British, notably Winston Churchill, also eventually came to accept the American method of bombing by day, and it would grow into a formidable 'round the clock' bombing strategy that would contribute decisively to the defeat of Germany. Churchill knew that without America's vast manpower resources and industrial might Germany could never be defeated and he welcomed American particiaption from the outset. American troops had begun arriving in war-weary Britain in the months immediately after Pearl Harbor.

The GIs, as they were known because of their own derisive term of 'Government Issue', created a culture shock, blazed a colourful chapter in British history and shared a close attachment with the inhabitants that only wartime can create. Young American bomber and fighter crews made a particular impact in the parochial parishes and towns in rural East Anglia that is still remembered today. They had well-cut uniforms, new accents and money, glamour and a devil-may-care attitude, which came from knowing that every day might be their last. The civilians were all involved in the war effort – as shipyard workers, Red Cross and Land Army, farmers and firemen. Above all, they were stubborn, determined fighters who had already endured three years of war. Into these lives came the sights and sounds – particularly the jargon – of the 'Yanks', as they were universally known. They came from the big cities and the backwoods, up state and down town, from California to Connecticut, the Deep South to Dixie – Delaware to Dakota – Frisco to Florida, Mid-West to Maine – the mighty Mississip' to Missouri – New York, New England, Ohio and Hawaii, the Pacific, Philly and the Rockies to the Rio Grande – from Texas to Tallahassee – Wyoming, Wisconsin, the Windy City and way beyond.

Walking around in the blackout was a new experience. Most Americans found England's fog and rain very hard to get used to. It was often very damp and seldom did one see the sun. Blackouts made it difficult to navigate at night with no lights. Money was always a problem. The GIs were paid much more than their British counterparts, but they had difficulty understanding English 'funny money'. There was 4 dollars to the pound conversion, then 20 shillings to the pound. So there were about 20 cents to a shilling, $2.00 to a half-crown. Beyond that, few could understand the language. 2 and 6? Two and six what? Thrupp'ny bit? Hay penny? Florin? It might as well have been a foreign language. 'How were we to feel about being invaded by thousands of brash, flashy young men [with] too much money to spend?' said one publican's daughter. 'They wanted to take over everything and everybody ... too friendly, too quick ....'

East Anglia was well endowed with historic old inns. GIs liked the public houses and many grew to become impressed with the seemingly timelessness of everything. The train rides to London enabled them to view the quaint beauty of the small towns and rural countryside of England. To many, the deep-green hedgerows, rolling fields and slow-flowing streams of East Anglia were scenes out of eighteenth century pastoral paintings. The music hall joke was that Yanks were 'Over fed, overpaid, oversexed and over here'. Some believed that the 'Four Overs' were justified in many cases. Many Americans had entered the service just out of school or college. They had never had a paying job before. Suddenly, they became better fed and better paid than ever before. Moral restraints from the American family, church and friends disappeared and 'everything' seemed to be available for the buying, asking or taking. Boasting seemed to be a popular pastime. They believed that America really was what was depicted in movies and the magazines. At least, that was

5

what most teenage girls and young women generally believed. In their well-cut greens and pinks (uniforms) they seemed like movie stars and the average GI usually had money to spend on chocolates, flowers and stockings, or even a silk parachute, which could be used to make underwear. American airmen were very generous. They had things English kids didn't because everything was rationed. They gave them ice cream, peanut butter and chewing gum. A child's often favourite question was, 'Any gum chum?' The response was often, 'Got a sister Mister?'

One English 'kid' who became involved in a friendly banter as to the role of the RAF, was told that only the Americans dared to fly in combat during the day and that the British only operated under the cover of darkness.

We retaliated by saying that the B-17s and B-24s couldn't even fly at night – that they could get lost over Britain even in daylight. Also that our Lancasters carried 15,000 lb of bombs in comparison to the 5,000 lb of the B-17 and B-24. These friendly arguments were usually replaced with references to pub-crawls, drinking, gambling and English girls, but not necessarily in that order. If, as a very young teenager, I was not aware of the facts of life, I became very much aware by mixing with guys who gave the impression they were all Romeos and Clark Gables, or so at least they thought. This is all part of how we saw the average American GI.

Home comforts were important to aircrewmen whose lives were measured in weeks rather than months. At 0300 hours on a chilly morning it does not seem like a good time to get up. Each officer and enlisted man faced the black morning in his own way as the pilots, navigators, bombardiers and gunners got into their flying outfits. No two men dressed alike, but normally it was heavy underwear first, then bright blue electrically heated 'zoot suits' of flannel, OD trousers or fleece-lined leather leggings and a sheepskin jacket, heated gloves and boots, Mae West and helmet. The flyers had problems with their heated suits; there were plenty of malfunctions and bad frostbite. Cold was often the number one enemy in the air and on the ground. Those lucky enough to be billeted at pre-war built ex-RAF stations lived the high life compared with those on the wartime bases, where living conditions were often described as 'rugged'. The Class A type airfield consisted of three intersecting runways, with the main runway aligned to the prevailing wind, being 2,000 yards long and the other two 1,400 yards long. Each runway was standardised at 50 yards wide and a 50 feet wide perimeter track or taxiway encircled the runway and joined the end of each. Branching off the taxiways were fifty hardstands and dispersal points for the bombers. The type of hangar varied but the T2, a rectangular, steel-framed 240 foot long building, 39 feet high and 120 feet span, clad with corrugated steel sheet and with sliding doors at each end, was the most numerous. The total number of personnel on a base was approximately 2,500 men. Passing vehicles showered the men with mud as they walked and cycled from their Nissens to the mess halls and briefing rooms before take-off. In winter, interminable rain and fog so thick you had to cut it before you could walk made life unbearable.

Bill Ong, an American Army engineer involved in building airfields in England, recalls, 'Training in the sunshine of Texas is one thing. Building airfields in the desert was easy – in East Anglia it was sure something else . . .. We weren't really popular with the local population. They didn't take kindly to us Americans moving in and tearing up their countryside. I tell you, what with the weather, the cold, the mud – well, fighting the Germans would have been child's play compared to all this. But we didn't blame the people for feeling the way they did. They knew that we were there to ruin their land and when we had ruined it would then fly hundreds of aeroplanes from this base and low over their homes. The land that we were building on had been requisitioned by the British Air Ministry and the Government had promised the owners that as soon as the war was over the land would be returned to agricultural use. Hogwash! We knew it would take years to reconstitute the land after the war, if it could ever be rescued properly at all. But that wasn't our problem.'

In 1942 most of the bases proved something of a disappointment. Barracks required strenuous cleaning, sanitary facilities were poor and not all living sites had bathhouses. Food upon arrival and for about a month following was a monotonous diet of mutton, potatoes and Brussels Sprouts. Romantics like John S. Sloan looked to the England of his schoolbooks, of King Arthur and Robin Hood and Cromwell and saw it as the beginning of a great adventure', adding 'morale was buoyed up by an excitement that neither mud nor minor discomforts could dispel.'[2]

In June 1942 a new three-star general, Dwight D. Eisenhower, an advocate of air power, was appointed as the US Army's European Theatre commander in place of Major General Chaney. That same month, Major General Carl 'Tooey' Spaatz, 8th Air Force commander, arrived in England from Washington. He moved into 'Widewing', his headquarters at Bushy Park, in the suburbs 15 miles south-west of London at Teddington. Spaatz told gathered newsmen that his intention was to bomb Germany by day. However, Eaker could call upon only a few B-17 Flying Fortress and B-24 Liberator bomb groups when the USAAF fully entered the fray in Europe. Eaker was used to meeting a challenge. When on 18 January 1942 he had been summoned by General Henry H. 'Hap' Arnold, Air Force Chief of Staff, and told that he was to organise the 8th Bomber Command in England, Eaker had been taken aback. When he reminded Arnold that he had been in fighters all his life, Arnold had replied, 'That's why I chose you. I want you to put the fighter spirit in our bomber force.'

German day-fighters now had to drive the heavily armed and armoured American bombers from the skies by co-ordination of fighter formations and closed formation attacks and flak. Flak, an acronym of the guttural German words *Flieger Abwehr Kannon*, or anti-aircraft guns, became equally as feared as the fighters. At the target there was no escape from the barrage. Crews had to endure a nerve-racking 60 seconds when the whole sky was stained with smoke and millions of shards of exploding steel fragments that could rip through a thinly skinned fuselage with impunity. A navigator who watched a

Liberator hit by flak start to burn and fall out of formation described the monstrous explosion as the plane literally disappeared before his eyes.

The motors were torn from the wing and went tumbling through the sky with the props windmilling as they fell. The wings and tail were torn to shreds. As the pieces of aluminium drifted and twisted while they fell with each turn the sun was reflected off their surface back into his eyes like they were mirrors. It was like watching a thousand suns turn on and off in rapid random fashion. The most spectacular sight was the gas tanks, which had been torn from the wings. They did not explode their gasoline but rather it burned in huge orange flames streaming out behind the tanks as they fell in a wavy fashion towards the earth below.

The box barrage, as it was called, was shaped exactly like an oblong shoe box, or a coffin, and the bombers had to plough through it, their speed cut as they flew into the head wind. Bomber crews were not trained to take evasive action to make themselves hard to hit. They had to fly straight to give the bombardier the 40 seconds necessary to fly the bomber on the Automatic Flight Control Equipment (AFCE) then aim and release his deadly cargo. With the bombs away, the pilot once more could take evasive action that might make the difference between life and death to the ten men in the crew. Crewmen who became jumpy and nervy were termed 'flak-happy'. As early as December 1942, evidence of mental stress, ranging from simple flying fatigue to serious psychological disorders, began to appear in some of the units.

At the end of June the first American heavy bombardment Group (the 97th) was on its way – by air. Three B-17s were forced down on a Greenland icecap. One of the crews managed to survive by cutting off the blades of one twisted propeller with a hacksaw, then using that engine to furnish heat for the plane and power for the radio generator, until a Navy flying boat, landing under extraordinarily hazardous conditions, rescued them. The other crews were also saved, one from a small island and the other from the sea. Two other Fortresses, caught by bad weather off Greenland, were forced down. Again, both crews were rescued. By early August the Group had been joined by the 92nd and the 301st in England. Ground Echelons came by sea across the sea lanes of the North Atlantic, which were infested with German U-boats that could, and often did, sink ships of every description. Troop ships were not immune.

Of the three new groups only the 97th, commanded by Colonel Frank A. Armstrong Jr, a cool, tough, no-nonsense North Carolinian who had been the only regular officer in Eaker's original contingent of nineteen staff officers, was considered operational. At the end of July Eaker asked him to take over command from Colonel Cornelius Cousland, who was sacked for running a 'lackadaisical, loose-jointed, fun-loving, badly trained (especially in formation flying) outfit', which was 'in no sense ready for combat'. Armstrong's West Point training, his erect bearing and wind-tanned face – for the last fourteen of his thirty-nine years most of his time had been spent in the cockpits of military aircraft – commanded the respect of those who served with him. He had worked closely with his RAF counterparts during the early, formative days at High Wycombe. With the help of officers like Major Paul W. Tibbets, Armstrong soon turned the 97th into a very effective outfit and his group had the honour of flying the first heavy bomber mission on 17 August, when a dozen B-17s attacked Rouen. Six other Fortresses flew a diversion. Major Paul W. Tibbets, who flew as Armstrong's pilot, recalls:

It was just past mid-afternoon when we lifted off into sunny skies. We started our climb for altitude immediately and had reached 23,000 feet, in attack formation, by the time we left the coast of England and headed south across the Channel. I wondered whether or not all aircraft would make it or whether there would be aborts. However, it was a banner day with no aborts. As we departed the English coast out over the Channel, the RAF escort of Spitfire Vs joined us. Group Captain (later Air Chief Marshal) Harry Broadhurst was leading the RAF escort fighters and it was an emotional, spine-tingling event. We were off to do battle for real and fighters were there to give us protection and comfort . . .. We caught the Germans by surprise. They hadn't expected a daytime attack, so we had clear sailing to the target. Visibility was unlimited and all twelve planes dropped their bomb loads. Our aim was reasonably good but you couldn't describe it as pinpoint bombing. We still had a lot to learn . . .. By the time we unloaded our bombs, the enemy came to life. Anti-aircraft fire, erratic and spasmodic at first, zeroed in on our formations as we began the return flight. Two B-17s suffered slight damage from flak. Three Bf 109s moved in for the attack but were quickly driven off by the Spitfires that accompanied us. The only German planes I saw were out of range and I got the impression they were simply looking us over . . .. A feeling of elation took hold of us as we winged back across the Channel. All the tension was gone. We were no longer novices at this terrible game of war. We had braved the enemy in his own skies and were alive to tell about it.

On 19 August the 97th supported the Allied landings at Dieppe when twenty-four B-17s hit the airfield at Abbeville-Drucat in northern France. It was here that *Hauptmann* Karl-Heinz 'Conny' Meyer's 5th and 6th *Staffeln* of 2./JG26, or the 'Abbeville Kids' as they were known, were based. When they were not relaxing in their quarters or in the *Casinos* (pilots' messes) this elite *Luftwaffe* unit flew yellow-nosed Fw 190s. Fortunately, the *Luftwaffe* was heavily engaged over the Dieppe area and did not show.[3] Two of the B-17s aborted because of mechanical failures. The rest plastered the airfield, scattering the ground crews, or *Schwarzemänner* (black men, so-called because of the colour of their tunics) who were going about their daily routines, destroying a hangar and severely cratering or 'postholing' the runways. British High Command reported that sixteen fighters were either destroyed or damaged as a result of the bombing strike and the airfield itself was put out of action for a vital 2 hours. In addition, the controllers of the whole of the fighter area remained out of action until that evening.

Four more small-scale raids on Dutch and French ports followed without loss. When on 29 August the JG26 fighter base at Wevelgem on the outskirts of Courtrai in western Belgium was bombed, results appeared good. Even the British press, which had at first been cautious of American claims, now openly praised them. On 5 September the 301st joined the 97th in a raid on the marshalling yards at Rouen and all thirty-seven bombers returned safely. On 6 September Eaker mounted his largest bombing mission so far, to the Avions Potez factory at Meaulte, using for the first time the 92nd Group, which scraped together fourteen B-17Es and crews, filling in with ground personnel, some of them privates. They joined twenty-two B-17Fs of the 97th in the main strike, while the 301st flew a diversionary raid on St Omer-Longuenesse airfield. Thirty Fortresses crossed Meaulte, but early-warning radar and radio intercept services monitoring any major increase on the American radio frequencies were alerted and they passed the word to the German fighter control organisation. German radar could detect formations before they crossed the English coast. Fw 190s of II./JG26 were encountered continuously from the French coast to the target and the escorting four squadrons of Spitfires failed to *rendezvous* with the bombers. JG26 intercepted the Spitfires and shot down three, while about fifty Fw 190s and a handful of Bf 109s bounced the Flying Forts. 'Conny' Meyer shot down Lieutenant Clarence C. Lipsky's Fort of the 97th north-west of Amiens for the *Luftwaffe*'s first American heavy bomber victory of the war. Four parachutes were seen to open.[4] *Baby Doll* flown by Lieutenant Leigh E. Stewart of the 92nd was pursued by at least five Fw 190s before finally *Oberfeldwebel* Willi Roth shot the B-17 down into the sea north-west of Le Treport. RAF ASR launches searched the area, but without success. Two other Forts were attacked by Fw 190s, which killed two gunners, mortally wounding another and wounding five other crew, one of whom died of his wounds three days later in hospital.

Two smaller scale raids were flown in September for little reward. Then on 2 October, forty-nine Forts were despatched to the Potez factory at Meaulte and St Omer/Longuenesse airfield. Lieutenant Charles W. Paine Jr, pilot of *Phyllis* in the 301st, was one who flew to Meaulte and he recalled:

> When the signal for the take-off came, I was so scared that I could hardly talk. Somehow though, I managed to make it. We were in vee of vees all the way to the target. Our ship was 'Tail-end Charlie', the rearmost left-hand ship in the formation and hence the last to bomb. We hit scattered heavy flak on our way in but it was slight and did no harm. We got well over our targets, in formation and unmolested and the bombing part was easy. But that's when the enemy fighters started to pour it on. The Germans' strategy was obviously to pick on the last ship and shoot it down. All the gunners in the crew started calling through the interphones, 'Enemy aircraft at 3 o' clock, Lieutenant . . . . At 5 o'clock . . . . At 9 o'clock . . . .' They were all around us.
>
> The fighters were employing two tactics that were new to me. When they peeled out of their formation to attack, they came in so close together that by the time one ship had shot up and banked away, the next in line had his sights on us. The other dodge they used was to pretend to come in on one of the other ships and then do a twenty-degree turn and

shoot the hell out of us. Mostly they came from the rear but at least one of them came up under us from in front, stalled and as it fell off, raked us the length of the Fort's belly. I could feel his hits banging into us. As a matter of fact I could feel the effect of all their fire. It was rather like sitting in the boiler of a hot-water heater and being rolled down a steep hill. There was an explosion behind me as a 20 mm cannon shell banged into us just behind the upper turret and exploded and I kept thinking, 'What if it hit the flares?' If it hit the flares and ignited them, I knew we'd go up like a rocket. Then I looked out at the right wing and saw it was shot to hell. There were holes everywhere. A lot of them were 20 mm cannon holes and they could tear a hole in the skin big enough to shove a sheep through. The entire wing was just a Goddamn bunch of holes.

One of the waist gunners yelled through the interphone, 'Lieutenant, there's a bunch of control wires slapping me in the face', which meant that the tail surface controls were being shot up. The right-hand outboard engine 'ran away' and the engine controls were messed up so we couldn't shut it off. The left-hand inboard engine also quit and the whole left oxygen system had gone out. I tried to get the ship down to 20,000 feet to keep half my crew from passing out. One gunner passed out from lack of oxygen and the radio operator, seeing him lying by his gun, abandoned his own oxygen supply and put the emergency mask of the walk-around bottle over the gunner's face. The gunner revived just in time to see the radio operator pass out. He in turn took the emergency mask off his own face and revived the radio operator with it.

The ship went into a steep climb, which I couldn't control. There was something wrong with the controls. I motioned to the co-pilot to help me and between the two of us we managed to get it forward and assume normal level flight. Then I started to think. The enemy fighters were still shooting us up. We had a long way to go to reach England and safety. We were minus two engines and it took almost full left aileron to hold that damaged right wing up. It was time, I decided, to bale out of the aircraft. So I yelled into the interphone: 'Prepare to abandon ship.' But just about that time the top gunner slid out of the top turret and fell between the co-pilot and me. His face was a mess. He was coughing blood. I thought he had been wounded in the chest. It later proved that he wasn't, but he was clearly in no condition to bale out of the airplane. I called for the bombardier and navigator to come up and help us with the top turret gunner and they did. Back in the waist one of our gunners was manning two guns despite a bad bullet wound in his leg. I don't know how many fighters we damaged or destroyed. There wasn't time to worry about that. We got over the Channel, finally, and a flight of Spits came racing out to meet us. Brother, they looked mighty good. We nursed the Fort across and made a belly landing at Gatwick, the first airdrome we could find. We nicked a hangar on the way in but somehow we made it.[5]

On 9 October, 108 B-17s and for the first time B-24 Liberators of the 93rd were despatched to the vast steel and locomotive works at the Compagnie de Fives, Lille. Also flying their first mission this day were the 306th from Thurleigh, Bedfordshire. Early in the morning Colonel Charles 'Chip' Overacker Jr, the CO, in a Fortress with Captain James A. Johnston and his crew led twenty-three crews. Each plane had a crew of nine as a second waist gunner was not thought necessary. As the Forts circled the field, Lieutenant Albert (Al) W. La Chasse, the bombardier of *Snoozy II* flown by Captain John Olsen, waved goodbye to his buddy, 'Butterball' Jones. His aircraft was grounded because they were using some of their parts to fly the mission.[6] The large formation of B-17s with the Liberators falling in behind began crossing the coast of England at Felixstowe. At about the same time III./JG26 *Kommandeur*, *Hauptmann* Josef 'Pips' Priller was leading his pilots off from their airfield at Wevelgem and heading north to intercept the bombers. Priller, who was short in stature at only 5 feet 4 inches, nonetheless has been described as a 'giant' in the fighter cockpit. A veteran of the French campaign and the Battle of Britain, his style of leadership was marked by a quirky sense of humour and he was reputed to be the only fighter leader who could make Hermann Goering laugh when things were going badly. Two of Thurleigh Group Forts aborted the mission before reaching the enemy coast. Nearing the target, flak enveloped the formation. Colonel Overacker's Fortress was hit in the No. 2 engine and he was forced to relinquish the lead. Al La Chasse recalls:

> Some smoke and dust covered the target area. As we continued the run a line of B-24s out of position were coming across the target area from the east, heading towards England. Flak hit our right inboard engine and set it on fire. Norman Gates, the co-pilot, somehow extinguished it. Flak increased. I was surprised it came in so many colours. On the bomb run Olsen trimmed the ship before turning the control over to me. I released the bomb load, not knowing there would be several malfunctions causing bomb rack problems. The plane lifted, lightened by the bomb drop. The B-24s were now behind us. It was 0942, time over the target as per mission plan. For *Snoozy II* the war was about to begin, and end. With only three engines pulling, we began a silly 360 degree turn into enemy territory. Where were the P-38s? None! As we came off the target about fifty of the 'Abbeville Kids' attacked from the rear and head-on. At about 1,000 yards at 3 o'clock there immediately appeared, in line astern, a gaggle of Bf 109s stalking us with four years' war experience. 'Ass-end Charlie' was about to become a 'sitting duck'! The interphone came alive with voices.
>
> Top turret: 'Jerries climbing into the sun behind me.'
> 'Red lights flashing on the instrument panel; four bombs hung!'
> I couldn't bring the doors up with the armed bolts still there. One stray armour-piercing bullet in the right place and boom, no anything!
> Bandits were everywhere. Where are those Goddamn P-38s? Sounds like typing on loose paper indicated that enemy shells were ripping into the ship's skin surfaces. *Snoozy II* began to lag behind the rest of the

formation. 'Honest John' McKee's ship tried lagging back with us. Good old 'Honest John'. He tried.

Tracers were coming and going in all directions. 'How can I toggle armed bombs in a canted ship?' I thought. They hadn't taught me that in cadet training. I thought, 'Salvo! That's it: dump the whole damn load, bombs, shackles and all.'

Now we were headed west, towards the white cliffs of Dover. Then suddenly, Staff Sergeant Bert E. Kaylor, the tail gunner, screamed, 'Jerries at 6 o'clock!'

I thought, 'Boy that's right up our butts.' Out of the sun the bastards came. I could feel each gunner's position as they fired. Tail, ball and waist gunners each took turns. Again, where are those ******** P-38s?

Now only Truman C. Wilder, the ball turret gunner, was still firing. Uh, oh, a belly attack was coming. All at once a German fighter flew right by our nose with a dirty yellow belly and nose with a white prop' spinner and black-painted corkscrew lines like a top. I tried to contact anyone on intercom but there was no sound. From behind came a hell of a thumping noise. We had taken a full burst of 20 mm cannon into the flight deck. Shortly thereafter the sun went by the nose as the ship went into a flat spin. We were lucky: it could have been in a tight vertical spin. Gise got caught in the centrifugal force of the spin. Everything loose flew through the air and plastered on the side of the ship. We finally made it back to the escape hatch to bale out into the 'wild blue yonder'. I followed Gise out after some trouble with the hatch. God must have opened it. The ride down was just like the book on parachutes said it would be, scary but nice. I was alive.[7]

Oberleutnant Otto 'Stotto' Stammberger and his 9./JG26 pilots had just landed at Wevelgem, when they were scrambled and told to climb in the direction of St Omer.

We spotted a quite large formation of formidable fat bluebottles and they were not flying in tight formation. Above were vapour trails of fighter aircraft. To the south of Lille I at last got into a firing position. We came in from behind, charged into the single vics in pairs, throttled back and fired our guns. The things grew bigger and bigger and all our attacks were commenced and broken off much too early, as we were afraid of flying into the 'barn doors'. I was wondering why I didn't register any hits until I thought about the size of the lumps: a wingspan of 40 metres! Therefore, charge in at much closer range and so fast that nothing would happen to us anyway. Then commence firing, starting with the engines in the left wing. On my third pass both engines were on fire and I hit the right outer engine as well, which belched forth smoke and the '*Kahn*'[8] plunged down in wide spirals. Four or five men baled out and to the east of Vendeville and the '*Kasten*'[9] crashed. I watched and then decided to go after the others. Miraculously, the sky was empty! Anyway, I was out of ammo for my cannons so I backed out towards home.[10]

Hauptmann Klaus Mietusch, meanwhile, led his *Staffel* in an attack on the American bombers, which he mistook for RAF Stirlings, and claimed a bomber shot down near Lille. Mietusch then pursued another B-17. Return fire downed his wingman, *Unteroffizier* Viktor Hager, who baled out badly wounded, but he could not open his parachute and he fell to his death. Mietusch made a second pass and damaged the B-17. This may have been a 306th Fortress, which crash-landed at Manston, or the one flown by Lieutenant Donald M. Swenson in the 301st,[11] which was ditched in the Channel and ASR rescued the crew. Or it may have been Lieutenant James M. Stewart's *Man O'War* of the 92nd, which lost the No. 2 engine, then both outboard engines began to overheat and lose power. Stewart nursed the ailing ship to the Channel and was also prepared to ditch until a lone RAF Spitfire turned up and guided him safely to Manston.[12] Only sixty-nine bombers hit their primary targets and many of the bombs failed to explode. The inexperienced groups had placed many of their bombs outside the target area, killing a number of French civilians. Traffic control was bad and some of the bombardiers never got the target in their bomb sights. During the post-mission interrogations crews revealed that they had made 242 encounters with *Luftwaffe* fighters and put in fighter claims for forty-eight destroyed, eighteen probably destroyed and four damaged. With so many gunners firing at the same targets it was inevitable that 'scores' would be duplicated and when the heat of the Lille battle had died away the American gunners' scores were whittled down considerably. Even so, the Germans lost only one fighter. At the time the figures did much to compensate for the largely inaccurate bombing.

On 20 October Brigadier General Asa N. Duncan, Chief of the Air Staff, issued a revised set of objectives to be carried out by 8th Bomber Command. In part it stated, 'Until further orders, every effort of the 8th Bomber Command will be directed to obtaining the maximum destruction of the submarine bases in the Bay of Biscay ....' On 21 October eighty-three B-17s and twenty-four B-24s of the 93rd were despatched to the U-boat pens at Keroman, about 11 miles from Lorient, while seventeen B-17s of the 11th CCRC were to bomb Cherbourg. The two forces flew a long over-water flight in the Bay of Biscay to reduce the threat of *Luftwaffe* interception. However, thick cloud at their prescribed bombing altitude of 22,000 feet forced all except the fifteen Fortresses of the 97th to return to England. The 97th bombed the target, but just after re-crossing the French coast they were bounced by a swarm of yellow-nosed Fw 190s. The attacks were ferocious and incessant and centred upon the rear of the formation. Three B-17s were shot down[13] and another six B-17s were badly damaged. The 97th now had the highest losses of any group to date.

On 7 November sixty-eight B-17s and B-24s, including for the first time, Forts of the 91st commanded by Colonel Stanley T. Wray, went to the U-boat pens at Brest. 'Wray's Ragged Irregulars', as they became known, had moved into the pre-war RAF base at Bassingbourn with gusto after looking the place over and it would remain 'their' base until the end of the war. The force returned without loss, although the 306th came under attack from fighters in the target area. Captain John Ryan's Fort was jumped by two fighters and gunners aboard Lieutenant George Buckey's ship fought off three Fw 190s, one of which was claimed shot down. One Liberator crashed at Exeter after sustaining battle damage.[14] 'Chip' Overacker's Group seemed to emerge from the encounter over Brest with renewed confidence, but for the next two consecutive days morale at Thurleigh took another dent when Fortresses were sent to bomb Abbeville-Drucat airfield and Lille and then St Nazaire. Twenty B-17s took off from Thurleigh for the Lille raid, but seven aborted, leaving thirteen to continue to the target where enemy fighters took advantage once the Spitfire top cover, low on fuel, left. In half an hour thirty fighters made at least 200 attacks on the five planes in the 369th Squadron. Incredibly, four of the bombers survived, but Captain Richard D. Adams' plane, which suffered a flak hit in the left wing between the two engines, was easy prey for the fighters. Fuel sprayed out of the wing and one of the engines was on fire. Adams tried in vain to shut down the engine. The flight controls were inoperative and the increasing bank angle was getting dangerously steep. The instruments and oxygen system were also out and with the plane at 20,000 feet, Adams rang the alarm bell and called over the interphone for the crew to 'abandon ship'. Adams only pulled his ripcord at 2,000 feet, but the long delayed jump might have been the reason Adams was saved from being captured, a fate which befell four of his crew.[15]

The next day, B-17 and B-24 crews were shocked to learn at briefing that they were to make their bomb runs on the U-boat pens at St Nazaire from 7,000 to 8,000 feet! 'Chip' Overacker phoned HQ to protest but it fell on deaf ears. The hard-pressed Colonel retorted, 'If my crews have to fly the mission, I'll lead them!' He did, and chose to fly the mission in Captain Henry W. Terry's plane, who went along as his co-pilot with his normal crew. Overacker's four squadron commanders refused to send their men unless they were with them and they flew too. Three Fortresses were lost in rapid succession to the flak over St Nazaire and they all came from Overacker's Group. *Man O' War*, flown by Lieutenant James M. Stewart went down with all of the crew killed. *Miss Swoose*, flown by Lieutenant John R. Barnett, was shot down after 'bombs away'. Lieutenant Loyal M. Felts' Fort was hit on the bomb run when the first flak bursts knocked an engine off its mounting. One of the bursts shot away the Plexiglas nose, knocking Lieutenant Andrew L. Graham Jr (bombardier) off his seat, back against Lieutenant Forrest D. Hartin (navigator) and the bulkhead at the back of the forward fuselage. Then the Fort tilted over into a dive and Graham fell out. Fortunately, he was wearing a seat-type chute and he managed to pull the ripcord and land safely. Hartin was trapped for a time but worked his way free and he baled out despite having been hit by flak while in the aircraft. Germans shot at him while descending and on landing he sprained both ankles.[16] Co-pilot Robert J. Jones was knocked out of the plane by the force of the explosion and survived. The seven other men in the crew died. The intense flak succeeded in breaking up the formations and they flew back to England in disarray.

'Wray's Ragged Irregulars' returned without loss but ten planes were damaged and eleven men wounded. *Quitchurbitchin*, flown by Lieutenant

Charles E. 'Red' Cliburn, a Southerner from Hazlehurst, Mississippi, took a direct hit from a 40 mm shell, which struck just aft of the ball turret, almost cut the plane in two and wounded both waist gunners. Captain John R. 'Tex' McCrary, a PRO and Photographic Officer, described Cliburn as having a 'Mickey Rooney grin'. He moved 'slow', talked 'slow', his eyes blinked 'slow', he chewed his food 'slow' and he even shot pool 'with a slow poke'. Nevertheless, somehow Cliburn got the crippled bomber back across the Channel on two engines. He force-landed *Quitchurbitchin* at RAF Exeter, was recommended for the DFC and was awarded the Air Medal. McCrary did not suppose you would say Cliburn 'thought fast – he just reacted ....'[17] 'Red' Cliburn's diary entry describing the raid was equally succinct: 'Went to St Nazaire today. A little rough.' A repair crew from Bassingbourn took a week to get *Quitchurbitchin* airworthy again.

At Thurleigh, where twelve Forts had returned badly damaged, an inspection by the engineering department revealed that Overacker's plane was severely damaged with hits in both wings, the bombardier's compartment, the left elevator, the bomb bay doors and two engines. Thurleigh was fast becoming the home of an 'unlucky' outfit. Missions to St Nazaire on 16 and 17 November passed without loss to any group, though on the latter date three Forts returned with damage and one man killed. The 306th were scheduled to bring up the rear with twelve B-17s. Three planes returned early with supercharger and gun problems and only nine remained. All went well on the bomb run and the start of the return home, but 20 miles north-west of the target fifteen Fw 190s singled out the small formation at the rear as easy pickings. *Chennault's Pappy* flown by Captain Robert C. Williams, the slightly built 423rd Operations Officer in lieu of Lieutenant William H. Warner, who was ill, was badly shot up. The bomber had been named by Lieutenant Raymond J. Check, an original pilot and a very popular member of the squadron, who thought that the large B-17s were fit to father the P-40s made famous in China by the Flying Tigers of Major General Claire Chennault.[18] Cannon fire tore away an elevator and in the next fighter pass Williams and his co-pilot, Lieutenant Warren George Jr, had to use their combined strength on the controls to keep the nose level. George braced both legs against the control column to keep *Chennault's Pappy* in a reasonably normal flight attitude. Williams and George and the gunners aboard the plane weathered the storm and force-landed at Exeter with a dead top turret gunner. Three other crewmen had to be hospitalised and the bomber never flew again. Lieutenant John M. Regan managed to land his badly damaged Fortress at Membury after taking a direct hit in an engine, which ripped off the cowling, and after some maintenance he took off for Thurleigh later on three engines.[19] That night at Thurleigh General Eaker presented medals to men in the group.

The next day when sixty-five B-24s and B-17s (the 303rd – the Hell's Angels Group – flew its maiden mission this day) were despatched to Lorient, St Nazaire and La Pallice the Thurleigh Group's run of ill luck continued. *Floozy* was shot down by a combination of flak and fighters and crashed in the Bay of Biscay. Nine of Lieutenant Ralph J. Gaston's crew survived and all were taken prisoner. Later, the German fighter pilots that had shot them down visited the survivors in hospital. The B-17 flown by Lieutenant Robert W. Seelos also came in for heavy attention by enemy fighters and flak. Fragments from an 88 mm shell hit his navigator Lieutenant Charles G. Grimes in the small of his back. 'Pappy' as he was affectionately known because he was older than most, managed to call on the intercom to his pilot, 'Seelos, I'm hit bad', before he died. John King, the co-pilot, was wounded by the same burst of flak. Robert Dresp, the co-pilot in another ship, was severely injured in the buttock and he also suffered massive internal injuries, but despite his wounds he tried to help his pilot James M. Ferguson handle the plane on the way home. After landing, Dresp was taken to the 2nd General Hospital at Oxford, where he died several weeks later. The return home of the bodies of good friends like Pappy Grimes had a greater impact on crews and ground personnel than the loss of a plane and crew, and his death hit the group hard. At Thurleigh, respiratory ailments were rife and the enlisted men grumbled about unsanitary conditions and the poor food on offer. Every army has its complainers and backsliders, but feeling sorry for oneself is not a condition that can be tolerated for long, especially if higher command identifies that the condition is widespread and constitutes a serious morale problem. On 25 November, the 306th was removed from the battle order, only resuming combat missions again on 12 December.

Meanwhile, on 22 November Colonel (later General) Curtis E. LeMay's Group flew it first mission, part of a force of B-17s and Liberators to Lorient. It was not a memorable debut. Only eleven B-17s of the 301st formation managed to bomb. On almost every mission bombers were hitting the target, but not in large enough concentrations to damage them seriously. LeMay, who had been a lieutenant at Selfridge Field in Michigan in the 1930s before the US really had an air force, was a single-minded and methodical officer, whose credo was, 'If you destroy the [enemy's] capability to win war, then the will to wage war disappears also'. LeMay decided to try and achieve greater bombing accuracy by flying a straight course on the bomb run, instead of zigzagging every 10 seconds, a tactic that had been designed to spoil the aim of the German flak batteries. He put the plan into operation on the next day, 23 November, when over fifty Fortresses set out from their advance base at Davidstowe Moor for the raid on St Nazaire. Bad weather and mechanical problems forced several bombers to abort and LeMay's fourteen remaining B-17s from the twenty despatched flew the longest and straightest bomb run yet flown in Europe. They placed twice as many bombs on the target as any other group. Despite his crews' worst fears, LeMay lost no crews over the target to flak or fighters, but in the Hell's Angels Group *Lady Fairweather* was shot down in flames near the target and in the 306th Lieutenant Clay Isbell's Fort was shot down on the bomb run. Isbell and seven of his crew were trapped when the Fortress exploded. The worst casualties, though, were suffered by 'Wray's Ragged Irregulars', whose formation had been reduced from ten ships to five because of aborts. A number of the group's Forts were still at other bases because of bad weather the day before and could not make the mission. At the *rendezvous* point no other planes were seen so the five Forts continued on alone. Shortly after crossing the French coast *Sad Sack*, which was named after Sergeant George Baker's famous cartoon character in *Yank* magazine, was forced to return with a feathered propeller. Thomas McCormick's crew and Major Victor Zienowicz, his squadron commander, were never heard from again. When the four remaining Forts arrived at the target area, the entire Brest peninsula was covered in clouds and there were no gaps to bomb through. At this point a formation of Focke-Wulfs attacked.

On previous missions the B-17s had been intercepted from the rear where enough guns could be brought to bear on enemy fighters. *Luftwaffe* experiments had now proved that the frontal area of a B-17 offered very little in defensive firepower. Despite the dangers of very high closing speeds, this was now considered the best method of shooting them down. *Oberstleutnant* Egon Mayer, *Kommandeur*, III./JG2 (who led the attacking fighters this day) and *Oberleutnant* Georg-Peter 'Schorch' Eder, *Staffelkapitän*, 12./JG2, are credited with developing the head-on attack, where the bomber armament was weakest. Determining whether an attack was exactly head-on or not when the targets were tiny dots in the distance was difficult, so Mayer and Eder[20] refined their tactics. They tailed the Forts to determine their exact course, altitude and speed, before moving out to a safe distance on one flank and overtaking the bombers, reaching a point about 2 miles ahead, before turning for a head-on pass. *Pandora's Box* was mortally hit and crashed into the sea about 30 miles north-west of St Nazaire with no survivors. The three remaining B-17s fought off repeated fighter attacks, and badly shot up and with wounded and injured on board, limped back to English shores. Captain Kenneth Wallick managed to put his severely damaged Fort down at RAF Chivenor. Lieutenant Nathan N. Corman Jr tried to crash-land *The Shiftless Skonk* on the outskirts of Watford, but at about 15 feet off the ground he clipped a high-tension tower and the plane crashed near Leavesden, killing three men instantly. Two more died later of their injuries. Only *Quitchurbitchin,* flown by 'Red' Cliburn, made it back home, but no one knew how. The rudder controls and elevator tabs were shot away, the wings and fuselage were riddled with holes and Cliburn, his co-pilot, Clyde DeBaum and the radioman were wounded after a 20 mm shell exploded in the cockpit. DeBaum was removed from his seat and the bombardier, Phillip Palmer, assisted Cliburn in getting the badly damaged plane back to Bassingbourn, where Cliburn put *Quitchurbitchin* down on the grass when the tail wheel refused to lower. Cliburn, who was awarded the DFC for bringing his ship back, was given another Fort, *The Bad Penny*, a 'jinx ship', which had been named by someone who had been shot down on the raid, while *Quitchurbitchin* underwent extensive repairs. Red's description of the raid in his diary was brief: 'Back to St Nazaire again. Rough again.'

Pinprick raids continued to be made on the U-boat pens and airfields in France. Eaker was not helped by the decision to send three squadrons of Liberators from Hardwick to North Africa on Sunday 6 December when over eighty B-17s headed for the Atelier d'Hellemmes locomotive works at Lille. One Liberator was lost and *Cherry* in the 305th left the formation in flames 10 minutes from the target. On 12 December when the Forts attacked Rouen Sotteville, the 306th returned to combat status, putting up eighteen Fortresses for no loss. There then followed another week's rest from combat for all bomber crews, missions resuming on 20 December when Bomber Command carried out its heaviest raid since Lille, sending 101 bombers[21] to strike the airfield and *Luftwaffe* servicing base at Romilly-sur-Seine, 100 miles southeast of Paris. Twelve squadrons of fighters flew escort as far as Rouen. At this point II./JG26, led by *Major* Gerhard 'Gerd' Schöpfel, who had paralleled the American formation waiting for the escorts to leave, attacked the leading B-17s of 'Wray's Ragged Irregulars' head-on.[22] A B-17 flown by Lieutenant Robert S. English and *Danellen* went down immediately.[23] For an hour the enemy fighters attacked in relays and did not break off until the withdrawal escort appeared over the Channel. *Chief Sly* was hit badly in the fighter attacks and limped back across the Channel. Lieutenant Bruce Barton crash-landed at Fletching, Sussex, with a seriously wounded navigator, Lieutenant Paul Burnett, who had received a bullet wound to his thigh. *Rose O'Day* was hit badly by flak and fighters, but thanks to Barton and his gunners aboard *Chief Sly*, together they fended off the attacks and pilot Captain Ken Wallick got *Rose O'Day* home to Bassingbourn and landed safely. *Chief Sly*, however, was fit only for spare parts. *The 8 Ball* in the Hell's Angels Group was also hit badly and crash-landed at Bovingdon after eight of the crew had baled out over Maidstone. *Unteroffizier* Hubert Swoboda made a lone attack on a B-17 in his Messerschmitt Bf109 and was hit by return defensive fire. His guns jammed and four P-47s arrived on the scene so Swoboda approached the Fortress at speed from the right and rammed the Fort, striking the rudder and damaging the fin before it finally went down.[24]

At Thurleigh eighteen Forts had taken off but three – all from the 367th Clay Pigeons Squadron – were missing. Their nickname originated from an American war correspondent who, writing in *The Saturday Evening Post*, said that the squadron reminded him of a bunch of clay pigeons. The name stuck! (Between October 1942 and August 1943 the 367th suffered the heaviest losses of any group.) *Leutnant* Otto Stammberger leading 9./JG26 attacking with *Hauptmann* Egon Mayer's III./JG2, saw a B-17 flip end-over-end before its tail section broke off and the Fortress fell away. Fighters raked the B-17 with 20 mm cannon fire shortly after the target and shells exploded in the nose, cockpit and throughout the fuselage. As the aircraft fell away from the formation, it went into a flat spin and rolled over. Lieutenant Danton J. Nygaard, a recent replacement pilot, who was burned on the face and arms, went out of the nose hatch, followed by the bombardier. The only other survivor was Lieutenant Frank Leasman, the navigator, who was caught under debris until the engineer freed him. With the B-17 still upside down and at about 4,000 feet, Leasman climbed out of the nose hatch and then jumped up as the Fortress passed under him.[25] Stammberger, meanwhile, had picked out his own target. It was *Rose O'Day*, flown by Lieutenant John R. McKee, one of the original nine pilots in the *Clay Pigeons* Squadron. As Stammberger started a second head-on pass, McKee's crew began baling out at short intervals. Eventually, there were nine chutes.[26] The third loss was *Terry and the Pirates*, piloted by Lieutenant Lewis McKesson, the former squadron operations officer. McKesson and six of his crew survived. The *Clay Pigeons* Squadron's original complement of nine crews now numbered just three. American gunners claimed fifty-three enemy fighters shot down. These claims were later reduced to twenty-one confirmed, but in fact JG26 lost one fighter and its pilot, while III./JG2 lost two pilots killed. As far as the bombing went, just seventy-two of the heavies were effective over the target at Romilly – one of the bombs dropped had hit a German mess hall, killing 200.

In France, meanwhile, changes in German fighter tactics and the disposition of units were afoot. It was announced in *Luftwaffe* circles that JG26 was to transfer to the Russian Front, where it would trade places with the Green Hearts *Geschwader*, JG54. However, the transfer was only partially complete when in the spring of 1943 the growing might of Bomber Command prompted *Generalmajor* Adolf Galland to cancel the move. At this time the *Luftwaffe*, unhappy with the relatively small numbers of bombers being shot down, revised its tactics. On 20 December it had made its attacks from dead ahead, or 12 o'clock level. Closing speeds of around 550 mph made it difficult to keep targets in effective firing range for more than a split second and there was always the fear of collision at the back of the German pilots' minds. Larger attacking formations and simultaneous attacks by fighters, rather than in trail, were to be used. While they would still use the head-on approach, the angle of attack would be from ten degrees above the horizontal – otherwise known as 12 o'clock high – which in experiments was found to be more effective. As before, the best chance of knocking a bomber out of formation was to kill the pilots in the cockpit.[27]

Christmas 1942 arrived – the first for the men at an overseas station – and the gift for all combat crews was a week's respite from combat missions until 30 December when the B-17s set out to bomb Lorient. The Thurleigh Group got its Forts in the air, but one abort after another forced the 306th to abandon the mission when fewer than nine ships remained airborne. Captain John B. Brady had taken off a few minutes after the group and did not find the formation in the murk over England, so he joined the 305th formation instead and proceeded to the target with them. On his return around the tip of the Brest peninsula enemy fighters attacked the B-17s and Brady's Fort was set on fire. All the crew baled out and were reported to have been fired on while descending in their chutes. All the crew died either shot by the fighters or drowned in the icy waters of the Atlantic. Two other Fortresses were lost on the raid.

New Year's Eve was party time too and missions did not resume again until 3 January, when the B-17s were despatched to St Nazaire. Eaker now abandoned individual bombing, which had been SOP (Standard Operating Procedure) from the outset, in favour of Group bombing[28] and the Forts dropped most of their bombs smack on the target. While none of the Group's B-17s were lost, two were so badly shot up by flak that they were left at Talbenny, Wales. Seven Fortresses failed to return and forty-seven were damaged. These were the highest losses thus far. Two of the Forts lost came from the Thurleigh Group, whose navigators were now in such short supply that some of its B-17s flew without one. Major William Lanford, 368th Squadron CO, led the remaining ships back to England, where bad weather forced them to seek shelter in Cornwall. Three days later they set off for Thurleigh but the formation strayed south, over the Channel Isles, and they were bracketed by flak. One Fort was lost. It was not until 8 January that the formation finally made it back to Thurleigh. By then the Group had a new CO.

On 4 January Eaker had set out for Thurleigh from Pinetree, with his A-3 (Operations and Training) Colonel Frank A. Armstrong Jr and Lieutenant Colonel Beirne Lay Jr in tow. Lay, the red-headed, Yale-educated pilot and writer, was one of Eaker's original six staff officers, who had also accompanied the general to England early in February 1942. Lay had penned the classic *I Wanted Wings*, which, in 1941, had been made into a successful movie by Paramount and will be remembered as the movie that made Veronica Lake famous. It was written originally to tell the story of what happens inside a boy who 'just has to fly'. Hence assigned as 8th Bomber Command's first historian, Lay also filled in at first with the additional duties of 'Mess Officer and egg forager, PRO, aide and officially, also a member of A-3 and Athletics Officer'.[29] Now he and Armstrong found themselves accompanying Eaker to Thurleigh. 'Things are not going well up there,' he told them. 'I think we ought to take a look around.' (Things obviously had not improved since Eaker's last visit to the Group on 14 November when HM King George VI and top ranking US officers toured Alconbury, Chelveston and Thurleigh. At the main gate a sentry who neither saluted nor checked the occupants' AGO cards casually waved past Eaker's Humber staff car flying the red flag with two white stars of a major general).[30] Eaker toured the base with Chip Overacker. The general, who was not impressed with what he saw, later recounted, 'As we visited hangars, shops and offices, I found similar attitudes as seen at the front gate. The men had a close attachment to their CO and he to them. But there was a lack of military proprietary and I could not help feel that this might be part of the problem that was being revealed in combat.' The 306th had lost nine Fortresses on its last three missions. On their return to the Thurleigh base HQ Eaker relieved Overacker of command. 'Chip,' he said 'You'd better get your things and come back with me.' The General then turned to Armstrong and announced, 'Frank, you're in command. I'll send your clothes down.' Eaker's purge of the Thurleigh outfit, which on 13 January lost two more B-17s, did not stop there. The General summoned William Lanford to his HQ on 17 January and relieved him of his post.[31] Two days later, Armstrong transferred Lieutenant Colonel Delmar Wilson, 306th deputy commander and brought in as operations officer 28-year-old Major Claude Putnam, who like Armstrong was a veteran of the 97th's early days in England. They began rebuilding the combat-decimated Group and within a few days had begun to restore the fading morale.

Armstrong was selected by General Eaker to lead the first American bombers over Germany on 27 January to attack Vegesack, an event that would forever tag the 306th with the proud boast, *First Over Germany*. Armstrong had earlier led the 97th on the first all-American bombing raid of the European war and it was appropriate that he performed a similar role again. Flying with Armstrong, as co-pilot was Major Claude Putnam, group operations officer, with Robert Salitrnik, navigator, and Frank Yaussi, bombardier. Eighteen B-17s of the 306th headed five bomb groups, making up sixty-four B-17s and Liberators, which was more of a morale booster than a surgical strike on the German war effort, and the raid proved most attractive to journalists. Andy Rooney of *Stars and Stripes*, for example, flew in the nose of Captain William J. Casey's plane. Poor weather, which held fast over the primary target at Vegesack, forced the bombers to head for the naval base at a partially obscured Wilhelmshaven on the north-west German coast instead. Having lost their way over the North Sea, the Liberators wrongly identified Lemmer in Holland as Wilhelmshaven and they dropped their bombs to the north of the harbour town. Wilhelmshaven was reached by the Fortress crews who were attacked by about fifty fighters and a Fort (and two Liberators) were shot down. Charles Red Cliburn got *The Bad Penny* back to Bassingbourn with all the control cables shot away except one elevator and the ailerons. For a plane that was supposed to be a 'jinx' ship, Cliburn did remarkably well and he flew the plane on sixteen occasions in all. American gunners claimed twenty-two destroyed, fourteen probably destroyed and thirteen damaged. However, all bomber claims made during the first half of 1943 must be taken with a grain of salt. Despite a new and much improved method of establishing claims, they were still affected by many confusing circumstances and they continued to run high.

It was not an especially well executed mission. The next morning at a First Wing meeting at his Brampton Grange headquarters, General Hansell, his group commanders and staff felt that the combat formations did not keep close enough together to give shielding protection, one to the other. Fifty-four aircraft were not enough aircraft to be able to defend themselves and it was deemed that poor formation flying resulted in aircraft becoming separated and an easy prey to fighters. Poor visibility at the target made the bombing very difficult and a target as small as this should only be assigned when the weather was very clear and visibility good. Many things that later became standard operating procedures were discussed. Despite the criticisms, the raid caused disquiet in Germany. *Luftwaffe* night-fighters were now put into action against American day formations whenever the latter flew without escort. The first use of night-fighters of NJG1 against American formations took place on 4 February, when eighty-six bombers attacked Emden, Hamm and Osnabrück. It was believed that the heavily armed Bf 110 night-fighters would bolster the day-fighter arm and prove effective against American day bombers. *Hauptmann* Hans-Joachim Jabs led eight Bf 110s of IV./NJGI into action against the American combat boxes.[32] Jabs, *Oberfeldwebel* Heinz Grimm and *Unteroffizier* Alfred Naumann claimed three B-17s shot down in the ensuing combat – among them *El Lobo*, a 305th Group B-17 flown by Lieutenant Cornelius A. Jenkins, with five men killed. All eight Bf 110s were badly damaged and two made belly landings on Ameland and near Leeuwarden. None of these aircraft would be serviceable to combat the RAF night bombers. The 305th lost a second B-17 when an Fw 190 slammed into *What's Cookin' Doc?* flown by Lieutenant William K. Davidson. All the crew were killed. Three more B-17s were lost on the mission.

Feldwebel Erich Handke had joined 12./NJG1 with his pilot, *Feldwebel* Georg 'Schorsch' Kraft, in October 1942 and they were amongst those *Nachtjagd* crews ordered to fly against the American combat boxes in early 1943.

> February 4 was a memorable day when for the first time the Americans mounted a massed daylight attack on Emden. Four of our sections took off to intercept them on their return flight. We caught a formation of sixty Boeing Fortresses. *Unteroffizier* Alfred Naumann accompanied by *Unteroffizier* Bärwolf achieved his first daylight *Abschuss*. Together with *Leutnant* Karl Heinz Völlkopf he attacked the formation head-on and shot a Fortress out of it, which dropped its undercarriage.[33] One engine smoked, the Boeing dropped back. Naumann turned back and renewed his attack from behind. As a result both went down in flames. But Naumann was able to ditch his aircraft on the northern shore of Ameland. *Hauptmann* Hans-Joachim Jabs, commander of the 11th *Staffel*, also shot down a Boeing with his section. *Unteroffizier* Scherer attacked the formation all alone. He reported: 'Contact with fifty Kuriere and making *Pauke, Pauke*.'[34] Then he flung himself into the formation. He fired at one but then he had to break off, as his face was full of splinters; his radio operator Mehner even had the entire altimeter in his face.

> Then it was our section's turn, *Oberfeldwebel* Heinz Grimm and I. We were directed by [GCI][35] station *Eisbär* (Polar Bear) and were the last to reach the formation at 7,000 metres, 20 km west of Texel. Suddenly we spotted the sixty Boeings in a heap before us. I must admit that I had a slight twitch when I saw them! We felt so small and ugly compared to these 'flying fortresses'. We attacked from the side, with the section leader leading. But he turned in too soon so that we were not able to fire, passing behind the formation with everyone firing at us. We then attacked the last aircraft alternately from behind and above until we were both riddled. At Grimm's final attack a Boeing caught fire and crashed later on. All of Grimm's windows were shot to pieces, the radio operator, *Unteroffizier* Hans Meissner, wounded, the port engine had stopped. We also had to feather our port engine as it began to smoke. Both port tanks *and* the starboard rear one were shot through, the coolant and petrol pipes to the port engine and Schorsch Kraft's bullet-proof windscreen were also gone. So both of us returned on one engine. As Grimm's starboard engine also failed he had to make a belly-landing.[36]

The Liberators continued to fly some shallow penetration diversion missions to aid the Fortresses. The Flying Eightballs' hurried afternoon mission, to Dunkirk, on 15 February, was to try to bomb the *Tojo*, a German night-fighter control ship, which was being moved up to the German Bight to fill a gap in the Ostmark area. An exceptionally long bomb run had been ordered in an attempt to ensure hits, but none came close. All it did was to enable the gunners to send up an accurate flak barrage. *Betty Anne/Gallopin Ghost* the lead ship suffered a direct hit by an 88 mm under the flight deck at about the nose wheel section and it ripped the nose clean off. For a few moments the noseless bomber flew on, only to fall away to starboard with the port inboard engine aflame and the right inboard ripped from its mounting. Finally, the starboard wing fell off and a huge explosion scattered debris among the formation.[37] *Railway Express*, piloted by Lieutenant Rufus A. Oliphant Jr, was hit and crippled and slowly lost altitude coming off the target. *Oberleutnant* Erich Hohagen, *Staffelkapitän* of 7./JG2, easily caught the B-24 and shot it down. There were no survivors. *Captain and his Kids*, piloted by Captain Tom Cramer was also damaged by flak. With three men dead, Cramer crash-landed on the beach at Sandwich without flaps or landing gear. In Dunkirk harbour the *Tojo* remained afloat.

On 16 February when the bombers were dispatched to bomb the U-boat pens at St Nazaire, German fighter controllers waited until the American escort fighters turned back before unleashing their fighters and six Forts were shot down. *Leutnant* Otto 'Stotto' Stammberger, leading 9./JG26, and *Feldwebel* Edgar Dorre hit a Fort flown by Lieutenant Joseph A. Downing of the Clay Pigeons Squadron, which had three engines hit or crippled by flak over the target. Downing put his ship into a steep dive from 10,000 to 4,000 feet, when he found some desperately needed clouds to hide in. Stammberger saw the B-17 fall from formation, although, as he was subsequently shot down by a *Viermot*[38] he was unable to observe the kill and it was not confirmed. Just west of Ploermal, *Unteroffizier* E. Schwarz downed a Fort in the troubled 306th Group and four of Lieutenant William H. Warner's crew baled out before the bomber crashed at Ploermal. Two men evaded and two were captured. American air gunners claimed twenty enemy fighters shot down but only Stammberger's aircraft (a shell smashed his cockpit and fragments hit his left hand) had to be written off. Two B-24s collided over the Channel, bringing the day's total losses to eight. Thirty heavies returned battle-damaged.

Technical Sergeant John R. Parsons, engineer in *Lightning Strikes* in Wray's Ragged Irregulars recalls the raid on 21 February.

> We were doing exceptionally well; a good formation, a tight box and we got to the target area. The lead navigator was somewhat of a cowboy and they decided, since we were all a little bit off the target, a little bit to the south and to the east, that we should make a 180 and drop, i.e. come back across the target and drop coming across. It sounded like a good idea and it was, except the lead navigator turned too short and as he did that, it completely scattered the formation. We were in a high box or high composite. We were in a helluva lot of flak and we made our turn. We were hanging out to dry, so to speak. There were nine airplanes behind ours and I saw two of them blow up right off. I looked up at the damnedest mess of fighters you ever saw; they swarmed in like bees. There were a lot of them shot down but we were in a position where we had to fight for our lives.
>
> They came in close. One would be attacking the rear and another would be attacking the right or left side. Most of them came in from the left and, oh, God, we had an Fw 190 come in right over the tail gunner. I

told Paul Goecke our tail gunner, 'Fight for your life'. Everybody was shooting everything they had. This guy comes in and I think he was the one that really hurt us. It was a 20 mm explosion in the No. 3 engine. It blew the whole cowling off and three of the jugs were blown out. You could look down and see the guts just flying around in the engine. Of course, you couldn't feather the darn thing and when they all started going, it didn't help us at all. We had a hole in the No. 3 reserve tank and it was as big as a large lampshade, a helluva of a big hole. Of course, gas was coming on board; it was burning. We had good communication up to a point but the attacks kept coming. I saw tracers fly through that airplane and I don't know how or why it didn't kill anybody but it didn't.

I said that if our communication does go out, we'd ring the bell and if we heard the bell going constant, '*Get out*'. At that time, as luck would have it, we lost our communication. The radio was completely dead. Simultaneously, our controls froze. The airplane went into an attitude of just a slight rate of climb and would shake, jiggle back and forth like it was trying to go but couldn't go and well . . . . Paul asked me if it was all right? I got down out of the top gun turret and said, 'I don't think so – it's going to go'. So he rang the bell. I felt the air come up through the bottom so I knew the bombardier and navigator were already out. I grabbed Clyde McCallum, the co-pilot and said, 'Mac, go'. He was a tall man. He got down to an area between the seats where he could stand up straight, reached over, put on the pilot's parachute, which was a clip-on and looked at his number. His should have been D2 and the pilot's was D1. Mine was D5. He looked at the number on that and took it off, set it right politely in place and reached over and put on his own and turned around. He was a big man and he was sitting there with his rump sticking up. I stepped on him and he flew right out the hole. I got back up, sat down in the co-pilot's seat and thought, 'With this thing going like that and burning like mad, we don't have a ghost of a chance'. So I told the pilot, 'No, it ain't gonna go, let's get out.' He said, 'All right, go.'

Well, I didn't think that he was going to get out, so I got down there by the escape hatch and waited and waited. He didn't come, so I went back up and I said, 'Are you coming?'

He said, 'Yes, get out.'

I saw his legs come over the seat, down into the opening and when I saw that, I went out. All this time I was trying like hell to get my oxygen mask off but it was clipped too tight and it was dragging a long hose. It must have been 6 feet long. It wouldn't come off. I was dragging it along. I hit the air and the sensation was unbelievable. Of course, back in No. 2 engine, it was going full blast, right out in the slipstream. I rolled like a rag doll. 1 thought my arms and my legs were going to be in knots. I finally got far enough away and I don't know why, I guess by instinct but I folded my arms and I put my feet in a diving position. I looked down and I was turning in a slow circle. We went out of that airplane at about 20,000 feet. The temperature was 60 below and I just didn't realise I would have to go through what I went through just by gliding here and rolling over, gliding and rolling over again. I got down and we started through the undercast. I thought, 'Now's the time.' I was lying on my back and I reached over and pulled the D-ring. Well, the chute came out. It had a little pilot chute which pulls the main chute out and it was stretched out there like you can't believe but the rest of the chute stuck together, had too much oil, wouldn't open up. I thought, 'Well, I don't know what I'm going to do now' but it stayed up because the pilot chute was holding it up. I reached over and pulled the shroud line and held it out far enough so that it did catch air and blossomed open, just like lying in a feather bed. I was really happy that damn thing came open. I was then going through the undercast and could see slightly, things becoming more clear, like houses and that sort of thing. As I came out the bottom, there came a damned old B-17. I mean, the engines just sounded terrible. They were unwound and running as fast as they could. It rolled over. I couldn't touch it but I was awful close as it rolled over bottom up, hit the ground and just exploded. I had the opportunity to look and I didn't see any hatches open. I felt bad that there might have been a full crew aboard that thing.

I almost got shot on the way down; there was so much fighting, so much machine-gun chatter and I'm just surprised any one of us made it. I didn't get shot on the way down. True to form, I always thought, 'I'm going to get out of this damn place'. But if I wait until I chute, the better position I'm going to be in at landing and I can just evade.

The increase in bomber missions did not escape the notice of the German pilots, even fresh ones like *Leutnant* Eberhard Burath of IV./JG1, who noted that 'during February operations became more frequent. The *Viermots* penetrated ever more deeply over the continent'. Burath did not have his first contact with the American bombers until 26 February when the Focke-Wulf aircraft factories at Bremen were the target for the day. Submarine facilities at Wilhelmshaven were the secondary target if weather conditions made it impossible to attack the primary one. At six air bases in eastern England ninety-three B-17s and B-24s taxied out for the mission. Eleven B-24s of the Flying Eightballs, including *Sad Sack*, flown by Lieutenants Robert H. McPhillamey and Wilbur F. Wockenfuss, and *Maisie* flown by Captain Howard Adams taxied out at Shipdham. Adams' mascot, a little wooden doll of the same name, swung gently from the cabin windshield in front of him and his co-pilot. The crew had also found room for Robert Perkins Post, a *New York Times* war correspondent, the only one of seven in the 'Writing 69th' who had asked to fly with the Eightballs on the mission.

In Holland, meanwhile, 30-year-old *Hauptmann* Ludwig Becker, *Staffelkapitän*, 12./NJG1, a great night-fighting tactician and the top-scoring *Nachtjagd Experte* with forty-four *Abschüsse*, waited at Leeuwarden to fly his very first daylight mission. Shortly before taking off in pursuit of the American daylight raiders in a formation of twelve Bf110s, again led by *Hauptmann* Hans-Joachim Jabs, Becker was informed of the award of the Oak Leaves to his Knight's Cross.[39] At Jever-Wangerooge 22-year old *Leutnant*

Heinz Knoke in I./JG1 waited to tangle with the enemy bombers. Knoke, like the Pied Piper who was followed by the children who were never to return, hailed from Hamelin, an industrial town in Lower Saxony on the Weser River and he lived on the same road, which was known as the Koppenstrasse. The son of a policeman, who had served as an infantry sergeant, young Knoke joined the Hitler Youth in 1935. In August 1939 he took command of about 4,000 boys of the *Jungbann* in the Hamelin District (Kreis). By 1940 he was under training as a fighter pilot and on 18 December 1940 he was one of 3,000 officers of all services who heard Goering and Hitler speak at the Berlin *Sportpalast*. The next day, Knoke was posted to JG52. In June/July 1941 he flew combat sorties in Russia during *Barbarossa*, but did not score any victories, before being posted to JG1. He scored his first combat victory, a Spitfire, on 5 March 1942.

Now, almost a year later, 26 February, Knoke was in the mood for 'a good scrap with a swarm of Americans' and he was boosted by the weather, which was ideal. The sky was clear and cloudless blue. At first, everything over Great Yarmouth was quiet so he and his fellow Bf 109G pilots lay around outside on the tarmac wrapped in up blankets, enjoying the warmth of the first spring sunshine squinting idly up at the sky. Two big loudspeakers had begun blaring out dance music, which suddenly stopped. Knoke was summoned to the telephone to be told that fresh enemy concentrations were reported in map sector 'Dora-Dora'. Soon the pilots of JG1 were racing to their fighters. The canopies closed and the black overall clad *Schwarzemänner* swung the starters. The engine on Knoke's *Gustav* thundered into life and he and the eleven other aircraft took off together in formation. Knoke turned on the radio and called base. 'Bodo' vectored him towards 'heavy babies' at Anton-Quelle-eight, a grid reference on the map. Heinz Knoke turned north and he spotted the mass American formation ahead grouped together, 'like a great bunch of grapes shimmering in the clear blue sky'. As he drew closer he observed that most of them were Liberators, which looked as if their 'fat bellies were pregnant with bombs'.

The Liberators had been scheduled to join the Fortress formation at Fakenham, but a variation in predicted winds caused a delay and they were unable to catch them until the Forts were about 100 miles out to sea. This placed the 66th Squadron at the rear of the whole formation. The First Wing, led by the 305th, having started with ninety-three Forts, was reduced to seventy-three when twenty B-17s returned early with mechanical or other problems. The formation continued to climb until the B-24s reached an altitude of 29,000 feet. A German radar installation on the island of Texel in the Netherlands located the American bomber formation and about 8 minutes later the bombers were attacked by a lone Fw 190 of IV./JG1 flown by *Leutnant* Eberhard Burath, who recalls:

> During the usual – mostly unsuccessful – search for enemy formations I had, flying right out on the starboard wing and while continually scanning the sky, missed my formation's turn to port and had continued straight ahead far out over the North Sea. I noticed it too late and now

looked for my own lot. They appeared back there and I went after them with full power. Then they grew ever larger, much too large for fighters. Can that be possible? There they were, the *Viermots*, sixty to seventy of them in close formation. What now? Fear comes only with experience and that I did not have. Without thinking I turned into the formation and attacked from ahead. Firing with all my guns I flashed right through them. Turn in, pass parallel to them ahead. In doing so I was nearly hit as a projectile, aimed with just the right deflection, came towards me like a red tomato. Nice that the fellows then still used tracer, enabling me to jink away just in time. I zoomed once more through the formation, and then it was time to return to the coast, which was still 100 kilometres away. What might the Yanks have thought about this 'massed attack by German fighters'? At least they had provided me with an alibi by a hit in the engine, but the 801 continued to run smoothly even on thirteen cylinders.

Shortly after Burath's lone effort, other Focke-Wulfs joined the attack, one of which, piloted by *Oberfeldwebel* Bach, claimed to have shot down a B-17. It seems likely that this was *Lucy Belle* of the Hell's Angels Group but Lieutenant Lloyd Driffin the pilot evaded the fighters by diving into low-lying overcast. The bombers reached the German mainland near the North Sea islands of Baltrum and Langeoog. As the formation moved inland over Ostfriesland, the attacks intensified as Bf 109s joined the attack. IV./JGI had taken off from Leeuwarden and intercepted the B-17s and B-24s. They returned, claiming two shot down, but Becker's Bf 110 was lost without a trace. *Feldwebel* Georg 'Schorsch' Kraft's *Bordfunker*, *Feldwebel* Erich Handke of 12./NJG1 recalls:

Hauptmann Becker's failure to return from a daylight sortie ... was a heavy loss for the *Gruppe*. We had always been of the opinion that Becker was not suited for daylight operations and now he had not come back from his first one. We had taken off with twelve aircraft for the box *Schlei* with Becker leading. Quite unintentionally he was suddenly on his own. So there was no one there when it happened. We searched the sea with all aircraft until dusk but found nothing. He had simply disappeared, together with his *Bordfunker*, *Feldwebel* Staub. Josef Staub had been decorated with the German Cross-in-Gold, as the first night-fighter radio operator for his part in forty victories.

On this sortie we were able to shoot down our fourth enemy. The Americans had flown into north-west Germany and were now on their way back. From Schlei our flight was sent to the north and then far to the west, until at 4,000 metres and 10 km ahead we spotted six Liberators, of which the last one was some 1,000 metres behind. It was already being attacked by several Focke-Wulf fighters without success. Our flight now attacked one after the other. We had been ordered to attack only from head-on, but no one adhered to this; all attacked from the side, from the teat, above and behind and mostly fired from too great a range, concentrating on the breaking off at the end. We almost had to laugh as each, after his attack, peeled off down, only levelling off 1,000 metres below. By the time they were back up we had completed our three attacks and the Liberator was down. We attacked precisely according to regulations, first twice from ahead. Schorsch flew on ahead to port and above until the leading Liberators had commenced firing. Then I said, 'Turn in', for Schorsch was unable to see behind him. After his starboard turn he closed the throttles, pushed down and fired. We flashed past the Liberator some 30 metres above it and repeated the attack from starboard ahead. Cannon strikes flashed in the wings. While I was changing magazines he now attacked from behind as the rear turret was already out of action. I did not even realise that he was attacking, I only heard the guns firing. I had just finished loading the cannon when we had approached to 100 metres. So he was able to empty these magazines as well. That was enough for the Liberator, it dived steeply into a bank of cloud. By the time we came out below the cloud, it was already in the water. It went vertically down with all engines running. No one got out.

Things had also gone well for Heinz Knoke. After sighting the Liberators he had picked out one of the B-24s as his target and decided to make a frontal attack. Knoke described the attack thus:[40]

> The Yank is focused in my sights. He grows rapidly larger. I reach for the firing buttons on the stick. Tracers come whizzing past my head. They have opened up on me!
>
> Fire! I press both buttons, but my aim is poor. I can see only a few bits register in the right wing.
>
> I almost scrape the fat belly as I dive past. Then I am caught in the slipstream, buffeted about so violently that for a moment I wonder if my tail plane has been shot away. I climb up steeply and break away to the left. Tracers pursue me, unpleasantly close.
>
> Blast all this metal in the air!
>
> Thee hundred heavy bombers carry a total armament of 4,800 super-heavy machine-guns. Even if only one in ten have a chance to fire that still means we run into quite a barrage.
>
> I come in for a second frontal attack, this time from a little below. I keep on firing until I have to swerve to avoid a collision. My salvoes register this time.
>
> I drop away below. As I swing round I turn my head. Flames are spreading along the bottom of the fuselage of my Liberator. It sheers away from the formation in a wide sweep to the right.
>
> Twice more I come in to attack, this time diving from above the tail. I am met by heavy defensive fire. My plane shudders under the recoil from the two cannon and 13 mm guns. I watch my cannon shell-bursts rake along the top of the fuselage and right wing, and I hang on to the stick with both hands.
>
> The fire spreads along the right wing. The inside engine stops. Suddenly, the wing breaks off altogether. The body of the stricken

monster plunges vertically, spinning into the depths. A long black trail of smoke marks its descent.

One of the crew attempts to bale out. But his parachute is in flames. Poor devil! The body somersaults and falls to the ground like a stone.

At an altitude of 3,000 feet there is a tremendous explosion, which causes the spinning fuselage to disintegrate. Fragments of blazing wreckage land on a farm 200 or 300 yards from the Zwischenahn airfield, and the exploding fuel tank sets the farm buildings on fire.

In a terrific power dive I follow my victim down, and land on the runway below. I run over to the scene of the crash. A crowd of people are there, trying to fight the fire in the farmhouse. I join in the rescue work and bring out furniture, animals and machinery from the burning buildings. Smoke blinds and chokes me; my flying-suit is scorched by the flames, as I drag a fat pig out by the hind-legs, squealing like mad, from the pigsty, which is completely gutted by the fire. The farmhouse and barns are saved.

Strewn all over a cow-field lies the wreckage of the Liberator. The explosion threw clear the crew in mid-air. Their shattered bodies lie beside the smoking remains of the aircraft.

One hundred yards away I find the captain's seat and the nose wheel. A little doll, evidently the mascot, sits undamaged between the shattered windows of the cabin ....

Just two crewmen aboard *Maisie* survived. Adams and Perkins Post, the war correspondent, were among the dead.[41]

An hour later Knoke landed at Jever where his men carried him shoulder-high to the dispersal point. It was Knoke's fourth combat victory on his 164th combat mission. His friend Dieter Gerhard was credited with bringing down his seventh victim, his second heavy bomber, while fellow pilots *Unteroffizier* Raddatz,[42] Hans Wenneckers and Dobrick were also credited with a victory each. Either *Unteroffizier* Heinz Hanke of 9./JG1 in an Fw 190 or *Unteroffizier* Hans Wennekers of 2./JG1 in a Bf 109 had claimed the apparently doomed *Night Raider*[43] flown by Captain Beattie H. 'Bud' Fleenor, as their first victory. The Liberator had been seen as easy meat as it limped away from the target area with a supercharger out, flak holes in its fuselage and a pair of useless tail guns, which had frozen tight after only eight rounds. Fleenor's B-24 was then attacked again and again by Hanke and Wennekers, who claimed the apparently doomed B-24 as their first victory. But incredibly, *Night Raider* made it back to crash-land at Ludham, Norfolk, with a badly wounded crew, no hydraulic system, punctured tyres, a 15-inch hole in the right tail flap and 177 shell holes in the aircraft. One ground crew man said, 'This one shouldn't have come back'. *Sad Sack* and Robert McPhillamey's crew did not make it back. They were shot down by one of these two German pilots.[44]

Wray's Ragged Irregulars lost two Forts and the 305th three. About 15 minutes later Bremen Lieutenant George E. Stallman's ship, the lowest in the entire formation, came under attack from two Bf 109s. They made several passes and the Fortress took hits in the right wing and No. 4 engine, knocking the ship out of formation. A burst of flak hit Stallman's bomber as he tried in vain to catch up with the rest of the formation over Wilhelmshaven and the crew were ordered to bale out. Five men were killed and five made PoW. As the Fortresses turned off the target the bombers performed a very steep turn and as a result those following had a difficult time maintaining formation. Major Joseph J. Preston, pilot of the lead plane, said later, 'This was the strongest fighter opposition so far'. Two of the Forts were victims of flak and fighter attacks. *Arkie*, flown by Captain Everett E. Tribbett, was shot down just south of Wilhelmshaven. Two crewmen were captured and made PoW and the other eight evaded. *Devil's Playmate*, flown by Lieutenant Isaac D. Benson, was lost over the North Sea with all ten crew.

Despite the victories, Knoke could not help thinking about the bodies of the American crew. 'When will our turn come? Those men share in common with ourselves the great adventure of flying. Separated for the moment by the barrier of war, we shall one day be reunited by death in the air.'

Bremen was the last mission of the month for the Eightballs. February had been a bad month for the 66th Squadron, which had lost three ships and their crews.

On 4 March while fourteen B-24s flew a diversionary feint, seventy-one Fortresses were dispatched to the Hamm marshalling yards, the first US raid on the Ruhr. There was very bad visibility over East Anglia and the North Sea and the groups had difficulty finding each other. Twenty Forts took off from Bassingbourn led by Major Paul L. Fishburne in *Chief Sly II* to lead the groups to Hamm. Four of the formation aborted and over the North Sea thick layers of cloud prevented the planes from rendezvousing with the three other groups, so Fishburne decided to continue to Hamm alone. Unbeknown to him, shortly after crossing the Dutch coast two of the other groups turned south to bomb the Wilton Feyenoord shipyards near Rotterdam while the 306th returned without bombing.[47] As Fishburne's formation proceeded the clouds began to break up and by the time the target was reached they were in clear skies. As they approached the IP some fighters made a few attacks before the Forts were in moderate flak over the Ruhr Valley. Charles Giauque, pilot of *The Eagle's Wrath*, could not maintain formation because of his flight leader's evasive action and his flight began dropping back. Not wishing to become a straggler and an open invitation for enemy fighters, Giauque went full power ahead and tacked onto another ship. As he did so the vertical stabiliser was hit by a 20 mm shell, which jolted his foot 6 inches off the rudder pedal and the radio operator took a light wound. They remained airborne and got back with one engine feathered. Lieutenant George Birdsong and the crew of *Stormy Weather*, which they had climbed aboard after *Delta Rebel* had developed problems after take-off, also received punishment but they, too, would make it home, just.

Captain Oscar O'Neill, born in Brazil, 'mother Spanish, father Irish and who looked like George Raft', was flying *Invasion II* as usual. On 30 December 1942 the former Colgate graduate and dental supplies salesman had brought the plane home with Major Edward P. Meyers, his CO, dead in the co-pilot's seat beside him after head-on attacks by enemy fighters. Proudly displayed on the left hand side of the nose was Uncle Sam's 'rigid digit', the distinctive symbol, which had been introduced by the Group CO Colonel Stanley T. Wray that winter. Sergeant Jack Gaffney, assistant to crew chief Master Sergeant Bob Dalton, had lovingly painted it on the nose above the name of the aircraft and he was also responsible for the yellow bombs denoting missions flown. Back at Bassingbourn, Gaffney waited to add a seventh bomb to the lengthening row of mission symbols. Captain John R. 'Tex' McCrary was on board *Invasion II* to get some good newsreel photography of fighter attacks and he certainly got more than he bargained for as he recalled.[45]

Weather over our target was 'the best this side of Cahuenga Boulevard, Hollywood'. Our bombs plastered the target ... but there was a story between the lines .... It seemed so placid up there, in the radio room hatch of a target-bound Fortress. Far less belligerent than it used to be at the ringside, Madison Square Garden, where I used to slip in among the professional news photogs and click a furtive amateur camera at the weaving fighters inside the ropes. Then the radio gunner lurched against my back, knocking me through the passageway, down onto the curved top of the revolving ball turret. My foot caught in the turret gears. A little panicky, I tried to yank it loose. But looking at my hands, I saw blood washing down the rubber-matted floor and curling over my fingers. I had never seen so much blood before. I didn't know where it could have come from. It was strangely impersonal – just so much red paint. And then I looked beyond my hands, slowly, crumpled on the floor was the radio gunner – the strong legged boy who had just snapped on my oxygen mask for me not 10 seconds ago. I saw his face. It was twisted in pain. The red that was sogging my gloves and flying boots was burbling out of a wound in his back. A slug had struck him squarely. There was nothing impersonal, nothing detached about this war now. Not any more. I didn't know the boy's name.[46] I had reached the plane just in time for the take-off. No time to swap names. But seconds ago he had been offering me chewing gum to relax the popping of my ears. Now he had fallen across my oxygen lines – that's serious 5 miles up. Without oxygen, you can't help anybody else; you become a liability to the others. But there was no time to fix the lines. Time only to rip off my parachute, dive for the first aid kit, claw at the unfamiliar dressings and scissors, start hacking at his clothes. This job needed the help of fingers more skilled than mine. I grabbed two spare film packs, took careful aim and threw them at one of the waist gunners down inside the bomber. I was afraid I might never make it back that far without oxygen. One film hit its target. The gunner looked around. His wits were as quick as my fingers were slow. He grabbed a walk-around oxygen bottle, came back and helped administer the pathetically inadequate first aid. Two hypos eased the boy's pain. All I could do was wish I had paid more attention to the flight surgeon's lectures at gunnery school – or that I had been a doctor instead of a newspaperman. And then the war muscled in again. We were over the target now. Not until then did I realise that we were alone – just our group. Having missed the briefing, I didn't know that the other groups had turned off for another target. And then the Jerries really piled into us.

As Fishburne's little assemblage was returning over Friesland Province in northern Holland they were attacked by Bf110s normally engaged on night-fighting duties. Gunners put up stiff resistance in the face of overwhelming odds but *Hauptmann* Hans-Joachim Jabs of IV./NJGI and his three wingmen finished off a straggler, which had repulsed at least thirty attacks before finally going down. *Hauptmann* Lütje then claimed a B-17 and shortly after four Bf110s had finished off another. These two were probably Lieutenant Harold H. Henderson's which was last seen on fire and in a spin 10 miles north-west of Munster and *Rose O'Day* captained by Lieutenant Ralph A. Felton Jr. The battle raged on for another 10 minutes and *Excalibur* finally fell victim to a Bf110, probably flown by *Leutnant* Kostler of IV./NJG1. Lieutenant Allen Brill ditched the heavily damaged bomber in very rough seas 40 miles west of Texel and it broke in two. Brill and his co-pilot Allen Lowry tried to pull men clear of the aircraft before it sank but they were swept away. The only other loss was the ball turret gunner who had been swept away shortly after ditching. Late in the afternoon an ASR Walrus finally picked up the seven survivors.[48]

Nine Forts headed back to Bassingbourn in a damaged condition with seven men wounded in action. One of the seriously wounded was the radio gunner aboard *Invasion II*, which according to McCrary:

... throbbed with O'Neill's confidence, which pulsed back through the ribs and muscles of the bomber, transfused from his hands on the controls. He made *Invasion II* buck and dive the way Tommy Hitchcock used to handle a polo pony. My knees buttered later – when it was all over. I wasn't really scared while the show was on. There wasn't any room for terror on O'Neill's ship. And besides, there was that boy on the floor.

Could our combat crews stand the strain of heavy casualties? I got the answer later. When you try to translate one actual casualty right before your eyes into terms of icy logic, you can't.

What had seemed like creaking hours had in fact been minutes. I expected it to be at least 5 pm when we finally raced to a landing. Captain O'Neill had poured on the coal to get our wounded gunner back to base. The take-off had been an early one – 8 am. I was several hours wrong on the elapsed time.

We got down fast and hard and taxied quickly off the runway, toward a waiting ambulance. No sooner were we off than I saw another Fort steam down where we had just been. Steam is the right word. No brakes – it boiled right over the end of the runway, into the barbed wire and brush.

The medicos raced out to our bomber from the ambulance. Men swarmed inside. Our gunner was stretchered out through the side entry as gently as men who admire courage can lift a mortally wounded boy. He died a few minutes later. He never had a chance. His spine was severed.[49]

Fishburne and Captain James Bullock, his navigator, were awarded the DFC for successfully leading and completing the mission and the 91st received a Distinguished Unit Citation. Although the American gunners claimed thirteen fighters destroyed, only two Bf 110s were missing. The planes were patched up and Jack Gaffney added another yellow bomb mission symbol to the nose of *Invasion II*, no doubt taking time to glance at the No. 4 engine where he had painted the word *Judith*, the name of his favourite girl back home in San Bernadino.

Two days later the Eightballs flew their fiftieth mission, a diversionary raid on a bridge and U-boat facilities at Brest while the Fortresses headed for the U-boat pens at Lorient. All the Liberators returned, but three B-17s were shot down. Two days later the Liberators set out on another diversion mission. This time twenty B-24s headed for the Rouen marshalling yards as the B-17s attacked another marshalling yard at Rennes. Three squadrons of RAF Spitfires and for the first time P-47C Thunderbolts escorted the bombers. Twenty-four-year-old Lieutenant James E. O'Brien from Monongahela, Pennsylvania, led the Eightballs in *The Rugged Buggy* with Lieutenant Colonel James Posey aboard, but he was forced to return to base when one of the gunners passed out through lack of oxygen. Captain Clyde E. Price in *Miss Dianne* took over the group lead and Lieutenant Bob W. Blaine moved up to the deputy lead. Fw 190s of II./JG26 led by *Oberleutnant* Wilhelm-Ferdinand 'Wutz' Galland, brother of *Generalmajor* Adolf Galland, led fighters in a tight turn to go *von Schauze auf Schnauze* (snout to snout). *Miss Dianne* and Blaine's B-24 both went down immediately. Only three gunners survived from Price's ship, which crashed in flames with the bombs still in their racks. *Unteroffizier* Peter Crump, who had fired a long burst at the B-24 from long range and could clearly see a number of hits in the cockpit area, had singled out Blaine's ship. He dived away in a split-S, then saw to his horror that he was immediately in the way of Blaine's jettisoned bombs. Crump managed to miss them in a tight turn but lost sight of his target and could not say which of the falling aircraft was his kill. (Blaine's B-24 crashed at Barentin. There was just one survivor.) He saw one of the doomed Liberators crash in a patch of trees north of the Seine, but without a witness, Crump would not be awarded confirmation of his victory. Instead, it went to *Oberfeldwebel* Willi Roth. The Spitfire escort, which had had their hands full with fighters led by Major Josef 'Pips' Priller, who had been promoted to *Kommodore* of JG26 on 11 January, finally showed up in time to prevent further losses. Even so, two Liberators barely made it back to Shipdham and *Peg*, a 93rd Liberator, which was attacked by *Oberleutnant* Johannes Naumann of II./JG26, limped back across the Channel and crashed at Bredhurst, Kent.

On 12 and 13 March, the Liberators again flew diversions for the Fortresses. Then on 18 March a maximum effort involving ninety-seven Fortresses and Liberators, the highest number of bombers so far, was mounted to attack the

Bremer Vulkan Schiffbau shipbuilding yards on the Weser, which were ranked the fourth largest producer of U-boats in Germany. At Jever, operation orders for I./JG1 arrived, telling pilots to intercept and attack a formation of heavy bombers approaching the coast of Germany. *Leutnant* Heinz Knoke and his comrades had been practising for a few days previously on bombing the tight formations of American bombers from above with 100 lb bombs. *Oberleutnant* Dieter Gerhard, his friend since fighter school days and a colleague in Russia, had thought of this idea and in the early morning Gerhard and Knoke made a practice flight off Heligoland, each dropping four 100 lb bombs on a sack, which was towed by a Ju 88. Gerhard's third bomb scored a direct hit but the *Alarmstart* (scramble) at 1412 hours gave the pilots of 5./JG1 too little time to arm their fighters with bombs and so Knoke and Gerhard would have to rely on their guns and cannon on this occasion. Before he closed his canopy, Gerhard called over to Knoke that he wanted to shoot down the formation leader. Knoke asked him, laughing, if the Yanks had recently taken to painting the wings of their planes with rank-badges.

JG1 established contact with the American formation at 25,000 feet in the Heligoland area. Knoke led the *Gustavs* in close formation for a frontal attack and he opened fire on a B-24 flying low right. It was *Hot Freight* flown by Lieutenant Howard E. 'Tarzan' Kleinsteuber in the 93rd, which immediately caught fire and fell away to the right like a crippled beast. Knoke pursued it, attacking from the rear, then from head-on. His aim had never been better. Suddenly, *Hot Freight* exploded, hurling wreckage through the sky. Sergeant Louis A. Webb was the only survivor. Knoke hurled his Fw 190 into a power dive to escape the flying engines and debris and only just managed to miss the falling fuselage of the doomed Liberator, which fell into the sea 12 miles south-east of Heligoland. It was his fifth victory. Knoke climbed back to 25,000 feet for another attack on the Liberators, but suddenly his heart almost stopped beating for Gerhard was in the middle of the bomber formation holding his *Gustav* steady, following the same course. Knoke thought that his close friend's first Liberator had gone down a few minutes earlier, but *Eager Beaver*, which although badly hit and seen to drop from formation with a smoking engine, made it back to England. Knoke knew that Gerhard wanted to put the formation leader in the North Sea and he thought that he must have become 'completely insane as he kept hard on the tail of his quarry, blazing away at it as tracers from every side converged upon his *Gustav*'. Knoke dived down through the formation towards Gerhard, firing indiscriminately at any bombers in the vicinity, then his close friend suddenly broke away in a steep dive and 3,000 feet below his Bf 109 began emitting a trail of smoke. Gerhard opened his canopy and baled out. Knoke flew past close to him and could see that his face was contorted with pain and he was gripping his body. Gerhard died of his wounds in his dinghy. That night Knoke took a bottle of brandy from his friend's clothes locker. There was another bottle in his own locker. It had been agreed that these bottles were to be drunk by the *Gruppe* in memory of whoever was first to fail to return from a mission.

Vegesack was officially described as 'extremely heavily damaged'. The bombers had dropped 268 tons of HE smack on the target and later photographic reconnaissance revealed that seven U-boat hulls had been severely damaged and two-thirds of the shipyards destroyed.

On 22 March Knoke was on alert again when eighty-four Liberators and Fortresses assembled in map reference sector Dora-Dora off Great Yarmouth. Their destination was the Marienewerft U-boat yards at Wilhelmshaven, but when the alert was sounded there was no time for JG1's aircraft to be bombed-up. The *Gustav* pilots got airborne but 7 minutes later they received orders to land. The American bombers had turned about and were now heading back in a westerly direction. After landing, the Bf 109s were refuelled immediately and the German pilots, anticipating another alert, stood by. Knoke's ground crew used the delay to attach a 500 lb high-explosive bomb under his *Gustav*, but when JG1 were ordered to take off, the bomb was not ready to go. *Unteroffizier* Hans Wenneckers took over, waved his hand in recognition, and rolled down the runway followed by the other *Gustav* pilots in close formation. Sweating *Schwarzemänner* worked flat out under the belly of Knoke's *Gustav*, as he remained strapped in his seat, flaming with impatience. Finally, his machine was ready, but with the bomb fitted he could not take off downwind and his Bf 109 rumbled awkwardly down to the far end of the runway. Turning at the perimeter of the field, his *Gustav* suddenly listed heavily to the left. A tyre had burst. Knoke fired off a red signal flare and thirty *Schwarzemänner* piled into a truck and raced over to him. With the engine still running the port wing was lifted up on powerful jacks and the wheel changed in a matter of seconds. The *Schwarzemänner* scattered as Knoke opened the throttle and started rolling with gathering speed. The *Gustav* again began to list to port, but he managed to pull it off the ground after a run of 600 feet and cleared the roof of No. 2 Hangar by a few centimetres. Knoke climbed at full throttle into the cloudless sky heading out to sea. Overhead were the vapour trails left by German and American aircraft and combat had already ensued. At 22,000 feet Knoke's *Gustav* reacted sluggishly under the heavy load and climbed wearily up to 30,000 feet, taking 25 minutes to do so. Knoke continues:

> The Yanks have bombed Wilhelmshaven, as I can tell from the smoke and fires below. They are over Heligoland on the return flight now. I edge forward slowly until I am over the tip of the enemy formation, which consists entirely of Fortresses. For several minutes I am under fire from below, while I take a very rough sort of aim on my target, weaving and dipping each wing tip alternately in order to see the formation below. Two or three holes appear in my left wing. I fuse the bomb, take final aim and press the release button on my stick. My bomb goes hurtling down. I watch it fall and bank steeply as I break away. Then it explodes, exactly in the centre of a row of Fortresses.

Liberty Bell, a Fort on its first combat sortie in Wray's Ragged Irregulars went down, followed by the torn wing 'fluttering down like an autumn leaf' 20 miles off Heligoland, scattering the two others in the same vic. All eleven men in Captain Hascall C. McClellan's crew perished.

Lieutenant Charles 'Red' Cliburn, who by now seemed to have a reputation for flying 'jinx' ships no one else wanted to fly, but who 'did not go much for superstitions' himself, flew *The Sad Sack* home on two engines. One engine blew up over the target and five twin-engined fighters put out another engine on the same wing over the North Sea. Cliburn managed to latch on to another formation and using about 15-degree flaps to keep the ailing bomber flying and with the airspeed dropping to 125 mph, he got home. After repairs *The Sad Sack* became known as a lucky ship and in 1944 she went home on a war Bond tour of the States. C. E. DeBaun, 'Red' Cliburn's co-pilot, who flew Cliburn's old ship *The Bad Penny* after Cliburn completed his tour and was moved up to a Combat Wing job, said of his pilot:

> He was one of those men who simply didn't know how to give up. Four times he had every reason to make a landing on enemy territory, to save his neck ... but he always brought his ship home, no matter what the odds were against him. His crew would have flown through hell with him, because they knew he would always bring them home.

Two Eightball Liberators failed to return. *Maggie*, flown by Captain Gideon 'Bucky' Warne was damaged by flak over the target area and was shot down by *Oberleutnant* Sommer, the intelligence officer of I./JG1 for his second victory. *Cactus*, flown by Lieutenant Virgil R. Fouts, whose crew were flying their first mission, was shot down into the sea off the coast of Holland by *Leutnant* Pancritius of 8./JGI for his third 'kill'. Back at Shipdham, Lieutenant Jim O'Brien counted twenty-nine separate holes in *Rugged Buggy*, while at Hardwick *Teggie Ann* returned with no fewer than 368 holes in the aircraft. Colonel Ted Timberlake, the CO, narrowly escaped death when a 20 mm shell entered the cockpit and missed him by only a few inches.

Shortly after noon on 28 March over 120 bombers set out to bomb the Rouen-Sotteville marshalling yards, but the Liberators were recalled early because of poor weather. The Spitfire escort at first failed to *rendezvous* with the bombers and they flew a triangular course in mid-Channel. When the Spitfires finally arrived they were low on fuel and had to return, leaving the B-17s to fly on alone to the target. Fighters tore into them and damaged nine over the English Channel. *Leutnant* Georg-Peter 'Schorch' Eder of 12./JG2 shot down a B-17 in the 91st and none of Lieutenant John A. Coen's crew survived. Eder was injured by return fire but he was able to force land his badly damaged Bf 109 at Beaumont-Le-Roger.

Three days later just over 100 bombers took off to bomb the wharves and docks area at Rotterdam. *Ooold Soljer* and *Two Beauts* in the Hell's Angels Group were lost when they collided in mid-air near Wellingborough and fourteen men died. *Satan's Chariot*, a Liberator in the 93rd was shot down 60 miles off Ostend with no survivors by *Oberleutnant* Otto Stammberger for his fourth victory. Four of the six bomb groups that set out were recalled because of strong winds and thick cloud, which all but blotted out the target, and many Forts, blown off course by strong winds and bad visibility, missed their objectives completely. Some bombs hurtled down into the streets of Rotterdam, killing 326 civilians. JG1 intercepted the 305th formation and made one pass before their fuel was expended. *Unteroffizier* Peter Crump attacked *Southern Comfort* piloted by Captain Hugh G. Ashcraft over the North Sea. During the latter stages of the aerial battle the radio operator was firing his gun when he saw that the rudder was hit. He looked down and saw fire between the two inboard engines. At first the fire was behind the vents, inside the wing and then it started coming out. As the German attack slackened, Ashcraft turned out of formation and swung back toward the English coast. Ashcraft announced over the intercom 'Those who want to, please pray'. Solid overcast swallowed the Fortress. The fire, apparently feeding on oil and not gasoline, was now 'very persistent in character'. The rear gunner recalled that at the time it didn't bother him much, because having flown a few missions he knew what it was. With plenty of time to arrange everything, he just sat there waiting for the signal to leave. Most of the rest of the crew gathered into two groups, one around the navigator's escape hatch in the forward end of the Fortress and the other about the door at the rear of the fuselage.

Southern Comfort was in the clouds at about 15,000 feet, dropping fast and on instruments. The crew could not see a thing, but the navigator said it was about time that they were over the coast. He gave Ashcraft a heading to fly, but the tail was a little shot up and he could do little. Ashcraft looked at the wing and could see the metal buckling and the flames getting around so he decided that 'all God's children ought to have wings'. As the alarm bell rang, the radio operator, who had been sending SOS signals, was waiting for an answer. He screwed his key down and prepared to jump with the rest. They were all out in less than a minute, each man instantly disappearing into the thick bank of clouds. Ashcraft waited until the last man had jumped, or until he thought the last man had jumped, and then he trimmed the B-17 so that it was flying level and followed the others overboard through the forward escape hatch. The left waist gunner, the last man to leave by the door at the rear of the ship, delayed to change his parachute. When he looked around and found himself in a pilotless and deserted aircraft he left immediately. The only fatality among the crew was *Southern Comfort*'s top turret gunner, who apparently slipped out of his parachute harness as he neared the ground. Three times the burning B-17 gracefully circled Wickham Bishops, a small village, and then crashed in a field, the last considerate act of a gallant lady.[50]

Bad weather grounded the bombers until 4 April, when nearly 100 B-17s headed for the Renault works in the Billancourt district of Paris. Most of the bombs that hit the factory were released by the leading 305th formation, led by Major Tom McGehee in *We the People*, flown by Captain Cliff Pyle and a thick pall of smoke reaching to 4,000 feet blotted out the whole area. Groups in the rear of the formation were not as accurate and many bombs caused a number of civilian casualties. North of Paris, fighters led by Spanish Civil War veteran Major Walter 'Gulle' Oesau, *Kommodore*, JG2[51] made several head-on passes before the Forts reached the Rouen area where more fighters began attacks on the formation. Cannon shells smashed through the windshield of *Dry Martini III*. Martini was temporarily blinded and his co-pilot was wounded and momentarily knocked unconscious. The B-17 dropped

1,000 feet before they could bring the plane under control. One engine was out and they were alone, easy prey for the fighters, or so they thought. They massed for the *coup de grâce*, but although they riddled the fuselage with 160 cannon and bullet holes and hit the right wing and left aileron, they could not bring the aircraft down. The right main wing-spar had been all but shot through but, incredibly, *Dry Martini III* made it home and her gunners were credited with the destruction of ten enemy fighters, a record for a bomber crew on a single mission. The Fort flown by Lieutenant Herschel B. Ellis went down in flames. Ellis and seven others of his crew baled out and were captured but the bombardier and ball-turret gunner died. *Available Jones* flown by Morris M. Jones and Harold P. O'Neill's B-17 were also lost. In the Hell's Angels group *Holy Mackeral!* went down with six of the crew. *Hauptmann* 'Wutz' Galland of II./JG26 claimed two of the B-17s and *Oberleutnant* Karl Borris and Oesau one each. The Spitfire escort reappeared to provide withdrawal support but six of their number were shot down in a 7-minute battle without loss to the *Luftwaffe*. American gunners claimed forty-seven German fighters destroyed, but the real losses were two pilots killed and one wounded. After the raid, photographs smuggled back to England by the French Resistance showed that the Renault works had been severely damaged. For its action this day, the 305th received a Distinguished Unit Citation. Pronounced beyond repair, *Dry Martini III* never flew again and instead was used as a 'hangar queen' at Chelveston.

Returning to Thurleigh from the Paris mission, Lieutenant Robert W. Seelos, pilot of *Montana Power* in the 368th Squadron went to consult Doc Shuller about his ears, which were bothering him. Seelos was diagnosed as having a head cold and the pressure at high altitude was making his ears ache, so Shuller said that he was grounded for a few days. For medication Seelos went to the officers' club and after a couple of drinks he felt all right again. Then the usual unwelcome announcement came over the loudspeakers: 'All armament personnel report to the flight line.' This meant that the Forts were going to be loaded up again for another mission the next day. Then, word leaked out that the mission would be a short milk run. Just over 100 bombers were going to be despatched to Belgium to bomb the ERLA VII aircraft and engine repair works at Mortsel, near Antwerp, where 4,000 Bf 109s were under repair. Seelos recalls, 'Naturally, I figured I shouldn't miss the chance to get my 19th mission in, leaving me with only six more to go. So I immediately went to Doc Shuller and had him "unground" me'. Seelos advised his squadron commander that he was ready to go but that he did not have a navigator. He told Seelos not to worry; a replacement crew had just arrived from the States that night and he could have the navigator.

The next morning after briefing I had the crew all in place, the engines warmed up and waiting for the red flare to signal us to start taxiing – but still no navigator. Just before the signal, a command car skidded around the corner and let out the new navigator, who was pulled up into the nose. We started to taxi immediately. I didn't even get introduced to my new crewmember. I learned later that his name was James E. Murray and that he had been married just prior to leaving the States. We took off and formed the Group.

Brigadier General Frank Armstrong returned to Thurleigh to fly on this mission as an observer with his former group, which was putting up eighteen Forts. Armstrong climbed aboard Captain John M. Regan's *Dark Horse*, which also carried Lieutenant Colonel Jim Wilson, appointed Executive Officer just three days earlier. The 368th Squadron flew lead, the 423rd high and the 367th Clay Pigeons flew low. One of the B-17s turned back after a cylinder head failed and supercharger buckets blew off. A second Fort turned back because the No. 4 engine went out and the aircraft could not keep up. At 22,000 feet the rest of the group headed south-east and crossed the English coast at Dungeness. About halfway across the Channel they made a 180-degree turn and headed back to Dungeness in a diversionary manoeuvre, which was designed to draw up and confuse the German fighters. Just north of Dover between Ramsgate and Margate at Foreland, the Forts headed almost due east across the Channel to the Belgian coast, near Ostend. Twenty-one Forts and Libs turned back due to various mechanical problems before reaching the enemy coast where, from then on, the leading 306th bore the brunt of head-on attacks by Fw 190s of JG26 and JG1, which continued all the way to the target. Obviously, the diversion had not worked.

III./JG26, went charging in but the *Kommandeur*, *Hauptmann* Fritz Geisshardt, who had been decorated with the Knight's Cross with Oak Leaves for his 102 confirmed victories, was hit in the abdomen by return fire. He was able to make a wheels-up landing in his Fw 190 on the airfield at Ghent but died from loss of blood early the following morning. *L'il Abner*, flown by Lieutenant Clarence Fischer was hit by flak over Ghent *en route* to the target and finished off by Major 'Pips' Priller. The crew baled out before the Fort exploded at Wilrijk. It was Priller's eighty-fourth victory. Lieutenant Kelly Ross's aircraft was badly hit on the way into the target by cannon and machine-gun fire from *Hauptmann* 'Wutz' Galland and Ross gave the order to bale out. All except the tail and waist gunners survived. It was Galland's thirty-eighth victory. North of the Scheldt another Fortress was claimed by *Oberfeldwebel* Adolf 'Addi' Glunz of IV./JG26 as his thirty-second of his eventual seventy-one-victory tally. Lieutenant William H. Parker and four of his crew were killed. Navigator Paul Spaduzzi's parachute was popped open by the force of the explosion before the crippled bomber spun in. North of Antwerp, *Oberleutnant* Otto Stammberger, found a faltering B-17 squarely in his sights. It was *Montana Power* flown by Robert Seelos.

I would guess that we were about halfway between the coast and Antwerp when I took a direct hit in the prop dome of my No. 1 engine. It was running wild, and with the feathering mechanism destroyed, there was no way I could do anything about it. With the old style props and the drag from the No. 1 engine, I had to use full power on the other three engines to stay with the group, which seemed to me to be in anything but a tight formation. At least three other planes were in trouble and trying to hang in there for more firepower and protection. I called the group lead ship and told them to slow down, that we were in trouble. I got no response. For some reason I kept thinking – if only our old squadron commander, Bill Lanford, was leading the group – he would have slowed it down and tucked the cripples in like an old mother hen, and would possibly have got us all back at least as far as the Channel. By now I was so mad and busy trying to keep going to the target, I really didn't have time to get scared or worry that we weren't going to make it. Just after our bombs were released I took a direct flak hit in the No. 4 engine. I immediately made a flat left turn in hopes the group lead would try to pick me up as they made their turn off the target at least a half mile ahead of me. But they seemed to be heading full power for the coast. In the meantime the German fighters were spraying the hell out of us. I had hopes of reaching the Channel and trying to ditch in the water but the No. 4 burst into flames. I told co-pilot Alex Kramarinko to tell the crew to bale out at once.

Stammberger raked the B-17 from head-on with a burst from his four cannon and two machine-guns. Stammberger had to pull up quickly because the Fortress suddenly nosed downward. He watched the survivors bale out and saw the pilotless ship carry on for a short time before finally crashing at Kalmthout. It was his fifth victory. Seelos came down on the edge of the town of Wuustwezel, Belgium, and was captured. He eventually ended up at *Stalag Luft III*. Seven of his crew managed to evacuate the doomed ship but the top turret gunner, a waist gunner and Lieutenant Murray were killed. In a bomb group reputed for its high turnover rate, Murray had the shortest tour of all in the 306th – a matter of hours only.

Seelos concludes:

By the time I got out I was well away from the others. I came down on the edge of the town of Wuustwezel, Belgium. As I was descending I could see I was going to go through the top of a tree. I braced myself and gritted my teeth – so hard that I bit through my cheek. The chute collapsed and I hit the ground so hard that I was knocked out momentarily. When I came to I was looking into the eyes of a perfect doll of a Belgian girl – long braids, blue eyes, wooden shoes. Blood was coming out of my mouth, and she thought I had been shot and was bleeding internally. She was trying to find the bullet hole and I had a hard time convincing her there wasn't any. When I was finally able to get to my feet, I had her hide the parachute in the brush. I then tried to tell her I wanted to get the hell out of there and hide someplace. But just then about a dozen German soldiers appeared with their little machine-guns. I wasn't about to try to run or do anything foolish. They proceeded to march me to their headquarters at the local city hall. A crowd of Belgian people was gathering and following with us and giving me the *V-for-Victory* sign, much to the annoyance of the Germans. The blonde girl stayed right behind me all the way to the city hall. I had eased my escape kit from my pocket and managed to give it to her without the Germans noticing. Just prior to reaching City Hall, I slipped off one of my dogtags and gave that to her also. The following morning, my family in Montana received the standard MIA telegram. When no more word was received after more than a month, my family was about to give up hope. On Mother's Day, the blonde girl was in Brussels and went to the equivalent of our Western Union. Using the address from my dogtag, she sent this cablegram to Mrs Seelos, Philipsburg, Montana, USA: 'Dear Auntie, Robert was here visiting, was in very good health, and sends his love to his darling relative.' Unbelievably, the message got through, untouched and uncensored. It was one fantastic Mother's Day gift to my mother. She called the War Department, and they informed her that they still had no information about me but they would check with the Swiss Red Cross. They called back shortly and said that my name was on the latest PoW list.[52] The Germans took me to a fighter base at Deurne on the outskirts of Antwerp. I learned later that my navigator, whom I hadn't even met, had been killed. We also lost our top turret gunner and one of our waist gunners.[53]

Well-aimed bombing was not possible due to the persistent fighter attacks, which forced many bombers off course. This serious situation was aggravated by problems with the Norden bomb sights in two of the Bomb Groups and the B-17s that got their bombs away dropped most of them on Mortsel where over 3,000 houses were destroyed, killing 936 inhabitants and injuring 1,342. Only four bombs hit the works, which killed over 300 workers and within a few weeks aircraft and engine repairs were back to the normal level at Mortsel.

Dark Horse was hit by cannon fire from an Fw190 attacking head-on during the bomb run, but Wilson and Regan got the Fortress safely home to Thurleigh. Captain Robert Salitrnik, the lead navigator, who had flown with Armstrong on the first American raid on Germany on 27 January, was in a critical conditon. Salitrnik had been hit in the leg by fragments from a can of .50 calibre ammunition, which exploded when hit by 20 mm fire from an Fw190 during the head-on attack. Armstrong administered first aid to the navigator as he shared a walk-around oxygen bottle with Regan. Salitrnik had received four pints of plasma in the plane and was further treated at the dispensary at Thurleigh and then taken to the hospital at Diddington. He was out of shock the next day but he developed gas gangrene on 15 April. The young lead navigator died the next day.[54]

On Friday 16 April, the first mission since Antwerp, over seventy Fortresses and Liberators bombed Lorient and Brest. One Fort was lost and the Flying Eightballs had eight B-24s damaged, but the heaviest fighter attacks by JG2 seemed to be aimed at the Travelling Circus, which lost four B-24s to Fw190s attacking from the rear of their formation at the target. *Liberty Lass* was the first to go down, followed by the crew of *Ball of Fire Jnr*. Captain Bud Fleenor and crew (who had crashed at Ludham on 26 February) in *Missouri Sue* went down in the Channel after the bombardier had baled out over France. *Judith Lynn* was also lost. *Yardbird* crashed at St Eval. Repairs were made to the battered bombers, replacement aircraft and crews were assigned and next day a record 111 heavies set out for the Focke-Wulf factory at Bremen.

Intense fighter attacks by just over 100 fighters were encountered and sixteen Fortresses failed to return. Ten of the bombers and 100 men – thirty-four of them killed – were from the 306th Group. 'It was like a feeding frenzy of sharks' Donald J. Bevan, a gunner on *Unmentionable*, later recounted. Everyone aboard was calm and remained at his post until Warren George Jr the pilot finally said over the intercom to the crew, 'All right, I guess we better bale out'. George and his engineer never made it. Some of those that did make it home were basket cases. Captain Pervis Youree got *Old Faithful* back to Thurleigh, but it was a mystery to him how they made it. The Fort flown by Lieutenant Kenneth A. Reecher in the Clay Pigeons Squadron came home with the body of the bombardier dead in the plane. Lieutenant Harold E. Lane had been hit in the groin by a 20 mm cannon shell, which severed a main artery, and he had soon bled to death. Many familiar faces like Captain 'Wild Bill' Casey, an original pilot who was on his twenty-second mission at the controls of *Banshee*, were gone. News later came through that all Casey's crew were safe, but morale, already dented by the loss of the four B-17s of the Clay Pigeons Squadron twelve days earlier, was shattered and the Thurleigh group was 'stood down' indefinitely after this devastation.[55]

The other six Fortresses lost all came from the 401st Squadron in the leading 91st Group formation. *Hellsapoppin*, which was almost certainly named after the Universal Studios movie of 1941, was hit by flak and crashed at about midday with the loss of pilot, John Wilson, and four of the enlisted crew. *The Sky Wolf (II)* flown by Nicholas Stoffel and his crew went down on what was their fifth mission. *Thunderbird*, which originated from Great Plains' Indian folklore and Harold Beasley's crew, failed to return. The Fort had flown just three missions since Beasley first flew the plane on 31 March to Rotterdam. *Short Snorter III* and Nathan Lindsey's crew went the way of the first and second *Short Snorters* on the crew's eighth mission. A Short Snorter was a popular good luck charm comprising bank notes from various countries that an airman passed through when deployed overseas, pasted end to end and covered in signatures along the way. *Short Snorter III* had lasted just ten missions and no more bombers in the group carried the name after this. *Rain of Terror* flown by Lieutenant Robert Walker on his first mission as pilot, having flown only two previous ones as a co-pilot, also fell victim to the German defences. Walker survived but two of his crew were killed.

About 4 minutes west of the target *Invasion II* and Captain Oscar O'Neill's crew – on their eighteenth mission – left the formation with the front section of the fuselage and both inner wing sections on fire as a result of flak hits. At their hardstand at Bassingbourn Bob Dalton and Jack Gaffney waited anxiously. Captain John R. 'Tex' McCrary who was in London, laid up with sinus problems, called up Bassingbourn to see how the mission had gone. He was anxious to find out the outcome. By now he had got to know O'Neill's crew well. McCrary was also concerned about Colonel Ordway, boss of 8th Air Force Intelligence Section, who was to have made his first mission that morning. McCrary had told him, 'Go with Oscar O'Neill. That guy will bring you back if he has to get out and carry *Invasion II* home.' McCrary called the base at about 8 o'clock and got the operations officer on the phone.

There was a lot of music, and very loud laughter in the background.

'Listen Colonel – can you hear me? How's Oscar? Did he get back okay – and the crew?'

Before he answered, I knew what the answer would be. It came, awkward, slow.

'Oscar? Well – guess he didn't make it. Yes he went down. Colonel Ordway? No, he's okay. He decided to go with somebody else. Well, it was pretty rough – we lost six. Oscar was leading the low flight. Flak must have hit him. The boys say his wing men followed him down. You know how they always followed Oscar because they always figured he knew what was best. And then the fighters must have got them, wiped out the whole flight. Last anybody saw of Oscar, he was still going down. But he seemed to have his ship under control ....'[56]

Incredibly, O'Neill and all his crew baled out safely. Before it was lost it was rumoured at Bassingbourn that *Invasion II* was being considered as the star to appear in the William Wyler's movie, which later starred *Memphis Belle*.[57] Although *Invasion II* and Oscar O'Neill never became movie stars, his daughter Jennifer later became a movie star in her own right.

Early May saw several raids on St Nazaire and the Ford and General Motors plants at Antwerp. In the mid-afternoon of 13 May Fortresses of the First Wing attacked the Avions Potez aircraft factory at Meaulte while Fourth Wing, flying their first mission, attacked St Omer-Longuenesse airfield. The Snetterton Falcons lost a B-17 when it crashed into The Wash at the start of the mission and the Group failed to bomb the target owing to a misunderstanding by the formation leaders. The straggling 351st formation abandoned the mission in mid-Channel. A 305th ship was shot down by flak with the loss of five crew killed. Major Pips Priller and *Leutnant* Helmut Hoppe of JG26 claimed two 91st B-17s. *Vulgar Virgin* crashed and exploded at Abbeville with the loss of eight crew and the Fort piloted by Lieutenant Homer C. Biggs Jr was lost with seven crew. Six men were taken prisoner from the two Fortresses. Eleven Forts, including one badly damaged by a bomb dropped by an Fw 190, returned with battle damage. The next day simultaneous attacks were made on the Krupp shipyards at Kiel, Wevelgem airfield and the Ford and General Motors plant and locks nearby at Antwerp.[58] Large numbers of Spitfires and P-47s escorted the bombers but they could not prevent heavy losses at Kiel.

Heinz Knoke and 5./JG11 again went looking for victories with their belly-mounted bombs. Several times Knoke attempted a formation attack 30,000 feet above Holstein, but each time the bombers weaved out of the way below. Over Kiel the *Gustavs* ran into heavy flak from their own Naval guns and the shooting was so accurate that they were considerably disorganised. Knoke also had time to observe the Americans dumping their loads right on the Germania shipyards. He was impressed by the precision with which 'the bastards bombed ... fantastic'. His chance of bringing off a formation drop had gone by now so he sent the *Gustavs* in one at a time. His own bomb failed to explode but hits were claimed by *Feldwebel* Erich Führmann,[59] *Feldwebel* Jonny Fest, 'a tall fair-haired' pilot, and *Unteroffizier* Biermann. *Hell's Angels* in the 91st was last seen just over the sea west of Armum Island heading back towards England, under control but with one engine out and a large hole through the rudder. All ten crew perished at sea. *FDR's Potato Peeler Kids* in the Hell's Angels Group suffered the same fate while a 92nd Fort crashed at Rendsburg, all nine men being made PoWs. Once again relying on his guns, Knoke dived for a frontal attack against a detached formation of thirty Fortresses. Almost at once he felt a hit in the fuselage and as a result he had to abandon the attack. His Daimler-Benz engine continued running smoothly, however, and all the controls seemed to be working so he attempted another frontal attack. His first salvo registered right in the cockpit of a Fortress. It reared up like a great animal that had been mortally wounded and dropped away in steep spirals to the right. At about 10,000 feet a wing broke off and it crashed near Husum. Knoke got home with several holes in his fuselage and tail.

The Flying Eightball crews flying in the rear of the formation behind the slower B-17s had been briefed to bomb from 21,000 feet but constant zig-zagging over the North Sea put them over Heligoland Bay at 18,000 feet. As they turned into the strong wind for bombing they were down to 160 mph, almost stalling speed. The Flying Eightballs cargo of incendiaries had required a shorter trajectory and a two-mile longer bomb run than the Forts. Flying a scattered formation, the Flying Eightballs were exposed to fighter attack. Altogether, five Libs were shot down. Worst hit was the 67th Squadron, bringing up the rear of the formation, which lost three bombers in quick succession. There were only two survivors from *Annie Oakley* and only six men got out of *Miss Delores*, which was hit by flak over the target. *Little Beaver* was shot up after leaving the target and three explosions rocked the ship, killing Captain Chester L. 'George' Phillips and six crew. Eight other B-24s were damaged and twelve men were wounded. *Margaret Ann* returned to base with one gunner mortally wounded and three seriously wounded. *Ruth-less* was very badly damaged but made it back, although pilot Lieu-tenant Frank Slough finally had to crash-land in Northern Ireland because Shipdham was so congested that it could not take any more aircraft in trouble.

Meanwhile, the attack on Wevelgem airfield had fared better. It was so heavily damaged by bombs dropped by the Forts that III./JG26 was forced to move to Lille-Nord. On the bombers' return east of Ypres they were attacked en masse by fighters. II./JG26 shot down two, *The Annihilator* and another 351st B-17. Flak bracketed the Antwerp force and fighters picked up the pieces. *Oberfeldwebel* Bach of II./JG1 applied the *coup de grâce* to a 9th Fort that spun out of formation at 2,500 feet and crashed on North Beveland Island, killing all the crew. *Oberleutnant* Horst Sternberg of JG26 claimed another over the Scheldt estuary. JG26 lost two pilots to return-fire from the bombers and *Hauptmann* Karl Borris was forced to bale out at 22,000 feet after coming off worse against a bomber. He was fortunate to survive when his parachute failed to open properly. The day's missions cost twelve bombers. Hans Wenneckers claimed a victory to take JG1's score to fifty heavy bombers. Later in the afternoon, *Generalleutnant* Galland signed the unit's visitors' book with his good wishes and congratulations on their 'Fiftieth Heavy Baby'.

Over the next few days, targets at Emden, Heligoland, Wilhelmshaven and Lorient were bombed. On 19 May just over 160 B-17s hit Kiel and Flensburg for six Forts lost; three of which were ripped to pieces by bombs dropped from above by *Feldwebel* Jonny Fest,[60] *Feldwebel* Erich Führmann and *Unteroffizier* Biermann of 5./JG1. *Leutnant* Heinz Knocke's bomb failed to hit a *Viermot* but he brought down a B-17 with his cannon and machine-guns near Husum. *Leutnant* Martin Drewes, a former *Zerstörer* pilot who was transferred to *Nachtjagd* at the end of 1941, served as a pilot in 7./NJG3. By early 1943, his tally stood at three victories and he was one of those young nightfighter pilots who were ordered to fly against the American bombers. He recounts a particularly fraught daylight sortie on 19 May:

> Late in the morning I had flown from my operational airfield Kopenhagen-Kastrup to Stade, to settle various things for the *Gruppe*. My radar operator had immediately gone to the big hangar to take a shower. Then all of a sudden – *Alarm!* – a strong formation of *Viermots* was reported flying in the direction of Kiel. A *Hauptmann* told me that the order for take-off was only for a specific number of aircraft of the unit that was based at the 'drome. Still, I felt that I *HAD* to scramble and walked towards my Bf 110. An officer mechanic asked me if he could fly with me and confirmed that he knew all about how to operate the R/T and the weapons systems. So, we took off at 1313 hours.
>
> The last machine to take off before me was flown by the excellent *Oberfeldwebel* Leschnik. I tried to catch up with him but he was climbing with full power and the distance between us wasn't reduced. Weather: bright sunshine, good visibility and at a height of some 1,000 metres an 8/10th veil of cloud. We climbed to a height of 7,000 metres. Leschnik, who flew some 500 metres in front of me, had come into shooting distance of the last Pulk of Boeing B-17s. I watched the exchange of fire, then Leschnik's machine plunged down steeply – no parachutes.
>
> Without any doubt, a number of 'Gun Ships' flew along in the Pulk. I was now alone with the thirteen B-17s in the last box and fired off a burst at the bomber that flew in the middle and in the back and registered some good hits. Suddenly I received strong return fire and heard bullets smashing into my machine, from the frame of my canopy creeping back to the tail unit. I glanced into the mirror but couldn't see my companion any more and the intercom remained silent. He must have bought it . . . . My Messerschmitt was responding to the controls, so I went into the attack again. The Boeing that I fired upon was sheering out of the formation, and jettisoned its bombs ... suddenly it turned onto its back and dived down steeply in order to reach the safety of the layer of cloud. I went after it and despite strong return fire I shot it on fire with a couple of bursts. It then plunged down. The clouds prevented me from observing it to crash into the sea.

I flew back to Stade. While I overflew the base, one signalled to me from the ground that my tyres were in one piece. A quick touchdown and I taxied towards the hangar. Then I suddenly saw the pale face of my companion appearing in the mirror. Thank God, he was still alive. I switched off the engines and already he jumped out onto the wing. He exclaimed, 'I will never fly with you again!' and off he went. What had happened? After he saw the aircraft in front of us going down, he had laid himself flat on the floor of his cockpit. The burst of gunfire that next hit my Bf 110 had flown over him with only inches to spare. The intercom was shot to pieces.

I drew up my combat report, *Abschuss* of a B-17 at 1412 hours some 80 km NW of Heligoland. I explained to the officer in the Operations Room that the aircraft had gone down and thus never would drag any more bombs to Germany. As far as I was concerned, that was the main point. I requested that he took care of the further formalities, as I really had to leave.

Although I had had a companion on board, who was not injured, he had observed nothing! A flak ship had heard the air combat raging overhead at the same time I claimed the *Abschuss* and further confirmed that the bombers were not on their way back yet. One had fished some smashed pieces of aircraft out of the water. Still, no firm claim could be submitted due to the layer of clouds.

From a superficial inspection of my machine it appeared that although it had been hit numerous times, no vital parts seemed to have been damaged. The route back to Copenhagen was monotonous, as shortly before I had been in combat, even though I was told not to. Really pleased with myself, I travelled along on a straight course, at a height of 300 metres. A wide turn before reaching Malmo, approach, touch down, the machine bounced ... bounced ... bounced. At the dispersals, the NCO in charge of the ground crews was of the opinion that anyone could perform a bad landing from time to time. I told him to climb onto the wing and to get hold of the control column. During touch down and the pulling back of the column, the elevator control cable had completely snapped; it had obviously been severely damaged during the air combat. Only the slightest sudden manoeuvre during the flight back to Copenhagen would have caused my machine to have crashed immediately into the ground. For a long moment I kept sitting quietly in my aircraft and did not take off on a mission that night![61]

Attacks on Wilhelmshaven, Emden and St Nazaire followed. In June Eaker was able to send his bombers on two-pronged attacks against north German targets at Emden, Kiel, Bremen, Wilhelmshaven and Cuxhaven on a single day. On 11 June the B-17s set out to bomb Bremen, but the target was covered with a solid layer of low cumulus clouds down to about 5,000 feet and they also partially covered Wilhelmshaven. Twenty fighters attacked the low groups for over an hour by Bf 109 'gunboats' with MG 151/20 cannon in large underwing gondolas, which brought down one Fort. During the bomb run the leading Hell's Angels formation was bracketed by flak. Colonel Chuck Marion, the CO, lost two engines and following aircraft had to manoeuvre violently and reduce speed dramatically to avoid a collision. Just at that moment the *Luftwaffe* took advantage of the now scattered formation and made repeated head-on attacks. *Pappy* was rammed by an Fw 190 that failed to pull out in time. The 379th, flying only its second mission, bore the brunt of the attacks, losing six of the eight Flying Forts that failed to return. Over sixty others returned damaged. Gunners claimed to have shot down eighty-five enemy fighters, but only seven were destroyed or damaged and two pilots injured.

Oberfeldwebel Karl-Georg Pfeiffer a night-fighter pilot in 6./NJG2 at Leeuwarden,[62] recalls:

The *Gruppe* was considered to be the best night-fighter unit, especially as their aircraft, mostly Bf 110, were already equipped with *Lichtenstein* radar. My radio operator was *Gefreiter* Willi Knappe from Berlin. In January 1943 sortie followed upon sortie, daylight ones as well, as the Americans began to come in broad daylight in formations of several hundred aircraft. We all thought that they would never return from Germany but they were Flying Fortresses (B-17s), feared by the German day fighters because of their defensive fire. In any case, the American concept succeeded and until the end of the war the Americans continued to attack the 'Fortress Europe' and the day fighters had their hands full. The British came by night and Leeuwarden was a main base of the German defence. The American bomber attacks on Germany in the spring of 1943 was really the end of our best times in Leeuwarden, especially for pilots. Until then the crews, if there were no test flights to be carried out or no battle training took place, could nip into town and have an ice cream on the roof terrace of '*Vroom und Dreesmann*' or go dancing in the 'Valhalla' and have some fun. But now the pilots – alone and without radio operators – had to take their turn daily at readiness in case they had to take to the air against the Boeings and Liberators. For this purpose we had been allocated four Fw 190s, of which I had put one down on its belly. Once at 1600 hrs on 22 March 1943, I had contact with about sixty Boeings in the vicinity of Terschelling. But the defensive fire was too strong and I did not dare get too close. I fired a couple of bursts at one on the fringe but he did not go down.

But standby duty also had a positive side: At this time there were for the first time German airwomen on communications duty, quite a new sight for us. Previously, no females had been permitted on the airfield, for security reasons. As long as there were no operations, we had flirted a lot with the girls and some of us had fallen in love there and even married. As the Americans came in ever increasing numbers and the day fighters were unable to cope with them on their own, the entire *Gruppe* under Major Jabs carried daylight sorties as well. For this purpose the flame dampers, which were good for night operations, were removed from our Bf 110s. This made the machines 50 km/h faster and more manoeuvrable. It was always a grand spectacle: 100, 150 and more four-engined, silver bombers in bright sunshine over the mirror-like North Sea and us in sections of four against this overwhelming force! During this time we also flew regular day sorties against the Boeings and Liberators. Unfortunately, this senseless arrangement – our aircraft were much too slow for daylight operations – led to quite a number of German night-fighters, among them a few aces like *Hauptmann* Becker, being lost, so it was discontinued after a while.

On 11 June once again hundreds of American Boeings and Liberators had flown in over the North Sea to Germany and caused great damage. It was the time when the day fighters in the *Reich* were too few to shoot down or at least distract the bomber formations and the night-fighters had to help out. We were supposed to catch them on their return flight. I was wingman to *Oberleutnant* Rudolf Sigmund. I believe we were all very apprehensive of the great number of Flying Fortresses, which were considered to be immune because of their powerful armament. We climbed as a close section from Leeuwarden in a north-easterly direction to more than 7,000 metres. Over the North Sea we then spotted the silver bombers, several groups of 40, 50 and more aircraft. *Oberleutnant* Sigmund headed for a formation on the port fringe and announced over the radio: 'I dive first, then you . . .!' I saw him diving down at an angle of about 45 degrees and turn in onto one on the fringe. But I could also see that his bursts missed, while the Boeings returned strong fire from the rear and upper guns.

At this moment Willy my *Bordfunker* quietly remarked: 'Now it's our turn!'

But I thought, wait a few seconds, otherwise we catch the full load from the *Amis*, for they were still firing after *Oberleutnant* Sigmund and at us as well. I counted slowly to ten, then forward with the stick, full power, to automatic, a final look at the gun lights: they were on and were therefore ready to fire. The Boeing I had selected came ever closer. The entire bomber formation now also went steeply down and therefore I was not catching up as quickly as I had expected. I still held my fire, but as the *Amis* opened up I gave a few bursts with suitable deflection. The bomber grew ever larger and I noticed that the deflection still did not suffice to hit it fully. By then we had at least 650 on the clock. At this speed I had to use all my strength to pull the machine into a greater deflection and now gave continuous fire. Now the projectiles must strike! And then we had passed beneath the bomber. I ceased firing and went into an almost vertical dive. The most difficult part was always the breaking of contact with the enemy. More than one had caught it fully while turning away. With a sigh of relief I reduced power and levelled off once we were out of range. I had not noticed any strikes. When we looked up we could not believe our eyes: suddenly the entire tail section of 'my' Boeing broke away and went tumbling down. At this moment five parachutes opened up, the crew had baled out. The crewless aircraft continued to fly without catching fire, did a bunt, then stood for a moment with running engines pointing vertically.

Then it went spinning down into the North Sea. We suddenly heard over the radio that the sortie was over and we should fly back to Leeuwarden. We were still dizzy from the experience and I made a pretty rough landing. *Oberleutnant* Sigmund came up to me to congratulate me for my *Abschuss*. 'A Boeing is not easy to get,' he said, a little embarrassed because he had missed. I appreciated his noble gesture. We had always got on well and he was a fine fellow![63]

On Sunday 13 June just over 220 heavies set out for the U-boat yards at Bremen and Kiel. The 94th, 95th and 96th Bomb Groups were to take off from their bases at Earls Colne, Framlingham and Andrews Field and on their return from Kiel, would land at the former B-26 bases at Bury St Edmunds (Rougham), Horham and Snetterton Heath respectively. (Heavy losses in the Marauder groups had prompted their transfer further south to Essex so that fighter cover could be improved.) The 95th Group led the Kiel force with Brigadier General Nathan Bedford Forrest III riding in the co-pilot's seat of the command aircraft flown by Captain Harry A Stirwalt. Forrest was the grandson of a very famous Confederate cavalry general in the American Civil War, whose motto had been 'To win – git there fustest with the mostest'. On Forrest's instigation, the 95th formation were flying a hitherto untried 'flat' formation, wing-tip to wing-tip, supposedly to be able to concentrate firepower ahead, below, above and to the rear more effectively. Both bomber forces were unescorted, the short-ranged P-47s being used instead on diversionary sweeps off the Belgian coast. It was hoped that the two bomber raids would split the German fighter forces, but while the Bremen force lost four B-17s, almost all the German fighters attacked the Kiel force before they crossed the enemy coast. Many of the gunners in the 95th were unable to return fire as their guns, which were lubricated with a new type of oil recommended by Forrest, had frozen. A massive diving frontal attack raked the lead aircraft with cannon fire from one end to the other and Stirwalt's ship fell out of formation and spiralled down. All thirteen men aboard baled out but only the group navigator survived. A strong offshore wind carried Forrest and the eleven other crewmen to their deaths in the cold Baltic Sea. Forrest was the first American general to be lost in combat in Europe. He and Stirwalt's crew were probably among the victims of *Hauptmann* Kurt Ruppert, adjutant of III./JG26, who singled out the low squadron and made a rear pass, shooting down four of the six Forts in split seconds. Ruppert's Fw 190 was hit by return fire and he was forced to bale out. He tried to open his parachute too quickly and the speed of his descent ripped his old hemp harness, throwing the twenty-one-victory ace to his death. Five further B-17s lost took the group's losses to ten. The 94th was also hard hit, losing nine Fortresses, including *Shackeroo!* flown by Major Lewis Thorup, whose crew was rescued by ASR after 11 hours in the open sea. All told, the Kiel force lost twenty-two B-17s and twenty-three others returned damaged with twenty men wounded in action.

At his Daws Hill Lodge HQ at High Wycombe, in a large square room with a high ceiling buried beneath 30 feet of reinforced concrete, General Eaker referred to the mission as a 'great battle' and said that 'he was satisfied with the results obtained'. Thirty-eight-year-old Brigadier General Frederick L. Anderson, whose 4th Wing headquarters at Elveden Hall, the beautiful country mansion on the fringe of Thetford Forest, could not be more different to Pinetree, said:

> It was a privilege to lead such men, who but yesterday were kids in school. They flew their Forts in the face of great opposition like veterans.[64]

Notes

1. *Here We Are Together, The Notebook of an American Soldier in Britain.*
2. *The Route As Briefed. The history of the 92nd Bombardment Group USAAF 1942–45.*
3. JG26 was in action over Dieppe all day. The three *Gruppen* of JG26 flew no fewer than 377 sorties, both against the Allied aircraft and against sea and ground targets. For six Fw 190s lost, the *Geschwader* claimed thirty-eight aircraft shot down, plus another eleven probables.
4. The Red Cross reported on 17.10.42 that Lipsky and five of the crew were PoWs.
5. B-17 41-24397 *Phyllis* was salvaged for scrap.
6. La Chasse never saw him again. He fell out of his ship's bomb-bay on a mission to the submarine pens in France after his ship was forced into the water by enemy fighters.
7. Olsen and Gates died in their blood-spattered cockpit. Technical Sergeant Erwin Wissenbeck, who was knocked out of his top turret, came to and found Olsen was leaning far out of his seat bleeding profusely and Joseph N. Gates was slumped over his wheel. Also dead were Technical Sergeant Thomas W. Dynan, the radioman, Staff Sergeant Bruce Nicholson, waist gunner, Wilder and Kaylor. La Chasse, Bill Gise (navigator) and Wissenbeck were the only three to bale out.
8. *Luftwaffe* slang for ship.
9. Slang for very large aircraft.
10. Stammberger's victim was either *Snoozy II* or the B-17 flown by Lieutenant Francis H. Chorak in the 92nd BG, which went down in the Channel.
11. 41-24362 of the 419th BS.
12. Officially, *Bathtub Bessie/Big Eagle* of the 93rd BG flown by Captain Alexander Simpson was shot down by flak and crashed near Lille but this may be the kill claimed by Priller. Simpson and two others survived. One crewman evaded. Six were KIA. Or it may have been the 93rd BG B-24, which actually crash-landed at Northolt.
13. *Francis X*, flown by Lieutenant Francis X. Schwarzenbeck in the 342nd BS, *Johnny Reb*, piloted by Lieutenant Milton M. Stenstrom and 41-24344 flown by Captain John M. Bennett, both in the 414th BS.
14. *Hellsadroppin* of the 93rd BG piloted by Lieutenant Julian A. Harvey.
15. Five men were killed aboard 41-24472. Adams successfully evaded and later returned to England on 24 April.
16. Hartin evaded and spent five days at large in France before being rescued by the Underground. He was eventually escorted to Spain and safety.
17. *First of the Many.*
18. Check was KIA on 26.6.43 while on his twenty-fifth and final mission.
19. Liberator *Katy Bug* in the 93rd BG crashed at Alconbury killing four of the crew.
20. Eder had joined JG51 on the Channel coast in December 1940 but he did not achieve any kills. Transferred to the East for *Barbarossa*, he destroyed ten Soviet aircraft before being badly wounded on 24.7.41. In 1942 he returned to operations with 7./JG2.
21. Eighty B-17s of the 91st, 303rd, 305th and 306th BGs and twenty-one B-24s of the 44th BG.

22. Schöpfel, who had scored twenty-two victories in 1940, including four Hurricanes on 18.8.40, was credited with a B-17 kill to take his score to forty-six. He left the *Geschwader* on 10.1.43 to become Operations Officer of Jafü Brittany, the fighter control unit defending the U-boat bases, and survived the war with forty victories. 'Pips' Priller, who at the time had eighty-one victories, replaced Schöpfel as JG26 *Kommodore*.

23. Three men in English's crew died and nine men were killed aboard *Danellen* piloted by Lieutenant Dan W. Carson. The four other men in these two crews baled out and became PoWs.

24. *Green Fury II* of the 96th BG, piloted by Lieutenant Stanley P. Budleski. *Green Fury II* dived out of control, crashing on Nordeney Island with the loss of six crew. Four men were made PoW. Swoboda baled out and reached the ground uninjured.

25. For a time Leasman evaded capture after being rescued by a French girl in the Resistance but he was captured later. On 9 February Trost crossed the Pyrenees on foot into Spain. He eventually reached Gibraltar on 21 April and was back in London within three days.

26. McKee evaded capture and was back in England on 26.1.43. The eight men in his crew who baled out were captured.

27. The new tactics were tried on 23.1.43 when Lorient was attacked. Five bombers were shot down and two more crash-landed in England.

28. The lead crew concept and the 'stagger formation' developed by Colonel LeMay, CO, 305th BG, had been tried at group level on the 30.12.42 raid.

29. Lay clamoured for a command appointment and on 28.2.44 he was given command of the 487th BG, which flew B-24s. Lay was shot down over France on 11.5.44. He baled out safely and evaded capture. In 1946, while many people's thoughts turned to peace, others were still thinking of war. Lay, who was working for MGM on *Above and Beyond*, another aviation film, received an interesting approach from Sy Bartlett, who as a major, had been General Spaatz's aide. Bartlett was now working as a screenwriter at 20th Century Fox Studios and he wanted Lay to co-write a book and screenplay about the air war called *Twelve O' Clock High*. The central character was 'General Frank Savage' who was modelled on none other than Brigadier General Frank Armstrong, with whom he had struck up a close friendship during the Second World War. It was Lay who came up with the fictionalised 918th BG commanded by Savage, which he arrived at by taking the 306th BG and multiplying it by three. In 1948 with the novel nearing publication Fox became very interested in the possibility of a screenplay of the same name and studio head Darryl F. Zanuck promptly purchased the movie rights. The central theme in the movie version would be the gradual and ultimate destruction of General Savage, played superbly by Gregory Peck. *Twelve O'Clock High* draws upon the 306th Group's troubled early combat history and its effect on the combat crews. Savage's ship, *Piccadilly Lily*, was named after the 100th BG B-17 that Lay flew in as an observer on the Regensburg mission on 17.8.43. His classic *I Saw Regensburg Destroyed*, which appeared in the 6.11.43 issue of the *Saturday Evening Post*, is among the finest pieces of literature in the annals of aviation. *Twelve O'Clock High* was finally completed on 1.7.49 and, when edited, ran for 133 minutes. This most famous of black and white aviation movies was premiered at Grauman's Chinese Theater in Hollywood on Christmas Day 1949. Gregory Peck summed up the movie perfectly when he said, 'It is gratifying to be part of a movie that is still being shown 25 years after we made it, I think the picture still has meaning for audiences because of its integrity. We managed to dramatise a true story without resorting to false theatrics and sentimentality.'

30. Eaker's aide James Parton confirms in *Air Force Spoken Here*, his biography of Eaker, that he was unimpressed with Overacker's outfit, which unlike the other two groups appeared slovenly and undisciplined. Parton indicated as much to Overacker and the Royal visit then went 'pretty much like the others, but there was a notable absence of spit

and polish'. Eaker told 'Tooey' Spaatz that he had better relieve Overacker, but the general waited six more weeks, by which time the 306th's bombing and loss record was the worst in 8th BG. Something had to be done.

31. Lanford later flew in Italy with the 483rd BG, 15th AF, and was shot down on his seventeenth mission to finish the war as a PoW in *Stalag Luft III*.

32. Jabs was a seasoned combat veteran who had his first taste of action during the Battles of France and Britain when he served as a Bf 110 *Zerstörer* ('Destroyer') pilot in ZG76. He quickly became one of the leading fighter pilots in the Bf 110 day-fighter force with seven a/c shot down during the Battle of France and another twelve Spitfires and Hurricanes over England during the summer of 1940. Decorated with the *Ritterkreuz* October 1940 he thereupon successfully led his 6./ZG76 during the campaign in Crete. His *Staffel* became 9./NJG3 in November 1941 and on completion of night fighter training Jabs became an operational night fighter pilot. He went on to claim his first night kill (a Stirling) on 25/26.6.42 and was appointed *Staffelkapitän* of the elite 11./NJG1 at Leeuwarden in November 1942. By the end of 1942 he had shot down four RAF night bombers. Jabs survived the war with fifty (twenty-eight night and twenty-two day) victories.

33. Völlkopf, a 22-year-old *Experte* with six confirmed *Abshusse* in 5./NJG2 and 9./NJG1 was killed when his Bf 110G-4 G9+GT crashed whilst flying at low level near Rheine/Wesfalen airfield on 21 June 1943. His *Funker* Uffz Heinz Huhn Huhn survived his three pilots – *Oberleutnant* Gildner (KIA February 24/25.43), *Leutnant* Oskar Köstler (killed, April 9/10.43) and Völlkopf – but after Völlkopf was KIA Huhn decided he had had enough and he never flew again. For the remaining years of the war he served as Operations Officer at Bergen/Alkmaar and St Trond airfields.

34. Kettledrums, Kettledrums – going into attack.

35. Ground Control Interception (radar).

36. *Leutnant* Heinz Grimm of IV./NJG1 died on 13.10.43 from wounds sustained over Bremen from his own flak defences. He was awarded the *Ritterkreuz* posthumously on 5.2.44 for his twenty-six night kills and one B-17 on 4.2.43.

37. Pilot Captain Art T. Cullen and three gunners were the only survivors. Among the dead was his CO, Major Donald MacDonald. Cullen was eventually repatriated, in September 1944.

38. *4-mot* or 4-engined bomber.

39. This had been bestowed on him on 1.7.42 after his twenty-fifth night victory. Becker, born in Dortmund in August 1911, volunteered for the *Luftwaffe* in 1934 and became a *Stuka* pilot before joining the Bf 110 *Zerstörer* and becoming a night-fighter pilot in July 1940. In 1941–42 Becker became one of the leading *Experten* in the *Luftwaffe* night-fighter arm. He shot down forty bombers in 1942 and taught the new and young crews from his experiences. To them, Becker 'The Night Fighting Professor' was an inspiring fatherly figure. He was instrumental in introducing the *Lichtenstein* AI radar into the night-fighter arm in 1941, though most night-fighter aircrew were sceptical about it (they liked to rely on the 'Mk I Eyeball').

40. *I Flew For the Führer*, by Heinz Knoke.

41. Wayne Gotke, navigator, was picked up after dangling between two trees about 20 feet in the air for about 25 minutes, afraid that if he unbuckled he would fall badly. At the first-aid station he saw the only survivor, Staff Sergeant Mifflin, assistant radio man.

42. KIA 10.2.44.

43. Also called *Heavenly Hideaway*, a 93rd BG B-24H, the first H model in the ETO.

44. McPhillamey baled out and landed near a small village close to Oldenburg and was captured immediately after a couple of shots were fired in his direction. He ran into

Lieutenant Wilbur E. Wockenfuss, his co-pilot and three others of his crew at a police station in Oldenburg.

45. *First of the Many*.

46. Staff Sergeant Edward N. Yelle.

47. The formation got as far as Texel Island. In the 306th BG Captain William E. Friend's B-17 was badly damaged and set on fire by Fw Flecks and Uffz Meissner, both of 6./JG1, and fell out of formation. The crew probably jettisoned the bomb load while under fighter attack: nine bombs hit two schools and two houses at Den Briel near the Hook. Four Dutchmen were killed and sixty to seventy children were dead or missing. The fire took hold and Friend gave the order to bale out over the sea. Seven parachutes were counted, yet no survivors were ever reported.

48. Brill and Lowry were posthumously awarded the DSC.

49. *First of the Many*.

50. The two other Fortress losses this day, *Kickapoo* flown by Captain John Swais and *Short Snorter II*, piloted by Lieutenant Beman E. Smith, came from the 91st BG.

51. Oesau, who claimed ten aircraft in the Spanish Civil War, was the third German pilot to reach 100 victories, on 16 October 1941. After a short spell on the Easten Front he returned to the West to lead JG2, then JG1. Physically and mentally exhausted, he was shot down and killed in combat with P-51 Mustangs and P-38 Lightnings on 11.5.44. He had 125 victories.

52. The girl who sent the cable to his mother was Elsa Moors. Seelos was able to thank her in person, many years later.

53. Kramarinko and Staff Sergeant William E. Baker evaded capture and together reached Spain, only to be caught and handed over to the Germans.

54. On 17.2.43 Armstrong was promoted to brigadier general and made deputy commander, 1st Wing. Command of the 306th BG passed to Claude Putnam. Moving to the Pacific Theatre, Brigadier General Frank Armstrong assumed command of the 315th BW (Very Heavy) on 18.11.44 and he remained at its helm until January 1946.

55. In all, thirty-nine B-17s suffered battle damage, two men KIA and four WIA. Gunners claimed sixty-three enemy fighters shot down.

56. Writing in *First of the Many*.

57. Major William Wyler, the famous Hollywood director, was sent to England late in 1942 to make a documentary about 8th AF operations, principally for American cinema audiences. Filming for the morale-boosting documentary began early in 1943 after bad weather had delayed its start. Five combat photographers were lost aboard B-17s during filming in the spring of 1943. Several B-17s at Bassingbourn were running neck and neck for the honour of being the first to complete twenty-five missions (a combat tour for the crews). One Fortress, which caught Wyler's lens more than most, probably because of its emotive and eye-catching name, was the *Memphis Belle*, piloted by Captain Robert K. Morgan. During crew training in the US he had met Miss Margaret Polk of Memphis, Tennessee, and the romance between the pilot and the Memphis girl flourished for a time, but Morgan and Margaret later married other partners. However, the *Belle* would become legendary. The crew flew the twenty-fifth and final mission of their tour on 17.5.43 and it was duly recorded in 16 mm colour and used with great effect in the documentary, which first appeared in 1945.

58. A fourth raid was to be made on a power station at Ijmuiden, Holland, by twelve B-26s from Rougham near Bury St Edmunds. The Marauders returned safely but missed their target at Ijmuiden completely.

59. KIA 19.11.43.

60. KIA by Thunderbolts on 6.8.44.

61. *Oberleutnant* Martin Drewes never received official confirmation of his B-17 *Abschuss* on 19 May 1943. A few days after this episode, he was posted to 11./NJG1, which he led as *Staffelkapitän* from August 1943. He shot down two B-17s on 26 July 1943 (going down at Bremervörde and Leer) and B-17 42-30603 of the 423rd BS, 306th BG on 26.11.43 (crashed between St Nicolaasga and Doniaga). On 5.1.44, he shot down a B-24 100 km north of Nordeney, followed by two more B-17s destroyed on 11 January, his adversaries crashing at Nijverdal (42-30782 of the 369th BS, 306th BG) and into the sea 20 km NW of The Hague. These victories made *Oberleutnant* Drewes the top scoring *Nachtjagd* pilot in the daylight battles with the 8th AF 1943–44. Drewes, who was awarded the *Ritterkreuz* on 27.7.44 and *Eichenlaub* on 17.4.45 ended the war with the rank of Major and a score of forty-three night and six day victories (including four claims for B-17s and B-24s) in ZG76, NJG3 and NJG1.

62. After his fourth night *Abschuss* (a Lancaster) Pfeiffer had been awarded the *EK I*. (*Eisernes Kreuz I* or Iron Cross 1st Class). The radio operator received the *EK I* after a sixth victory.

63. *Hauptmann* Rudolf Sigmund, *Kommandeur*, III./NJG3, was killed when he was hit by flak over Kassel on of 3/4.10.43. He had twenty-eight victories. On 11.6.43 the 8th AF lost eight Fortresses, of which three went down over the North Sea. The 379th BG lost five to enemy action and a sixth crash-landed at RAF Coltishall, Norfolk on the return. It seems that the B-17 Pfeiffer shot down was a 379th BG Fort flown by Lieutenant Noel R. Britten, whose entire crew baled out safely. None of the other Forts lost this day, including one in the 303rd BG and one in the 95th (*Lonesome Polecat*. Lieutenant Malcolm B. Mackinnon ten KIA) had five or more survivors. Pfeiffer's final score was ten night victories and one day *Abschuss*.

64. Anderson, like many other American generals in 1943, had never held an important combat command. Before the war he was a graduate of West Point and Kelly Field, San Antonio, but he had contracted tuberculosis after a plane he was flying lost its engine and crashed into the sea off San Francisco. He made a remarkable recovery and served five years in the Philippines and later directed bombardier instruction at the Air Corps Tactical School before becoming Deputy Director of Bombardment at AAF HQ in Washington DC in January 1942.

CHAPTER 2

The 'Bloody Hundredth' –
Blitz Week and Beyond

*The Hundredth was known throughout the land not because we were
superhuman but rather because we were human. Our fame and notoriety
spread not just because of Regensburg or Berlin or the Russian mission but
also because of our losses, and yes, even because of our faux pas.*

Bill Carleton, Engineering Officer

For nine days following the Kiel debacle no bomber missions were flown,
but changes were in the pipeline at all levels of command. Brigadier
General Frederick L. Anderson would succeed Eaker as Chief of
8th Bomber Command when Eaker moved to command 8th Air Force and
his tenure at Elveden Hall would be taken over by the new 4th Wing CO,
Brigadier General Curtis E. LeMay. At group level, Colonel John 'Dinty'
Moore, CO of the 94th, and Colonel Alfred A. Kessler, commanding the 95th,
were replaced by Colonel Fred Castle and Colonel John Gerhart, respectively.
Gerhart, who had been one of the 8th's original staff officers at its activation in
January 1942 and Castle, who had been one of the officers Eaker had brought
to England in February 1942, had yearned for combat. Now their experience
would be needed as they set about lifting the morale of crews who resented the
loss of their established commanders. When General LeMay visited Rougham
'he gave us the usual welcome talk', said Captain Franklin 'Pappy' Colby, at
41 years of age the oldest combat pilot in the 8th Air Force 'and left the
impression of being a bit hard-nosed about things. But he had flown a lot of
rough ones and had a good record. And he was trying to improve the poor
formation flying which had been so troublesome'. The fresh appointments
and the group moves to new bases in Suffolk heralded a new era for the 4th
Wing. The area around Bury St Edmunds is very historic and it offered
some interesting new vistas for men during their off duty hours. Culford Hall,
6 miles away, was built by the Marquis of Cornwallis, whose surrender at
Yorktown in 1781 meant victory for the Americans in the War of Inde-
pendence. At Newmarket there was horse racing and at Lavenham the old
wool town was famous for its half-timbered houses, which dovetail into
winding streets. Now the 4th Wing was adding to the history, gaining three
more groups. The 100th moved from temporary accommodation at Podington
in Northamptonshire to just inside the Norfolk border at Thorpe Abbotts,

which was found to be more incomplete than Podington had been. Many of the buildings were unfinished and even 'the mud was 'thicker'. The 385th arrived at Great Ashfield and the 388th at Knettishall near Thetford, birthplace of Thomas Paine, one of the sons of the American Revolution.

In time the 100th would become probably the best known of all the bombardment groups in East Anglia. Often referred to as the 'Bloody Hundredth', in the short time the group was in action, the outfit lost 229 Fortresses, 177 men missing in action and fifty-two from 'other operational losses', the third highest total among all units. More precisely, it had the highest loss rate among its sister groups for the twenty-two months it was operational.

The group would achieve its legendary status in August 1943. A crew who lowered their undercarriage as a mark of surrender and then shot down the German fighters escorting the battered Fort to enemy territory, so upset the *Luftwaffe* that the 100th became a 'marked' group. Thereafter, they believed they were singled out for 'special attention'. In reality, the high loss rate was caused mostly by poor formation flying, but the group's reputation as a 'bad luck' outfit was assured. Other groups learned to keep their distance whenever possible. One pilot in the 100th was to recall one mission when many ships could not find their own groups and tacked on to anyone they could for protection. He heard one pilot tell his group that he could not locate them so he was going on in another group. His commander called back and asked which group he was with. He replied that he did not know but that they had a square 'D' on the tail. Someone said, 'Oh that's the "Bloody Hundredth"'. The interloper immediately left formation in the squadron in front of him. Needless to say, it did not make the pilots in the 100th feel any better. No replacements looked forward to being posted to Thorpe Abbotts either. When it left England the Bloody Hundredth had earned the dubious reputation of being perhaps the most infamous and 'jinxed' outfit in the 8th.

The future seemed as bright and promising as the weather on Wednesday 22 June 1943 when the 100th first sent its Forts off on a mission. Only six got airborne before further participation was scrubbed. Then word came through that it was on again and crews were to wait by their planes. Finally, after about an hour's delay caused by ground mist, about twenty planes got off but they only flew over the North Sea before returning.

At ten other bases in eastern England just over 230 crews were briefed for the raid on the chemical and synthetic rubber plant at Hüls in the flak-infested Ruhr Valley. Crews had been briefed for a raid on the plant near Recklinghausen the day before, but the mission had been scrubbed. At Bassingbourn Tex McCrary had sat through the briefing with 'a knot the size of hangman's noose' growing inside his throat'. When the A-2 officer, former New York State Senator John McNaboe, had started his running commentary on the target 'sleepy lids opened no wider' and 'chins hung on chests' until he said that over 400 fighters were expected to oppose the mission. Then half the crews whistled, 'the special whistle' that meant 'Jeeeee-sus-keee-rist!' McCrary had hoped to fly the mission with Lieutenant James Baird's crew in *Piccadilly Commando*, but as they taxied out the mission was put back 5 hours and later it was scrubbed. 'Nobody knew whether to be fed up or happy.' The same feelings probably persisted on the Wednesday morning as twenty-two crews returned to the briefing rooms, blinking at the light and filling up the benches. Father Hunt the Catholic chaplain as usual was by the door, silver cup in hand and his purple cloth under the leather jacket he wore to keep out the early morning chill. Clean shaven operations staff in neatly pressed uniforms waited patiently to update the crews. Captain 'Sunshine' Atwell, the met officer, who used to be a football coach at Princeton, stood by to give a weather report. The briefing room doors were locked and Major Alford from Rising Star, Texas, drawled out the flight plan. McCrary would fly the mission with 'Smitty' Smith's crew in *Our Gang*. 'At 26 this boy was already gnarled and weathered and toughened. His strong fingers were laced in the coat of his dog Skippy, sprawled on the table before him.'

Another war correspondent wrote[1] that [the crews]:

... are nervous now, like a relay runner waiting to take over the baton. Later, when their time to carry the action comes, they will be calm. But now they are nervous. And they are sleepy and filled with breakfast ... they sit waiting – talking, yawning, watching the little group of officers clustered before the map. When the Old Man turns and faces them there is a sudden hush. Through the blackout curtains there drifts, in the moment of silence, a sound that reaches every ear in the room. It is far away and muted. It is the sound of a Fortress engine at its dispersal point. The line crews are on the job. The combat men stiffen for a moment. Then they relax. They look up at the Old Man, who stands facing them gravely ... 'Our target is the synthetic-rubber plant at Hüls, near Recklinghausen. A smaller force will be attacking the Ford and General Motors plants at Antwerp, approximately half an hour before your Time Over Target. There will be an RAF fighter sweep over this part of the Dutch coast at 1035, an RAF diversion in here, and one of our own Groups will fly a diversion to this point in order to draw off enemy fighters from this area ....'

S-2 [the intelligence officer] takes the stand, pointer in hand. The lights are lowered. A picture of the plant at Hüls is flashed on the screen. 'This is the plant at Hüls. It produces approximately 29 per cent of Germany's synthetic rubber and 18 per cent of its total rubber supply. With Germany at present so short of rubber that she's trying to bring it through in blockade runners from the Far East, I don't need to emphasize the importance of this target. The plant area is a square, approximately 3,500 feet on a side. Your approach will be in here. Your aiming point is here, on the gas plant. This is the butadiene plant and this ... across these railway sidings, which will be on your right as you cross the target, you will see the Auguste Viktoria coal mine, which serves the plant. This Group will be bombing from 25,000 feet. After bombing you will continue to this point, where a turn to ....'

The Flak Officer stands before the map of enemy anti-aircraft batteries, using a billiard cue as a pointer. He is apologetic, as flak officers usually are. 'We've routed you today so that the flak you get will be, in general, just deterrent.' He waits for a laugh – and gets it. 'Here, where you cross this island just off the German coast, there's a four-gun heavy battery. If you stick to your course you'll be out of range. There'll be moderate heavy flak here and ....'

It is 0450 as the gunners pile aboard the jeeps and trucks for the dispersal points. The eastern sky is pale with dawn now, though the field still lies in darkness. In the main briefing room Flying Control has concluded the preparation with the time-tick, during which the crews set their watches. '20 seconds before 0447, 15 seconds ..., 10 seconds ..., 5 seconds ..., 4 ..., 3 ..., 2 ....' The navigators have adjourned to an office and are laying out the routes on their maps. The bombardiers are in session with the Group Bombardier, studying the target pictures. The radio operators have collected the flimsies giving the call signals of the day – rice-paper sheets to be eaten in case of capture.

The planning is over now .... The sky is filled with the sound and the stately, shifting movements of Fortresses as they find their places in formation and move off in ever-diminishing perspective. By 0732 they have gone. The Old Man remains staring at the sky where his planes had been. 'I hope,' he says finally, 'all those boys come back.'

At around midday ground personnel at each of the ten bomber bases gathered in bunches along the hangar lines waiting for the return of the Forts. Crews began touching down at Bassingbourn and 20 minutes later the last Fort was down and taxiing back to its hardstand. Refuelling crews and maintenance men went to work immediately and the Engineering Officer counted noses of the Forts out of action and those that could be ready for combat the next day. At five dispersal points, line crews wandered aimlessly, waiting in vain for the return of bombers and crews they had waved off only a few hours earlier. *Royal Flush* flown by Marcel Fountain, *Nightshade*, *Mary Ruth*, *Old Ironsides* and 'Slats'. Slattery's Fort had been shot down and his crew dead or captured. *Old Ironsides* had only just been repaired after its right-hand stabiliser and elevator had been knocked clean off by two bombs dropped from above on the Bremen mission. Lieutenant Buster Peek ditched *Old Ironsides* in the North Sea after fighters had knocked out an engine and most of the controls and hydraulic system. Chauncey Hicks, the bombardier, was wounded by an exploding 20 mm shell. It pierced his eardrum and badly lacerated his face, but he continued to man his guns and continue firing. Everyone except the tail gunner, who drifted away and was drowned, was picked up by ASR and returned to Bassingbourn.[2]

The combat crews trooped into the Briefing Room, coffee mugs and sandwiches in hand. The war correspondent that was present described the scene:

... they mill around. Little groups form, dissolve and re-form. There is some talk and laughter but not much. These are tired men. Their faces are drawn, their hair is matted and tangled, and in their eyes is a deep weariness. They scuff about awkwardly in the heavy flying boots or sit with hunched shoulders, staring at the floor. Later they will come alive but now they show only patient acquiescence as they await their turn for interrogation ... each crew at one of the big tables scattered around the room. Bombing altitude? Position in formation? Number of enemy fighters seen? Where did you hit flak – altitude, position, time? How was the bombing? Encounters: How did he come in? When did you start firing? Do you claim him as destroyed? Any flame? Did the pilot bale out? Did you see the ship crash? Any suggestion or comments on the operations? The questions are brief and pointed. The answers, at first, are terse. Then the crews loosen up and become more voluble as they relive their part. The Interrogation Officer waits, looking from one to the other, jotting down the pertinent facts on his form. Two stories conflict. They are contrasted. A compromise is reached. Finally it is over and the crew straggles away from the table. Another group takes its place.[3]

Hüls was severely damaged and smoke from the plant rose as high as 17,000 feet, but sixteen Forts were missing and four more lost on the raid on the Ford and General Motors Works at Antwerp. Major 'Pips' Priller claimed *Iron Gut Gert* of the 381st, while another ship was jointly claimed by *Oberfeldwebel* Adolf 'Addi' Glunz and *Unteroffizier* Niki Mortl. *Oberfeldwebel* Johann Edmann was hit by return fire and he crash-landed near Woensdrecht with severe injuries. Another Fort suffered a runaway propeller, staggered across the target badly shot up, but made it back to crash-land at Framlingham. *Little Chuck* crash-landed at North Foreland in Kent with six crew injured and *Salvage Queen* was ditched in the Channel with the loss of seven crew. Another Fort crashed in Holland with four crew dead. An official report later concluded that:

> Indications are that this plant is at present inoperative. A high proportion of the bombs dropped fell within the target and considerable damage is seen throughout the plant. The full extent of the damage to several buildings cannot be completely assessed from photographs. Many of the most important plants and buildings have been damaged, including the Arc, Converters Plant, the Butylene Glycol Plant, the Aldol Plant, the Aerylonitrile Plant, the Butadiene Plant, the Acetaldehyde Plant, the Polymerisation Building, and the Gas Compression and Fractionation Building ... ..

Production was curtailed for a month and full production was not resumed for five months after that.

Three days later 275 Forts were despatched to bomb Hamburg and other targets in north-western Germany. Cloud hampered bombing at Hamburg, splitting up the formations and scattering some of the groups around the sky. It was an open invitation to fighter attack and eighteen Forts were shot down and over sixty damaged. Gunners claimed scores and scores of fighters destroyed, but only a dozen were really lost and six damaged. Cloud interfered on 26 June also when Triqueville airfield and an aircraft factory at Villacoublay in the Paris area were bombed. Five B-17s – all from the 384th – were shot down by Fw 190s, including one, which fell to the guns of Major 'Pips' Priller, *Kommodore* of JG26. Two days later another two forces went to St Nazaire to bomb the lock gates and port area and Beaumont Le Roger airfield further inland. German controllers waited until the Spitfire escort had turned back and then sent *Hauptmann* Egon Mayer's II *Gruppe* into the fray. Eight Fortresses of the St Nazaire force were lost and flak damaged fifty-seven others. The force attacking Beaumont Le Roger came through unscathed. Raids on airfields in France were the order of the day in July for the heavies. On 10 July 185 B-17s escorted by eighteen squadrons of Spitfires and eight squadrons of P-47s hit airfields at Caen, Abbeville and Le Bourget. Bombing was largely ineffective and three Forts were lost, including *Exterminator*, which was shot down by *Leutnant* Helmut Hoppe west of Rouen in his first pass.[4] Wutz Galland's fighters continued to attack the bombers for another 10 minutes until low fuel forced them to break off.

With missions coming so hot and so fast, for those that survived them the only respite was the occasional flak leave at a 'flak shack' in a quiet backwater in the quaint English countryside or a 48-hour pass in the capital, where the surroundings could not be more different. Unfortunately, after a time even London ceased to arouse most people. The aircrews tended to be more interested in finishing their tours and going home. In short, the novelty had worn off. London was famed for its American Red Cross clubs, the most well known being Rainbow Corner on the corner of Piccadilly Circus and Shaftesbury Avenue. One radio operator recalled:

> At Rainbow Corner there was this lovely lady in an American Red Cross uniform who sat at a desk in one of the rooms. A sign on the desk read, 'Have Adele Astaire write a letter home for you'. Adele Astaire was the sister of Fred Astaire, the famous movie tap-dancer. She was also Lady Cavendish, having married into British nobility. I was one of the fascinated guys who went over to ask her to write a letter home for me, but I really did it so I could stare at her; I think she had the most gorgeous set of legs I've ever seen in my life.

Lalli Coppinger, a volunteer hostess for about two years at The Washington Club on Curzon Street says that though smaller than Rainbow Corner, it was 'cosier' and 'more intimate'. It was a place where:

> ... homesick Yanks could sit on a couch in a fairly quiet lobby and write letters home. They could get a room for about the equivalent of two dollars, eat in the cafeteria, dance up a storm to a good band and maybe meet a nice girl who wouldn't steal their wallet. I learned a lot about the young American male, far from home, 1940s type. They weren't the kind that we English girls had become familiar with through American movies. Sure, they were from big cities, some were sophisticated, but they were also from every small town and hamlet in the USA. Their average age was 19 to 23. I met a few who were even younger than 19 – they'd lied about their age. And there were many who had never tasted hard liquor or smoked, and had little or no adult sexual experience. At the most vulnerable time of their lives, with adrenaline pumping, raging hormones and all, they were let loose in London, at that period the largest city in the

world, with just about every temptation known to man available to them. London was renowned for its wide variety of entertainment as many an unsuspecting GI found out, not always to his advantage. But they learned fast and these were the men who frequented the Red Cross Clubs, the 'safe havens' from the blackout!

Pretty Jo Sippy from St Louis, Pennsylvania, who before the war had been an airline hostess, was a Red Cross volunteer at Rainbow Corner. Jo held a pilot's licence and she liked planes and the men who flew them. Not surprisingly, they liked her too. One of her best friends was John H. Perkins, a light-hearted lieutenant from Chicago who flew *Windy City Challenger* in the 305th Group at Chelveston. He had started out as a co-pilot on Forts but when his pilot and bombardier had completed their tour and went home, Johnny had been given his own crew. He missed his friends. When in London they would team up with Jo, take in the sights and go on all the tours together and she often visited Chelveston loaded down with bundles for local children and made and cancelled dates, theatre tickets and hotel reservations for men going on leave. She particularly enjoyed the riotous base dances. Perkins, whose father was English, had once taken Jo Sippy to Cornwall to spend a weekend with his great aunt after one particularly rough mission. Johnny had completed eighteen missions when on Bastille Day, 14 July, he and the crew of *Windy City Challenger* were awakened for another rough one to France, part of a force of over 100 B-17s attacking the Fw 190 repair facility at Villacoublay. Another 100 aircraft would head for airfields at Amiens-Glisy and Le Bourget.

All three targets were well hit – at Villacoublay, hangars and seventy Fw 190s were destroyed – but over 150 Forts were damaged by the German defences and five had failed to return from the raids on the two airfields. Two more failed to return to Molesworth and Grafton Underwood, while at Chelveston sixteen of the twenty Forts that had taken off returned damaged and one was missing. *Staffelkapitän* Georg-Peter Eder of 7./JG2 had singled out *Windy City Challenger* south of Paris. Eder recalls:

> I pushed the black button on the right of the panel and the three yellow rings and cross flicked on in the sight glass. We were doing about 450 km per hour now and were coming down slightly, aiming for the noses of the B-17s. There were about 200 of us attacking the 200 bombers but there was also the fighter escort above them. We were going for the bombers. When we made our move, the P-47s began to dive on us and it was a race to get to the bombers before being intercepted. I was already close and about 600 feet above and coming straight on: I opened fire with the twenties at 500 yards. At 300 yards I opened fire with the thirties. It was a short burst, maybe ten shells from each cannon but I saw the bomber explode and begin to burn. I flashed over him at about 50 feet and then did a chandelle.[5]

Perkins and six of his crew were killed. Three other crew and a photographer aboard survived and were taken prisoner. Jo Sippy had two burning ambitions. More than anything she wanted to fly on a raid in a B-17 and then go home in one as hostess. Before *Windy City Challenger* went down, she and Johnny Perkins had a plan to send the plane home to Chicago like the *Memphis Belle*. At Chelveston meanwhile, a Fortress was christened *Windy City Avenger* in the crew's honour.

Despite continuing losses the addition of more groups allowed Eaker to send a record 322 bombers to Hanover on 17 July and on 24 July a week-long series of heavy bomber raids, later called 'Blitz Week', went ahead. The offensive began with a raid by just over 200 B-17s on Heroya and Trondheim in Norway. One failed to return and scores were battle damaged. The next day 218 bombers attacked Hamburg, devastated the night before in the great RAF Bomber Command fire raid, and Kiel. Cloud cover and the huge smoke pall from the still burning fires at Hamburg caused a third of the force to abandon their strike. Three Forts were shot down during the approach to the Elbe estuary and over the North Sea fighters picked off three stragglers. Major Karl-Heinz Leesmann, *Gruppenkommandeur*, III./JG1, crashed into the sea after one attack and his body was washed ashore on 16 August. Altogether, nineteen B-17s – seven of them in the 384th – were shot down and over 100 returned battle-damaged, two crashing on landing.

On 26 July more than 300 heavies were despatched to bomb rubber factories at Hanover and shipbuilding yards at Hamburg. Thick cloud over East Anglia hampered assembly and many groups became scattered and had to be recalled. Only two combat wings won through to their targets, while other elements bombed a convoy and other targets of opportunity along the German coast. The 92nd lost three B-17s and it could have been more. Co-pilot John C. Morgan, a 6 foot red-haired Texan, somehow got *Ruthie II* back after his pilot had the back of his head blown off and lay slumped over the controls for 2 hours. Morgan, who put the battered ship down at RAF Foulsham in Norfolk, was later awarded the Medal of Honor for saving the plane and the crew. Another pilot from Texas, Lieutenant Alphonse Maresh of the 369th Fightin' Bitin' Squadron in the Thurleigh group got the shattered *Dixie Demo II* to near Cromer, where he ditched just off the Norfolk shore. Fightin' Bitin' was the creation of lead navigator Kermit B. Cavedo, who liked the numerical connection between his squadron and the Fightin' 69th Regiment of the First World War. So, using a little literary licence, he used the name Fightin' Bitin' and two insects sparring and applied it to the nose of his crew's Fort. The crew of *Dixie Demo II* felt a little embarrassed because having got into their dinghies, they discovered that the water was so shallow that it only came up to their waists. Captain Arthur Issac, the Jewish bombardier from Brooklyn, was relieved to have made it home. Isaac carried three sets of dog tags on missions. One had his correct name, another was stamped 'Otto McIsaac', which he carried in case he was ever shot down over Germany and the third set had the name 'Francois d'Isaac' in case he baled out over France! The Brooklyn bombardier always swore that the first thing he would ask for if he was shot down in Germany was the nearest church where he could hear a Catholic Mass said over him. The crew were sad because the

Fightin' Bitin' Squadron had flown forty-two consecutive missions without loss and they had killed the record. However, next day *Dixie Demo II* was pulled ashore by an Air Service Command Mobile Repair Unit so, technically, they had made it home.

Two other Forts also ditched and their crews were rescued but twenty-one other B-17s failed to return. Four came from the 95th and five were from the 388th, although most of the crew of *LaChiquita*, which went down in the North Sea, survived after being picked up by German ASR. Another crew returned to Knettishall after being picked up by a British rescue launch. *Mister Yank* and two other ships exploded over the target area. Sixteen men survived from these three Forts and one of the navigators by the name of Wiegman, was picked up by German civilians and taken to a beer hall. Knowing that his escape kit would have German marks in it he ordered beer for everyone a couple of times. As he was about to pay, two German soldiers entered and to his surprise his escape kit had French francs in it. One of the Germans had to pay for the beers while Wiegman was taken prisoner! Once again, losses could have been higher but the pilot of *Impatient Virgin* put down at Foulsham with numerous flak and 20 mm shell holes, no oxygen system and the vertical fin half torn off.

After stand down on 27 July, just over 300 bombers were despatched on the 28th to bomb the Fieseler aircraft works at Kassel and the Fw 190 factory at Oschersleben. Bad weather interfered with the missions and only a fraction of the forces managed to hit their targets. Twenty-two B-17s were lost, including seven in the Snetterton Falcons and three more in the 95th, to take their losses to seven in two days. *Leutnant* Eberhard Burath of 1./JG1 singled out *Spook III*, flown by Lieutenant Francis J. Reagen, which was finished off by *Gruppenkommandeur Hauptmann* Emil-Rudolf Schnoor for his third victory. *Spook III* ditched in the North Sea with the loss of all ten crew. Lieutenant James F. Rivers' Fort crashed at Hoehausen and he and his crew survived. *Exterminator* crashed at Lathen, Germany, and all Lieutenant Fred D. Hughes' crew were also made PoW. In comparison, it would seem that the 306th, which officially lost two, got off lightly, but bland statistics often clouded the true facts. Twenty-four Forts led by the 367th Clay Pigeons Squadron had taken off from Thurleigh but six planes had aborted early into the mission with turret and engine problems. Before reaching the target, the formation loosened up in heavy weather, an open invitation for fighter attack and one which the *Luftwaffe* accepted with alacrity. *Peck's Bad Boys* had two engines knocked out and set on fire and Stephen W. Peck, a veteran pilot, ordered the crew to bale out. Everyone got out safely, but most pulled their ripcords too soon at around 25,000 feet and seven men needed medical treatment after landing. Anti-aircraft fire over Kassel claimed *Bab's Best* and only four crewmen in Jack Harris' crew survived. Three Forts crashed on their return to England and every plane in the formation suffered flak damage, three so badly that they had to be transferred to 8th Service Command for repairs.

At Thurleigh, Major Thurman Shuller had no doubts as to why losses among the crews in his group were mounting. As a doctor he recognised that the flight crews were 'terribly tired'. He also doubted whether some of them had slept at all when the Company Quartermasters (CQs) were in the barracks at 0430 on Thursday morning, 29 July, to get the crews out for another long haul, this time to bomb the U-boat yards Kiel. A smaller force was to hit the Heinkel aircraft factory at Warnemünde. Shuller concluded that, 'It was all a vicious circle resulting in poor flying by the pilots, poor bombing by the bombardiers and high losses. There was a human element to this thing that Bomber Command seemed to fail to consider.' Twenty-year old Eric G. Newhouse, a waist gunner in Flight Officer Berryman H. Brown's crew in the Clay Pigeons Squadron, probably had more to consider than most. Eric Newhouse had been born a Jew in Vienna on 5 May 1923, but raised as a Catholic. His father ran a chocolate shop on the Esterhazystrasse, which was targeted by the Nazis after the Wehrmacht occupied the country in 1938. Newhouse slipped away to Czechoslovakia and on to Greece and finally Palestine, where he lied about his age and joined the British Army. Meanwhile, his parents had fled to France and then to Mexico and finally America. On 7 December 1941, the day the Japanese bombed Pearl Harbor, Newhouse, though he was not yet an American citizen, tried to enlist in the AAF. He was rejected, but he turned up at his enlistment at Wausau, Wisonsin, for 120 consecutive days until they finally accepted him. He became a gunner in the AAF and went to England, where in June 1943 in London he met a 'pretty and nice' girl born in Paris of French and English parents and they were to be married on 30 July. Dave E. Scherman, *Life* photographer, was planning to be at the ceremony to photograph the happy couple. On 29 July, when the briefing for the raid on Kiel was over the young Austrian, who had flown six Fortress missions, took a coloured glass-headed pin from the briefing map and stuck it in his leather bomber jacket beside the other six mission pins. Then Newhouse joined the rest of Berryman H. Brown's crew and went out to *Big Jack*, waiting at dispersal along with seventeen other Forts.

Doc Shuller had observed that the maintenance crews were tired too and they could not keep the planes in shape for so much combat. Five ships aborted just after the mission began but *Big Jack* was not one of them. Captain George E. Paris Jr, a lead pilot in the Fightin' Bitin' Squadron, flying as the low squadron, led the group to Kiel. Everything was quiet until Heligoland Island when the unlucky thirteen came under mass attack by more than 100 fighters and the proud record held by Fightin' Bitin' was at an end. III./JG26 at Nordholz, which had been alerted an hour earlier by radar warnings, hit the little assemblage in a vicious head-on pass and first in the Fightin' Bitin' Squadron to go down was *Jeiavad* – a name made up of the first letters of the names of the wives of the seven married men in the crew – after an attack by *Oberleutnant* Paul Schauder. Two crew were killed. Lieutenant Keith Conley; a twenty-two-mission veteran from Portage, Utah, and seven of his crew, baled out. Next to go down was *Fightin' Bitin'* and Lieutenant Donald R. Winters' crew. They were replacements for the regular crew, among them radio/gunner Billy Brown, a 30-year-old former Coca-Cola soda-fountain salesman from Hollywood, who were on pass. A fortune-teller had told Brown that there 'wasn't anything on the Germans' side that would harm him in this war'. *Oberfeldwebel* Heinz Kemethmüller raked the Fort with gunfire and the right wing came off and went down. Winter and five of his crew were killed. A few minutes after *Fightin' Bitin'* went down, *Hauptmann* Hermann Staiger singled out another Clay Pigeon and raked it with cannon and machine-gun fire. It exploded, killing all ten of Flight Officer Carl D. Brown's crew. It was Staiger's thirtieth victory. The *Luftwaffe* ace then attacked *Big Jack* and knocked out two engines before it, too, went down. Eight men got out but Harry W. Lofgren, ball turret gunner, and Eric Newhouse were killed.

Two days later Bomber Command announced a three-day stand down from combat, but it had come too late as far as the Thurleigh group was concerned.

On 30 July just over 180 Flying Forts went to Kassel in central Germany. Altogether, twelve bombers and six US fighters were lost. Just over 100 Thunderbolts arrived on the scene to prevent further losses. The 388th lost three B-17s, including *Classy Chassis*, which went down just before reaching the target, and *Bobbitt*, which was shot down south of Antwerp by *Leutnant* Göhringer. *Lucky Lady II* flown by Lieutenant Carmelo P. Pelusi in the Snetterton Falcons jettisoned its bomb load and had two engines knocked out by flak over Belgium before being shot down over Flanders by *Feldwebel* Ernst Christof for his ninth and final victory. Christof was shot down and killed 2 hours later by an American fighter. Lieutenant Guerdon W. Humason's B-17 in the 381st came under attack from five Fw 190s and Major Wilhelm-Ferdinand 'Wutz' Galland put three engines out of action. Four crewmen baled out before the doomed plane descended into cloud near Ascheberg. One of the men was almost certainly killed when he hit the tail. Six men remained aboard as Humason brought the aircraft in for a crash-landing at Deelen, where it was strafed by at least one of the Fw 190s. *Hauptmann* Johannes Naumann was credited with the destruction of *Man O' War* flown by Lieutenant Keene C. McCammon in the 91st.[6] This Fort was probably the oldest in the group and had suffered a series of mechanical problems and malfunctions over the past few months. Near Arnhem, *Feldwebel* Peter Crump claimed a B-17 and *Unteroffizier* Wiegand's claimed another west of Eupen. Hans-Walter Sander shot down *Dry Run* flown by Lieutenant Andrew Miracle II in the Snetterton Falcons. The nine-man crew and photographer Sergeant Bruce who called themselves *The Miracle Tribe* lived up to this name, being picked up by ASR.

The next day, 31 July, a three-day stand down from combat was announced. In a week of sustained operations, about 100 aircraft and ninety combat crews had been lost.

Losses in men and machines were made good and over 300 bombers were sent to attack targets in Holland and France on 15 August as part of the *Starkey* deception plan. This was to make the Germans believe that an invasion of the French coast was imminent, to relieve some of the pressure on Russia and halt troop movements to Italy. Strikes against enemy airfields in France and the Low Countries continued on 16 August. Then early that evening, base operation staff throughout eastern England awaited details for the anniversary mission next day. Eaker and his planners had conceived a most ambitious and daring plan to attack, simultaneously, aircraft plants at Schweinfurt and Regensburg. The *Luftwaffe*'s operational fighter strength on the western front was showing a significant increase and Regensburg was the second largest aircraft plant of its kind in Europe, the largest being at Wiener Neustadt near Vienna. The original plan to bomb all three plants on one day, 7 August, had been disrupted by bad weather so the plan had been modified to bomb each target when the opportunity arose. Production at Regensburg was estimated at 200 Bf 109s a month, or approximately 25 to 30 per cent of Germany's single-engine aircraft production. It was estimated that the total destruction of the Regensburg plant would entail a nine-month delay in production. Immediate results would be felt in operational strength, it was hoped, between one and a half to two months. The double strike was a bold move as, hitherto, the campaign against the German aircraft industry had been waged within reasonable striking distance from the British mainland.

Leading the 1st Wing to Schweinfurt would be the 91st with the Group Commander, Colonel Clemens L. Wurzbach in *Oklahoma Oakie* piloting and the Air Task Force Commander, Colonel William M. Gross, in the co-pilot's seat. Brigadier General Robert B. Williams, the 1st Wing Commander, would fly in the co-pilot's seat of *Lady Luck*, the deputy lead ship. Colonel Curtis E. LeMay, meanwhile, would lead 4th Wing to Regensburg, flying in the Snetterton Falcons formation. Williams, a Texan who was a stickler for military discipline, usually carried a swagger stick and was easily recognisable by his moustache and only one good eye; the other was lost while serving as an observer during the Blitz on London. He had won his wings and commission in 1923 and in 1936 at Langley Field, Virginia, he had been operations officer of the first group to fly the Fortress. Williams' force would return to England after bombing Schweinfurt, but Le May's would fly on to North Africa after hitting Regensburg to minimise attacks from enemy fighters. Crews learned all the details at briefing. One of the crewmen at Thorpe Abbotts who flew the raid was James P. Scott, Jr, Lieutenant Donald Oakes' radio operator of *High Life* in the 351st Squadron, whose crew were veterans of twelve previous combat operations over Germany. Scott recalls:

At the briefing, in the early morning darkness, the crews were stunned when the curtain covering a huge map of Europe, was pulled back. A red line stretched from England to Regensburg in Eastern Germany and then south over the Alps, across the Mediterranean to North Africa. Expressions of surprise, dismay and doubt filled the room. 'Aw, hell! Who dreamed this up?' 'My Gawd, we'll never make it.' 'This one should count as two missions.' After these outbursts, silence, disbelief and resignation, as we listened to staff officers outline the mission. One hundred and sixty planes of the Fourth Wing would bomb the Messerschmitt 109 factory at Regensburg and continue on to Africa while 170 of the First Wing would attack ball bearing plants at Schweinfurt and return to England. This would be the beginning of the end of the German war machine, or so we were informed by our S-2 (Intelligence officer). As happened all too frequently, take-off was delayed by fog and clouds over the coast and the English Channel. Less than usual small talk and banter was exchanged as we waited for the signal to 'start engines' or word that the mission was scrubbed. Each man was pondering the odds of returning from a raid so deep into the Third Reich. Those odds were high at best as the losses per mission were averaging 10 per cent. After an hour's delay, the fog started to lift. Engines came to life and the group lined up for take-off. Seventy minutes later the wing was assembled in combat formation over the English Channel. The sky seemed filled with B-17s as we headed east towards our target. Lieutenant Thomas E. Murphy, a commercial airline pilot from Waltham, Massachusetts, and pilot of *Piccadilly Lily*, was squadron leader for this mission, with *High Life* flying off his right wing.

At St Trond on 17 August *Unteroffizier* Otto Fries, a Bf 110 night-fighter pilot in 5./NJG1,[7] had only got to bed after sunrise and he intended to sleep through lunch in the mess, as he was not due to take off before late afternoon for target practice in area *Kolibri*. For the last six nights Fries had had barely more than 4 hours' sleep but towards 1030 hrs his *Bordfunker* (radio operator) Fred Staffa hammered against his door and chased him out of bed with the words 'cockpit readiness'. Fries shot up and tore off his pyjamas. In no time he was dressed and had put on his fur-lined boots. He had not washed, shaved, or cleaned his teeth. He strapped on his pistol and ran off. As he passed the washroom he stopped briefly to clear the sleep from his eyes with a handful of water. Downstairs, in front of the cadet school the crew bus was waiting with the engine running. It filled up in no time at all. The door was barely closed when it turned into Luiker Street to speed along to the crew room opposite the airbase gates. They rushed out of the bus and dashed into the barrack hut and to the cupboards holding their equipment. Flying trousers and jackets were hurriedly donned, signal pistol ammunition belts were strapped on and flying boots fastened, gauntlets and *Bordfunker*'s satchels torn from the shelves. Then they went off at a jog trot across Luiker Street to the operations room behind the guardroom to the left. The *Kommandeur* and the *Staffelkapitän* were already there. The adjutant checked and reported the complete assembly of the crews of the II *Gruppe*.

Despite the planning, Eaker and his subordinates knew the B-17 crews would have a running fight on their hands, but hoped that the fighter escort would keep losses down. Four P-47 groups were scheduled to escort the Regensburg force, but only one group rendezvoused with the bombers as scheduled. The overburdened Thunderbolts could not possibly hope to protect all seven groups in the 4th Wing. The long, straggling formation stretched for 15 miles and presented the fighter pilots with an awesome responsibility. Fortresses in the rear of the formation were left without protection at all. Fw 190s of JG1 and JG26 began their attacks 30 km east of Brussels.

At St Trond, meanwhile, *Unteroffizier* Otto Fries had waited for the off after the 'Old Man' (Major Walter Ehle[8]) had reported that several American bomber formations in England had taken off and they were already over the Channel approaching an unknown target. Following briefing, all crews had gone to cockpit readiness, just in case division ordered take-off, which would be signalled by the firing of a *Raclieschen*, a 'radish flare'. After take-off, they would assemble in a wide turn to port over the airfield, staggered in height: Staff Flight and 4th *Staffel* at 500 m, 5th and 6th *Staffel* each 50 m higher. Radio communication would be over the operations room frequency. After the take-off of the first aircraft, a continuous note of 30 seconds at 1 minute intervals would be transmitted for 10 minutes by operations for tuning-in purposes. There was to be general radio silence except for orders and instructions from the *Kommandeur*, who would also give out departure, course and height. Other exceptions were important reports from crews.

They ran to the bus, which turned at once onto the perimeter track to the dispersals – the 5th *Staffel* one was the last. Konrad, the mechanic of Fries and Staffa's G9+EM was already standing on the wing to help them put their parachute harness and seat belts on. He closed the cabin cover and struck it with his fist to indicate that he should not forget to lock it. Fries unlocked his shoulder straps to give him greater freedom of movement and switched on the electrics; Konrad had already connected the battery cart. Fries checked the instruments and the controls for freedom of movement and Staffa checked his radio gear. Having found everything in order, Fries turned off the electrics again. They did not have to wait long before the 'radish' flares went off into the air with a bang. Fries turned on the electrics again and pressed the starter button of the starboard engine. The rising tone of the centrifugal starter fascinated him each time. Fries pulled the clutch; the engine turned and gave a couple of puffs but it did not start. Fries repeated the process – again nothing. Engines were roaring everywhere. Angry, Fries tried again three more times – the damned engine simply would not start. The other aircraft were already taxiing out. He swore to himself and decided to try the port engine. At last, at the third attempt, coughing and spitting, the propeller began to turn. The mechanic signalled: the battery cart was empty! So Fries had to try to start the starboard engine using the generator of the port engine; fetching a fresh battery cart would take far too long. Fries tried it time and again, but the damned engine simply would not start.

The engines roared above the airfield. All the aircraft must have taken off. Fries decided to make one last attempt. If it did not work this time he would have to change over with a heavy heart to the reserve machine, one by no means popular with the crews and generally known as the *Staffel* 'whore' and that name said it all. Fries increased the revs of the port engine and pressed the starter button of the starboard one. Croaking and purring forth a blue-grey cloud, the engine came to life. 'Halleluia!' Staffa called out behind. Konrad pushed the battery cart to one side, removed the chocks and gave the clear sign. Slowly Fries taxied out of the hangar to the perimeter track, turned to the right and hurried to the take-off point. 'Lampion from Adler 98 – taxiing for take-off. *Tampen* (course)? *Kirchturm* (altitude)?'

'Adler 98 from Lampion – *Tampeo* one-zero-zero – *Kirchturm* four-zero – *Horrido* (tally-ho). Out.'

Fries paused briefly at the take-off point, locked his shoulder straps and set the take-off time on the clock – it showed 1130. He opened the throttles and took off. Having retracted the undercarriage and flaps, he set a course of 110 degrees. Fries flew at excess boost and a rate of climb of only 5 metres per second to keep up speed, as he wanted to catch up with the *Gruppe* as quickly as possible. Fred Staffa had tuned his receiver to the operations room frequency to keep a listening watch, but apart from background noises there was nothing to hear.

The cathedral of Tongres had long been left behind and they were approaching the River Meuse. Fries had reached 5,000 metres and trimmed the machine for level flight. They had already donned their oxygen masks at 4,000 metres. It was a glorious summer's day with no clouds in the sky and there was only a slight haze, which covered the countryside in a thin smoky-grey veil. Aachen appeared to port and some kilometres straight ahead in the haze Fries saw widely scattered aircraft of his *Gruppe* engaged with single Boeings. Why only single machines? Where were the formations? (Later he heard that individual aircraft had been cut out from a formation, whether by single-engined fighters or by the Aachen flak no one really knew.) Fries opened the throttles to take-off power and turned on the automatic propeller to utilise maximum power. The breeches of the guns clattered to the firing position as Fries turned the lever. Switching on the reflector sight, he noted with pleasure that Konrad had removed the night filter. He had forgotten to ask his mechanic about it before take-off, for it was important to be able to use the reflector sight as no tracer ammunition had been loaded (at night Fries preferred to use 'dark' ammunition). Konrad was a perfect mechanic who thought about everything!

Unteroffizier Otto Fries dived off his excess height and quickly approached the scene of the action. He decided to go for the group to starboard, as it was the closest. Two Bf110s were engaged with a Boeing, which had evidently already been hit for its starboard outer engine was trailing whitish-grey smoke. When Fries was within range, still 50 metres above the bomber, the two Bf110s had just made an attack in night-fighter fashion, from behind and below and had dived away to starboard. Fries, behind and to one side of the Boeing, broke off to port and let his sights run between the engines and along the starboard wing. A brief burst of fire and he saw the strikes in the wing. Then he dived away to port below the bomber. Whether he had been fired at he did not know; it had all happened so quickly and it had been so exciting to fly an attack on such a large ship in broad daylight. In any case, his machine had received no hits, for he knew that impertinent knocking sound only too well.

Fries drew his aircraft up again in a turn to port and saw the other two Bf110s attacking the bomber again. Its starboard wing suddenly burst into flames like an explosion. Bits detached themselves and before very long the first 'packages' dropped from the Boeing, plunging downwards and suddenly hanging on their parachutes. There was nothing left to do. Fries looked around to see where the others had gone but apart from a fire on the ground there was nothing to see. The other two machines circled the burning bomber. He did not want to wait for them and went back on to his old course. There were no aircraft to be seen. 'Listen out on your radio to find out where they've got to.' Staffa gave no reply; he had obviously switched off his intercom. He always did this when he was working his gear, seeking a transmitter or getting a beaming. Once when Fries had complained about this his *Bordfunker* had countered: 'You only interfere with your chatter and generally at the most inconvenient moment.' Fries briefly waggled his wings.

'What's up?'

'Try to get the fighter broadcast, they always give a situation report.'

'I am doing it already – just a moment, the frequency is jammed.'

Fries continued on his course of 110 degrees. He turned off the automatic propeller and went on to economic cruise to save fuel.

'They have turned off to the south; they are probably heading for the Rhein-Main area or Karlsruhe-Stuttgart.'

Fries went on to the south and increased power to gain more speed. They must be somewhere over the south Eifel. Down below another bomber was burning; it looked as though it would start a forest fire. The Mosel appeared ahead. Far off to port in the haze and just discernible, Fries saw the Deutsche Eck.

'Anything new on the fighter broadcast?' he asked Staffa after he had waggled his wings.

'No, they are still up ahead – can't you get your horses to run a bit faster?'

'Certainly, where are they now?'

'The map reference given should be north-west of Mainz. On the operations room frequency there is nothing except a constant rustling and odd words, which make no sense. I'm staying on the fighter frequency, if there is any news I will let you know. I'm switching you off again.'

'Very well, thanks!'

Fries gave a little more power and went into a slow climb so that if required he could exchange height for speed. He looked around him; there were no aircraft to be seen. Nahe appeared below, he recognised Mainz to port. Its inhabitants would all be in their air-raid shelters. Fries was approaching his home ground. The propellers turned, the engine noise was soothing and all instruments indicated what they should. The airspeed indicator showed just below the 420 km per hour mark.

Something appeared to be happening ahead to port. Fries opened up the throttles to the gate, turned 20 degrees to port and turned the propeller to automatic again. He crossed the Rhine and up ahead he saw a formation, which appeared to be surrounded by fighters swarming around like a bunch of hornets. Fries would have liked to whip up his horses some more, but he did not want to open his throttles beyond the gate. He gave a brief waggle.

'What's up?' asked Staffa.

'There's a heavy formation up ahead – let's see what we can do, our ammunition can't be exhausted by a long chalk yet.'

'Well, let's go then!'

Ahead and a little lower a single Boeing appeared, its port undercarriage leg hanging down. Three Bf 109s circled around it. Fries had the impression that they were out of ammunition. He approached very fast, much too fast, and snatched the throttles closed. Seconds later he peeled off to port and sent a long burst into the starboard wing. He passed the bomber close above him, opened the throttles again and took the Bf 110 around in a steep turn to port. When the Boeing came back into view he saw that the starboard wing was on fire and that parachutes were hanging in the air. The bomber continued briefly onward then went down over the starboard wing and exploded shortly before reaching the ground. The parts fell widely dispersed into a wood to the north-east of Mannheim.[9]

Weeks later, Fries heard by chance that the crews of the Boeings would lower their undercarriage if they wanted to surrender. The fighters would then cease their attacks in order to give the crew a chance to bale out. He felt very ashamed afterwards and cursed the fact that night-fighters were ordered up by day without making them acquainted with the usages of day fighting. It might be that the old sweats of his night-fighter unit, who had come from the *Zerstorer* units and had partaken in the early campaigns and the Battle of Britain, were familiar with these customs. He had come straight from night-fighter training and had only the faintest idea of the tactics and conduct of the day fighters. Fries' misdemeanour made him feel sad.

The three fighters were still circling the crash site and then they formed a Vic and flew off eastwards. Fries had lost contact. Apart from a few fires there was no sign of friend or foe. He turned his equipment to normal flight and set a course of 150 degrees. He saw the Königstuhl on his port beam. *O alma mater heidelbergensis* – would he ever return to the university? Staffa, who had been silent during this time, spoke up:

'That one won't drop any more bombs anyway!'

'You're right but I have lost contact – listen in to the fighter broadcast, they must still be nearby.'

'I'll call you right back!' The machine was approaching the Kraichgau and the silhouette of the Black Forest appeared in the distance. 'They have turned off to the east.' They were both so occupied with the bomber that they had not noticed it.

'The formations are supposed to be in map references *Toni/Toni* and *Toni/Ulrich.* That must be the area south of Würzburg. They are on an easterly course. We have gone much too far to the south.'

Fries looked at the map in his mind's eye: 'I assume that north-east would be about the right course?'

Fred Staffa took the navigation chart from his satchel. 'We are about north of Karlsruhe, I think 045 degrees would about do.'

Fries turned on to north-east and increased the speed and pulled out the plugs of the pneumatic fuel gauges to check the contents. He had more than an hour's fuel left. Fries never trusted the fuel gauges. It had happened more than once that they showed zero although he had only been flying for 1 hour. According to the elapsed time the gauges could be correct in spite of the increased consumption caused by the propeller automatic and the increased speed, for they had only been flying for just over an hour.

They crossed the Neckar. His thoughts went back to the past: how often had he paddled here at weekends and spent the night in a tent with his friends.

It seemed as if decades had passed since that time. *O Gaudeamus igitur ...!* When had he last sung it in the circle of his friends?

It would certainly not do to dream during a sortie against the enemy – stark reality recalled him at once: a formation of Boeings appeared over to port, they were approaching each other at an acute angle. 'What a bunch of bombers!' came Fred Staffa's voice. 'There must be more than thirty of them and not a single Bf 109 to be seen. What are you going to do?'

'I don't know yet!'

Fries had heard somewhere that day fighters would attack from ahead and above, take one of the leading Boeings into their sights, fire and then dive down and away through the formation. Then, if they had not been damaged themselves, they would pull up and around and repeat the process. The Bf 109 was a small and manoeuvrable aircraft, against which, his night-fighter Bf 110 seemed like a fat and lame duck. Would he be able to carry out an attack in a like manner? The chances of being hit appeared considerable, but they still had their parachutes as a final consolation! An attack from behind and above or in the night-fighter manner from behind and below were out of the question considering the firepower of thirty Boeings. That only left an attack from abeam, perhaps at an angle from ahead and above.

Fries did not know what would be the right method for him and his aircraft, but it was clear that he must do something and he wanted to. 'Well now I've had a few things going through my head. I believe it would be best that we pull up and make an attack at an angle from ahead and above – or have you a better idea?'

'Hardly and what are the chances of not being hit?'

'Very small; is your parachute harness secure?' Silence ....

'Your ideas have become superfluous – look there!' A Boeing left the formation and turned off to the south. Fries had to admit that he felt a great relief. 'Why is it turning away – does it have some special orders or is it damaged?'

'Perhaps they want to escape to Switzerland because they don't like this dangerous game!'

Though he was unaware of it, the B-17 was *High Life*. James P. Scott, Jr recalls:

> For those manning the gun positions, attention was focused on German fighters pressing their attacks.
>
> '109s at 3 o'clock low and climbing.'
>
> 'Number 5 plane of lead squadron burning, counted five parachutes.'
>
> 'Two Fw 190s coming in at 12 o'clock level.'
>
> 'Scratch one fighter, he's smoking and going down.'
>
> The plane shook constantly from the triphammer percussions of the fifty-calibre machine-guns as the crewmembers alerted one another over the intercom. There was no respite from the battle as fighters made their passes, half-rolled under the formation, turned and went around for another try.

Then, from the ball turret gunner, Leslie Nadeau, 'Number two engine losing oil fast.'

The top turret gunner, '109 coming in at 3 o'clock level.'

The plane shuddered as a cannon shell exploded in No. 3 engine. It misfired, ran rough and the wing began to vibrate violently.

Pilot to co-pilot: 'Feather number three before it shakes us to pieces.'

Joseph Harper, co-pilot: 'Feathering number three . . .. Damn, it won't feather; hydraulic fluid must be gone.'

So No. 3 continued to windmill after power was cut. *High Life* began to drop behind the formation. With two engines gone and one of them windmilling, our effective power was reduced to less than 40 per cent of normal. The pilot ordered the bombardier to jettison the bomb load, hoping it would lighten the plane enough to maintain formation. The gap continued to increase so we turned away towards the Alps, hoping we could make it to Sicily rather than bale out over German territory. Fortunately, the fighter attacks were ending, probably because their fuel supplies were running low. One lone Me 210 with longer range followed us, lobbing 40 mm cannon shells, hoping for a hit while staying out of range of our fifties. We had enough problems. The top turret operating mechanism was malfunctioning, the tail guns were out of ammunition and the waist gun stations had only a limited supply. However, the top turret got off a few rounds at the German and he turned back whether for lack of fuel or no desire to fight.

Fries put his aircraft into a steep turn to port and followed the bomber, which was about 50 metres below him. It appeared to have been damaged after all. As he got closer he thought he could recognise holes in the rear turret and the fuselage and the propeller of the starboard outer engine appeared to be turning only by the slipstream. 'I hope I have enough juice in the cannon. You can forget the machine-guns where such a heavy is concerned.'

'But you haven't fired that much so far, there must be enough left!'

'I hope so – hold tight!'

Fries was no longer excited, he was quite calm and turned the propeller to automatic again. He held his height and placed himself on the starboard quarter of the bomber. Why did they not fire? He was well within their range! Fries peeled off to port, aimed at the starboard inner engine and pressed both firing button and lever. Only one of his cannons fired a short burst and not all of the four machine-guns fired. Fries dived below the Boeing and pulled up his machine in a steep turn to port. 'Damn it! The cannons are empty and it looked as though only two of the machine-guns were working. What rubbish!' Angry, Fries flew two further attacks at the starboard inner engine with the remaining machine-guns. At the second attack only a couple of bullets stuttered out, then it was finished. 'That can't be true!' He turned the switch for the guns off and on again and tried both triggers. Nothing happened; the machine-guns and cannon remained silent. 'The devil! Such rot! Now it's your turn, Fred!' As Fries pushed the aircraft down two 'packages' dropped out of the Boeing and two parachutes opened. 'They seem to have given up after all!'

Fries sheered off to one side and waited, flying at the same height as the Boeing – 3 minutes – 5 minutes – nothing happened.

'Well, what's up with you my friends,' said the *Bordfunker*.

The bomber flew on as though nothing had happened; the starboard outer engine was obviously dead. 'I am now going to place myself below him and draw slowly ahead. You must direct me into the right position and then aim for the starboard inner engine. Then fire until nothing more comes out of your barrels!'

Fries went down a little, pulled over to port and increased his speed.

'Stop, that's good, you can go a little higher.'

Fries gently pulled on his stick.

'Stop! No higher!'

Fries held the machine rigidly on course and height – it was no simple matter as he was unable to see the Boeing. Four or five bursts clattered, then he heard the resigned voice of his radio operator: 'Any number of holes in the tin and the engine is still running. My ammunition's all gone.'

Fries sheered off to one side and they continued alongside the bomber for a short while to see whether the crew would give up after all but the Boeing continued steadily onwards. 'There's not much point in hanging on any longer; he'll surely go to Switzerland. 'Let's find a place to land. Our fuel might last as far as St Trond but I do not want to fly without ammunition. Perhaps Echterdingen with its Night-Fighter School might suit; the people there are familiar with the Bf 110.

'I'll see if I can find the frequency in my lists, then I'll give you a bearing. I'm switching off.'

Fries set course westwards and before Staffa had reported, he saw an *autobahn* ahead. It could only be the road from Munich to Karlsruhe, but was he now north or south of Stuttgart? Fries was not familiar with the area. It had been an age since he had flown around the area during his blind-flying training in a Ju 52 and then the windscreen had been obscured as, sitting beside his instructor, he had been practice flying on instruments. Instinctively Fries turned off to the north and minutes later he recognised the airfield of Echterdingen. 'You needn't trouble yourself any more, there's Stuttgart up ahead.'

Fries landed at precisely 1300 and taxied immediately to the hangars. The armourers found that one cannon and two machine-guns had been jammed by burst cartridge cases. As a change of guns would have taken far too long, he had the magazines of the remaining guns filled up and taxied over to refuel. They took off about 2 hours later and on the way he allowed himself a small detour to the north. When the Vogese came in sight, he swung along the edge of the hills to the north until the Weintor between Alsace and the Pfalz came into view. This was the beginning of the wine road of the Pfalz, which went through Winzerdorf, where Fries had been born. He circled three times at low level over the hill where, nearly 1,200 years before, his home village had been built. Everywhere in the vineyards people were waving; his mother stood on the stoop and waved too. Such digressions were officially called 'infringements against the aviator's proper behaviour', but without an accuser there could be no judge. And where operational crews were concerned, they usually turned a blind eye. Fries arrived at 1530 in St Trond, where he handed the machine over to the armourers. *High Life*, meanwhile, had headed for Switzerland as Fries had predicted. Scott continues:

Now we were alone but losing altitude and as we approach the mountains, it was apparent that the route south was effectively blocked. So the pilot orders the crew to prepare for bale out. At this point, the navigator spotted Lake Constance off to the West and informed the pilot that Switzerland was just across that body of water. We were down to about 10,000 feet as our crippled plane turned toward the lake and safety – 5,000 feet and almost there. Suddenly, we encountered a barrage of flak from below. We learned later that Friedrichshafen, which we were passing over, was the location of a training station for anti-aircraft gunners. Each battery used different coloured smoke to aid in scoring, so the sky was filled with bursting shells displaying every colour of the rainbow. The pilot took evasive action to spoil their aim, as the plane was buffeted like a leaf in the wind. Perhaps, this was a beginner's class as we were finally out of range over the lake with only a few more holes in the fuselage. Reluctantly, the pilot ordered the crew to jettison all loose equipment to slow our descent. Out the side windows went the remaining ammunition, the post-mounted machine-guns, large tools, toolboxes and emergency gear. Afterwards, we were told that one of the guns fell through the roof of a tavern and created considerable consternation among the customers.

Our pilot was looking for a reasonably flat, unsettled space to land and found an open field except for a lone farmer loading hay. The landing gear would not go down, so we cranked the wheels down manually only to discover one tyre has been hit by flak. Hastily, we cranked the wheels up again and assumed our designated emergency landing positions. There was a crash, the sound of tearing, crushing metal and the fuselage filled with dust and debris, as we ground to a stop. Then we scrambled through the various exits to good old mother earth. None of the crew had suffered so much as a scratch but *High Life* had come to the end of the road. We huddled together some distance from our Fort, hoping she didn't catch fire. Suddenly, Swiss soldiers, who seemed to appear out of nowhere, surrounded us. The officer in charge told us: 'For you, the war is over. You are in Switzerland.' We had landed on a Swiss fighter strip at Dubendorf, a small town near Zurich. Our plane was the first but many would follow before the war was over.

We were confined to a cadet barracks in individual rooms, searched, interrogated and informed of our rights as belligerents in a neutral country. After three days, we were taken to a small hotel in Macolin, a town near Bienne where we were joined by two more aircrews, one from the Schweinfurt mission and another from a raid over Italy. A Swiss officer and several militiamen were placed in charge and a representative from the military legation of the American embassy in Berne arrived to explain, in detail, what was expected of us during our enforced vacation.

About 250 fighters – twice as many as against the Regensburg force – were hurled against the Schweinfurt force from the moment it crossed the mouth of the Scheldt on their way in and cost thirty-six Fortresses. The worst hit were the 381st and 91st, which lost eleven and ten B-17s respectively. Thick inland mists had delayed the 1st Wing after LeMay's force had taken off. This effectively prevented a two-pronged assault, which might have split the opposing fighter force, which had time to refuel, re-arm and re-deploy to forward bases in Holland after shooting down twenty-four Forts of the Regensburg force, the 'Bloody Hundredth' losing nine ships. Nevertheless, the bombing at Regensburg was extremely accurate and Beirne Lay Jr who flew aboard *Piccadilly Lily* piloted by Tom Murphy could see that they had 'smeared the objective. The price? Cheap. 200 airmen.'[10] On the way to the Alps a few fighters attacked the surviving B-17s, some flying on three engines and many trailing smoke. LeMay circled his bombers over Lake Garda near Verona to give the cripples a chance to rejoin the wing. Red fuel warning lights were showing in every ship and it was a ragged collection of survivors with dead and wounded aboard that headed for North Africa. There, the almost non-existent maintenance facilities ruled out any further shuttle missions The *Luftwaffe* lost twenty-seven fighters, as against claims by the B-17 gunners and escorting fighters of 288 German fighters destroyed!

At St Trond *Unteroffizier* Fries lay down on his bunk and took stock of the events of the daylight sortie that had been a new experience for him. He felt exhilaration on the one hand and disappointment on the other because he had not succeeded in shooting down that last Boeing. Daylight operations against American formations appeared to make no sense at all. By the law of averages, his *Gruppe* would have hardly any aircraft left for night operations if it went on like this for another week.[11] Twenty-one German night-fighters were lost during the daylight operations on 17 August and fourteen crewmembers were killed or severely injured. Fifteen crews that were scrambled from St Trond shot down seven B-17s, but they lost four Bf 110s and one pilot to return fire and in combat with Thunderbolts. Almost all the other Messerschmitts returned with such severe battle damage that they could not be sent off to hunt for RAF Bomber Command aircraft.

From late summer onwards, fighter escorts accompanied the American combat boxes. These took an unacceptably high toll on the lumbering German twin-engined machines and crews and early in 1944 night-fighter crews were finally relieved of their day-fighting duties.

Notes

1. *Target Germany* (1944).
2. Peek was KIA on 31.8.43 flying *Eager Beaver*, when he was again forced to ditch in the sea. This time only the tail gunner survived.
3. *Target Germay* (1944).

4. This 95th BG Fortress crashed at Elbent with six of Lieutenant James R. Sarchet's crew dead. Two crew evaded and two were captured.
5. Georg-Peter Eder was shot down seventeen times and wounded on twelve different occasions. On 15.3.44 after leaving hospital after being wounded he took command of 6./JG1.and remained as its CO until 7.6.44. Awarded the *Ritterkreuz*, on 1.7.44, he was transferred to JG26. Eder finished the war with seventy-eight victories, thirty-six of them *Viermots*. Twelve of his kills were gained flying the Me 262 jet fighter with *Kommando* 'Nowotny' and JG7. His war ended in hospital after being shot down by P-51 Mustangs.
6. Eight of McCammon's crew were KIA. Two were PoW. Naumann's *Staffel* lost three Fw 190s and one pilot KIA to return fire from the B-17s.
7. Fries and his *Bordfunker*, Uffz Alfred (Fred) Staffa, had claimed their first kill, a Lancaster III south-east of Charleroi, on 11.8.43.
8. Major Walter Ehle had thirty-five night and four day victories in ZG1 and NJG1. He was awarded the *Ritterkreuz* but was KIA 17/18.11.43 in a crash near St Trond airfield.
9. *All Shot To Hell* of the 390th BG, the exploded remains of which, came down at Bringen, on the western banks of the River Rhine. All ten of Lieutenant Ashbrooke W. Tyson's crew survived and were PoW.
10. *I Saw Regensburg Destroyed. Piccadilly Lily* and Murphy's crew were lost on 8.10.43.
11. Otto Fries finished the war with fourteen night *Abschüsse*.

CHAPTER 3

To the Promised Land?

*'Son-of-a-bitch and this is my 25th mission!' Eyes turned towards the speaker
and there were expressions of sympathy and condolence until a baby-faced
pilot spoke: 'What the hell are you crying about? This is my first!'*

Colonel Budd J. Peaslee, CO, 384th Bomb Group,
Schweinfurt raid, 14 October 1943

In the hours following the raids on Schweinfurt and Regensburg, sten-
ographers were busy at Pinetree, Major General Frederick L. Anderson's
Headquarters at High Wycombe, where he had taken residence in June
after succeeding Eaker who moved to command the 8th Air Force.
Anderson's congratulations on LeMay's completion of an 'epoch in aerial
warfare' were transmitted to North Africa where 'Old Iron Ass' and his men
were now enjoying a change of scenery, living in tents and mud shacks at
desolate desert air strips. At night almost everyone at the French Colonial
base at Bône in Algeria and at Telergma, about 100 miles west of Tunis, opted
to sleep on the ground beneath the wings of their Forts. At Bône there were
hundreds of Italian PoWs nearby and Australian troops that sang songs that
made the British look like 'nuns in a convent'. The Americans traded soap and
mattress covers with the Arabs for eggs, chickens and water melons, while
some even got a donkey and fitted the animal with an oxygen mask for flying
back to England with them! They called her Lady Moe. By sheer luck the
animal survived the flight home, but it was killed soon after by a passing truck.
LeMay inspected his men and returned their snappy salutes left handed, while
smoking his customary long cigar clenched between his teeth. This legendary
leader had been in the same 1929 class at Kelly Field as Anderson when they
had taken flight training and won their pilot's wings. Anderson was sure that
'the 4th Bombardment Wing has continued to make history. The Hun now
had no place to hide'.

Despite the fine words the 19 per cent loss rate suffered on the Schweinfurt
and Regensburg missions was unacceptable on a sustained basis and there was
no disguising the utter desolation on the majority of Fortress bases in the
bitter aftermath. Fifty Forts that were damaged had landed in North Africa
and in their bloodied insides lay dead, dying and wounded. Lieutenant
Richard H. Perry was co-pilot of *Betty Boop the Pistol Packin' Mama* in the
390th flown by Lieutenant Jim Geary. The ship had been riddled by .30 calibre
armour-piercing shells in the waist section, one of which went right through

Sergeant Leonard A. Baumgartner's steel helmet. Perry went back to the waist to administer to him but Baumgartner took his last breath in his arms. Canadian-born Aubrey 'Bart' Bartholomew in *Raunchy Wolf* in the 385th was almost blown out of his ball turret at 19,000 feet after persistent fighter attacks during the bomb run. Bart's turret door flew off as a result of an ill-fitting hinge and only the toe of his left flying boot hooked under the range pedal of his guns saved him from being sucked out. Oxygen and intercom cables were severed and he lost contact with the rest of the crew. He somehow managed to pull himself back into the ball and attract the attention of a crewman who cranked him back inside the fuselage. Major Gale 'Bucky' Cleven, CO of the 350th Squadron in the 100th, put *Phartzac* down at Telergma after it had been riddled with 20 mm shells, which cut off both the radio operator's legs just above the knees and wounded the bombardier in the head and shoulders. Sergeant Norman Smith lost so much blood from the stumps of his severed legs that he died long before landfall. He had married shortly before leaving the States and his wife was expecting a baby at Christmas. A staggering 118 Forts of the Schweinfurt force had also returned damaged to East Anglia with wounded and dying men aboard.

The raids had failed to knock the plants out of action permanently and the bombers would have to return to Schweinfurt again and again before the war was over. On 14 October Anderson was forced to send 290 bombers back to Schweinfurt. After the raid General 'Hap' Arnold confidently told gathered pressmen: 'Now we have got Schweinfurt!'[1] Sixty Flying Forts were lost, 594 men killed or missing and over 130 bombers returned damaged with a further forty-five casualties.

Unfortunately, the scenes of carnage and bloodied and battle-damaged bombers returning to England in 1943 were commonplace. Bert Stiles, a B-17 pilot in the 91st, vividly recalled[2] the time he was at Bassingbourn when a ship came in with dead aboard.

> One flak shell had burst just outside the waist window. The waist-gunner wore a flak suit and a flak-helmet, but that didn't help much. One chunk hit low on his forehead and clipped the top of his head off. Part of his brains sprayed as far forward as the door into the radio-room. The rest of them spilled out when the body crumpled up, quite dead. The flak suit protected his heart and lungs all right, but both legs were blown off and hung with the body, because the flying-suit was tucked into electric shoes .... Nobody else on the plane was hurt. The waist looked like a jagged screen. The Fort got home okay .... I climbed in with the medico, and, getting through the door I put my hand in a gob of blood and brains that had splattered back that way. I took one look at the body and climbed out again, careful this time where I put my hands .... I felt no nausea, just a sense of shock, just a certain deadness inside.

The armoured flak vests made of heavy canvas covered with overlapping plates of manganese and steel protecting the chest and back had been developed by Colonel Malcolm C. Grow, Chief Surgeon of the 8th Air Force, in association with the Wilkinson Sword Company of Great Britain. When encountering flak, crewmen put on, or more to the point draped, the cumbersome 20–35 lb flak suit over themselves plus a large steel helmet with big steel earflaps that went over the earphones. As Ben Smith, a southerner from Georgia, and the radio operator gunner in Anthony 'Chick' Cecchini's crew in the Hell's Angels Group at Molesworth recalled:

> ... there was one part of the anatomy much beloved by the flight crews. This was shown by the extreme lengths they went to protect it – the groin. All who had sitting jobs in the aircraft sat on a piece of armour, as most shrapnel travelled upward. All sorts of ingenious methods were devised to protect the 'family jewels'. The fact that this fragile piece of equipment would avail them little if their head were blown off seemed not to matter; they surrounded it with armour plate. The married men were particularly solicitous in this behalf, although I am afraid that we all overdid this piece of business. I think that all these elaborate safeguards were more symbolic than protective. It was just one of the many things we did to foster the myth of our continuity.

Each base had a serviceable dispensary and sick quarters building with bed space for twenty-five to forty-five patents. Slightly injured men were kept in sick quarters until fit for duty, usually no more than five days. The more seriously injured were evacuated to General Hospitals but these were over 60 miles from any base. Emergency cases, which could not be hauled long distances, were treated at one of thirteen RAF or nearby Emergency Medical Hospitals. Sometimes men badly burned or mutilated in a crashing bomber were beyond help. One young captain who had the misfortune to witness the death throes of a B-17 near his base inspected the scene of devastation. The top of the cockpit was gone and it was all out in the open, heaped up higher than the rest of the surrounding debris. He just stood there looking.

> Everything was covered with whitish-brown foam from the fire hoses, and it moulded everything into one large mass of almost indistinguishable objects. My eyes suddenly stopped wandering. Yes, it was the co-pilot still sitting in his seat; his body could just be made out as it protruded from under the blanket of foam. It was sitting upright, with no head on its shoulders, its right arm at its side and its left arm raised and bent as if to protect a face that wasn't there. The arm was very badly burned, and still smoldering. Leaning against the co-pilot's seat was another form, the engineer. He was at his post between the pilot and co-pilot, his body horizontal, looking like a smoldering potato sack, crushed against the debris. Then I picked out the form of the pilot, lying on the floor of what had been the cockpit. A bent arm without a hand that protruded above the foam covering was all that indicated that the shapeless form had once been a man. I had seen enough, and turned away.

A navigator who came upon another scene of utter destruction of a once proud Liberator bomber found it difficult to describe.

Wreckage was scattered over a large area. I was the only person there except for the British Bomb Disposal Crew. The area was roped off, which I ignored. I proceeded to within a few feet of one of the craters caused by an exploding bomb. Not all bombs went off as I saw several scattered about, still unexploded. The bottom cone of the hole was filled with aluminium that had melted from the intense heat of the burning wreckage. Not too far away was a crew of three men, they had placed a rope around the trunk of the body of one of the pilots. Both of the unfortunate pilots were still sitting in their heavy metal bucket seals, their arms had been burned to stumps as were their legs. All their bodies including their heads were burned charcoal black. The clean-up crew gave a tug on the rope, expecting to extract the body but instead, the torso simply pulled apart like an overdone roast. I saw no other bodies, but on the way to my observation point, I saw an unburned electric flying glove. We always needed an extra glove so I was not above usurping this one for my emergency bag. When I picked it up, it took me no time to let it go again, as I noticed it still had a hand in it. One of the men pointed to my feet and said, 'Look what you are standing on, Governor'. I looked down; my left foot was on top of a man's skull, cut off at the hairline. Another man said I should move further away as they were going to defuse some bombs. By this time, I had seen more than I had bargained for. Even though I find words inadequate to describe the sights I saw that day, I'll never forget them.

Death would come in many ways, from the effects of enemy fighters and flak and either directly or as a result of shock brought on by wounds and blood positioning and other factors such as anoxia (oxygen starvation). Professional treatment was of course only available once the aircraft had returned to a permanent base. It was not uncommon for badly wounded men, who would not survive the journey home, to be pushed out of the aircraft with their parachutes on, in the hope that the enemy would treat them and save their lives. Combat crews were on pills to wake them up and get them going. Sleeping at night became so bad that men started taking pills from their escape kits. While over at the base hospital being treated for scabies, Ben Smith saw two air gunners who looked like lepers.

They were in a frightful condition, their faces swollen and shapeless. I found out that they were suffering from frostbite. These were usually waist gunners or tail gunners. Because there was no way to keep warm back there in the sub-zero weather we flew in, frostbite was a common occurrence. Sick Call was one function that was always well attended. It was not that the fellows were sick; it was the delightful medicine they served, terpinhydrate, called by its aficionados, 'GI Gin'. It was cough syrup with codeine in it. A guy could get bombed with a couple of swallows. There was always a long line and a lot of phony coughing going on . . . the first aid kits in the airplanes were systematically looted for their morphine syringes. This was a serious business but it continued to be a problem.

Heavy losses like those at Schweinfurt and Regensburg always affected morale and the signs manifested themselves in many ways, from a high abort rate to, at the very least, severe bouts of intoxication. A combat crewman recalled one of the boys from the Bronx who got drunk every chance he could because he knew he would get killed the next time out. Then one night he came back drunk but he went out to his ship in a stolen jeep, rounded up the Very pistols and burned up several wheatfields. He finally ended up in another barracks, opened one door and started firing Very pistol shots inside, setting fire to clothing and bedding. Because of the firing the occupants of the barracks got down on their hands and knees and crawled into the ice and snow. He was not sent home but was just confined to barracks. Conflicts often arose because crew huts were crammed with inhabitants with diverse life styles. There were the swingers, the club hounds, the sack rats who never left their beds except to fly or to eat, the eager beavers that followed every rule and restriction to the letter and the neatniks, the slobs and the pub-crawlers. Bill Rose, a pilot in *Fame's Favoured Few* recalled an occasion one night when the night before a mission he was in his barracks writing letters, and one of the officer crews packed all their belongings.

> It made me wonder what insight they must have had to know they would not survive the next mission. Sure enough next day they went down. We had another crew who went on a bombing mission to southern Germany. After bombing the target we turned around and came home but this crew took off for Switzerland. When we got back I checked their clothes in the hut. Everything was there except for their 'Class A' uniforms, which they had worn on the raid to prove their identity. They had just given up fighting.[3]

One pilot, who considered 'continuous perfect health an ever-present concern of every member of the crew', explained that:

> Should anyone become ill, a substitute would be assigned to fly and function in his capacity. Hangovers and the common cold could ground you and the flight surgeons were ever vigilant. Mental fatigue, VD, and other maladies were more easily detected. A sick man does not belong on a team in the sky. I didn't know it until we finished our tour of missions that one of my crew was a dormant syphilitic and experienced airsickness each time we were airborne. The rest of the crew liked this man so well they kept it a secret knowing full well that if I were aware of this condition, I would have had him taken off the crew and found a replacement. My crew was truly a family taking care of each other in the air and on the ground.

For those that came back physically unscathed after each mission often there was mental torment. Flight surgeons, aided by psychiatrists and psychologists kept a close watch for the first signs of crews becoming 'flak happy', otherwise referred to as 'battle fatigue'. Staff Sergeant Larry 'Goldie' Goldstein, a radio operator in the 388th, saw 'many men' who 'absolutely refused to fly another mission after seeing their buddies go down or were afraid of being victims of mid-air collision'. Ronald D. Spencer, a gunner in the Rackheath Aggies, recalled that the club officer was considered 'flak happy'.

He played the piano, not too well, but with great gusto; leading all of the profane singing that was common in the club. He at least kept the atmosphere lively. One day one of our hut-mates said the club officer was talking to him when he suddenly stopped talking while looking out the window. He then grabbed his .45 automatic, opened the window and started blasting away at something. It turned out to be a large rat. Apparently a poor marksman, he emptied the clip, slammed the window and began cursing that he had missed. Flak happy I guess he really was. But the classic was a pilot whose favourite expression was 'Heil Hitler, just in case we lose'. I probably heard him say it a hundred or more times. Unfortunately, he and his crew were shot down and killed or made prisoner. In any case, a couple of days after they were shot down the pilot was heard on the German radio extolling the virtues of his captivity and how well he was being treated. Our reaction was, 'Jesus, he really meant it all along.'

Ben Smith recalls:

Every combat crewman was issued with a .45 automatic pistol. I never figured out why. They were useful for celebrations and shooting out lights. Sometimes that was the only way to terminate a poker game. I once shot them out myself. It got to be a sort of a tradition. Nobody got excited about a few rounds being fired off. Almost every morning before the mission somebody would accidentally fire off a machine-gun. A round came through the dispersal tent one morning narrowly missing us.

John A. Holden, a navigator, recalled the crew that they resided with who were on their twenty-eighth or twenty-ninth mission when they all went 'crazy'. One in particular would wake up in the middle of the night and shoot his .45 off at mice.

Upon the recommendation of their flight surgeons, enlisted men and officer crewmen had separate 'rest homes', more commonly known as 'Flak Homes', to which they were sometimes sent for up to seven days when combat fatigue was diagnosed. These breaks were supposed to prevent breakdowns and promote morale and efficiency. When Cliff Hatcher, a pilot in the 94th was sent for a 'flak furlough' at Coombe House shortly after the Group lost eight B-17s, he and his crew were in such bad shape that their flight surgeon, 'Doc' Miller, went along with them! He too was getting 'flak happy' riding along with his boys. Howard E. Hernan, an air gunner recalled that, 'After the Schweinfurt raid we got to go to a rest home run by the Red Cross, which was much needed. The officers went to Stanbridge Earls while we went to Moulsford Manor. We were treated royally and got to wear civilian clothes. There were butlers, waiters and maids to take care of us.' But not everyone got to go to a 'flak shack', Larry Goldstein for one. 'We reached seventeen missions without anybody suggesting a rest home to us.' Further, 'If a crew survived eight to ten missions at this time they were considered lucky.' Leaves were often issued upon the completion of ten to fifteen missions. In RAF Bomber Command mental breakdowns caused by operational flying was caustically termed LMF – Lacking in Moral Fibre. But RAF bomber crews, unlike their American counterparts, were expected, after a period of rest, to fly a second or even a third tour of operations. It had long been recognised that to counter combat exhaustion and stress, anxiety or emotional breakdown, morale would be improved if crews flew a fixed limited tour of combat missions. However, as will be seen, this combat tour was repeatedly increased as laid down by the top brass in Washington and carried out at command level in England. For the time being a tour in 1943 was twenty-five missions.

At Chelveston on 18 August Lieutenant Ralph R. Miller, pilot of *Lady Liberty*, waited to fly his thirteenth mission. A few more and he and his crew would reach a point 'from where they could see that Promised Land of twenty-five missions completed, then *finis* and they would all be past and only memories'. Fortress crews had been stood down for just one day after the Double Strike mission. Now, on the morning of 19 August 170 crews waited to be despatched to bomb Brussels and the airfield at Woensdrecht. All crew-members were at their places in the ship waiting for the tower's instructions to taxi out for take-off, but all morning they waited because weather ships were reporting that Brussels was covered with clouds. Miller knew that they might have to take their secondary target, Gilze-Rijen airfield on the coast of Flushing Island, Holland. It was early afternoon when the order to finally taxi came. Miller recalls:

Co-pilot John Meade and I were chatting in the pilot seats. 'John, I certainly am happy to have this milk run for the thirteenth mission,' I said, 'it's so soothing to the nerves to have our fighters all the way[4], I don't mind the flak if we don't have to look at those fighters.' John agreed, but expressed his non-belief in superstition. Just two days before we had returned safely from one of the greatest air battles ever fought, the first twin raids on Schweinfurt and Regensburg. All set, down the runway and throttling up to join the squadron in formation now seemed like old stuff, a new confidence had been born in us. Squadron joined with group, group with wing and as wing joined with other wings we were high over England, 21,000 feet, heading straight for Brussels. What a rosy feeling it was to look out and see our own fighters dancing all around us and knowing that they would be there all the way. We did not expect to fire a single shot; they even sent a photographer along in the ship next to ours to get a picture of our bombs coming out. Many ground officers of the group that had been able to talk operations into a ride had crowded into the planes: five of these and they would receive an Air Medal.

Brussels was covered by clouds; we saw the wings in front turning left toward Flushing Island. Boy, what a milk run, not an enemy fighter in sight! Then only a few minutes passed before we saw the bombs dropping from the wings far in front. In hardly any time Joseph McGinley, bombardier, on intercom, 'Bomb bay doors open,' moments later, 'IP 2 minutes to target'. Then Rudy Emil Radosevisch in the tail, 'Flak, two bursts, 6 o'clock level.' Then McGinley again, '30 seconds to target.' At this moment, over the roar of the engines and in spite of the fact that my steel helmet pressed hard against my earphones, I heard a thunderous explosion. I did not think of it for at the same moment the plane lurched upward and as automatic as formation flying can be I threw the wheel and stick forward. They were as limp as anybody's dish rag. As I realised that I had no control, the ship flopped into a vertical dive. All engines sounded as if they were running away, the screams of the dive sounded like a mess of wildcats. I jerked the throttles back, nothing happened; I tried to hit the alarm bell, I couldn't move; the wheel and stick were pushing against me and the speed on the dive had me pasted to the seat like the paper on the wall. Five, six, seven seconds sitting there, helplessly watching the ground come up. What a shock to realise that you had just 'had it', not just watching someone else as it had been before. What a ghastly, sickening feeling to have time to realise that you would he dead in a few seconds. Then all thoughts stopped.

I opened my eyes with the sudden realisation that I was alive, I couldn't believe it and I had a vivid picture of those last frightening seconds. I took time for the peaceful quiet to impress me and I realised that I was in a car with two *Luftwaffe* guards, an officer and a driver. My wet clothes, open parachute and half-inflated life preserver were under my feet. I was dressed in a strange fatigue-type suit and had heavy bandages on my head. I began to feel the severe cuts there. My left ankle was sprained and there were wounds on my legs. 'What happened, how am I alive, where is the rest of the crew?' It was to be a long time before I had the answers to all of these questions.

I asked for a cigarette and the officer obliged. 'Are you English?' he asked.

'No, American,' I said.

'Are you a pilot?'

'Yes,' I answered.

'Are you a fighter or a bomber pilot?' he enquired.

'I am not allowed to answer that,' I said.

He enquired further: 'What happened to your airplane?'

'I would like to ask you the same thing. How did I get here?' He smiled as if I was well aware of what had happened and said:

'Some people took you from the sea, you came in your parachute but you have been unconscious for a long time.' I can only estimate that it had been about 6 hours since I had known anything, as the long twilight of central Europe was now becoming dusky.

That night I was placed in a small clean jail cell and I could think of nothing but 'What happened, how am I alive and what is the fate of the others?' The next morning as I was being led from my cell, there was Radosevich; he had been in the same jail. 'Rudy,' I yelled, as I grabbed his hand and shook it, 'what happened to us?' Mastering the understatement Rudy said:

'I was at my tail gun and heard the explosion of flak. I looked toward the front of the ship and there was no front of the ship there, so I opened the escape door and baled out.' I knew then what had happened. The third burst of flak had exploded directly in our ship, cutting it in half.

Later in prison camp, where I was to spend nearly two years, I began to solve the second mystery – 'How am I alive?' As other unfortunate crews arrived from my group, they told me of watching us 'get it' and of the exceptional pictures of the ship going down in two pieces. The photographer did not catch our bombs dropping that day but he photographed our *Lady Liberty* in pieces. Many Americans saw the pictures; they were published nationally in 1944. In talking with eyewitnesses and studying these pictures, I am sure now that the speed of the dive caused the ship to disintegrate, throwing me through part of it. Miraculously something caught my chute, opening it, as also is the case of my half-inflated life preserver. The third mystery – 'What happened to the others?' – stood for a long time. I had learned early that Sergeant Crabtree's body had been recovered. At the war's end, Rudy and I knew that we were the only survivors.[5]

The Schweinfurt losses were still having a mighty effect on the B-17 groups and during late August and early September missions mainly consisted of shallow penetration raids to bomb airfields in France, protected by heavy formations of escorting fighters. Strength was regained and on Monday 6 September the target for the bombers was the VKF instrument and ball bearing plant at Stuttgart, but as the Forts advanced across France the cloud became very heavy and at the target smoke screens covered the area. Many groups in the bomber stream began to break up and crews sought targets of opportunity in France and Germany. Twenty-one Forts in the 388th formation were flying as the low group in the slot more commonly known as 'coffin corner'. They were singled out for intense attacks by about 150 fighters that lined up 2 to 3 miles in front, then came in level from 11 o'clock to 1 o'clock at 20-second intervals. At 300–400 yards the fighters began their barrel rolls through the squadrons, three and four at a time before peeling away. Crews believed that the German pilots were using the cloud layers to their advantage. But the thick cloud actually made the bombers harder to find and, once attacked, they tended to disappear into the lower layers. *Wolf Pack* was hit on the bomb run and caught fire before five of the crew scrambled out. *Impatient Virgin II* and *Sky Shy* headed for Switzerland, but only the *Virgin* made it. Nine of the ten men aboard *Sky Shy* baled out safely near Ulm, with the radioman being killed by German civilians on the ground. *Lone Wolf* was last seen near Troyes and crashed with its cockpit on fire. *In God We Trust* also went down near Troyes. The pilot successfully evaded but the rest of the crew were captured. *Silver Dollar*, *Shedonwanna?*, *Slightly Dangerous* and three other Forts went down over France and Germany. *Slightly Dangerous* was reportedly attacked by two yellow-nosed fighters of JG26 at La Chapelle-Champigny about 60 miles south-east of Paris. Five crewmen were killed, but the two pilots were able to escape and returned to England via the French underground. By the time the group reached the safety of Bernay and a covering force of over 100 Spitfire escorts, eleven Forts were missing. Four planes in the 95th and three in the 100th, including *Raunchy*, piloted by Sam Turner, crash-landed on Lake Constance in Switzerland, were also lost. Captain Sumner Reeder got *Squawkin' Hawk* back after heavy fighter attacks from head on and high during the bomb run, shattering the nose and hitting the co-pilot Harry Edeburn in the chest and right shoulder. The 20 mm cannon shell exploded against the armour plate of his seat back and flying fragments wounded Reeder in the head and body. Two shells that entered the nose compartment and exploded near the navigator tore out one of his eyes and severely wounded the bombardier in the head and body. Somehow, Reeder and his crew got the plane to a fighter strip on the south coast where the pilot put the shattered plane down without brakes.

The next day a message from General Eaker was distributed widely at Knettishall. Eaker said: 'The spirit of the 388th in bearing these [heavy losses] and coming back with fighting hearts is a matter of great gratification to me.' The words brought little comfort to the group, which had just lost eleven planes and 109 men, and the mission went down in group history as 'Black Monday'. Six of the Forts lost were from the 563rd Squadron. Still reeling from the disaster, the 388th entered into a series of missions that would earn the name 'Black Week' for its losses and personnel and aircraft.

On 4 October, when over 300 Forts were despatched to targets mainly at Frankfurt, Wiesbaden and Saarbrücken, Heinz Knoke and his fellow pilots in JG1 at Marx were at their dispersal area. Knoke had to glance through a folder bulging with papers, but his thoughts were far away, already considering his coming 'tangle' with the Fortresses. Turit, his faithful hunting dog that he had brought back from Norway, chased down the runway barking angrily at some seagulls that had flown in from the sea. The day before, Knoke had taken Turit rabbit hunting. Suddenly, the music from the loudspeakers faded and announced, '*Achtung!, Achtung!* Stand by for take-off.' *Schwarzemänner* poured out of the hangar and ran over to the *Gustavs*, followed closely behind by the pilots. As usual Turit was sitting on the left wing of Knoke's Bf 109 as he fastened his safety-harness. Only after the engine started did he allow himself to be blown from the wing by the air pressure. Then he ran along behind his master's *Gustav* until Knoke disappeared into the sky with forty fellow fighter pilots, heading on a course of three-six-zero heeding the words of their commander, *Hauptmann* Sprecht, to try and make a frontal attack in close formation. Slowly, the Messerschmitts climbed. Radio silence was seldom broken. At 22,000 feet the Daimler-Benz engines began leaving long moisture-trails. It was cold and the pilots' breath began freezing on the oxygen masks in front of their faces. At intervals Knoke had to slap his thighs vigorously in order to keep warm. Then, finally, they sighted several hundred bombers far in the west. The mission leaders were 100 miles off course. In the air battles and skirmishing that ensued, twelve Fortresses were lost, including three that ditched in the sea while another crash-landed near Margate on return. North of Holland, Sprecht singled out a formation of thirty-plus bombers, which it transpired, were Liberators of the diversion force. The

Gustavs tore into the bombers with every gun blazing. In the confusion the 392nd lost *The Drip* and the Flying Eightballs' *Holiday Mess* in mid-air collisions, one of them possibly going down as a result of a head–to-head with a Bf 109. All three aircraft and their crews perished in the North Sea. Knoke, meanwhile, had headed at full speed for the nose of one of the B-24s. He fired and then ducked away sharply beneath the giant fuselage to avoid a collision, but kept on going right on through the formation to pull up hard in a climbing turn to the left before returning for another attack. Knoke's salvo had had its effect. His victim swerved, dropped out of the formation and headed away in the opposite direction. But Knoke had other ideas.

> Whoops, my friend, that is not the idea! You are not to go home now. As soon as my Liberator is separated from its brethren and beyond the range of their guns, I close in under the fat belly and continue firing until it is in flames. The Liberator burns very much faster than the more streamlined Fortresses. Eight men immediately bale out. The parachutes mushroom in the air and hang there swaying. The heavy crate glides away down. I draw up alongside and stay within 60 to 100 feet of it, certain that no living soul can still be aboard. I can distinctly see the great holes punched by my cannon-shells in the nose and tailplane. Suddenly I notice the flashes in the dorsal turret. Too late! A salvo of fire smashes into my crate. My engine bursts into flames at once. There is no response when I move the controls. Once again it is time for me to hit the silk; jettison the canopy; unfasten the safety belt. My plane stalls, plunges, rights itself again ... and then I am thrown clear as if by some giant hand .... Somehow my parachute must have opened, although I do not remember puffing the ripcord. Several hundred feet below I observe the other parachutes. This is one time the Americans and I go bathing together.

Knoke eventually managed to get into his inflatable dinghy. About 2 hours later he was picked up by a rescue service Focke-Wulf *Weihe* or 'Kite' single-engined floatplane, the airborne ambulance that *Luftwaffe* personnel dubbed the 'Leukoplast Bomber' or adhesive tape bomber. There were no survivors from Knoke's downed Liberator, which was either *Satan's Flame* or *Mac's Sack*, both of which failed to return to Wendling.

During the night of Thursday 7/Friday 8 October there was a red alert on the East Anglian bases as enemy aircraft bombed between Bungay and Norwich. Personnel at Thorpe Abbotts saw ack-ack and a dozen aircraft were reported shot down within a few miles of the airfield, several in flames. An early radio report announced that 175 enemy aircraft were over England. At 0500 hours the 'Bloody Hundredth' was alerted again, this time to be briefed to lead the 13th Wing to Bremen. Captain Everett E. Blakely, a lead crew pilot, Lieutenant Harry H. Crosby, lead navigator, and Lieutenant James R. Douglass, lead bombardier, had received two days of pre-briefing during secret trips to Elveden Hall and so they knew what was planned. Crosby recalled that the general idea was that, 'many hundreds of planes of heavy bombardment were out to "Hamburg" Bremen'. Blakely would pilot the lead aircraft, *Just a Snappin'* with Major John B. Kidd, who had led the 100th on the Regensburg raid, was the command pilot sharing the piloting duties with Blakely. The co-pilot, Lieutenant Charles A. Via, would ride in the position of tail gunner, serving the vital function of formation control officer. Major 'Bucky' Cleven, the 350th Squadron CO, decided to fly the mission in *Our Baby* with Captain Bernard 'Benny' DeMarco's crew. Squadron commanders were required to fly ten missions but Cleven was on his twentieth and he had never bothered to call for the DSC awarded to him for gallantry on the 17 August raid on Regensburg. Just before take-off the co-pilot, Flight Officer James 'Skip' Thayer, had been instructed to proceed to London to receive his commission as a second lieutenant. After chatting to Cleven he was given a choice – 'fly or go get the commission'. Thayer decided to fly the mission. 'He'd get the commission tomorrow.' Thomas Murphy, an original pilot, was flying *Piccadilly Lily* on what was his twenty-fourth mission with Captain Alvin Barker, the 351st Squadron Operations officer taking co-pilot Marshall F. Lee's seat. Lee would go along as ball turret man to observe the formation. Murphy's radioman and right waist gunner had completed their tours four days earlier so Derrel Piel, whose regular crew had failed to return from the 3 September mission to Paris, and Elder D. Dickerson, whose regular crew had completed their tour on 16 September, were drafted in as replacements.

The mission was planned as a two-pronged attack with more than 350 bombers in an attempt to fool the German controllers. Third Division would approach Bremen from the north-west, across the North Sea, while the First would fly across Holland to the target.[6] In an attempt to minimise damage from flak, forty B-17s in the leading Groups would carry radar jammers for the first time to interfere with the German gun-laying radar. After the bombing, both Divisions would return by way of Holland. Meanwhile, Liberators were to attack the U-boat building yards at Vegesack. As the formations flew over the North Sea, it seemed that everything was going according to plan. However, the German defences accurately judged the height and speed of the bombers and had no need to alter these calculations as the 100th sailed over the target at much the same height and speed. Frank McGlinchey, the bombardier in Bill MacDonald's crew in *Salvo Sal*, said it was the most intensive flak he had ever seen. *Just a Snappin'* was hit repeatedly and lost 3,000 feet before Blakely and Kidd regained control. An Fw 190 flown by *Leutnant* Hans Ehlers, a 29-year-old fighter pilot in 2./JG1, collided with *Marie Helena*. Everett Blakely saw the collision and was left with a 'very sobering feeling in the pit of the stomach'. All ten men aboard were KIA. Ehlers survived the mid-air collision and baled out with various facial injuries and a double fracture of the right thighbone. Following the collision, *Phartzac* was torn apart from what appeared to have been an explosion in the bomb bay area. Minutes later *War Eagle* left the formation under control with an engine on fire and crashed shortly after. *Our Baby* also went down. 'Benny' DeMarco, 'Bucky' Cleven and the nine other crew survived and were made PoW.

A minute or so after bomb release, *Piccadilly Lily* was hit by flak, which damaged the navigator's compartment and caused a fire in the No. 3 engine and the oxygen system. Alarmed crewmembers on the right side of the plane could clearly see the right main landing gear hanging down. Flames were spreading from behind the engine firewall, which meant that the fuel line or oil tank feeding the No. 3 engine had been ruptured. Murphy gave the order for the crew to bale out and the alarm bell was rung. Piel and Dickerson were killed by flak before reaching the target. Charles C. Sarabun, the navigator, destroyed the *Gee* equipment by pushing two buttons simultaneously on the panel of his equipment and for good measure fired a round from his .45 calibre pistol into the console. He and Floyd C. Peterson, the bombardier, went out the nose hatch and landed safely, although Sarabun suffered a sprained ankle. John J. Ellen, the top turret gunner, Reed A. Hufford, the ball turret gunner, and Gerald O. Robinson, the left waist gunner, got out safely. Aaron A. David, a quiet, small-framed cowboy from Oklahoma, evacuated his tiny tail gun position, which bore the inscription 'House of David' beneath a Star of David on either side of the emplacement, and baled out but his parachute failed to open properly and he was killed. *Piccadilly Lily* went into a steep dive and exploded, killing Tom Murphy, Captain Barker and Marshall Lee, who having got his parachute pack, had gone forward to help the pilots.

Flak hit Herbert Nash's ship and it plunged to earth and exploded. Nash and three crew were killed. The rest of the crew who were on their third mission baled out but the engineer died after they were rounded up. *Salvo Sal* flew on alone. Frank McGlinchey scanned the sky and looked for their two wingmen but he saw no one. Shocked, he realised that their whole squadron of nine ships had been 'knocked out'. German fighters finished off *Salvo Sal*, which had already been badly hit by flak and one waist gunner bled to death after being hit just after the attack began. With the plane rapidly losing altitude, MacDonald gave the order for the crew to bale out.[7] Ed Stork flew *Hot Spit* back for 400 miles on one engine. An exploding 20 mm shell blew away the top of the mid-upper turret of *Sunny II*, which after landing was found to have bullet holes in all four propellers. Walter 'Big Chief' Moreno got *Messie Bessie* home with its rudder smashed by flak and landed at Thorpe Abbotts without brakes and with a badly damaged hydraulic system. A sea of despondency descended on base operations when it became known that the 'Bloody Hundredth' had lost seven B-17s. Seventy-two combat crewmen were missing and thirteen more were in the base hospital suffering from wounds. There was only one crumb of comfort. Word reached the base that the crew of *Just A Snappin'*, which had been wrecked in a crash-landing at Ludham, were alive and that four wounded men were being treated at the Norfolk and Norwich Hospital. (Waist gunner Lester W. Saunders, who had been hit by a 20 mm shell, which tore through the left waist window into the pit of his stomach and hurled him back against the other side of the plane, succumbed in a hospital bed one week later.) Everyone had thought that the crew were 'done for' and that they were one more casualty on a day of high losses. In all, thirty bombers were missing.

Maintenance crews at Thorpe Abbotts worked around the clock but they could get only sixteen Forts ready for the mission the next day when the CO, Colonel 'Chick' Harding, a graduate of West Point and a famed football coach for the Army, led them to Marienburg. No planes were lost, but unserviceability problems mounted when three ships aborted. Only fourteen ships and their crews were available for the next mission to Münster on Sunday 10 October. *Rosie's Riveters* was still under repair following Robert Rosenthal's debut on the disastrous mission to Bremen, so he would fly his third mission in three days in *Royal Flush*. When Major John 'Bucky' Egan, CO 418th Squadron, returned from leave in London to hear the news that his close friend 'Bucky' Cleven had been lost on the mission to Bremen he was determined to avenge his loss. Egan demanded and received permission to lead the group. Egan, who would fly the mission with John Brady in *Mlle Zig Zag*, wrote:

> The briefing was the same as usual, until the S-2, my good friend Miner Shaw, flashed the photo picture of the old walled city of Münster on the screen with his Bell Opticant. Shaw's voice droned on that we were going to sock a residential district. At this point I found myself on my feet cheering. Others who had lost close friends in the past few raids joined in the cheering. It was a dream mission to avenge the death of a buddy. The mission had not been set up for me to kill the hated Hun but as a last resort to stop rail transportation in the Ruhr Valley. Practically all of the rail workers in the valley were being billeted in Münster. It was decided that a good big bomber raid could really mess up the very efficient German rail system by messing up its personnel. Crews were told, 'Your MPI will be Münster Cathedral ....'

The fighter attacks began just short of Münster and they paused only when the flak opened up at the approach to the target. They resumed their attacks again after the *Zerstören* waded in with rocket attacks to add to the carnage. Thirteen Forts in the 'Bloody Hundredth' formation reached the IP and they were met by fierce level attacks by Fw 190s and Bf 109s of JG26, which closed to 50–75 yards before flicking over and diving away. In just 7 minutes six of the Forts had been destroyed and six others were turning back with smoking engines from a combination of fighter and rocket attacks. *Mlle Zig Zag* went down after a direct hit in her belly with the body of one of the waist gunners aboard. The rest of the crew had incredible escapes, not least the bombardier, Howard 'Hambone' Hamilton, who had been hit in the back by a 20 mm cannon shell, which destroyed his flak suit, damaged his right shoulder, punctured a lung and wounded him in both hands. Hamilton was too weak to release the mechanism on the nose compartment door to bale out. After struggling with it, he stood on the door, which opened outwards, twisted the handle and fell through. Unfortunately, his right shoulder strap caught on the handle and he found himself hanging in space with the inboard propeller whirling around near his head with the fighters still circling and firing. The co-pilot finally released him and, once free, Hamilton opened his chute and landed safely in a clump of high trees. He and ball turret gunner Roland Gangwer, who had a very bad leg wound, were captured by two German soldiers and then taken by ambulance to Münster about 30 miles away, where they spent many weeks in hospital. Gangwer was eventually repatriated. Egan landed in a wood and evaded for a time before he was caught and sent to PoW camp, where he was reunited with his buddy 'Bucky' Cleven (who escaped to England in 1945).

Invadin' Maiden flown by Charles D. Walts went down under fire from *Hauptmann* Walter Höckner of II./JG1, a German ace who had scored seventeen victories on the Eastern Front, including six in one day as CO of 1./JG26. As he dived his Fw 190 under the doomed bomber, his engine was hit by return fire from the ball turret gunner and he was forced to bale out. Six of the Fortress crew got out, some of them escaping certain death when the bomber exploded and broke in two. The engineer, who was badly wounded, died later of his injuries. As Höckner drifted down attached to his parachute, he saw another Fort spiralling down in flames, then lose its right wing before it exploded. It was *Slightly Dangerous*, which was shot down by fighters with the loss of three crew killed and seven taken prisoner. *Shackrat* exploded over Xanten and spiralled down, with only two men surviving after being blown out of the doomed ship. Only two days after coming home from Bremen on one engine, Ed Stork and his crew ran out of luck when *Forever Yours* was set on fire; it slowly heeled over and went down. The navigator and radio operator died, but the rest of the crew were taken prisoner. All ten men aboard *El P'sstofo*, which went down in two rocket attacks by Bf 110s, also survived. *Lena*, which had aborted on the Bremen mission with a malfunction in the top turret gunner's oxygen system, went down with its right wing on fire and the controls shot away. *Sexy Suzy, Mother of Ten* was hit in the left wing by a Bf 109, which failed to pull out in time, and the Fort went into a vertical dive and exploded. *Sweater Girl*, which remarkably had returned undamaged from Bremen, was involved in the same collision and also went down. *Aw-R-Go* went down shortly after bombs away after a fierce blaze, which broke out near the radio room, took hold and blew the ship apart. *Stymie* was hit by flak and went down on the deck, but was hit by fighters over Holland and was belly-landed near the German border. After bombing the target the crew of *Pasadena Nena*, which had also returned undamaged from Bremen, found themselves on their own. John Justice, the pilot, dived for protection to another formation about 6 miles distant, but when this group came under attack, *Nena* was hit in an engine and went into a spin. Fighters finished her off. Justice came down by parachute and evaded capture with the help of the Dutch underground. He was back in England at Christmas time.

By now only *Royal Flush* remained. Two engines had been knocked out over Münster and a rocket shell had gone through the right wing to leave a large hole, but Robert 'Rosie' Rosenthal completed the bomb run and instigated a series of violent manoeuvres to throw the aim of the flak guns. Rosie's Fort was the only ship that returned to Thorpe Abbotts. Two badly wounded gunners were removed from the shattered aircraft as fog rapidly gathered around the base like a shroud and they were taken to hospital. One of the gunners who had some shrapnel lodged near his heart was later returned to the United States for treatment. Later an unexploded 20 mm shell was found rolling around in one of the self-sealing fuel tanks. The tail gunner noted in his diary: 'by the grace of God we were the only ship to come back. Our pilot brought us home safely.' Planes from other groups put down in emergency at Thorpe Abbotts and when one of them taxied in with empty fuel tanks, Colonel Chick Harding got on the radio and asked where the rest of his group was. When informed what had happened, the Colonel refused to believe it. Captain Keith Harris, who had flown the mission with another group landed *Stork Club* at just after quarter past five. He recalled that 'Thorpe Abbotts was a sad, sad place ....' It was another black day for the Third Division, which lost twenty-nine B-17s and the Black Week had cost the 'Bloody Hundredth' twenty-one planes and over 200 casualties, including two squadron commanders. Some crews were now convinced that the *Luftwaffe* was singling out their planes on each mission. A few hours later Rosie Rosenthal decided to 'wind down' at the Officers' Club and he found it to be 'a very lonely and silent place ....' The next morning, when senior officers were debriefed at Elveden Hall, Rosenthal told General LeMay and his staff what he had witness at Münster. The room remained silent as he quietly explained how the flak had decimated the formation on the bomb run and how fighters overwhelmed them. A few hours later Rosenthal and his crew were on their way to the 'Flak Home' at Coombe House in the peaceful Dorset countryside.

Lieutenant Lowell H. Watts and his crew in their final Stateside training at Madras, Oregon, could not realise how badly groups needed replacement crews. Watts had just won his wings and had been assigned as a co-pilot when the 388th had reached its full complement of combat crews at Wendover, Utah, in April 1943. 'By a favourable nod of the gods of war', as he put it, he checked out as a first pilot and he was assigned his own crew. It would be their destiny to fill in one of the gaps left in the 562nd Squadron as the combat losses mounted, but only after they had completed their pre-combat training and ground school in England. When they finally reached Knettishall on 16 November, Watts' diary entry was brief and uninspired: 'Arrived at base at 1800. It isn't so hot. No barracks. No blanket. No heat. Slept in a cold room and about froze.' At that moment Watts really envied the crews that had come in with the original group movement. The next day things began to improve. He turned in all their papers at headquarters and reported to Major Goodman, CO of the 562nd Squadron. Watts took an immediate liking to him and that helped. A couple of oil burning heaters and two candles for light at night were produced then Watts and the other officers in the crew were assigned to a Nissen hut, which was partly occupied by Lieutenant Montgomery Givens' crew. Circumstance had thrown Watts and Givens' crews together and though they did not know it, their fate would be intertwined.

> On our second day on the base we got to fly a 2-hour group formation practice mission. It was good to get back in the air again. I got to meet some of the other pilots but it was on a business-come-first basis. I was more concerned with learning what was expected of me and where everything was located than in anything else. We located the mess hall, Officers' Club, quarters for their airmen, the briefing and personal equipment room, the Flight Surgeon's office, Link trainer and the hangars,

control tower and flight line. I was interested in the posting of crews, pilots' names and number of missions each had.

Our crew was written up on the crew list in operations. On 20 November, just four days after we reported in, we were assigned a new B-17G. The 'Gs' were now beginning to come in to replace the older B-17Fs. Major improvements were the chin turret with its two .50 calibre guns, electronic turbo controls and enclosed waist windows. We named her *Blitzin Betsy* in honour of my wife. We were immersed in ground school and in checking everything about our new plane. We spent time with our ground crew headed by Harry Allert, a crew chief I would come to respect and value as a friend and one upon whom our crew could depend with utmost confidence.

By this time I had met the other pilots in the squadron. I did not feel that they conveyed a sense of superiority. Nor did they show enthusiasm for us either. We were just there, a part of a big machine, and it would be up to us to earn our place in the system. I had the impression that I would make only a couple or three very close friends and the rest would be seen as spots in our formation that were important to the strength of our group. The primary thought of most of the aircrews was survival. There was little place for long-term friendships. Eventually, I would come to know all the pilots in our squadron, but never would really know those in the other three squadrons.

On 23 November, I was briefed for my first mission. I would fly as co-pilot with Lieutenant Duncan since it was customary for each crew commander to fly his first mission as co-pilot to get some sense of the techniques of aerial assembly and the combat environment. I slept poorly the night before that mission. I would be the only one in our hut flying and was afraid the CQ [Charge of Quarters]might not find me to wake me in time for briefing. I did not need to worry about that.

We were briefed to bomb the Air Ministry in Berlin. I knew from the groans and comments that this was a super tough mission. I did not know at the time just how special and how difficult a mission it could have been. We would have only short-range fighter cover. The mission could be deadly but I tagged dutifully along with Duncan as we checked the plane and taxied out for take-off. Then came the red flares from the tower and the mission was scrubbed. I've often wondered what our losses would have been had we actually flown that mission.

On 26 November we were again alerted. This time Major Goodman asked if I'd feel okay flying as first pilot, which of course I replied in the affirmative. The Eighth wanted maximum effort and there was little time to waste getting crews in the air. Our new plane was still being refitted and we were assigned a B-17F named *Quarterback*.

I felt that our training had been as adequate as could have been expected in the time frame of the war. I did not yet consider our crew as a real part of the Group. We needed combat to achieve that relationship. But I felt that the Bovingdon ground school had given us as much knowledge as possible of what we would face and what was expected of us. I thought the formation practices with the Group had been adequate and was comfortable with the personnel who were in command positions at the 388th. Now it would be up to us to prove we could carry out the tasks expected of us.

Our target that day was Bremen. We were given a slot on Colonel William B. David's [the CO] left wing, one of the easiest spots in the Group. Assembly was easy for our position and everything went along as briefed. As we climbed to altitude and crossed the enemy coast it became more difficult to keep up with our lead plane. At our new altitude our number three engine simply would not draw the manifold pressure we needed. Very slowly we slipped behind, dropping back to fly with the second element of our Group. Then we were back with the low squadron and still falling behind.

One dominant theme drilled into new pilots was that we must never, never become a loner. Your protection is with your buddies. Fly alone and you are dead meat for the *Luftwaffe*. So here I was on my first mission unable to stay up with the formation. Reluctantly we turned back, hoping for clouds that were not quite as solid as we wanted.

Luck rode our wings that day. We saw only one fighter and he did not press a serious attack. It was the first mission for all the crew. Emmett J. Murphy, our navigator, was next put on notice that I needed a heading for home. After all our jockeying and no longer in sight of our Group, Murphy gave me a heading. When we saw the coastline, nothing seemed quite right. It turned out to be the coastline of Scotland, well north of our intended landfall. Finally we got squared away and landed at Knettishall after all the other planes were in. Ah, the joy of a first mission.

Our second mission on 29 November was also to Bremen. It was a fairly easy mission but weather kept us from dropping our bombs. The next day we were briefed for the steel mill in Solingen. We were carrying incendiaries. Ed Kelly, my bombardier, was grounded with ear trouble and we took a replacement named Mecum, a stocky bombardier I had not met before. Bad weather caused serious mix-up in our assembly. As we broke out above the clouds I failed to see any flares from our Group lead. Continuing to climb as briefed, I finally saw the flares of the 96th Bomb Group. I flew over to the 96th and found a spot in their formation. I'd begun to feel a bit more at ease about everything. But now I wondered what happened to green pilots who couldn't find their correct formation.

Flak was fairly heavy over the target. Only few fighters bothered us. But then something else bothered me and it was a big something. Three of our incendiaries had hung up in the bomb bay. I called Mecum to cut them loose. As he struggled with the bombs he pulled his oxygen hose loose and passed out. His body hung over the catwalk chain. The bomb bay doors were open. The three bombs swung back and forth as wind gusts caught them; the air coming in that bomb bay at 26,000 feet was almost 60 degrees below zero and Solingen was way, way down there below Mecum. Joe Ramsey, our engineer, and Ivan Finkle, our radio operator, joined forces to haul Mecum back into the radio room and give him some oxygen. Now Mecum was safe, but we still had those bombs. Ramsey finally cut them loose without setting one of them off. Now we were back together again, but coming home with the wrong group. After landing, we learned that our Group had been unable to assemble and only ten of us had actually made a good mission. That made us feel a whole lot better.

Our next mission was a replay for formation assembly above the cloud deck. The target was Emden. Our pilots were having to learn to hold a briefed heading and climbing rate until they broke above the clouds and could form together. We did better on this mission, but those of us in my Group never did form into a Group. Once again we had to tie in with another Group. Weather would be almost a constant problem during the winter months. For me, the descent in low visibility when we came back at the end of a mission was a more demanding task than the take-off and assembly, but getting the formations together was an arduous and time-consuming part of any mission.

By this time our crew was beginning to feel more comfortable with our assignments. We had seen fighters and flak. We had blundered through clouds to make a mission out of chaos. We had almost salvoed our bombardier. We no longer felt an outsider in our Group. Now we felt ready to face the weather, the *Luftwaffe* and the flak during the winter of 1943–44. This was just as well since tougher missions were coming up.

Amid all the death and destruction, occasional chivalry was shown. One of the B-17s that flew the 20 December 1943 mission was *Ye Olde Pub* of the 379th at Kimbolton, flown by Lieutenant Charlie L. Brown, whose crew were on their first mission. As an inexperienced combat crew they were given the No. 3 (left wing slot), second element, low squadron, or what was more commonly called 'Purple Heart Corner'. Everything was uneventful until they reached the IP for the bomb run at 27,300 feet. As the group was leading the strike force, there were no aircraft in front and all Brown could see was the rapidly expanding black cloud from flak bursts, which gradually became a black oily carpet as they got closer to the target. A veteran combat pilot had told Brown that you were in serious trouble when you were close enough to see and distinguish the orange and red centres of the flak bursts! About 2 minutes before bombs away, immediately in front he saw several of what appeared to be fantastically beautiful, deadly, black orchids with vivid crimson centres. Brown knew they were in trouble and they were. *Ye Olde Pub*'s nose section was hit and almost destroyed and the oil pressure suddenly dropped in one engine. Brown initiated engine shutdown procedures and feathered it. Then another ran away. At that point, the aircraft suddenly lurched skyward just as the bombardier called out 'Bombs away!' They were a 'cripple' and a 'straggler' with a feathered engine. As Brown says, 'Either condition normally attracted German fighters somewhat like blood attracts piranha or sharks.' There was little delay. The cry, 'Enemy fighters, 10 o'clock; bandits, 12 o'clock,' was called as the intercom came alive with multiple reports of sightings of German fighters in front of them. Brown quickly looked up from the instrument panel to see eight Fw 190s forming a line slightly above and just ahead. Just then the tail gunner called out, 'Enemy fighters, 6 o'clock!' The fighters made pass after pass at the crippled B-17. An engine was shot away, although the oil pressure and engine temperature remained stable and the engine continued to produce about 60 per cent power. Hundreds of machine-gun bullets and 20 mm cannon shells peppered the Fortress. Then at some point during their continuous twisting, turning, climbing and diving man-oeuvres, the attacks finally ended.

Flying in very close formation with Brown's B-17, about 3 feet from their wing tip, was a Bf 109. For a moment Brown thought that he had lost his mind and if he briefly closed his eyes it would disappear. He tried, but the German pilot nodded and appeared relaxed. At this point, only a single gun in the top turret was functioning out of the original eleven guns on the B-17F, with the other weapons in the 'guns down' or inoperable condition. The Bf 109 closed in slowly from the low rear and finally, he came up on their wing, so close that his wing actually overlapped the B-17's wing. The Bf 109 pilot looked across, motioned with his right hand as if to say, 'I salute you. I gave you my best and you survived.' When the fighter pilot saw the engineer's head appear in the top turret, he saluted, rolled over and was gone. It was an abrupt end to one of the briefest, but most unusual, encounters in the short history of the heavy bombardment as a major weapon of war.

Incredibly, Brown managed to get *Ye Olde Pub* across the North Sea and 350 miles back to England, where he landed at Seething, south of Norwich. Staff Sergeant Hugh Eckenrode was dead.[8] Yelesanko was in a critical condition with a major wound to his leg (which later required amputation), Blackie was unable to walk because of frozen feet, and Pechout could not use his hands. There was no rudder control possible due to the severe damage to both the rudder and vertical stabiliser. Also, both elevators had been damaged and one horizontal stabiliser was almost destroyed. In addition to the three damaged engines, every major component of the aircraft had suffered severe damage. The Plexiglas nose section was almost gone. There were hundreds of flak and bullet holes and one large hole possibly left by an 88 mm anti-aircraft shell that had miraculously passed through the wing without exploding. The radio compartment was almost destroyed and the mid-section of the aircraft had suffered extensive damage. The aircraft was described by one military onlooker as a 'flying wind tunnel that looked like it had been designed by a Swiss cheese manufacturer'.

Charles Brown never forgot the encounter and in 1989 he wrote an article about it for the German fighter pilots' association. On 10 January 1990 *Leutnant* Franz Stigler, former *Oberleutnant* in 6./JG27, responded by letter from his home in Surrey, British Columbia (he had emigrated to Canada in 1953). After considerable investigation, it was confirmed that Stigler was the pilot of the lone Bf 109 who did not attempt to finish off the helpless B-17.[9] Stigler had already downed two B-17s that day and his Bf 109 was being refuelled when Brown flew over the edge of his airfield. The German pilot immediately cut short the refuelling and went after the Fort. Upon catching up with the bomber, he positioned himself to fire on the Fortress from the rear

(Stigler's fighter was fully armed at the time of the encounter; he was not out of ammunition as previously thought by Brown's crew). When the tail gunner did not raise his guns and there was no defensive fire from the bomber, Stigler went closer. As he came alongside and surveyed the damage he could hardly believe what he saw.

> It was like a sieve and there was blood everywhere. I could see the crew were having a terrible time dealing with their wounded and struggling to stay in the air. I was amazed that the aircraft could fly. I saw two wounded men on board, rather than just the airplane, which was our normal target. It was one thing to shoot an airplane, but in this case I saw the men. I just couldn't do it. I thought to myself, how could I shoot something like that? I cannot kill these half-dead people. It would be like shooting at a parachute.

Stigler later described the aircraft as 'the most badly damaged aircraft he ever saw, which was still flying'.

At least twice he turned his fighter into the front of the bomber in attempts to get Brown to turn back into Germany and surrender. After Brown had ignored his efforts he decided to escort the plane out over the North Sea, hoping the pilot would turn towards Sweden, only about a half-hour flight away. However, after clearing some islands Brown turned towards England, instead of Sweden. Stigler then thought, 'Stupid guy, I hope he makes it home and gets medical help for his crew.' Then, in one of those rare moments of compassion in an otherwise brutal war, Franz Stigler did an extraordinary thing. He saluted, rolled his fighter and departed. It was a decision that could have resulted in severe punishment, possibly even execution, had his superiors known.[10]

On the 30 December 1943 mission to Ludwigshafen twenty-three bombers were lost. One of them was *Satan's Sister* in the 388th, which went to the IG Farbenindustrie chemical works at Ludwigshafen. At the IP another Group had cut in front of them and they experienced severe prop wash. *Satan's Sister* initially tipped up 180 degrees on her right wing, came back down, then went up and rolled over on her left wing. In other words, it made a slow roll with a full bomb bay! Returning crews reported that the ship had exploded on entering the clouds 5,000 feet below the formation. Lieutenant Art Carlsen's crew had been on their seventh mission. For 21-year old Larry 'Goldie' Goldstein, the Brooklyn-born radio operator in B. J. Keirsted's crew, it was the crew's 'darkest day'. The missing crew were close friends whom they had trained with and shared a barracks with since arriving in Britain aboard the *Queen Mary* from New York, along with 15,000 other Army Air Corps personnel. Belford J. Keirsted was a strong quiet man from Uniontown, Pennslyvania, a tough coal town. 'BJ' had a dark, brooding look about him. He and his sister Dorothy had toured the country before the war as the ballroom dance team of 'Jan and Janis' (Belford and Dorothy apparently lacked pizzazz). 'BJ' had asked his crew to work hard, become proficient at their jobs and possibly some day one of them might be responsible for the rest of the crew's survival. He along with co-pilot 'Ace' Conklin prodded the crew to achieve perfection and at the same time were also working hard to sharpen their skills. Conklin was a Jock from New Paltz, New York. When Conklin was assigned to Keirsted's crew he was crestfallen. He thought, 'I don't want to be with this crew – we've got a ballroom dancer for a pilot!' but Keirsted proved he had more on the ball than a set of twinkletoes. Quiet, reserved, he exuded a calm authority that was universally respected and admired. More than that the men liked Keirsted. 'He was just a nice guy, period,' Conklin would say. 'He never had a bad thing to say.'

Our crew gelled immediately, and we worked well together, but with any group of men there were individual personalities to deal with, but when we were flying our sole aim was to help the crew survive, nothing else mattered. Personally I had a great deal of faith in the abilities of 'BJ' and 'Ace' as pilots and I felt safe with them at the controls and they seemed to be aware of potential trouble that was always around us, and prepared to handle an emergency if it happened. This was a comforting thought when flying because there always was the element of danger present. Beside the pilots, our crew was composed of Kent Keith the bombardier, a sheep rancher from near Ekalaka, Montana. Phil Brejensky, navigator, was also Jewish and from Brooklyn too. In training Kent Keith had given him the nickname 'Bloodhound' joking that there was a dog on his Montana ranch that could find his way home better than Brejensky. Jack Kings, waist gunner, from Huntington, West Virginia had never met anyone Jewish before. As a kid he fished for food. It was something to eat besides rice and beans. In the depths of the Great Depression his family was too poor to afford new shoes so they stuffed cardboard soles in the old ones. 'We kind of came up the hard way' he recalled. Later, in combat his attitude was, 'If you got hit, you were hit. If you didn't, you made it. I could never see any point worrying about it.' E. V. 'Pete' Lewelling the other waist gunner was a good ol' boy from Zolfo Springs, Florida. The tail gunner, Bob Miller, a lunk from Chicago, Illinois, and a loner. Howie Palmer, engineer, was from New Hampshire. Eddie Kozacek, an immigrant's son and farm boy from Coxsackie, New York, a gunner, was added as a replacement.

With twenty-nine other crews Keirsted's had been assigned to a replacement pool and after five days they were rushed to Knettishall as replacement crews for those lost. When they entered the barracks that cold dreary night all they saw were empty beds. When they asked, 'Why the empty beds?' they were told they were left by the men who had gone down recently, which they found 'rather discouraging'. Suddenly flying status did not seem that appealing. Someone said out loud, 'And we volunteered for this?' Goldstein recalls:

> Men living together as closely as we did made us feel almost like family. To lose a friend and to actually see it happen was devastating to my crew and myself. Our morale was at its lowest point, especially when we returned to our barracks and saw their empty beds. We did not know whether they had survived the parachute jump, or had been killed. We did not have time to mourn their loss because we were called out for

another mission the very next day and as was the case, our own survival was on our minds. It was about this time that I realised that this was a dangerous game I was a part of. Was the glory of being a combat crewman worth it? I never knew if I was a brave man, I had never been tested. Our crew never once discussed the possibility of our chances for survival, but I am sure that we all thought the same thing. When we first began flying together our goal was to not take chances and to put our faith in our pilots. 'BJ' kept repeating that we would make it and on one occasion when we met our first ground crew chief when our own plane was assigned to us, 'BJ' asked him how many crews he had. He said you are my third, the other two went down. 'BJ's' answer to him was, 'We will make it, you can mark it down'. We were not as sure as he was, but his self-confidence rubbed off on us. When I saw another plane get hit and go down, I watched for the parachutes to open. I immediately felt sorry for them but just as quickly I found myself saying, better them than us. Self-survival can play mean tricks with the mind.[11]

New crews did what everybody else did. They tried to blend in and be invisible. Traditionally, replacements were subjected to the 'flakking process' as it was known and shouts of, 'Here comes the fresh meat!' and 'I see they've lowered the standards again,' was quite unnerving. One new air gunner moved his gear into a barracks and threw it onto one of the lower bunks, which was conveniently near one of the two warm 'pot-bellied' stoves. One of the men said, 'You can take that bunk if you want but it belonged to our engineer who got it through the head on a mission a couple of days ago.' With no further comment the gunner selected another bunk, farther away from the heat of the stove. A replacement crew at one base who entered their uninsulated tarpaper and wooden hut, which was falling apart, were not prepared for what confronted them. Inside were cots for the gunners of five crews – thirty men. There were a few double-decked bunks as extra beds. The hut was full except for six empty cots. The crew quickly claimed their spaces and were widely separated from each other. The mid-upper gunner was not prepared for the sinister silence that greeted them, nor the green-tinged faces and the tired, listless eyes. His crew looked out of place in their best uniforms and bright, expectant faces. Strangely dressed reclining figures, one more outrageous than the next, allowed themselves to be scrutinised and took no notice. They wore rumpled fatigues, assorted parts of summer and winter uniforms. Some had hats on, the knitted infantry wool cap, fatigue hats with the brims snapped up, fleece-lined leather caps. One guy was even wearing a steel flak helmet! The whole picture was disturbing. The rest of the crew tiptoed around trying not to upset anybody. Confidence slowly oozed away. What a bunch to live with – all in each other's laps. These men were all insane.

When Ben Smith in 'Chick' Cecchini's crew had been at the Combat Crew Replacement Centre at Bovingdon waiting for a posting to an operational group, they began to get 'disquieting' news. They heard about a hard-luck group called the 100th, which was continually being wiped out. They fervently prayed not to be sent to the 100th. When finally it was their turn, Cecchini's crew were sent to the Hell's Angels Group at Molesworth, but it was still something of a shock as Ben Smith recalled.

> We did not fly to our base; we took the train from Bovingdon to a station near Molesworth and were ignominiously carried there in trucks. When we came to our squadron area, we were not greeted by the familiar, 'You'll be sorry', the customary greeting on the Stateside. The men we saw gave us only a few incurious glances and said nothing to us. Our hearts sank. We were assigned a barracks shared by two or three other crews. Six empty cots gaped at us. These had been occupied by a crew that had not returned from the mission the day before. We were not prepared for this sobering reality.
>
> In progress was a non-stop poker game. The players did not look up or acknowledge our presence in any way. We were accorded a few glum nods from some others who were lying in their sacks reading. About that time the door flew open and a bevy of uproarious drunks fell inside. It was the lead crew – Captain Brinkley's crew. I had seen many drunks, but this was a different kind of drunkenness. These men were veterans of the great missions of Schweinfurt and Oschersleben. They had seen too much and it showed. I had the sudden feeling that things were far different from what I had been led to believe. I was right. The lead crews were specially trained crews used to lead the missions. Only the bombardier in the lead crew used the bombsight, along with a deputy lead in case the lead crew was shot down. All the other airplanes dropped their bombs simultaneously with the lead ship, it being the point of the formation. In addition, the navigator in the lead ship navigated for the entire group. The lead radio operator did all of the transmitting from air to ground, his first transmission being the strike message after Bombs Away.
>
> We were not referred to as Cecchini's crew. Instead, we were called the 'new crew', which continued to be our status until we had flown about eight combat missions. New crews were given the most vulnerable places in the formation and had a way of disappearing after a few missions. We heartily resented this callous treatment; but, after winning our spurs, we were as bad as the rest.

At least Cecchini's crew's prayers had been answered and they had not been posted to the 'Bloody Hundredth'. Of course, there were other crews that were. One of the replacements at Thorpe Abbotts was Crew 13 and Technical Sergeant Earl Benham was the radio operator. On arrival, they were told, 'You fellers are Crew 13. This is the 13th Wing. You're assigned to airplane No. 13. Oh yes, your airplane is named *Hard Luck*!'[12]

Notes

1. It was only when the city was finally overrun by US armoured divisions in 1945 that America could at last confirm that it had 'got Schweinfurt'.
2. *'Blood on my Hands', Serenade To The Big Bird.*
3. On 7.8.44 the 492nd BG was withdrawn from combat having lost fifty-four aircraft from May to July 1944. This was the heaviest loss for any B-24 group for a three-month period.

4. A force of 175 P-47 Thunderbolts would fly penetration and withdrawal support missions for the bombers.

5. Donald J. McGowan, navigator (only married officer) and Sergeants Bynum Crabtree, mechanic/gunner, Fulton Horn, radioman-gunner, Edgar G. Lott waist gunner, Bill Crough, waist gunner, Al Miller, belly turret gunner. Crabtree and Lott were married.

6. On 13.9.43 the 1st, 2nd and 4th BWs became the 1st, 2nd and 3rd Bomb Divisions respectively.

7. MacDonald and McGlinchey were captured at a border post in the Pyrenees trying to cross into Spain but Carl Spicer, the navigator, made it.

8. Posthumously awarded the DFC for remaining at his frozen guns until his death to warn of impending fighter attacks.

9. At various times a *Staffelkapitän* of 3 *Staffeln* – 6, 8 and 12./JG27 – he was credited with twenty-eight victories in JG27 and over thirty probables. Stigler ended the war as technical officer of General Adolf Galland's famous *Jagdverband* 44 of *Experten* (aces), flying the Me 262. He was credited with 487 combat sorties, was wounded four times and was shot down seventeen times: four times by fighters, four times by ground fire and nine times by American gunners on bombers. He baled out six times and rode his damaged aircraft down eleven times.

10. Stigler met with Brown and two of the surviving crew members, Sam Blackford, the ball turret gunner, and Dick Pechout, the radio operator, during the 379th BG Association Reunion, at which the ex-*Luftwaffe* ace was a guest of the Association. Brown and Stigler, not surprisingly, have remained friends ever since.

11. Eighteen-year-old tail gunner Bob Scalley and three other EM were the only survivors.

12. B-17F 42-3413 *Hard Luck* was a lucky ship despite its name, derived from the date of its arrival – Friday 13.8.43 – and the serial number. Seven of Crew 13 finished their tour. The navigator was KIA after Benham, who flew twenty-eight combat missions, went home to the USA in 1945. The bombardier and one of the waist gunners were grounded with wounds. *Hard Luck* held what must have been a record in the 8th AF, its first fifty missions being flown with original engines. Crew chief Master Sergeant 'Zip' Myers was extremely proud of 'his ship' and refused to allow inexperienced pilots to fly it – 'that is if it could be avoided!' *Hard Luck* flew missions for a year and a day, being lost on its sixty-third mission, on 14.8.44. Donald Cielwich's crew baled out and were taken prisoner.

CHAPTER 4

The Lucky Bastards

Lucky Bastard Club – a club for those bomber crewmen who have completed a specified number of missions and so can return to the Zone of the Interior.

Abe Dolim

At Snetterton Heath on 4 January 1944 at about 0030 hours, George, the Squadron clerk, turned on the lights in Bishop Ingram's Quonset hut and said, 'Maximum effort today.' Ingram's crew felt that they were veterans of Europe's air war as Stanley Peterson, the navigator, recalls.

We even had the thrill and excitement of a New Year's Eve raid on St Cloud, a south-western suburb of Paris. Our B-17 lost an engine due to flak about 10 miles south of the Eiffel Tower and we made a solo flight back across France and the English Channel and those beautiful White Cliffs of Dover to an RAF Spitfire base in time for an English dinner and too many scotches. The German fighter pilots started New Year's Eve celebrations early because we limped back across north-west France by ourselves and everybody ignored us.

It was the beginning of a long quest to complete their missions and join the ranks of the 'Lucky Bastard Club', a club for those bomber crewmen who completed a specified number of missions and so could return to the United States. There was even an award certificate to go with the honour of making it. Peterson felt that it was not an alarming designation to be a replacement crew, since he assumed that aircrews were completing their assigned twenty-five missions and heading home. But, as he was to recall:

The awful truth was that only about one-third of the crews were completing their tour and replacements were badly needed. We hadn't been on station 24 hours when we heard the two words. 'Big B'.

As we dressed on 4 January very little was said and we headed for the mess hall breakfast at 1 am. After a couple of cups of coffee we all spoke freely about today being 'Big B' day. General Jimmy Doolittle had been named 8th Air Force Commander and the famed Tokyo raider was ready to send his troops to Berlin and only the President of the United States kept him from leading the assault. After the briefings we all headed for the sleeping aircraft about 5 am. Our crew was short two gunners. The experience of the Paris raid was too much for them. We were assigned replacements and made ready the trip to 'Big B'. The weather was terrible and getting worse as the morning progressed. Finally, at about 0830 hours the mission was scrubbed. By February our crew with replacements was considered sixteen mission veterans. We received a new airplane and a new replacement pilot. Ingram needed rest and his crew was needed in the campaign. [We were] The crew of *The Saint*, a name chosen by Mosier, who was to die in the co-pilot's seat and whose mortal remains are interred at Cambridge Cemetery.

Early in 1944 the *Luftwaffe* was still a force to be reckoned with, especially when one considers its day-fighter *Geschwaders* of conventional fighters could, and did, shoot down dozens of bombers on a single mission. In addition, night-fighter pilots like *Leutnant* Peter Spoden, a 22-year old pilot, also bolstered the *Luftwaffe* on daylight missions in 5./NJG5. He started his night-fighting career with four RAF heavies shot down in August and November 1943. Spoden comments:

I flew several missions in daylight during the first months of 1944. Only crews with few night victories were selected for these sorties, as the aces were too valuable for the powers that be. We youngsters usually just came into readiness at night, as in the Himmelbett night-fighting system; the most successful crews were scrambled in the first waves. Nevertheless, those daylight missions were quite exhausting, as we were also at readiness at night. What's more, we were too slow in daylight with our 110s equipped with Lichtenstein and flame-dampers, and tactically we were at a disadvantage due to our approach from behind. When we came into firing range of the heavy defensive fire of the American bombers, it was like flying into a shower! The 109 and 190 on the other hand attacked the *Pulks* from head-on and out of the sun. Consequently, the losses among our night-fighters were horrendous.

On 7 January Peter Spoden's *Gruppe* was scrambled to intercept a force of 502 bombers bound for Ludwigshafen:

This time we night-fighters arrived on the scene too late and all I could see were pieces of wreckage and between seven and ten American airmen in life jackets floating in the sea. They signalled towards us. They were in the sea between Bremen and Heligoland: we immediately alerted the German coast guard and stayed with the Americans, who kept waving towards us. And now the terrible thing happened; by the minute the movements of the men in the water became slower and in the end they didn't move any more at all. We could already see the German marine craft approaching and flew as low as we dared in an effort to keep the men awake. We were later told that no one survived and that all had died of hypothermia. From that day on I always flew with a one-man dinghy, which was firmly attached to my body, even on baling out.[1]

Baling out, especially over water, was everyone's worst nightmare whether they were German or American. Even the most experienced fighter pilot could lose his nerve in the face of death and the growing list of friends lost. In JG1

Eberhard Burath joked that, 'Before take-off, one risked getting lost in the cigarette smoke. The majority of pilots were withdrawn, unapproachable. There was only Major Bär who did not change.'[2] When on 10 February 169 Fortresses were despatched to Brunswick escorted by 466 Lightnings, Thunderbolts and 9th Fighter Command Mustangs, 'Pritzel' Bär, who was leading II *Gruppe*, knocked down a Fort and a Thunderbolt. JG1 lost five pilots – two of them killed – as a result of combats with American fighters. *Leutnant* Rudolf Kasischke and *Unteroffizier* Hans Hitter both died in their fighters. Eberhard Burath, who flew as wingman to an experienced *Oberfeldwebel*, met up with a formation of B-17s over Brunswick. His comrade attacked alone and immediately shot one of the Forts down. Burath approached another victim close in and fired a long burst, which hit the right wing, causing flames to appear. The American gunners continued firing accurately at their attacker and the Fw 190 was hit all over. Burath recalled, 'Like lightning flashes the bullets ripped into the fuselage. Soon there was no response from my joystick or from the other controls. I did not know what to do to get out! I had already jettisoned the canopy, but like a stamp on an envelope, I remained stuck to the armour plate in the cockpit.' Burath finally managed to extricate himself from his Focke-Wulf fighter and he baled out, landing in a snow-covered field, on all fours with the parachute silk wrapped all round him looking like 'a pig trying to find a truffle'. *Unteroffiziers* Harald Feist and the promising Helmut Stiegler belly-landed their Fw 190s and also lived to fight another day.[3]

Once the B-17s had been picked up on German radar in sector 'Dora-Dora', Heinz Knoke had been ordered to take off and climb to 25,000 feet over the Rheine. Over Lake Dümmersee he sighted Fortresses flying eastwards. He described the sight as 'a truly awe-inspiring spectacle'. Knoke picked out a group of Forts flying on the left flank of the main body and closed in for a frontal attack, but as he did so they altered course slightly and his attack was in vain. Swinging off to the right and round in a wide arc, he waited until his *Gustavs* were again flying ahead of the bombers and then he came round for a second frontal attack. He wanted his forty fighters to cut a swathe through the ranks of the Americans. By radio he urged his pilots to remain calm and make every shot count. The *Gustavs* kept close together. Knoke noticed Thunderbolts behind, but the American fighters were unable to intercept the Bf 109s before they dived into the formation of bombers. *Unteroffizier* Raddatz held his *Gustav* flying almost wing-tip to wing-tip alongside Knoke's. Then, suddenly, there was a bright flash and Raddatz immediately plummeted down vertically. Knoke continued closing in on his Fortress, firing at the cockpit until he had to pull up sharply to avoid a mid-air collision. But his gunfire had its mark. The Fortress reared up on its tail and others swerved out of its way. Then the left wing dropped and the Fort went down out of control in its final death dive to disintegrate thousands of feet below. In all, twenty-nine Fortresses and nine US fighters were lost on 10 February. Though he was twice set upon, first by eight Mustangs, and then by a pair of Thunderbolts, Knoke managed to shake them off and he landed back at Wünsdorf, where he learned that Raddatz was dead.

Long-range P-51 Mustangs, which could accompany the bombers to their targets and back again, formed a highly effective fighter shield, but on occasion even they were powerless to prevent German fighters causing carnage on a large scale. On 10 February, when Brunswick was the target for the Third Division, the German defences destroyed twenty-nine Forts despite over 460 escort fighters being despatched. For B. J. Keirsted's crew in the 388th, which lost three ships, it was their nineteenth mission and a significant one for Larry 'Goldie' Goldstein, whose twenty-second birthday it was. The young radio operator considered the mission the roughest so far. He saw quite a few planes go down and even saw his own fighters 'taking it on the chin'. Goldstein was not ashamed to say that he was scared and 'never prayed harder to come through'. Keirsted's crew now had six more missions to fly and they would soon come quickly. Escort fighters were available now in huge numbers and General Carl 'Tooey' Spaatz wanted to a mount a weeklong series of co-ordinated raids on the German aircraft industry at the earliest possible date. Operation *Argument*, as it was called, would be the first battle involving the mass use of bomb groups of the Strategic Air Forces, involving as it did, Major General Jimmy Doolittle's 8th Air Force and Major General Nathan F. Twining's Italy-based 15th Air Force. RAF night bombing would also play a part. *Argument* needed good weather and the forecasters predicted that good weather could be expected throughout the week of 20–25 February.

'Big Week' as it soon became known, began on Sunday 20 February when over 980 B-17s and Liberators in sixteen combat wings escorted by over 830 long-range American fighters and sixteen RAF squadrons were given twelve different targets in Central Germany. The target for over 300 Forts of the Third Division commanded by Brigadier General Curtis LeMay, was the Focke-Wulf assembly plant at Poznan in German-occupied Poland with Tutow airfield and targets of opportunity in the Rostock area as secondaries. At Knettishall one of the thirty-seven crews in the 388th that were awakened early for the mission was B. J. Keirsted's, who were flying their twentieth mission in the 563rd Squadron, in a B-17 called *Cock o' the Walk*. For Lieutenant Lowell H. Watts and the crew of *Blitzin' Betsy* in the 562nd Squadron, the mission would be their nineteenth.

Cold, distant stars flickered at us from a frosty sky as we entered the briefing building. Like on so many mornings in England, the sky was clear, but a few stray clouds drifting in from the North Sea gave promise of an instrument assembly above 10/10ths clouds by take-off time. In one respect, not yet apparent to us, this morning was different from the others. Our raid today was the beginning of a week which was to mark the biggest air battles of the European war, a week of 'all out' conflict between the USAAF and the *Luftwaffe*. Before the next six days were past, hundreds of American bodies would lie scattered across the continent; other hundreds would be in German prison camps and scores of our bombers would lie, bits of crumpled wreckage, in their own craters. But hundreds upon hundreds of Jerry fighters would drop from the flaming skies to rest in ruin as complete as that of many of the factories from which they came – the hoarded power of the *Luftwaffe*, built up during the winter, shattered into a fraction of what it was.

For Lieutenant Orlin 'Mark' Markussen, the 21-year-old co-pilot of *Ain't Mis Behavin'*, captained by Reginald Smith in the Bloody Hundredth in the 13th Wing at Thorpe Abbotts, it was his twentieth mission. Just five more missions and he could go home, but he had a premonition about this mission, one he never had before or after.[4] He may have been apprehensive because of the length of the mission, 13½ hours; he just didn't know. 'Something's going to happen today,' he told himself. After the early morning briefing he went back to the barracks and wrote his first 'To whom it may concern' letter about what to do with his belongings and a letter to his wife. Markussen had won some money playing cards and asked his crew chief to make sure his wife got it. He had always worn low-quarter shoes before on missions. This time he wore combat boots. He even went to church services and he was not a religious man.

Lowell Watts was also very careful that morning to leave his personal belongings in the safe keeping of the PW room at Knettishall. He felt that the chances of needing them that night seemed rather slim. Like Markussen he, too, had a sense of foreboding. When Watts viewed the map in the briefing room it was covered as always, but there was an extension on the right-hand side of it.

Our regular map, which reached from England to east of Berlin, was too small for this raid! The cover was pulled away and there it was! The red tape ran out from England, over the North Sea to Denmark, across it, out over the Baltic Sea, then back again in over eastern Germany and into Poland. Poznan was our target. It lay almost 1,000 miles away. 'Men,' Colonel William B. David [the CO] was saying, 'Your bomb load is 5,000 lb, gas load, naturally, maximum. Don't start your engines before you have to. You'll need all the gas you have. Altitude is 11,000 feet. Over the Baltic you'll climb to 17,000 which is your bombing altitude. If you lose an engine over or near to the target check your gas and, if you don't think you can make it, head for Sweden. Our wing is bombing Posen. The 13th Wing will go part of the way but are bombing about where you will hit the German coast, so you'll be alone all the way back. The rest of the 8th will be bombing targets all over central and southern Germany. You'll have no fighter escort so shoot at anything you see in the way of a fighter. Keep on the ball and good luck to all of you.'

Out at the plane we double-checked everything with unusual care and threw in a couple of extra boxes of ammo. For the first time on a combat mission we noticed a box of 'K' rations in the ship. We'd need some food before we got home on a haul like this one. Just before taxi time we started the engines. We'd run them up while lining up for the take-off. There was no point using any gas we could save. We took off, climbed through the clouds and assembled. The rendezvous time was cut in half and we started out over the North Sea, tightening up the formation more as we went along and climbing to 11,000 feet before levelling off. We used the lowest possible power setting and the lowest rpm possible and flew as smoothly as we could in an effort to make our gas last.

As almost 10,000 bomber crewmen and over 8,000 fighter pilots in eastern England prepared for the mission, *Luftwaffe* pilots on the other side of the North Sea in Germany and Holland readied themselves for combat with the *Amis*. Three *Gruppen* in JG1 had not seen combat for ten days but now *Oberfeldwebels* Reinhold Flecks and Rudolf Hübl, *Hauptmann* Harald Römer, 2nd *Staffel Staffelkapitän*, and his friend *Oberleutnant* Helmut Biederbick, a veteran of *Jagdgeschwader* 54 on the Eastern Front, waited to be called to action. Biederbick had found victories relatively easy to get in Russia, which he considered far less dangerous and nerve-racking than in the west where:

> Loudspeakers blared out military marches. We would gather near our aircraft, accompanied by the music, which was sometimes interrupted by news concerning the advance of the 'Dicke Autos' or 'Indianer'. We followed their progress on a map. Each *Staffelkapitän* had a telephone on the wing of his aircraft and linked to the *Stab* section. The music was interrupted: *Sitztbereitsschaft* – cockpit readiness. At any moment we could be taking off. A green flare over the airfield was the signal; engines would be started and we would take off.

When the alert sounded JG1's pilots usually had 5 minutes to prepare themselves, put on the obligatory life jacket and go to the toilet as nerves took a hold.

At Oldenburg on the north central German coast, meanwhile, a dense ground fog put 24-year old *Leutnant* Heinz Hanke and his fellow pilots at ease. Hanke's fighter *Gruppe* had moved from Husum to Oldenburg the day before because radio monitors had concluded that the entire American 'birdcage would be opened' for a flight into Germany. As Hanke's late morning breakfast eggs arrived, the alarm howled and he heard flak in the distance signalling that the mass American formation returning from Poznan was nearing the German coast. Hanke, a veteran of 1,088 sorties in almost two years of war, fought back 'dull thoughts' as he rushed out to climb aboard his Fw 190 *The Mule*. He expected something bad to happen and he had never before entered his cockpit with dull thoughts, not even before his first air battle when he had fought off twelve British Spitfires and landed with a frozen engine and a standing propeller. Since then he had downed four Allied aircraft. He told his *Staffel* commander that a 'big dog' (bad time) would come today. About 45 minutes after take-off Hanke's *Gruppe* lost ground visibility and a short time later they lost ground radio contact. The American bomber pilots, meanwhile, were having problems of their own. Heavy cloud cover obscured the target in Poland. Because the Americans could not bomb occupied territory unless the sky was clear, the formation turned toward its secondary target at Stettin, Germany. Led by radar-equipped pathfinder aircraft, the B-17s had climbed to 20,000 feet to begin their bomb runs, but near Denmark the clouds began breaking up and by the time the Forts crossed the Danish coast, it was clear as a bell beneath them, ideal conditions for enemy fighter pilots.

Lowell Watts watched a formation off to his left under heavy fighter attack and he saw two of his Group's bombers go down. The top turret gunner in Lieutenant Richard F. Reed's ship had been killed by enemy gunfire and the left wing hit by a 20 mm cannon shell, putting the bomber out of control. As the two pilots got the plane under control again, Reed opened the bomb bay doors for bale-out, but the Fort burst into flames and some of the crew were blown out. Lieutenant J. B. Payne, the pilot of *Barbara*, radioed Knettishall to say that they were returning because of a fuel leak and that was the last that was heard of them. Payne and eight of his crew died but the tail gunner was picked up wounded in action and made prisoner. Later, Watts saw ten chutes drop from another crippled plane but, pilotless as it was, this ship, slowly losing altitude, continued on eastwards and not until the formation was across the Danish peninsula did he lose sight of it.

The Fw 190s attacking us kept sweeping in until we were well out over the Baltic and the quaint red-roofed villages of Denmark had blended into the horizon behind us. We changed course to the south-east and climbed to 17,000 feet. Clouds were piling up beneath us again and they covered the German coast. On and on we flew. We were almost to Poland now and Ju 88s, Bf 110s and Me 210s had replaced the Focke-Wulfs, making steady, unrelenting diving attacks on our formation. Nowhere could we see a break in the overcast. There was a ruling that no target in an occupied country would be bombed except by contact bombing. Targets in Poland came under this category. So, after flying those hundreds of miles, many of them under fighter attack, we had to turn back, still carrying our bombs, tired, hungry, with the fighters still on us and a feeling of frustration in the knowledge that Posen's factories would still be turning out Focke-Wulfs on the morrow.

We checked our gas tanks. They were less than half full and we were still lugging our bombs. The loss of only one engine would be enough to make us run out of gas. As it was, it would be nip and tuck. We should just make it but maybe we wouldn't. We were still at 17,000 feet, using a lot more gas than we would had we dropped our bombs and gone back down to 11,000 feet. Sixteen of our twenty-one planes were still in formation. Our other two groups were a little better off. We had lost the left wing and the 'diamond' ships in our element, the second element of the low squadron. The VHF crackled to life. 'Wolfgang Yellow, Wolfgang Yellow, this is Wolfgang White calling. Open bomb bay doors. We're approaching our target.' Now over Germany, we were going to bomb a secondary target by PFF [Pathfinder Force] through clouds. Our bomb doors swung open as we fell in behind the 96th Bomb Group which contained the PFF ship. Suddenly, flak appeared – big, ugly mushrooming billows of black, blossoming out around the angry red flash of the shells' explosions. The flak became thicker and more accurate as we neared the point of bomb release. Our ship bounced as the sound of ripping metal brought a lump to our throats. A big jagged hole had made its appearance between our number one and two engines. The number two gas gauge still showed no indication of a leak. There were two rips in the number two cowling, but the oil pressure was up and the engine was running smoothly. Ahead, two long streams of white arched down beneath the lead ship in the 96th formation. Those were the marker bombs of the PFF ship. In a few seconds we were nearing those markers. As we passed them we dumped our bombs, happy to feel the plane leap upwards, free of its load. The flak pounded us for about a minute longer, then it began to disappear. At last we were heading home, free of our bombs and able to cut down on our power settings. Only a few Ju 88s were around. Now and then they would lob a rocket at us, careful to stay out of range of our .50s. One formation of the 88s lined up behind us and started pumping rockets at us. The projectiles sailed into the high squadron, bursting like flak. Fire broke out on the right wing of one plane. It flew for a minute longer, then rolled up on one wing and started down. Suddenly, there was a flash, a huge billowy puff of smoke and jagged pieces of broken, twisted metal fluttered aimlessly earthwards.

'Mark' Markussen in the co-pilot's seat of *Ain't Mis Behavin'* felt a jolt as flak ripped into the left inboard engine. He tried to feather the engine but he couldn't. 'It was like having a big brake windmilling out there,' he said. Reginald Smith called to the squadron leader for help. Normally, a formation would slow down to keep 'cripples' under protection, but according to Markussen the squadron leader panicked and directed *Ain't Mis Behavin'* to fall out of formation and head for the overcast clouds below. Sweden was 70 miles away, but as they were diving enemy fighters were coming up. Markussen saw them right away.

> I had never seen so many German aircraft. We always respected the German pilots and were impressed by the courage they displayed. It seemed to us, though, that it was almost suicide for them to press head-on attacks against the massive firepower generated by our massed bombers. It was just one tremendous air battle that lasted for hours with many aircraft from both sides going in.

Of the 140 interceptors that had taken off from Oldenburg, only seven remained. The rest either had been shot down or were on the ground refuelling and rearming. Heinz Hanke thought the six other Fw 190s were *Staffel* leaders and they were on *Ain't Mis Behavin'* in an instant, slashing away at the B-17, almost dead in the sky. Tracers blinked everywhere.

Markussen recalled:

> I was calling out fighter attacks when smash, there was this big explosion. They had shot off the whole top turret. When I turned to look over my shoulder there was just a big hole. I got up, took off my flak vest and went to see about the gunner Tom Egan. I was sure he was in shreds. The concussion had thrown him back but he wasn't even in shock. He didn't have a scratch.

As Hanke made his first approach at *Ain't Mis Behavin'* a warning light indicated that he had 8 minutes of fuel left at reduced power. Hanke decided to press the attack in the hope that he could, as a last resort, crash-land on the beaches of the Baltic. On his own now after a head-on open formation attack, Hanke roared in at high speed from the rear, attacking the B-17 with his four 20 mm cannons and two heavy machine-guns. Dodging pieces of the aircraft, he rolled in under the tail toward the left wing. Too late, he realised he was coming too fast and too close. Too late! Left waist gunner Ed Britko had him. Hanke flipped *The Mule* over on its back and tried to dive to safety. As he started down, Britko raked the Fw 190 with bullets. The cabin filled with oily smoke and aluminium dust and the engine screamed like a circular saw. With his throttle linkage shot away and a foot-long piece of his left wing gone, Hanke's only thought was to get out. Another round of fire pierced the armoured ring above the oil cooler. Hanke said, 'That was the end of it. I could not see out of the cabin, now dark with black-brown oil.'

Releasing the canopy and protected now only by the windscreen, the *Jagdflieger* tried three times to work himself out of his aircraft. He could barely see after a rush of oil slapped across his face. Finally, though, he was free, his shoulder and ankle brushing the rudder as he tumbled away from his whining aircraft. Markussen hardly had time to notice. By the fourth German pass *Ain't Mis Behavin'* was an inferno. The No. 2 engine and its 700 gallon main fuel tank were ablaze and the fire roared back into the bomb bay, radio room and the waist gun positions. The left horizontal stabiliser was gone, thanks to Hanke, cutting all manual control cables to the tail section. Except for a single .50 calibre gun at each waist position and the twin .50 calibre tail guns, *Ain't Mis Behavin'* was defenceless, her turret guns rendered useless after the first attack. Added to that, radio transmissions were shot. The pilot and co-pilot could receive transmissions from the rest of the crew but couldn't transmit. While Smith worked the elevator control button on the autopilot to keep the plane from spinning in, Markussen manoeuvred the ailerons by hand. Somehow, the aircraft limped through the sky, but not for long. She would soon career away, completely out of control but not before taking her toll. Another Fw 190 blew up in a hail of bullets, a victim of tail gunner Mike Udick's accuracy and right waist gunner Bob Dunbar was certain he decapitated an onrushing attacker who almost rammed the B-17. The other German flyers were forced to 'belly in' on the Danish beaches, out of fuel. Miraculously, not one of the crew was hit but the aircraft was completely on fire, its left wing melting. One by one the crew baled out over the Danish Island of Fyn and *Ain't Mis Behavin'* crashed on Funen Island. The crash was witnessed by some Germans at the radar station at Skovby. 'After all the noise, it was the most beautiful sound I've ever heard – dead silence,' Markussen said. He landed safely, standing up and was captured. After initial interrogation at an anti-aircraft site where he was held overnight, the following morning Markussen was taken to a German military headquarters in Odense, the birthplace of Hans Christian Andersen – ironically, Markussen's mother had also been born there – where he was interrogated by the *Luftwaffe* and the *Gestapo*. Eight other members of the crew were also captured. Ira Evans, the radio operator, hid in a forest and later escaped to Sweden aided by the Danish underground.

Hanke also parachuted safely on Fyn, landing between a fence and a flagpole and just missing telephone and high-tension lines. Once on his feet he lit up a German war cigarette. 'As terrible as it tasted, it was surely the best of my life,' he said. The Danes who greeted him weren't overly friendly when they found he was German, but he soon changed their opinion. He was taken to a large farm and asked what should be done with his plane, embedded deeply in the ground some 50 yards behind the house. 'When I looked into the hole, I realised the ammunition and oxygen bottles would explode any moment,' he said. 'Frantically I waved the people away and they began to run. Within 4 or 5 seconds, there was a huge explosion. Luckily no one was hurt. From that moment the people seemed to change their minds about me.'[5]

When the American bomber formations were sighted the twenty Fw 190 pilots of JG1 went into action, making three passes against the bombers with the third, in the region of Mulhouse, resulting in claims for three B-17s and two P-38s. Helmut Biederbick recalled:

> We flew for several seconds parallel to the formation in order to evaluate its strength and direction. We were aware of the escort fighters but often they did not attack at this moment. We picked up speed, swept wide of our target and carried out a 180 degrees turn. We were then head-on and opened fire while traversing through the bomber stream. During this move, our formation lost cohesion, and that was what the enemy fighters were waiting for. They then picked us off at the rear of the *Viermots*.[6]

Reinhold Flecks claimed one B-17 and a P-38, and Rudolf Hübl claimed a B-17, but *Hauptmann* Harald Römer and three other pilots of JG1 were killed in combat and two were wounded.[7] Römer's place was taken by his friend Helmut Biederbick. Heinz Knoke, meanwhile, returned safely but blamed his own poor shooting for failing to score any victories. Major Günther Specht, the *Kommodore* of 5./JG1, was forced down and had to make an emergency landing on the Danish Island of Aroe. He had lost an eye in a dogfight at the beginning of the war, and Heinz Knoke described[8] him as 'short' and 'a model of the conscientious Prussian soldier' with a 'dominating personality' with his one remaining eye making him look like a 'buzzard'. Lowell Watts and the crew of *Blitzin' Betsy* meanwhile, had come through unscathed.

> The hours dragged on. We'd been up almost 8 hours now and we were crossing Denmark with the North Sea still separating us from England. Leaving the coast we let down to 10,000 feet and loosened the formation as the fighters fell away. A glance at the gas gauges was anything but heartening. It would be a close one getting back today. We checked everything we might need if we should have to ditch. The sun was riding low in the west as we neared England. Every few minutes one of our planes would drop out of formation to save gas. A few we heard calling pitifully to Air Sea Rescue and soon, below us, one of the lone planes would glide with a splash into the sea, its gas exhausted. 'Pilot from

navigator, we're over England. You can see a spot of coastline off to our right through that little hole in the clouds.'

We watched the radio compass swing around, telling us we were passing over our field. Our squadron leader zoomed gently up and down. His left-wing ship peeled off and was followed by the squadron lead ship, his right-wing ship and then our plane. The ships were letting down on a heading of ninety degrees, disappearing one by one into the fluffy folds of white below us. Soon we were skimming the clouds, then we were in the soup, dark, lonely and uninviting. I was watching only the instruments now, heading 90 degrees, flaps one third down, wheels down, airspeed 150, vertical speed 500 feet per minute. Down, down, down we went, the gloom darkening each second. At 1,000 feet we were still on instruments. We were all dead tired but during the let-down we forgot it for the moment while eager eyes tried to pierce the murk for signs of the ground or other planes which might hit us. At 750 feet we broke out. It was raining but visibility was fair. We turned almost 180 degrees until the radio compass read '0' and flew on until landmarks became familiar. Finally, we saw flares up ahead and soon the runway became visible. A plane was on its approach. Another, too close to it, pulled up and went around again. We started our approach and let down with the fuel warning lights on and the gas gauges reading almost empty. We couldn't stay up much longer. Kennedy turned the turbos full on in case we should need the power if we had to go around again. Old *Blitzin' Betsy* settled down, floated a second, then touched the runway. We rolled to the end of the runway, another mission completed. Then we realised how tired we were.

B. J. Keirsted's crew also made it back safely to Knettishall in *Cock o' the Walk* as Larry Goldstein recalls.

There were quite a few enemy fighters but somehow they were not too eager and did not pester us. We landed at dear old Knettishall in a heavy late afternoon haze and in almost total darkness. I believe we stretched the B-17 to its maximum and as always it brought us home in one piece.[9] The mission count at this point was twenty. We started thinking about it but did not say it out loud: 'Can we as a crew make it through twenty-five?' No one talked about it but I'm sure we all thought about it.

In all, the Americans lost twenty-one bombers and four fighters. Three Medals of Honor (two posthumously) were awarded to B-17 crewmen.

The next day, 21 February, just over 850 bomber crews fought their way through dense contrails and biting cold to their targets at Diepholz, Brunswick, Hanover and Achmer. For B. J. Keirsted's crew at Knettishall, it meant another run to Brunswick, which eleven days earlier had been a nightmare trip for the crew. Larry Goldstein was sure that all his fellow crewmembers felt the same as he did. Would he survive this one? 'Will we come home to our own beds?' To him it seemed from past experiences that every time the 8th went to Brunswick, it was a 'bloodbath'. As it turned out, fighter support proved 'plentiful' and the radio operator considered that they did a 'magnificent job' protecting them. The rest of the mission he noted in his diary, 'wasn't too bad' and he put it down as an 'easy' mission, though they were very tired fliers. 'We had been flying many missions, mostly long flights to heavily defended targets and all major aircraft component plants.' Nineteen bombers and five fighters though were lost. Heinz Knoke of 5./JG1 had orders to draw off the escorting fighters 'at any cost' and keep them engaged in combat while other *gruppen* attacked the bombers. Five of the missing *Viermots* were claimed destroyed by II./JG1, three of them by Heinz Bär to take his score to 185 kills. However, the *Gruppe* lost five pilots killed and four wounded. In the 95th, *Liberty Belle* and *San Antonio Rose* were shot down by *Oberfeldwebel* Addi Glunz and *Unteroffizier* Gerhard Loschinksi and fourteen crewmen were lost. Three days later Loschinksi was shot down and killed in combat with a Mustang.

The German fighter wings were active again on 22 February when almost 800 bombers set out again for aircraft targets in Germany while 118 bombers of the 15th Air Force bombed the Messerschmitt assembly plant Regensburg, losing fourteen aircraft. The mission began badly for the 8th, which lost two Forts during assembly in a mid-air collision near Irthlingborough and eighteen men died. Bad weather prevented the Forts in the Third Division forming properly and they were forced to abandon the mission to Schweinfurt at the enemy coast. Then the Liberators were recalled when 100 miles inland and since they were over Germany it was decided to bomb targets of opportunity. However, strong winds caused them to fly over Holland and the bombs hit Enschede, Arnhem, Nijmegen and Deventer in error. This was a costly mission, the worst of 'Big Week', with forty-one bombers lost. Two of the Forts lost, part of a diversion attack on Aalborg West airfield in northern Denmark by Fame's Favoured Few, collided when one plane emerged from cloud and flew straight into the other. To Bill Rose it looked like 'a huge oil tank fire at 20,000 feet with nothing but black smoke'. There were no survivors aboard *Hot Rock*, which crashed into the North Sea, though nine survived from the other ship. Worst hit of the Groups were the 306th, which put up thirty-nine planes with nine aborts on the mission to the Ju 88 factory at Oschersleben and Bernburg. On the way home after the fighter escort left, German fighters tore into the Thurleigh Group, shooting down seven B-17s.

Heinz Knoke of 5./JG1 returned to Wunsdorf after a 90-minute sortie in his *Gustav*, during which he claimed a B-17 near his home town of Hamelin. He and *Obergefreiter* Kurt Krüger, who had only joined his unit two days earlier, attacked a Fortress in a formation of about thirty bombers head on. Knoke's cannon and machine-gun fire was accurate and shells penetrated the cockpit area. He flashed past, turned and came in again, this time diving down upon his victim from the tail until a collision was imminent. The pilot of the Fort tried to weave out of the *Gustav*'s line of fire and swerved sharply round to his left. It may have been the B-17 piloted by Lieutenant Colonel Robert P. Riordan, the *Fightin' Bitin'* Squadron CO from El Paso, Texas, who twice turned the group into the attacking fighters, forcing them to abandon their attacks and re-form for another pass. Knoke's shells continued to penetrate

115

the left wing and left side of the fuselage of his intended victim and flames began belching from the tail.

Lieutenant Fred J. Rector, leading the Clay Pigeons flying as the low squadron, looked out of the cockpit at the German fighters swarming around. 'They just kept coming. Although our gunners took a heavy toll, our left inboard engine was set on fire and we lost most of the control surfaces on the vertical and left horizontal stablisers.' Knoke pulled in closer to beneath the fuselage and continued to blast away with everything left in his magazines. Meanwhile, the brave if foolhardy Krüger took on another Fort to Knoke's left, the neophyte fighter pilot going in to within a few feet of 'his' B-17. By now the fuselage of Rector's ship was a blazing torch. 'We flipped over violently and dropped out of formation. We were able to level out considerably lower but when power was applied to maintain flight we again lost control and the plane had to be abandoned.' Knoke saw Rector's crew baling out. Rector, who was on his eleventh mission, and five others in his crew made it out but four died in the doomed ship, which made a wide sweep round to the left and began to go down. 'Its passage', noted Knoke, '[was] marked by a long trail of black smoke.' The blazing Fort dived ever more steeply and soon it was in a vertical spin. It crashed in a pasture beside the river at the southern end of Hamelin, where a tower of flame spurting high into the air marked the spot where it crashed. At that moment *White 10*, Krüger's Fw 190, crashed into a lumberyard at the south end of Hamelin on the premises of the Kaminski wagon manufacturing and repair workshops. Knoke took off again after the Forts when they were homeward bound, but he became embroiled in a dogfight with a pack of Thunderbolts and he did not have a chance to fire at any more bombers.[10]

Fred Rector evaded capture for four days, during which time he rode trains and walked for miles. American survivors were brought together at Geilenkirchen. Among them were men from the crew of the B-17 flown by Lieutenant Thomas W. Symons III, most of whom were on their thirteenth mission, and this ship may have been Krüger's victim. Symons was killed instantly in a fighter attack, which plastered the nose area with 20 mm cannon fire. A cannon shell hit the navigator, Lieutenant Robert G. Jobe, in the side where the front and back of his flak suit did not quite meet and he was killed. Lieutenant Robert F. Proctor, bombardier, was badly wounded on his entire right side from face down and both legs had been shot up. The plane tried to loop but came back to horizontal with a sheet of flame enveloping the right wing. Waist gunner Hayden M. Collier jumped an instant before the plane exploded. Proctor and two others were blasted out of the B-17 by the force of the explosion. When Proctor regained consciousness he had fallen through a cloud layer at about 1,500 feet and managed to pull the ripcord on his back pack with his left hand. He was knocked out again when he hit the snowcovered ground amongst young pine trees. Had he been wearing his usual chest pack, which was in for repack, Proctor probably would never have retrieved it in time to survive. Regaining consciousness again, an old man and a boy of about fifteen were standing over him, the boy waving a rifle menacingly at Proctor. The young German, who was almost as tall as he was,

Scattered around every airfield from Bassingbourn to Bungay and Rattlesden to Rackheath, typical corrugated Nissen hut. Huts were lined but not insulated so they were pretty cold in the wintertime. (*via Pete Worby*)

here is very little onversation at the e. Just drink your ee and pick at the od. Then it's back into the dark and cold night. A grey has started to fill he sky in the east. nother long walk the flight lockers. (*Author*)

NO UNAUTHORISED PERSONS ALLOWED IN THIS SECTION

REGULAR MEAL HOURS
BREAKFAST 6:45 TO 7:45
DINNER 11:15 TO 1300
SUPPER 1715 TO 1845

By Order Mess Officer

Chow. Fresh eggs confirmed that a combat mission was scheduled. (*USAF*)

At briefing men listened to the A-2 officer's running commentary on the target. (*USAF*)

Fortresses flying through Flak (*USAF*)

utnant Otto Stammberger, Staffelkapitän of
Staffel. (*via Eric Mombeek*)

Oberleutnant Georg-Peter 'Schorch' Eder,
Staffelkapitän, 12./JG2. (*Bill Donald*)

mann Hans-Joachim Jabs a seasoned combat
n who had his first taste of action during the
of France. (*via Theo Boiten*)

Hauptmann Ludwig Becker, Staffelkapitän,
12./NJG1. (*Theo Boiten via Rob de Visser*)

22-year old Leutnant Heinz Knoke of I./JG1 at Jever-Wangerooge. By late 1944 he had scored 44 victories in the west. On 9 October 1944 while travelling by road convoy from Austria via Prague, Dresden and Berlin to a new base at Anklam in North Germany, his Volkswagen was blown up when it ran over a mine in the road in Czechoslovakia and his left knee and right pelvis were shattered. He only just managed to avoid having his leg amputated but his career as a pilot was over. He was awarded the Ritterkreuz on 27 April 1945. (*via Eric Mombeek*)

Captain Oscar O'Neill, 'born in Brazil, mother Spanish, father Irish and who looked like George Raft', in the pilot's seat of Invasion II in the 91st Bomb Group at Bassingbourn, Cambridgeshire. O'Neill and his crew were shot down on 16 April 1943. (*USAF*)

Above: Hauptmann Dietrich Wickop, II.Gruppe Kommandeur, JGI, who was killed in action on 16 May 1943 following combat with P-47 Thunderbolts. Wickop had thirteen victories, including three B-17s. (*via Eric Mombeek*)

22-year-old Unteroffizier Gefreiter Ernst Schröder, pilot, II.Sturm/JG300 in the cockpit of his Fw 190 'Red 19'' Kolle-alaaf!' (Cologne-aloft - Schröder was born in Cologne). On 27 September 1944 Schröder destroyed one of the 25 Liberators in the 445th Bomb Group that failed to return from a raid on Kassel. Five more crashed in France and England. Only five made it back to Tibenham. (*Schröder*)

A B-24 Liberator hit in the wing on the bomb run goes down in flames. (*USAF*)

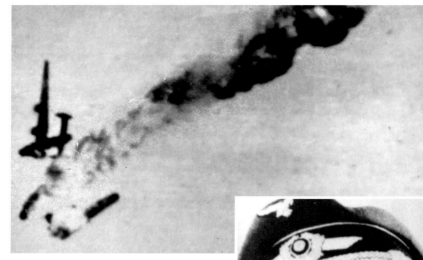

Staffelkapitän Oskar Romm of Sturm IV/JG 3 'Udet'. On 27 September 1944 he destroyed a B-24 of the 445th Bomb Group, the next day, he claimed 2 B-17 kills to take his tally to 85. (*via Heinz Nowarra*)

Bomb Bay doors open with contrails. (*USAF*)

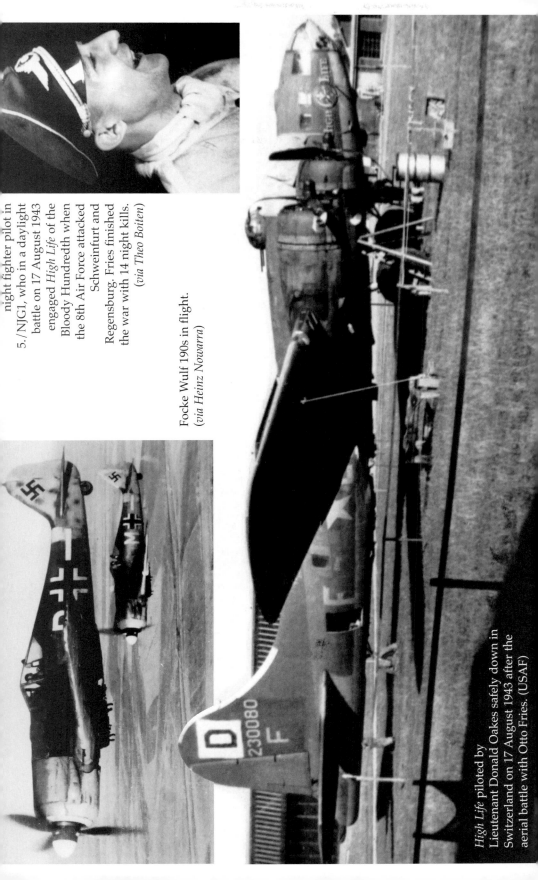

night fighter pilot in
5./NJG1, who in a daylight
battle on 17 August 1943
engaged *High Life* of the
Bloody Hundredth when
the 8th Air Force attacked
Schweinfurt and
Regensburg. Fries finished
the war with 14 night kills.
(via Theo Boiten)

Focke Wulf 190s in flight.
(via Heinz Nowarra)

High Life piloted by
Lieutenant Donald Oakes safely down in
Switzerland on 17 August 1943 after the
aerial battle with Otto Fries. (USAF)

The Bloody Hundredth was well known for its high loss rate. On 27 December 1943, a wet, cold, gloomy and foggy day, three Forts piled up landing on the short runway at Thorpe Abbotts. *King Bee*, *Flyin' Jenny* and a third plane were wrecked but amazingly there were no casualties. Behind is *Holy Terror*, which crash-landed at Detling on 31 January 1944. (*USAF*)

Lady Liberty of the 305th Bomb Group going down on 18 August 1943. There was no Promised Land for eight of Lieutenant Ralph R. Miller's crew. (*USAF*)

Focke Wulf 190A-7 'Black 3' of II./JG1 at Dortmund in January 1944. (*via Rob de Visser*)

Unteroffizier Heinz Hanke of 9./JG1 (far right) who shot down *Ain't Mis Behavin'* in the Bloody Hundredth on 20 February 1944. (*via Eric Mombeek*)

On 11 January 1944 ten of the 15 pilots of 11 Gruppe, JG1 led by Oberleutnant von Kirchmayr, claimed 11 Fortresses destroyed. L-R; Leutnant Fritz Wegner; Oberfeldwebel Leo Schuhmacher; Oberleutnant von Kirchmayr; Oberfeldwebel Rudolf Haninger; Oberleutnant Eberhard Burath; Feldwebel Max Sauer; Stabsfeldwebel Rudolf Martens (KIA 24 January 1944 by P-47 Thunderbolts near Tournai) and Feldwebel Schönrock. (*via Eric Mombeek*)

The *Worry Wart* crew of the 388th Bomb Group at Knettishall, February 1944. Back row (left to right) Lieutenants Philip 'Bloodhound' Brejensky, navigator; Belford 'B. J'. Keirsted, pilot; Clifford 'Ace' Conklin, co-pilot; Kent 'Cap' Keith, bombardier. Front row (left to right) Staff Sergeant Ed Kozacek, top turret gunner; Staff Sergeant E. V. Lewelling, waist gunner; Technical Sergeant Jack C. Kings, waist gunner; Technical Sergeant Larry 'Goldie' Goldstein, radio-operator; Staff Sergeant Robert Miller, tail gunner. (*Larry Goldstein*)

Technical Sergeant Larry 'Goldie' Goldstein at the radio position, Knettishall, 1943-44. (*Larry Golds*

Major Heinz 'Pritzl' Bär, Kommandeur, III/JG1 inspects *Miss Quachita* of the 91st Bomb Group at Bexten, near Saltzbergen after he shot the Fortress down on 22 February 1944 during a raid on Gütersloh. Two of 2/Lt Spencer K Osterberg's crew, were KIA. The other eight survived to be take prisoner. (*USAF*)

...ew of *Blitzin' Betsy* of the 388th Bomb Group at Knettishall, Suffolk. Back Row L-R: 1st Lieutenant ...well H. Watts, pilot; 2nd Lieutenant Robert M. Kennedy, co-pilot; 2nd Lieutenant Emmett J. ...urphy, bombardier; 2nd Lieutenant Edward J. Kelley, navigator. Crouching L-R: Technical Sergeant ... Ramsey, top turret; Staff Sergeant Ray E. Hess (KIA 6 April 1944), right waist; Technical Sergeant ...n Finkle, radio operator; Staff Sergeant Robert H. Sweeney (KIA) ball gunner; Staff Sergeant ...rold A. Brassfield (KIA), tail gunner; Staff Sergeant Don W. Taylor (KIA), left waist gunner. (Watts)

Major Heinz 'Pritzl' Bär. The top scoring NCO pilot in the Battle of Britain, Bär ended the war as the top scoring jet ace of WW2, with 16, and eighth overall on the list of experten with 220 confirmed victories. Bär was killed in a light aircraft crash in 1957. (USAF)

P-51D Mustang *Dopey Oakie* of the 352nd Fighter Group at Bodney, Norfolk. (*via Bill Espie*)

General Ike of the 91st Bomb Group at Bassingbourn. This Fortress flew its first operational mission on 13 April 1944; two days after General Dwight D Eisenhower christened it. Ike completed 75 combat missions, returned to the USA in June 1945 and was broken up for scrap. (*USAF*)

Lieutenant Abe Dolim, a Hawaiian born radio operator who flew two tours in the 94th Bomb Group at Bury St. Edmunds (Rougham). (*Dolim*)

"*Prowlin' Tom*" of the 390th Bomb Group, which crash-landed at Framlingham on 23 March 1944. It was repaired and was lost with Lieutenant Edwin G. Sechrist and crew on 8 June 1944 when it failed to return from a raid over France. (*via Nigel McTeer*)

B-24 Liberator over its target in 1944. (*USAF*)

Major Walter "Gulle" Oesau (left) who was the third German pilot to reach 100 victories. Physically and mentally exhausted, he was shot down and killed in combat with P-51 Mustangs and P-38 Lightnings on 11 May 1944. He had 125 victories. On the right is Oberleutnant Hans Ehlers who on 8 October 1943 flying a Fw 190 collided with *Marie Helena* of the Bloody Hundredth. All ten men aboard the Fortress were KIA. Ehlers baled out with various facial injuries and a double fracture of the right thighbone. He was shot down and killed on 27 December 1944 by Mustangs of the 364th Fighter Group. At the time of his death Ehlers had at least 55 victories including 23 Viermots. (*via Eric Mombeek*)

Swanner's crew in the 379th Bomb Group at Kimbolton who flew the D-Day mission on 6 June 1944. Front row, L-R: Frank J. Bagdon, flight engineer; Frank Marsh, tail gunner; Al Tenenzaph, radio operator-gunner; Al Smith, waist gunner; Otis Creighton, waist gunner; John Snyder, ball turret gunner. Standing, L-R: John L. Swanner Jr, pilot John East co-pilot; Frank L. Betz, navigator; Walter G. Collings, bombardier. (*Frank L. Betz*)

...berator on fire. (*Staff Sergeant Clifford Stocking Jr.*)

A Fortress goes down in flames at Merseberg on 2 November 1944. (*USAF*)

Oberstleutnant Josef 'Pips' Priller, Kommodore, Jagdgeschwader 26 "Schlageter" scored his 100th victory on 15 June 1944 when he shot down a B-24 Liberator of the 492nd Bomb Group. Priller survived the war with 101 victories. (*via Eric Mombeek*)

2nd Lieutenant Russell A. Goodspeed's crew in the 493rd Bomb Group at Debach, Suffolk. On 3[...] March 1945 the crew flew their first mission to the submarine docks in Hamburg when they wer[...] hit by flak. Returning they crashed at Little Walden where the right wing touched the ground an[...] the plane broke in half at the trailing edge of the wing killing five crew in the front of the Fortre[...] Goodspeed died 6 hours later. Only the flight engineer, the navigator and Lieutenant Roger D. L[...] the co-pilot (2nd from left, front row) survived. (*Roger Laib*)

B-17 on fire breaks up over Merseberg on 30 November 1944. (*USAF*)

Luftwaffe aircraft at an abandoned German airfield the end of the war. (*Author's Coll*)

seemed as scared as his prisoner. The old man said, 'I come from Cincinnati in 1934. Why do you bomb Germany?' Proctor had no reply, as all of his teeth on the left side of his mouth had been loosened. Also blasted out of the plane and to safety was Robert L. Woodruff, radio operator, and Joseph P. Fiddes, one of the waist gunners. When he saw the plane was on fire Woodruff, who was not wearing his chute, started to put on his parachute. The explosion blew him out and the shoulder strap wrapped itself around his wrist. In the air Woodruff saw that he was attached to his chute harness by the strap around the wrist and, knowing that he had nothing to lose, pulled the ripcord. The chute opened and the pressure created by his weight against the twisted strap kept it in place and he landed safely. Once on the ground, he shook his wrist and was free of the chute. Symons' co-pilot, engineer, ball turret gunner and Albert J. Dome, who had not gone on leave with his regular crew that day but had instead volunteered to fly, all died. The twenty-three B-17s that made it back to Thurleigh, including one with more than seventy flak holes and just two engines, were battle damaged.[11,12]

On 23 February in England crews received a much needed respite when weather conditions were the prime reason for keeping the heavies on the ground but the 15th AF destroyed 20 per cent of the ball-bearing works at Steyr, Austria. Maintenance crews worked around the clock, attempting to get every bomber possible ready for combat. They were needed the next day when Doolittle again dispatched in excess of 800 bombers to targets throughout the Reich. Third Division crews had to return to the Baltic coast to bomb Rostock, but hearts really sank at First Division group briefings when the curtains were pulled back to reveal their target – the factories at Schweinfurt! However, losses were light – eleven Forts were lost – and events were over-shadowed by the Liberator's success and high losses, at the Messerschmitt Bf110 assembly plant at Gotha. Flak was heavy over Holland and the escorting fighters were unable to prevent attacks on the B-24s by over 150 enemy fighters who shot down twelve Liberators in the 445th before reaching the target. The thirteen survivors, who had veered off course, continued alone to the target and executed an 8-minute bomb run. A thirteenth victim was shot down moments after 'bombs away'. Six 'Sky Scorpions' were also lost, making thirty-three Liberators lost in all. Heavy damage was inflicted on the Messerschmitt plant, intelligence sources later estimating that six to seven weeks' production was lost.[13] Heavy cloud at Rostock had prevented the Third Divison from bombing, forcing the B-17s to head for their secondary target at Poznan, which had been missed four days earlier. Larry Goldstein noted in his diary that they ran into some flak along the route and were hit in the right wing as well as by fighters. As they had no support all the way they had a battle on their hands and he did quite a bit of shooting. 'A few fighters kept pecking away at us and there were a few 17s that went down.' He added that the mission was 'long and tiresome' and that they were airborne for over 11 hours. Five Forts, including one in their group, failed to return from the mission but Keirsted's crew made it. They were so exhausted they could hardly get to the mess hall for the evening meal. Larry Goldstein concluded that 'at this point we as a crew figured that the next three missions to bring us to the magic number of twenty-five would by the law of averages, be simple, light missions. How wrong we were.'

'Big Week' ended on 25 February with 1,300 bombers and 1,000 fighters being despatched to aircraft and components plants in the deepest raid into Germany thus far. The Liberators were assigned the Bf110 component plant at Furth and the First Division the Messerschmitt experimental and assembly plants at Augsburg and the fighter plants at Stuttgart. Third Division crews learned at briefings that their target was Regensburg, which was being bombed for the first time since the devastating mission on 17 August 1943. The shadow cast by the high losses at Schweinfurt and Regensburg was still uppermost in the minds of all crews. This time the bombing would be shared with the Italy-based 15th Air Force, which would bomb Regensburg an hour before the England-based force arrived over the city. The Germans had given top priority to the reconstruction of the Regensburg plant and within six months had restored production to something like its previous output. Although most of the old buildings had been destroyed, several main build-ings had been rebuilt, including a long assembly shop on a site where three had once stood. News of the Regensburg strike came only hours after crews had logged 12 hours' flying time during a mission to Rostock on the Baltic coast at a cost of five Forts. It had not only been the longest raid they had flown so far, but also one of the roughest.

At Knettishall 'BJ' Keirsted's *Worry Wart* crew and Lowell Watts and the crew of *Blitzin' Betsy* were still very tired, as they all were, when they were roused from their fitful sleep at 0300 hours on 25 February. Keirsted's crew were assigned *Pegasus, Too*, which they had flown on their last two missions. For some, the prospect of flying to Regensburg did not seem to sink in. Watts recalls:

> Crews had arrived at that mental state, where one more extra long, extra tough raid, meant nothing to us. It was just another raid. As for myself, at least, I'd grown calloused. The tougher the raid now, the better I liked it.
>
> Beautiful weather greeted us as we assembled over England and headed off across the Channel. We crossed the coast at 21,000 feet, our formation assembled and everything was working OK. It was one of those rare days in the European theatre when fog, clouds, or haze did not limit visibility. Just as the enemy coast began passing beneath us, a murderous barrage of flak started coming up. We were supposed to cross the coast between Dieppe and Le Havre, but we were evidently too close to Le Havre. We'd been through heavier flak before, but the accuracy of this stuff was hard to beat. They had our altitude perfect. Then they began tracking us and in a matter of seconds those black puffs were riding right along with us. The ship jerked a little to the sound of ripping metal. We'd been hit and hit hard. Our left wing showed a big, ragged hole. A few more bursts got in close enough to leave other hits showing in the nose and fuselage. Monty Givens, flying our left wing, peeled off and headed for England. He'd probably make it back from our present position, but he hadn't lasted

long. Sweeney turned his ball turret to the front and looked over the bottom of our wing. 'Pilot from ball turret; there are a lot of holes in the wings, especially the left one, but I can't see any gas running out.'

All four of our engines kept purring away and we were seemingly in pretty fair shape as we flew out of range of the flak. It was time now for our fighter cover to be showing up but they were nowhere in sight. For another 30 minutes we kept flying to the east and still found ourselves out there alone. Something had gone wrong with the timing. Then we began to see fighters but they weren't our own, they were Jerries. Focke-Wulf 190s, Ju 88s, and Messerschmitt 109s were beginning to circle in ever increasing numbers, then they pulled up ahead of us and started their attacks. One B-17 dropped out of formation and lost altitude. Chutes appeared beneath it. As we watched him he started burning, leaving a long trail of black smoke behind. The crippled plane dropped fast then seemed to level out a little, sailed over the hills beneath and finally disappeared into a mass of flame and debris, which scattered itself over almost half a mile as it hit and exploded. Another B-17 was hit and exploded, almost in the formation. A B-24 seemed to fall apart as the Jerries took on one of the B-24 formations.

As time wore on we could see the Fw 190s peel off from their attacks, dive almost straight down, levelling off just above the ground, make a brief half circle and land on the nearest field. They would taxi in, sit there for 5 to 10 minutes and then we could see the dust behind them as they started up again. In another 5 minutes they would be back to the attack. It was sort of fascinating to watch that circle complete itself but at the same time very discomforting to realise that these fighters that were hitting us might follow us all the way in and out unless they were shot down. Of course, some of them were, but not enough. There was still no sign of our fighter cover.

It was almost 1200 when we sighted a column of smoke rising almost to our altitude. It was dead ahead. If that was smoke from Regensburg, then the 15th Air Force had hit it and no question about it. The Alps were clearly discernible to the north of us now. They reminded me quite a little of our own Rockies. About then, I was wishing they were the Rockies too. Upon reaching our IP we could easily see the 15th's target. All we had to do was follow that column of smoke down to the earth and there it was or what was left of it at least. We turned in for our bombing run and there above us was the most welcome sight I'd ever seen on a mission; a group of P-38s. At last, our fighters had found us!

Up ahead the flak was getting thicker and thicker. One of our squadron leads was hit and peeled out of the formation so quickly that his whole squadron was scattered. Only half his planes got back into formation during the bombing run. Back behind us his second element of three ships was trying to catch up with us but they were too far behind. Then the flak got too heavy for us to worry about anyone but ourselves. We settled down on the last of the bomb run. The target was spread out beautifully below us in perfect visibility. A chance like this was a contact bombardier's dream come true. The bombs went out, we closed our bomb bay doors and turned away from the target. Behind us were those three planes, making a bomb run of their own. They looked so vulnerable and all alone back there, but they made the run and pulled in with another formation without losing anyone.

Below us our target was rapidly looking like the other one which had been hit by the 15th Air Force before we had arrived. Smoke was pouring upward, rising to about 20,000 feet. The Jerries were still making things quite interesting, but with our own fighters in the skies, a lot of their attacks were diverted. Now the strain began to tell. We'd done a lot of combat flying during the week and we were beginning to feel its effects. Kennedy and I began trading off on the flying. Both of us were so tired that after about 15 minutes we just couldn't hold formation. Never in all my missions had I reached the stage where I was absolutely too tired to fly, but I reached it on this raid. During a lull I looked around the formation. Several ships were missing and in three of the missing spots was a queer-looking sight. Three P-38s were flying formation with us. Each of them had lost an engine and had pulled into our formation for protection.

Hours later we circled Knettishall and set *Blitzin' Betsy* down on good old terra firma once again. Every man on the crew was completely fagged, sleepy, stiff, sore, and just generally all-in. We taxied up to our hardstand and tumbled out. Those holes were even bigger and uglier-looking than we had realised. Quite obviously our wing was badly shot up. The gas tank had been hit in several places. Tired as I was, at that particular moment I could have taken my hat off to the engineers who had never seen combat but who had developed the bullet-proof gas tank. Our story of this particular day would have been quite different had those tanks never been designed.

Pegasus, Too also made it back safely to Knettishall. Larry Goldstein recalled:

The flak had been mostly scattered and ineffective but at one point over the target it was intensive and very accurate. Some aircraft were hit. Luckily not ours. A few enemy fighters pecked away but fortunately we were not the group to be hit. Our fighter support was supposed to be there but they only showed up when it was too late. This was one of those fouled up missions. The only thing right was our bombing. The raid was a great morale booster at a time when it was needed. As it turned out this raid was also important for the invasion, which was to come later. My brother was in the US Army tank forces and he later told me that when his unit entered Regensburg the plant was in a shambles.

A dozen Third Division Forts, including one claimed by *Oberfeldwebel* Addi Glunz, and four Snetterton Falcons failed to return and the First Division lost an unlucky thirteen planes bombing Augsburg and Stuttgart. On the way in, the 306th were greeted by accurate and unexpected flak from Saarbrucken, which split the Group wide open. Before it could properly re-form, two diving attacks by *Hauptmann* Klaus Mietusch and *Oberleutnant* Paul Schauder took out a B-17 on each pass near Charleville. German radar had picked up the American bomber formations in sector 'Dora-Dora' and fighter pilots went to their planes. Heinz Knoke and his pilots in 5./JG1 took off and received news that 'heavy babies' were approaching over the sea. High over Luneberg Heath, Knoke's fighters were joined by other *staffeln*. Ground control gave him the latest enemy position report saying, 'Heavy babies are now in sector Siegfried-Paula.' 'On your left – watch for heavy babies to your left.' But Knoke could see no sign of them. Nerves were tense. Suddenly, he could make out vapour trails ahead. There they were! 'I see them,' said Specht. 'Victor, victor' base acknowledged. Specht dipped his left wing tip and JG1 peeled off for the attack. Messerschmitt after Messerschmitt followed him down. Knoke recalled:[14]

'After them!' The radio is babel of sound, with everybody shouting at once.

I check my guns and adjust the sights as we dive down upon the target. Then I grasp the stick with both hands, groping for the triggers with my right thumb and forefinger. I glance behind. Thunderbolts are coming down after us.

We are faster, and before they can intercept us we reach the Fortresses. Our fighters come sweeping through the bomber formation in a frontal attack. I press the triggers, and my aircraft shudders under the recoil.

After them!

My cannon-shells punch holes in the wing of a Fortress.

Blast! I was aiming for the control cabin.

I climb away steeply behind the formation, followed by my Flight. Then the Thunderbolts are upon us. It is a wild dogfight. Several times I try to manoeuvre into position for firing at one of their planes. Every time I am forced to break away, because there are two-four-five-or even ten Thunderbolts on my tail.

Everybody is milling around like mad, friend and foe alike. But the Yanks outnumber us by four or five to one. Then some Lightnings come to join in the mêlée. I get one of them in my sights. Fire!

Tracers come whizzing in a stream close past my head. I duck instinctively.

Woomf! Woomf! Good shooting!

I am forced to pull up out of it in a steep corkscrew climb, falling back on my old stand-by in such emergencies. For the moment I have a breathing space. I check the instruments and controls. All seems well. Wenneckers draws alongside and points down at four Lightnings on our left.

'After them!'

Our left wing-tips dip and we peel off. We hurtle down towards the Lightnings as they glisten in the sun. I open fire. Too fast: I overshoot the Lightning. I wonder what to do about my excessive speed.

But now a Lightning is on my tail. In a flash, I slam the stick hard over into the left corner. The wing drops. I go down in a tight spiral dive. The engine screams. I throttle back. My aircraft shudders under the terrific strain. Rivets spring from the wing-frame. My ears pop. Slowly and very cautiously I begin to straighten out. I am thrust forward and down into the seat. My vision blacks out. I feel my chin forced down on to my chest.

A Lightning passes me, going down in flames. There is a Messerschmitt on its tail.

'Got it!'

It is Wenneckers.

A few moments later he is alongside me again. I wave to him with both hands.

Congratulations!

'The bastard was after your hide,' he replies.

It is the second time Wenneckers has shot a Yank from off my tail. After we land I go up to Wenneckers to shake hands, congratulate him on his success, and – but Wenneckers interrupts before I am able to thank him:

'No need for you to thank me, sir. I only wanted your wife not to be made a widow by that bastard. Besides, think what a nuisance to the Flight it would have been to have had to dispose of your remains!'

All the mechanics standing around greet this remark with roars of laughter. I dig the lanky lad in the ribs. We go together into the crew-room. Meanwhile, the others have also been coming in to land. This is one day we all come back.

Output at both the Me 410 assembly plant at Augsburg and the Bf 109 plants at Regensburg was severely reduced for four months following the raids. Nearly 20,000 tons of bombs were dropped on the aircraft industries of the Reich during the week long offensive. Though 'Big Week' had undoubtedly caused widespread damage to the German aircraft industry, the cost had been high with 226 bombers alone being lost. Losses had to be made up and bad weather helped keep casualties down as missions were scrubbed as Larry Goldstein recalled.

Between 25 February and 2 March we had bad weather and an abort on 29 February when the target was Brunswick. We added new crews and new aircraft to our depleted forces. We were veteran fliers and not many crews made it to this point. We had two missions to go; would we make it?

Unfortunately, a decision taken by General Jimmy Doolittle would give Keirsted's crew their sternest test yet. Doolittle concluded that 'Big Week' had dealt the German aircraft industry a really severe blow and he felt confident the 8th AF could strike at Berlin in the very heart of the Third Reich. The German capital had been scheduled for attack by the Americans on 23 November 1943, but this had been postponed because of bad weather. The momentous day arrived on the morning of 3 March and nearly 750 bomber crews were briefed at bases throughout East Anglia. At Knettishall 'BJ' Keirsted and his crew were alerted to fly their penultimate mission and were assigned *Pegasus, Too* again. One more mission and they could go home to the USA. Larry Goldstein recalls:

We were called out to a very early briefing. When we entered the briefing room the chaplains were very visible. This made us uneasy and we thought it must be something big. When the route and the target were explained to us there was not one man in the room who thought he would be sleeping in his own bed that night. At the revetment while we waited to board our aircraft, all of us constantly watched for a flare shot from the control tower scrubbing the mission. It never came. As we waited for our chance for take-off I tuned to Radio Bremen, which spoke in English. Here we were waiting to take-off for a raid over Germany and Radio Bremen was saying 'American bombers are on their runways in England now, waiting to attack north-west Germany'. How did they know? We finally got into our take-off position and rolled down the runway. Take-off was at 0730 hours. Soon after forming, the group was off on its way. I sat at my radio with my headset tight on my ears waiting for the abort signal but it never came. We used a tricky route to the target and were to bomb and get the hell out quickly. The weather was our friend. It turned bad and the mission was finally scrubbed after our target was socked in.[15] That night I wrote in my diary, 'One more to go. God be good to me on the next one!' However, on Saturday 4 March the extra early briefing attended by all three chaplains – Jewish, Catholic and Protestant – gave added importance to the destination. The briefing was a duplicate of the day before: back to Berlin for the first daylight raid of 'Big B'. Berlin was the worst possible news that the *Worry Wart* crew could hear.

After briefing we hoped the mission would be scrubbed and we constantly watched the control tower for a red flare. It never came. We went though our pre-flight ritual as we always did, but this one had a special meaning. Take-off and assembly were normal but we were a little bit more on edge. Over France and into Germany we had flak and fighters but no damage or injuries. Just before we reached the target for the second straight day the entire force was recalled, the best possible news that I could hear over my radio. The fact that we were going home was sweet music to our crew when I told them of the recall but someone said, 'Can we take our bombs home on our last mission?' We all said, 'No, let's unload on any target'. We dropped out of formation to make our bomb run on a railroad marshalling yard on the German-French border despite 'Ace' Conklin's warning that the formation was getting father and farther away. We unloaded our bombs and began our climb back to the formation, which now was miles ahead of us. Our bomb bay doors were closing and according to Kent Keith they were closed. My job was to check those doors visually. I did. They were open. Several more attempts to close them were futile so BJ gave the order for Jack Kings to leave his top turret and hand crank them closed. We were at about 25,000 feet. I watched to make sure he did not pass out. Suddenly, there was a loud explosion. A Bf 109 must have seen a straggling Fort and fired several 20 mm shells at us. BJ and Clifford 'Ace' Conklin took evasive action by falling off to the right. Every time we came out of the clouds the German fighter was there with a couple of shots across our nose. We levelled off in the clouds before taking a head count. No one reported any battle damage or injury. Little did we know that we were severely damaged.

We finally broke out over France. Our navigator, Philip 'Bloodhound' Brejensky was unable to plot a course and I was asked to get a heading. Our 'G Box' was out of order so I contacted the RAF distress channel for help. God bless them because they answered immediately in the clear with a course for England but the Germans immediately jammed it. A friend of mine, Wallace Gross, was flying as the alternate radio operator. Normally he was radioman on Wendell Hulcher's crew, but somehow he was one mission behind his crew and volunteered to fly the ball position. He was not eager to be there for the whole flight and was sitting on the radio room floor. He was a crackerjack radioman and immediately set up another frequency. Again I transmitted and again the receiver message was jammed. We began to panic but Wallace put in a third unit and we received a heading, which I gave to the navigator. When we broke out of the cloud we were over the English Channel and saw the White Cliffs of Dover; it was the most beautiful sight that I could ever hope to see. At this moment I did not realise the importance of my radio work, I had been too scared at that moment, but my training had paid off.

The rest should have been routine but it wasn't. We were probably the last aircraft to land. Everybody had seen us get hit and figured that we were lost. As we came over Knettishall our landing approach was normal until touchdown ... no brakes. We went off the end of the runway and did a slow ground loop coming to a halt in a farmer's ploughed field. The fire trucks all rushed to our aid but they were not needed. The medics wanted to know if the radio operator was hurt. When someone on our plane said I was okay one of the firemen pointed to a tremendous hole in the right side of the radio room. It was then that I realised that we had flown like that for 3 hours. I was probably too scared to realise how dangerous it had been. I was fortunate not to be injured. The hole was where my head might have been, but somehow I had ducked and lucky for me that I did. Nevertheless, it was twenty-five and home. We walked away from *Pegasus, Too* and said our own individual prayers of thanks. A few days later BJ came into our quarters and ordered us all to accompany him to the base chapel and there we really became one crew that was thankful for our completing our missions without a major injury.[16]

Severe weather en route had resulted in the recall and while 219 B-17s hit targets of opportunity thirty crews in the 95th and 100th Groups defied the elements to drop the first American bombs on 'Big B'. Excited newspapermen and press photographers 'swamped' Horham, where the Group had come through without loss and at Thorpe Abbotts too. One of the 100th ships had failed to return and Robert J. Shoens, pilot of *Our Gal 'Sal'* in the 351st Squadron did not feel like celebrating because the pilot, Stanley M. Seaton, had been his best man at his wedding in May 1943. Like so many others Shoens, had become calloused. He had flown his first mission on 4 January, to the Ruhr Valley or 'Happy Valley' as bomber crews called it. 'As green crews we were fed all kinds of stories and the Ruhr valley spawned a number of them because of its heavy anti-aircraft batteries. For example, the flak was to heavy you could put your wheels down and taxi on it!' Seaton became a PoW.

Robert J. Thornton and the rest of his crew got back to Rougham after leaving their Fort at an airfield under construction about one-mile inland following the recall at Kiel and returning with a windmilling prop. The wing was badly damaged by the fire and the plane was no longer operable. Thornton believed that they were now 'out of the bombing business'. Indeed, on 5 March the B-17s were stood down while the Liberators attacked targets in France but preparations went ahead for another attempt on Berlin on 6 March and Thornton still had one more mission to do. He was awakened at about 0300 hours and told, 'Get to briefing.' His reply was something like, 'I have no ship, no equipment; you have the wrong guy.' Wrong again. This was a maximum effort and every plane that was flyable was to participate.

> I was told that a composite group had been made up and I was part of it. This was to be my twenty-fourth mission. My crew, which had a great deal of combat experience, was split up and the ship [ironically called *Li'l Opportunity*] and crew [Lieutenant C. E. Johnston] that I was assigned to were foreign to me. All the equipment was assembled in a hurry. I was given a parachute harness and made the mistake of not adjusting it properly. Our job was to lead the composite group over 'Big B'.

At Knettishall 'BJ' Keirsted's crew were 'out of the bombing business' now. As they lay comfortably in their beds in the 563rd Squadron area at four in the morning there was a call for briefing and it was a great thrill and some satisfaction to all of them to just turn over and go back to sleep. Not so for Bernard M. Dopko's replacement crew who now shared their hut since arriving in Suffolk via the southern ferry route. Keirsted's crew were among those who cast envious eyes at Dopko's much cherished leather boots, which had been custom-made in Africa. Dopko's neophyte crew would fly their inaugural mission in *Little Willie*, which was something of a veteran. In other huts on the base another thirty-two crews that were on the bulletin board in the operations room were rudely awakened from their slumbers. In the 561st Squadron area John W. McLaughlin and the crew of *Shack Job* and Augustine B. Christiani's crew of *Shack Rabbits* had their names called. Montgomery 'Monty' Givens and his crew of *Susy Sag Tits*, which had obviously escaped the attentions of the censors, and Lieutenant Clarence A. Gridley's crew of *Duchess of Dixie* were among those roused from their cots in the 562nd Squadron area. So, too, were Charles D. Wallace and the crew of *A Good Ship and a Happy Ship*. As Lowell H. Watts pulled on his clothes in the

125

inky blackness of early morning, he felt that perhaps he should have had a premonition of disaster.

> If not then, maybe the briefing should have left me anxious and worried. We were all set for our final combat mission, the mission that would relieve the strain of combat and give us at least a month at home with our friends and families. How we looked forward to going home again. That trip was almost within our grasp. Just a few more combat hours, that was all. But those hours were to be spent deep on Germany over a city the 8th had twice before tried to bomb without success. Berlin, 'Big-B', defended in full force by the *Luftwaffe* and hundreds of flak guns manned by some of the best gunners on the European continent.

At briefing the crews at Third Division bases learned that they had been assigned the Robert Bosch Electrical Equipment factory at Erkner, a suburb of Berlin. They would 'trail the parade', filling in behind five B-17 wings in the First Divison that had the Erkner bearing plant as their target. Liberators would bring up the rear. Over 800 fighters would fly escort, but experienced crews knew that they would be hard pressed to cover a column stretching for 60 miles in the sky. As he listened to the briefing details, Lowell Watts' premonition seemed to be coming true.

> On the previous recalled missions to 'Big B' a dog-leg route had been planned. There would be no bluff on this mission. We were to fly straight in and straight out. In addition to this grim prospect, we were to lead the low squadron of the low group of the second section of our combat wing. In short, our squadron would be the lowest and furthest back and, there-fore, the most vulnerable spot in the wing to aerial attack. As I walked out to the briefing room Major Goodman, our squadron commander, gave me a pat on the back and said his good wishes. He was assured that *Blitzin' Betsy* would be back on the line that evening and, if not, it would have cost plenty to bring her down.
>
> I walked under a faded white half moon through the pre-dawn dark-ness to our equipment room. The stars seemed cold and unfriendly. I had gradually grown calloused to many of the dangers of combat. Sure, the fighters and flak brought out the sweat and a tinge of nervous energy, but the thought of actually being shot down seemed like something that just wouldn't happen. Still, there was one thing certain, no chances would be taken on this last mission. I was deadly serious in checking over every detail of our plane and equipment. Still, I could show plenty of con-fidence when I told Harry Allert, our crew chief, to expect a first-class buzz job over his tent when we got back.
>
> The sun crawled up and peeked over the eastern horizon, casting a pink tinge on the fluffy, scattered clouds that seemed to forecast a clear day. Had we known, could we have seen a few hours into the future, we would have taken that pinkish tinge as a portent of the blood that was to be shed above those clouds. But then, it just looked like another day with better than average weather.

Our take-off was perfect. We slid into our formation position without trouble, the rest of the squadron pulling up on us a few minutes later. Everything was working perfectly: engines, guns, interphone. Every man on the crew was feeling well and in good physical condition. We were all set for this final and greatest combat test. I wondered then if all this was a harbinger of a smooth mission or the calm before the storm. The question was to be answered very definitely within a very short time.

While we were assembling the wing and division formations over Cambridge, the lead ship of our section of the wing aborted. Our group took over the wing lead. I felt better then; at least we weren't in the low group now. We crossed the English coastline and the gunners tested their .50 calibres. The Channel passed beneath us, and then the Dutch coast dropped under the wings and fell away behind us. We sailed over the Zeider Zee and were almost over the German border when the storm broke.

Over the Dummer Lake, fighters concentrated on the leading groups of the First Division and they were given a thorough going over.[17] Next, it was the turn of the Third Division and the unprotected 13th Combat Wing caught the full venom of the enemy fighter attacks. Robert J. Shoens, pilot of *Our Gal 'Sal'*, part of 'Fireball Yellow', which flew lead, recalls. 'Ahead of us, probably 10 miles, there appeared to be a swarm of bees; actually German fighters. Guesses ran as much as 200. They were coming right at us, and in a few seconds they were going through us. On that pass they shot down the entire high squadron of ten planes.' Major Albert 'Bucky' Elton, who was leading the 100th, looked up and was stunned to see six of the high squadron ships 'afire in formation, trailing long sheets of flame from their engines'. As the fighters leaped in again all six 'peeled out' while others were in 'obvious trouble'. The lead ship had its nose shot away and both pilots died in a fusillade of shells fired from head-on. The bombardier was tumbled out from the nose with a parachute and the ball turret gunner was also killed. The rest of the crew, who were on their twenty-fifth mission, baled out and were taken prisoner.

In 30 minutes, twenty-three Forts were shot down or damaged so badly that they were forced to ditch or crash-land on the continent. Eight of the ships lost came from the 95th and one from the 390th. The rest were from the 100th. Shoens continues:

When an airplane went down you had to shut out the fact that it took men with it. On this raid it became most difficult because so many were lost. One loss in particular was an example of this. The crew from our own barracks were flying off the right wing of our airplane. Suddenly, during one of the fighter passes, their entire wing was on fire. In the next instant there was nothing there. The fighters made two more passes and when it was over *Our Gal 'Sal'* was all alone. The last airplane from the group that I had seen flying was Captain Jack Swartout in the 351st Squadron lead flying in *Nelson King*, piloted by Lieutenant Frank Lauro. He was struggling along with about 6 feet missing from his vertical stabiliser and was the only other airplane from the squadron who came back with us.[18]

We saw another group ahead of us, so we caught up with it. The airplanes had an 'A' in a square on the tail, so they were from the 94th. We flew on to Berlin with them and dropped our bombs. The flak was heavy but over Berlin the sky was black. The target was on the south-east side of Berlin. For reasons we couldn't figure out, the group we were with chose to turn to the left and go over Berlin. Since we were not part of the group we decided to turn to the right and get out of the flak. When we did that a Germany battery of four guns started tracking. They fired about forty rounds before we got out of range. None of them came close because of the evasive action we had taken. Higher up and ahead of us we saw another group, so we climbed and caught up with it. It was also from our wing, having a 'Square J' on its tail [390th]. We flew the rest of the way home with them without further incident. It was still a beautiful day and with a chance to relax we began to wonder what had happened to our group. It couldn't be that we were the only survivors of 'Fireball Yellow'.

The 94th lost just one Fort and as luck would have it, it was *Li'l Opportunity*, the one Bob Thornton was a fill-in for.

We hit the target. The enemy opposition was extremely heavy. It was very unusual to see fighters in the flak field. They were in there that day. The sky was black from, flak bursts. The Germans threw everything they had at us. We lost many planes. After bombs away all you could hear on the headsets was 'Let's get the hell out of here'. We had no problems until about 1430 hours. We took a hit from flak. It knocked us out of control. We went into a dive, on fire. The hit was between the cockpit and the bomb bays. Very serious situation to say the least. We dropped 5,000–6,000 feet out of control. For some reason the ship levelled off just long enough for the enemy fighters to pounce on us. Everyone was scrambling to get out, except the co-pilot. He took a direct hit in the head from a 20 mm. No head. I left the plane at approximately 17,500 feet. The ship was an inferno. When my chute opened, the loose harness hit me between the legs. I was knocked out. I regained consciousness just as I started through the clouds. I knew that I was hurt, but not how bad. My groin area was completely numb. My left leg was dangling. As I came through the clouds a Bf 109 almost hit me. He was using cloud cover to get to the formations. When he saw me he banked around and throttled back. I thought he was going to shoot me as I hung in the parachute. He came up along side, took a good look, saluted and went back after the formation. Whew, what a scare. The wind at ground level was high, the ground was frozen and the field I landed in was ploughed. I was swinging and my left side took the brunt of the landing. My left ankle broke (both sockets), my left leg was immobile and, needless to say, escape was impossible. I later found that I was 13 km from the border of Holland, near a small town named Lingen. My story from here on for the next fourteen months would fill a volume. From being almost bled to death during my first night of captivity to lasting through an eighty-seven-day death march at the end.[19]

Lowell Watts had witnessed the decimation 3 miles ahead of him.

Their formation had tightened up since I last looked at it. Little dots that were German fighters were diving into formations, circling and attacking again. Out of one high squadron a B-17 climbed slowly away from its formation, the entire wing a mass of flame. I looked again a second later. There was a flash, then nothing but little specks drifting, tumbling down. Seconds later another bomber tipped up on a wing, rolled over and dove straight for the ground. Little white puffs of parachutes began to float beneath us, then fell behind as we flew on toward our target. Our interphone came suddenly to life. 'Enemy fighters, 3 o'clock level!' 'Enemy fighters, 1 o'clock high!' They were on us. One could feel the tension, the electrifying impulse that swept through each individual crewmember when the Fw190s sailed through our formation. We were now fighting for our lives, for the plane and the crew, for the formation and for the group upon which much of our safety hung. Should that formation be badly chewed up now, we'd catch a great deal of hell during the next 6 hours.

Roy Island, flying on my left wing, peeled off and headed west. His place was taken by another ship flown by a swell kid with three missions behind him. This fourth one was all he'd get. Another of our planes feathered an engine and began dropping behind, the target for several of the fighters. Two silvery streaks flashed past us. They were P-47s; our fighter escort had caught up with us. As the P-47s came in the Jerries dropped away, making only sporadic passes. Once again we could breathe a little easier.

The rest of the way in we had good fighter cover. Violent dogfights flared up ahead of us, forcing several of our fighters to drop their tanks and head for home. With their cover spread more thinly the Focke-Wulfs picked up the pace of the attack. They hit us hard twice before we reached the IP, taking several of our bombers out. Near the IP I looked off to the left where Berlin lay, just north of a heavy, low cloudbank. One bomb wing, the 13th, was making its run, just entering the flak. A dark, puffy veil that hung like a pall of death covered the capital city. It was the heaviest flak I had ever seen. It almost seemed to swallow up the bomber formations as they entered it, but somehow the planes kept coming out of the other side. True enough, there were losses. One ship blew up from a direct hit and three others dropped away from their formations, but still they went on to drop their bombs. It didn't seem like anything could fly through that, but there they were, Flying Forts sailing proudly away from the scene of their devastation. It wasn't too comforting to realise that we were the next group over the hellish scene.

Our group leader opened his bomb bay doors and we followed suit. However, the turn into the target was not made. Instead we were making a wide, sweeping circle to the left around the city. Our leading groups were already out of sight, heading for home. But still we swung on around Berlin. Precious seconds mounted into minutes, and still we flew without a bomb run. Tempers mounted and the radio crackled with curses and challenges to the men aboard our lead plane. 'Get that damn thing headed towards the target. What in Hell do you think this is? The scenery may be pretty, but we're not one damned bit interested in it. If you ain't got the guts to fly through that, let somebody else lead the formation.' And so went the radio challenges to a crew who, through incompetence or some error, had lost us precious time and muffed a lead responsibility that posed no peculiar problems other than courage and a clear head. Finally, north-east of our target, our lead ship turned toward the centre of Berlin. Our bomb doors came open and we settled down for the bomb run. This was it with a capital 'I'.

For maybe a minute or two we flew on, flattening out and tightening up the formation. Then the flak hit us. They didn't start out with wild shots and work in closer. The first salvo they sent up was right on us. We could hear the metal of our plane rend and tear as each volley exploded. The hits weren't direct. They were just far enough away so that they didn't take off a wing, the tail, or blow the plane up – they would just tear a ship half-apart without completely knocking it out. Big, ragged holes appeared in the wings and fuselage. Kennedy, the co-pilot, was watching nothing but instruments, waiting for that tell-tale story on some instrument that would indicate a damaged or ruined engine, but they kept up their steady roar, even as the ship rocked from the nearness of the hundreds of flak bursts.

In quick succession the crew reported from nose to tail. Everybody was okay, with four of the crew on walk-around bottles. Flak was coming up as bad as ever, but increasing in intensity. Above and to the right of us a string of bombs trailed out of our lead ship. Simultaneously, our ship jumped upwards, relieved of its explosive load as the call 'Bombs Away!' came over the interphone. [The bombs hit a residential district between the marshalling yards and the Oranienburg Canal, just east of the Heinkel plant at Annahof.] Our left wing ship, one engine feathered, dropped behind the formation, leaving only four of us in our low squadron. A few minutes later, it seemed like a long time, the flak stopped. We had come through it all and all four engines were still purring away. After getting through that, nothing should be able to knock us down.

A call came on the VHF radio from our low group. They still had their bombs. As if things hadn't already been enough of a nightmare, we still had another bomb run to make! Wittenburg lay off to the north-west, a big, easily spotted factory visible on its outskirts. We headed over it with our other group and took another blast of flak while they dropped their bombs. A big column of smoke began pouring out of the factory as the bombs hit. [They fell on to a textile works on the banks of the Elbe.]

By this time we were 31 minutes late. It proved to be an eternity for a good many men. Our fighter escort had long since headed for home and our other bombers were nowhere to be seen. There we sat, two lone and shot-up groups in the heart of Germany with no friendly fighters in the sky. I checked the ships in the formation. We had fifteen. We should have had twenty-one. Only three ships still flew in our low squadron where there should have been seven. A check of our low group showed only fifteen planes there, a total of thirty in all.

As we settled down into the routine of the trip home I began to feel a glow of happiness. We had come through hell without an injury on the crew. Shot up as we were, the plane was still flying smoothly. We had been over Berlin and had contributed to the carnage. Now we were heading home. There was an immeasurable relief in knowing that a target had been crossed for the last time, at least in our present combat tour. No longer would we worry about the alerts that meant fitful sleep before another mission. On into the west we flew, while the minutes turned to hours and the miles clocked beneath us in endless and fatiguing procession. The sun swung low into our faces, streaming through the windshield in a bright but eerie light. Off to our right we could see the much-bombed cities of Bremen and Hamburg. In a few minutes Holland would be beneath us.

The interphone came to life. 'Fighters at 10 o'clock high! Hey, they're '47s.' Oh, what a beautiful and welcome sight they made as they swooped over us, dipped their wings and wheeled away. With our first sight of them a terrific sense of relief swept away the horrible feeling of loneliness and danger that had ridden the skies with us all the way from Berlin. We were now protected and in 20 minutes would be over the English Channel. I began to think about the buzz job that I was going to give Harry. Also, I wondered how I'd word the cable back home to Betty when we landed. For a second a wave of extreme and indescribable happiness swept over me. Completion of our combat tour in the 'Big League' of aerial warfare seemed at hand.

For us, the mission was a lot nearer finished than we realised. The P-47s, after their first pass over us, turned tail for England. We didn't know then that they had been sent out looking for us. Not until they were just about to return for lack of gas did they spot us. But the sight of them had been reassuring. With only 15 to 20 minutes' flying time to the Channel, we felt we could fight our way through anything and we hadn't seen a Focke-Wulf for almost an hour.

I had just settled wearily back into my seat, relaxing from the first tenseness of seeing the fighters and subsequent relief of knowing they were friendly, when I noticed the high squadron leader was relaxing too much. He was flying back out of position with his squadron by what looked to be 400 or 500 feet. Things settled down for that last weary haul across Holland and the Channel.

The interphone snapped to life. 'Focke-Wulfs at 3 o'clock level!'

Yes, there they were – what seemed in a hurried count to be about forty fighters flying alone, just out of range beside us. They pulled ahead of us, turned across our flight path and attacked from ahead and slightly below us. Turrets throughout the formation swung forward and began spitting out their .50 calibre challenge to the attackers. Some of the Focke-Wulfs pulled up above us and hit us from behind. Most of them dived in from the front, coming in from 11 o'clock to 1 o'clock low to level, in waves so close that only every second or third plane could be sighted on by the gunners. Still they came, rolling, firing and diving away, then attacking again. As the first of these vicious attacks began to ease off, flame shot from Gridley's plane, flying our wing. Chutes began dropping from it one after the other. 'Those poor guys,' somebody said. 'They've got in twenty-one missions too.'[20]

The stimulation of mortal combat took hold as we settled down to see this last battle through to its bitter, bloody end. I had old *Blitzin' Betsy* pulled into the tightest possible formation and was cursing the high squadron leader, who was still trying to get into a decent position.

The fighters began their second attack. I saw only what was visible from the corner of my eyes. I was flying formation, as steady and as tight as humanly possible. The Focke-Wulfs swept through our formation, especially between our lead and high squadrons. Somebody would pay for the gap left up there by lax flying. They couldn't get between the lead squadron and us, so they began concentrating attacks on our ship, now the lowest one in the formation. Enemy fire swept the nose and front of the cockpit. Dust began flying and the smell of powder from the exploding 20 millimetres was strong and pungent in my nostrils. The second wave passed and the fighters queued up for still another attack. Two more of our planes had been badly damaged and were dropping in flames from the formation.

Brassfield called from the tail position: 'I got one, I got one!' Then, with almost the same breath, 'I've been hit.' No sooner was the interphone cleared from that message when one more ominous crackled into the headsets: 'We're on fire!' Looking forward I had seen a Focke-Wulf come at us from dead level at 12 o'clock. Our top and chin turret fire shook our B-17. At the same instant his wings lit up with the fire of his guns. Twenty-millimetres crashed through the nose and exploded beneath my feet in the oxygen tanks. At the same time they broke some of the gasoline cross-feed lines. Flames, which started here, fed by the pure oxygen and the gasoline, almost exploded through the front of the ship. The companionway to the nose, the cockpit and the bomb bays were a solid mass of flame. While this happened, gunfire from Ramsey and Kelley's forward turrets began tearing the attacking plane apart. Flames could be seen, and as the fighter fell apart, throwing pieces of metal in his path, he swept a few feet over our cockpit, obviously finished and out of control.

I took a last look at Clark's plane on my right wing and our only remaining ship in the squadron. Then the flames blotted out all vision. I called the crew to bale out and started to set up the automatic pilot to fly the ship after we cleared the formation. I looked over to Kennedy's seat for help. He had gone. Ramsey had left the top turret, now nothing but a furnace. I had been too busy to even see them leave the cockpit.

Emmett J. Murphy, navigator, also flying his twenty-fifth and final mission, takes up the story.

The fighters attacked us six abreast from the front and fired their 20 mm cannon as soon as they were within range. One Fw 190 actually passed within 50 feet of our plane after firing and continued on throughout the formation. Some of us believed we hit him because we saw smoke from his engine, but we could not be certain as it all happened extremely fast. During the frontal attack we were hit by 20 mm shells in both inboard engines, with one shell coming through the Plexiglas nose, just missing Edward Kelley's, the bombardier, head and mine and exploding in the oxygen tanks below the pilots' cabin. We were also attacked from the rear as Taylor, one of the waist gunners, called out over the intercom that he had been hit in the eye. Everything began to burn, so Kelley went out through the front hatch and I followed, getting my eyebrows singed as I went out.

Meanwhile, Lowell Watts was not yet ready to give up the struggle. He shoved the ship's nose down to clear the formation and reached for the autopilot with his left hand. Just as he touched the switches he noticed for the first time that the two inboard engines were flaming out and there was no hope of stopping them. Suddenly, *Blitzin' Betsy* jarred, shuddered, and went out of control. Watts continues:

I didn't know what had happened. It was not until I talked with Monty Givens that I learned we had come up under our lead plane, piloted by Captain G. C. Job. Apparently, we rolled over upside down after hitting the other plane. It was this collision, I am sure, that smashed our windshield and knocked most of the top of the cockpit off. Because of the fire I did not see what happened and thought we were gradually dropping below the formation. The tail damage, which was reported to have shredded the tail fin, probably damaged our elevators and sent the plane out of trim, causing it to crash.[21]

My safety belt had been unbuckled after the P-47 escort found us. I fell away from the seat but held myself in with the grasp I had on the control wheel. After a few weird sensations I was pinned to the seat, unable to move or even raise my left hand to pull off the throttles or try to cut the gas to the inboard engines. My left foot had fallen off the rudder bars while we were on our back. I couldn't even slide it across the floor to get it back on the pedal. Flames now swept past my face, between my legs and past my arms as though sucked by a giant vacuum.

Unable to see, I could only tell that we were spinning and diving at a terrific rate of speed. With all the strength I had, I pulled back on the wheel. Horrible seconds passed and the controls failed to respond. I knew that Sweeney could never have gotten out of that damned ball turret. I fought the controls with no response. The fire was too heavy to even bother trying to jump from the nose hatch or the bomb bay. My chute would have burned off in nothing flat. I pulled my side window open, gasping for air. Then the 'Gs' began easing off. I thought of trying to jump out of the side window, but at best that was a tight fit and a rough way to bale out. I was still worried about Sweeney. He couldn't possibly have gotten out yet. Then I noticed that there was no windshield, no top turret and no roof to the cockpit! At least I could bale out by jumping through the roof.

The ship felt like it was levelling off, but still the fire kept me from telling just what our real position was. I thought I'd fight it out a few seconds longer to give the men in the back a better chance; then jump. I fully expected to see the earth crashing through the front of the plane. Which would it be: that, or death from the flames that were searing past? I couldn't help but feel sorry for Betty and her baby boy. I remembered with a flash of pain that Don Taylor had called from the waist less than 10 minutes before we hit to tell us his boy was a year old that same day. Death in itself didn't seem so frightening as I had imagined it might be. That wild, eerie ride down the corridors of the sky in a flaming bomber was to haunt my memories for the rest of my life. But it wasn't just the terror of death that would sear these memories across my brain; it was the unending confusion and pain of a hopeless fight and the worry of nine other men who were my responsibility. Contrary to the usual stories, my past life failed to flash through my mind. I was too busy fighting to keep that life.

As those thoughts combined with the struggle to maintain control of the plane, I felt myself suddenly catapulted through space, spinning so fast I couldn't pull my arms and legs into my body for several seconds. Something jerked heavily past my face. It was my flak suit. Then my oxygen mask flew off, followed by my goggles and helmet. Automatically, I reached for my chest. Yes, there was the ripcord, right where it should have been. Until then I hadn't once thought about my chute. I jerked the ripcord and waited. Nothing happened. I jerked it harder. There was a soft swish, then a hard, sharp jerk and I was suspended in space, hanging in the most complete silence I had ever known. I anxiously looked up at the billowy white nylon of my chute, fully expecting it to be on fire. I knew a great relief when I saw it intact. Above me the formation roared on into the west, the battle still raging. I looked for our plane. An engine went by, still burning. A few pieces of metal wrinkled on down, and farther away I caught sight of the bright yellow dinghy radio falling through space. What a screwy time to notice that radio but, ever since, the sight of it has stayed in my mind more clearly than anything else. I could see nothing else of our plane. Up above me were three chutes. There should have been nine. Just three. Damn! Sweeney never had a fighting chance.

Off to the west our formation faded from sight. As the sound faded, a surge of anger and helplessness swept through me. I had flown a solid 8 hours of formation. I took no chances. Our gunners had taken their toll. We had taken at least two, probably three and possibly four, German fighters down with us. We had done everything possible, yet here

I hung on the shroud lines of a parachute. There were three more chutes, and what of the others?

A Focke-Wulf swept towards me in a slow, deliberate circle. Then he came straight at me. I thought: 'Damn, do these bastards shoot guys in their chutes?' The fighter flew on until he was almost on top of me. I tried to swing the chute, feeling very helpless. Then I noticed he was still turning, going on by me. A few seconds later he crashed. Not until then did I realise that a dead pilot had just flown past me. I looked down and saw three other planes burning on the ground.

With a start I suddenly realised that I wasn't just hanging in space. I was drifting and backwards at that. My burns, which I had begun to notice, were forgotten as I swung up, hanging to the shroud lines. The ground came up faster, faster. I jerked on the shrouds. In a very definite but unceremonious manner I had set foot upon the European continent. As I tumbled onto the wet, snow-covered earth, the wreckage of *Blitzin' Betsy* fell in scattered litter around me. With it fell the hopes, the faith and the efforts of everything I had trained, worked for and built during the past year and a half. The miles back to Colorado seemed farther than human comprehension as I looked helplessly into the western sunset.

Emmett J. Murphy continues:

After Kelley and I got out Kennedy followed. He had to beat out the fire on his chest pack before putting it on. I fell to about 7,000 feet before I pulled the ripcord. When I last saw our plane, while hanging in my harness, it was on its back in a steep dive, burning like a blowtorch. Its four engines were screaming and running away. Then it exploded, blowing Watts, J. B. Ramsey, engineer/top turret gunner and Ivan Finkle, the radio operator, clear of the aircraft, where they pulled their ripcords.[22] When I came down in the chute I sprained my ankle badly. There were a number of people who saw me and two Dutchmen helped me to Edward J. Kelley, the bombardier, who had come down perhaps 500 metres away. We were met there by Finkle, who said Ramsey was injured and Finkle said he was going to get Ramsey to a convent. We exchanged some clothing with the Dutchmen and they helped us to Schnoing's home where we were hidden in a chicken coop, behind the house. We hoped to get with the Dutch underground. That night we were brought into the house and Schnoing's wife gave us food and then two Dutch policemen came. They said that too many people had seen us so they had to take us. We went on bicycles some distance to a local jail. The local police chief had a doctor come and look at my ankle, which fortunately was not broken. He had a daughter who could speak English and she was friendly and explained the situation to us. Kelley and I spent the night in a small cold cell behind the police chief's house. The next day the girl brought us some food. That evening the Germans came and took us away to Assen. The next day they moved us to Leeuwarden, then to Amsterdam, Frankfurt, then *Stalag Luft I* at Barth, Germany.

Stanley Peterson, navigator in the crew of *The Saint* in the Snetterton Falcons at the rear of the 45th Wing, witnessed the wholesale loss of aircraft in the 388th and 452nd. As he says, 'You would have to see it to believe it.' (No fewer than thirty-five Forts in the Third Division were shot down on the mission.) Peterson looked down the shadows the bomber contrails created on this clear day and estimated it was about 20 miles in width. To him, it was so symbolic of the approaching storm of defeat closing in on the Third Reich. Although the targets were in the suburbs of the capital, Big B had been reached at last. He looked down on the city and was surprised at how all this was possible. They flew past Templehof, past lakes and woods and then they began their bomb run. It was the only time he could remember that they continued to climb during the bomb run, as the anti-aircraft fire was extremely heavy. Peterson thought that this was a day neither the men of the 8th Air Force nor Hermann Goering and his leader would forget. Goering had promised the Berliners and especially Hitler that the American bombers would not appear over the capital city.

Staff Sergeant James H. McMahon, tail turret gunner of *Baggy Maggy* in the Travelling Circus squadron in the high element and 'coffin corner', looked down on Berlin with hate in his heart. He should have been as 'nervous as hell' but he thought of his brother Thom in a PoW camp and all the other fellows he had seen go down.

The sky was perfect, no clouds, which meant that the German fighters were going to come up and that the flak would be accurate. I figured if I came back, OK, but if I went down it would be for Thom. Thinking this I felt glad. I believed that I was going to die and was fully prepared to die right over the target. I felt that what I was doing *was* the most important thing I had done on all my nine previous raids. All of the men felt the same way. We felt that if we could hit Berlin and survive we would probably survive to go home. Of course, this was rationalising but it worked for a lot of us. Well, all the way in to the target the flak was bad and the Jerry fighters sure played hell. Our fighters sure gave them hell too. I didn't get any shots at fighters till the target. I saw one Fw 190 shoot down one of our B-24s, which went into a dive and went straight down. Then all hell broke loose. The flak was terrible at different places going to the target and coming out. It was very heavy over Berlin itself. It looked like we had flown through a black thundercloud as we were going away from the target area. The plane shook and was buffeted like we were in air turbulence and you could hear the shrapnel hitting the ship like a tree branch whipping a metal roof. German fighters were every-where. The group behind us was catching hell with fighters and I got in about ten squirts at them.

We kept flying through the flak and made two runs on the target (I believe that we went directly over the centre of the city). It took 20 minutes. All this time I could see Berlin and there were B-24s and B-17s all over the place. Our bombs hit smack on the target and my heart bled for those damned Krauts down there. The whole lousy place was on fire.

Everything was blowing up. Well after that for a 100 miles I could see the fires and smoke. It looked like all Berlin was on fire. Boy did I feel good. I was laughing like hell for some reason. I guess it was because I was still there. After I got back to base (after squirting those Jerry fighters all the way home) I got to sleep and dreamed about Thom. All the time over the target I was thinking about him and Dad and Mom and Sis. Everything was going through my mind at once. I sure felt good because we knocked the hell out of them. We didn't even get a scratch on the plane either and that sure was something for the books. I saw many, many planes burning on the ground and pieces of aircraft flying past my turret from ships that had exploded somewhere ahead of us. I remember many chutes floating down and watching some ships going down in flames after head-on fighter attacks. Most of the planes exploded into three or four balls of fire like Roman candles before they hit the ground. Typically they fluttered to the ground like falling leaves or spiralled into a ball of fire or just dis-integrated. I saw many, many German fighters passing under my turret and sometimes just above it. It was like a fast speed movie. Lots of the time I didn't get a chance to squirt them. Fighters going away were the hardest to hit. Returning to base, we were on the same path as when we went in and the fires were still burning on the ground. Some of them were ours and some of them were theirs. I had a feeling of hate for the Germans and I wished that I could have gotten a clear kill. I felt that we had killed many Germans and that perhaps our raid would pay them back in some way for the comrades and innocent people they had killed. I hoped that that raid would terrorise them as they had terrorised us. It was the beginning of the end for them and they knew it. We lost six planes on this raid.[23]

When Robert J. Shoens got home to Thorpe Abbotts his crew discovered that they were one of only five crews to return.

To say the least, we were upset, as was everyone on the base. Lieutenant Colonel Ollen 'Ollie' Turner, the CO, met us as we parked the airplane. He was in tears. Most of the losses had been from his squadron. It was hard to take, but this was what we had been trained for.

Apart from *Blitzin' Betsy*, seven other Forts had failed to reach Knettishall. *Shack Job* and John W. McLaughlin's crew had been hit by flak over the target and they had to drop out of formation. Enemy fighters jumped them and the crew fought them off until they had to abandon the aircraft. All the crew baled out near Quakenbruck and they were made PoW. *A Good Ship and a Happy Ship* left the formation in the vicinity of Wuskenbruck and was hit by enemy fighters. Charles D. Wallace headed for Sweden and landed near Rinkaby. The crew returned to England on 30 September. Augustine B. Christiani and the crew of *Shack Rabbits* went down under fighter attacks and flak hits and the plane sunk in a swamp near Zwolle in Holland with the loss of five of the crew. Christiani and four others were captured. *Duchess of Dixie* was last seen on fire and going down. Clarence A. Gridley and two others survived, though the ball turret gunner later died in captivity. *Susy Sag Tits* was hit by the Abbeville Boys and went down in flames near Darien in Holland, where Monty Givens and eight others who survived were thrown into the town jail. There was still one other Flying Fort unaccounted for, but some crewmembers were sure that *Little Willie* and Dopko's crew had gone down on their first mission. Keirsted's crew were lying on their bunks in the barracks they shared with Dopko's crew when someone said that Dopko's crew had gone down. There was a mad scramble as twenty-five men reached for the brand-new equipment and, above all, Dopko's custom-made leather boots from Africa! But, as Larry Goldstein recalled:

> ... later that evening after chow one of our barrack members said, 'Guess who I saw having late chow – Dopko's crew'. They had made it back home on the deck and had landed at another base and had been trucked over. We were embarrassed. Each of us who had taken some piece of equipment attempted to put it back. Unfortunately, we could not remember where all the items went so they were just piled on one bed. When Dopko's crew walked into the barracks the quiet was astounding. Although one of his crew complained to the CO nothing ever came of it. It seems this was an accepted way of life.

The crew of *Little Willie* finally showed up at Knettishall, laughing and joking about their madcap trip home from Berlin after a propeller ran away and the supercharger on another engine went out by flak hits over the heart of Big B. The stricken ship fell out of formation and was immediately attacked by two German fighters. Tail gunner Robert Haydon Jr returned fire and they broke off the attack almost as soon as it started. Then the fun began. To keep from being attacked again, Dopko pointed *Little Willie*'s nose to the ground and screamed down to 50 feet, where he levelled off and started dodging rooftops They skimmed chimneys down main streets of German towns and never more than 100 feet off the ground. They roared between two church steeples and went down the main road of one place so low that William G. Kelly the bombardier yelled to Dopko, 'Look out for the curb'. They whistled and waved at a German girl cycling down the street of one town and finally shot up all their ammunition at the German defences on the Dutch coast. 'Coming over another city we were flying along a road and came upon a man riding in a cart,' said Lieutenant Glenn R. Cederstrom, the navigator. 'When he saw us he jumped and dived into a ditch. If he hadn't we would have knocked him off, we were that low.' Approaching a German machine-gun emplacement, the crew spied a soldier running to his gun position. Then, apparently thinking better of it, he ducked quickly to the cover of a nearby ditch. Every member of the crew joined in shooting up German defences. Thoughtfully, Dopko rocked his big plane from side to side to give his gunners better view for strafing. *Little Willie* hobbled across the last stretch of the North Sea at the height of 10 feet and made it back to East Anglia.[24]

A record sixty-nine bombers and eleven fighters and 686 fully trained bomber aircrew were dead, missing or in captivity. Of the returning bombers,

316 suffered battle damage, 102 of them seriously.[25] The Snetterton Falcons returned without a single bomber missing. Stanley Peterson concludes:

> I can still hear the happy yells of our crew as England appeared and our air base came in view. Little did we realise that in another 36 hours our group and wing would lead the 8th back in the air heading east again to 'Big B' and again one more time another 24 hours after that.

All Bomb Groups were stood down on 7 March before the daylight offensive resumed on the 8th when 623 heavies escorted by 891 fighters were sent to bomb the VKF ball-bearing plant at Erkner in the suburbs east of Berlin. At noon JG1 were ordered into action. *Oberleutnant* Heinz Knoke and his fellow pilots took off on the first of two sorties and made frontal attacks on a Fortress formation north of his airfield. Knoke shot one bomber down and left a second in flames, but he could not watch it crash because he was fully occupied with several Thunderbolts trying to get on his tail. The P-47s shot down *Feldwebel* Veit and his body was found in a cornfield. Knoke shot down another Fortress on his second sortie during the first frontal attack when he aimed at the cockpit. He believed that both pilots were killed and the controls put out of action because the B-17 crashed without any sign of fire. Knoke's fighter was hit by the Thunderbolts and though he was forced to land on one wheel he got down safely. Just over 530 heavies got their bombs away over the German capital, which once again was heavily defended. The leading Third Division lost twenty-three B-17s, including one in the Bloody Hundredth.[26] Worst hit was the 45th Wing in the van, which came under mass enemy fighter attack and had sixteen bombers shot down, five of them in the 388th. The First Division lost five B-17s to fighter attacks and flak.

Heinz Knoke, meanwhile, had tried to summon up a reserve aircraft for a third sortie but it was destroyed in a low level strafing attack and two of his mechanics were seriously wounded. Undeterred, Knoke was assigned another fighter and he and Specht, accompanied by *Oberfeldwebel* Hauptmann and *Feldwebel* Zambelli as their wingmen, took off to attack Liberators over Luneberg Heath. Though nine B-24s were shot down the quartet did not add to the score because they were bounced by P-47s and in the ensuing dogfight the two wingmen were shot down, and Specht and Knoke escaped only with great difficulty. Gunners aboard the bombers claimed sixty-three enemy fighters shot down and the escorts a further seventy-nine, but only twenty-seven *Luftwaffe* fighters were lost. Zambelli, who played the accordion, had been in the middle of playing a lively dance tune when the alert came and Knoke returned to find the accordion still lying on the table and to receive news that Wennekers was in hospital after being shot down and seriously wounded. Specht's request that 5./JG1 be withdrawn from combat temporarily was rejected. It became very silent in the crewroom as Knoke and Jonny Fest sat alone in their two armchairs.[27]

Berlin was attacked again on 9 March by just over 360 B-17s, while 165 Liberators visited Hanover, Brunswick and Nienburg. Weather conditions kept the *Jagdwaffe* on the ground and for once the enemy fighters were noticeable by their absence. The 800 escort fighters returned without claiming any enemy fighters, while eight bombers were all lost to flak. By now most crewmembers, Stanley Peterson in the Snetterton Falcons among them, had flown three 'Big B' bomb runs in four days. Needless to say, on the evening of 9 March the bomber crews slept undisturbed for 15 hours and the crew of *The Saint* awaited its assignment for number twenty-five, the final mission. The young navigator would not have long to wait.

Smaller scale raids on targets in France and Germany followed and on 1 April 246 B-24s headed for the chemical works at Ludwigshafen. However, thirty-eight B-24s veered off course and bombed a Swiss town in error. The incident led to America having to pay the Swiss thousands of dollars in reparations. It was not until 8 April that the cloudy conditions abated and allowed the 8th Air Force to assemble in force. Thirteen combat wings consisting of 644 bombers were dispatched to aircraft depots throughout western Germany. Of the thirty-four heavies shot down, thirty were Liberators, of which eleven were from the 44th and six were from the 466th. The majority of the losses came down in the area of Brunswick due to persistent fighter attacks. On Easter Sunday, 9 April, 104 Liberators headed to the aircraft assembly plant at Tutow. Missions were being mounted with alarming regularity, but each one that a crewman returned from, especially if they were of short duration, increased the chances of completing a tour. On 10 April Sergeant Louis J. Torretta, a B-17 tail gunner in the 447th, was awakened at 0230 hours at Rattlesden to fly his twenty-first mission.

> We were briefed and boy was I surprised when I saw the ETR or the time of return. We took off at 0630, went into France and over to Belgium. We were briefed to bomb a plant but the weather was bad over that target and we found an airfield at Dietzshaven in Belgium to bomb with ten 500 lb demolition bombs from 18,000 feet. We made a direct hit. The temperature was 18 degrees below. We landed at 1230. It was a nice short mission. I wished I could get more like it but my twenty-second mission next day was an oil plant in Poland. We took off at 0530 and landed at 1700 – 11½ hours. Wow, what a ride! Again the weather was against us and we had to bomb the secondary target, which was an airfield at Airunwalde at Stettin in Germany. It was set out in the woods and we had a heck of a time finding it until the Germans tried to hide it with a smoke screen and that just gave it away. We had a good score. We ran into about twelve Bf 109s and we sort of took a beating. We lost Pauling's crew, who were very good friends of mine. About three weeks later we heard they had landed on the small island of Bornholm just off of Sweden, which was occupied by the Germans. Five out of ten escaped to Sweden and they were returned to us. The other five were never heard from again. They were either killed or taken prisoner.

The next day over 900 bombers attacked targets throughout Germany supported by over 800 fighters at a high cost of sixty-four Liberators and B-17s missing. Losses were always hard to stomach and it was no different for replacements like Wilbur Richardson, a gunner who had grown up in Long Beach, California, and who arrived at Rougham on 11 April with three other crews. 'Later in the Mess Hall we learned that four crews failed to return from Poznan, Poland. Such news to hear on arrival. For the month of April twenty-five crews were lost. What would our fate be?' Another gunner, Forrest S. Clark, in the Flying Eightballs, who went to Bernburg that same day, could have commiserated with Richardson. For him, Bernburg stands out above all others as an overwhelming feeling of disgust with war.

There's nothing heroic about war. War is disgusting and war in the air is no exception. The air war was a dirty business and aircrews, all good and honourable men, often went to their deaths, not only because of enemy fire, but also because of errors and mishaps in their own planes. I never went on a mission without this being brought home to me forcefully and brutally. I even got so I felt sorry for the enemy pilots that went down and the enemy crews. On many missions I saw both our men die and the enemy in the same fight. I recall sitting in −30 degree temperatures at altitude seeing our planes and those fighters of our enemy bursting in flames and going down and thinking to myself in the next instant; would I follow them in some blinding explosion? I would sweat under my flight suit and my hands would get wet from sweat, the sweat of fear, and a bone chilling type of fear. Some men vomited into their oxygen masks from fear and sickness and this could be dangerous and fatal by cutting off their oxygen supply. However, the war was turning slowly in our favour.

There was a little thing I did on each mission. One of our waist gunners had the habit of going off to one side of our dispersal area and when he thought he was far enough so there was no danger of fire he would light a cigarette. The next thing he would do was to pray. Once I found him doing this I started to pray. Most people don't think of heroes as prayers. But we were no heroes and prayer comes easy to those who are familiar with violent death in the skies. The images of that burning bomber are deeply burned into my memory and every time that image comes from deep inside me I answer it by praying.

Therefore this incident over Bernburg, Germany, is a frightening lesson for all of the sickening effects of war. It was a war fought in the skies at 1 or 2 miles above the earth where friends die in an instant and sometimes prayer is the only comfort, if any comfort there can be.

We had one strong and fierce attack by seven Bf 109s straight on and through our formation. You could see the enemy gunfire ripping through our group. As fearsome as this was, it was nothing compared to what happened to one of our own planes and crews. Flying near us in the formation, we saw one of our bombers catch fire. I saw the plane burning and then the tail blew off. What was left of the plane did a loop before exploding right in front of us. It was a miracle that we were not taken down with it. It was a sickening sight. Three chutes were reported coming out of the burning plane before it exploded. Our co-pilot Bill Tinsman said he saw one burning body go dangling through space with no chute. In many cases crewmembers did not have time to attach their parachutes, or forgot them in their panic to get out of burning planes. Many of them jumped to their deaths this way. The cockpit of the burning bombers was filled with flames and the crew never had a chance to survive this inferno. It was later said that the fire and explosion was because the bomber dropped its bombs through its bomb bay doors. Contact with bomb bay doors was enough to ignite high-explosive bombs and there were other reports of similar incidents. I knew the crew of that doomed bomber and remember them to this day. Some had been with us a few hours before back at the base, playing cards and singing in the barracks and then they were gone, burning in the skies over Germany. Such was war. There were no heroes, only the lucky ones, only those who survived and carried the guilt to their graves. Years later my co-pilot told me, 'I am not a religious man but I still pray and remember those who didn't come back.'

On 18 April well in excess of 770 bomber crews were awakened for all-out raids on targets in the Berlin area. Some, like Ben Smith in 'Chick' Cecchini's crew in the Hell's Angels Group, were flying their first mission, while others, like Sergeant Louis J. Torretta at Rattlesden where they were awakened at 0500, were flying their twenty-third mission. Ben Smith recalls:[28]

It was common to refer to a group by its place name – Molesworth, Grafton Underwood or Kimbolton – when conversing with crews from other groups. They all had euphonious names like Thorpe Abbotts, Chelveston, Steeple Morden or Snetterton Heath. I suppose this is why we liked to say those names. Somehow they added class to a pedigree .... My group had taken its name from one of the group's original airplanes. The old Fort helped make the group famous by becoming the first heavy bomber to reach the twenty-five-mission mark. Our leaders, even the generals, were all quite young. It was nothing to have bird colonels in their twenties ... the average age of the flight crews was about twenty. When a flier had attained 28 or 30 years, he was usually called Pop. We once had a Boston Irish toggelier called 'Pop' Lovett. He was only 32 but seemed ancient to us ... there was one thing different about our show. The brass didn't send us off to some bad places like Leipzig or Magdeburg. They led us there. On the really rough missions a general would be in the lead plane of each squadron. Really, it was necessary to have somebody in charge who knew the overall plan of the mission. This could not be done from an armchair on the ground. We respected these men. They were brave, intrepid leaders, sharing all the dangers and rigours of aerial combat with us. If we had any complaint about them at all it was that they were too valiant. Many times they went on to the target when it would have been better to turn back.

Cecchini's squadron had been alerted to fly the Berlin mission the night before. On the night of 17 April as Ben Smith looked up and down the row of bunks, there were many cigarettes glowing in the dark. There was not much sleep going on. In the early hours of the morning the doors to the Nissen hut opened and a cheery soul named 'Fluke' entered, switched on the lights and started calling off the crews who were to fly the day's mission. He yelled 'Cecchini's crew' and Ben Smith's heart sank. He felt like a condemned man.

We donned our flying coveralls, heated suits and boots, and headed to the mess hall down the road where the cooks were putting on a mission breakfast. The chefs were very solicitous, seemingly jovial. We could have pancakes, eggs sunny-side up or any way we wanted them. Sort of like, 'It's your last meal. You can have what you want.' To me it seemed a somewhat macabre occasion, and I found their jollity very disquieting and out of place. I could eat none of the breakfast anyway. Even to this day I have butterflies before breakfast.

All the crews, officers and non-commissioned officers were briefed together. The radio operators were also given a separate briefing at which time they received a canvas packet with coded data called a 'flimsy'. In the main briefing hall the target remained covered until the Intelligence Officer came in. He was a dapper individual, sporting a moustache and quite hearty in manner for a good reason: he didn't have to go. These intelligence officers were non-flying personnel with some useful information and a lot that was useless.

His first move was to peel back the cover from the map, an act that was always met with a loud groan from the assembled crews. They were a lively bunch, and time had to be allowed for them to get over the initial shock, sound off and 'cuss' a little while. After a time they subsided, and he began.

We could see that the red lines pinned on the map went deep into Germany. The target was the Heinkel plant at Oranienburg in the suburbs of Berlin. We were told that we could expect heavy fighter opposition, with flak at the target described as 'intense'. In other words, the target was heavily defended.

We could see from the diagram that we were flying Tail-end Charlie in the high squadron. There would be a lead squadron, a low squadron and a high squadron.

Catholic boys were receiving the Sacrament from the priest, Father Skoner. He was very popular with Protestants and Catholics alike, with none of the phoney piety often found in clergymen, just one of the fellows. Chick's crew were Catholic, Protestant and Jewish. We were descended from Irish, Italian, English, Scots, Hungarian, Jewish and German immigrants, truly an all-American bunch. Chick weighed over 200 pounds and had been a policeman in New York State. Italian to the core, he was red-haired and looked like a big Irish cop. He wore a perpetual grin and was quite a womaniser. The boy had a lot of charisma and personal charm. We adored him. . . . We were typical of the men who flew in the great bomber formations.

The briefing was over. We got up and started out. We climbed onto lorries and headed out for the hardstands where the Forts were parked. The ground crews swarmed over our B-17 getting it ready. The armourers were arming the bombs in the bomb bay. It was still pitch dark.

We put our machine-guns into their casings and attached the gun belts. When this was done, we went to the dispersal tent and lay down on the canvas cots, which were there for that purpose. We tried to log a little sack time before 'Start Engines'; the signal was a flare from the control tower.

These quiet moments in the dispersal tent were always the worst part of the mission for me. I was always afflicted with an unbearable sadness at this time.

I can still hear the clanking coughs of the aircraft engines as they struggled manfully in the damp mist and then caught up. We were on board and soon taxiing out in trail until we reached the end of the runway. Every 30 seconds a Fort would gun its engines and hurtle down the runway into the darkness. Finally, it was our time. We always sweated at take-off as we were heavily laden with gas and bombs.

We climbed through the mist on a certain heading until we reached a predetermined altitude. At 10,000 feet Chick told us to go on oxygen. Thereafter, we had periodic oxygen checks with each position checking in. We learned the value of this on a later mission when the ball-turret gunner did not check in. We pulled him out of the turret unconscious and almost dead. His hose had become disconnected.

At the appointed altitude the aircraft orbited around an assembly beacon, a ground installation emitting a signal. Each pilot knew his place in the formation from briefing. Take-off was in the same order. It remained only to locate the squadron leader or assembly ship. He would be firing a combination of flares like red-green. When the pilot saw his colour, he joined up, tacking onto the leader in his proper slot while continuing to orbit. When all the aircraft were in the combat box, it headed out towards the North Sea or English Channel, depending on where the mission was going. This is an oversimplification of the procedure, but it's basically how it was done.

During all this time there was complete radio silence, as the German interceptor stations were monitoring constantly. Looking back, I doubt if we ever fooled them. The planners would go to extreme lengths to conceal the mounting of a mission, but I doubt whether they could conceal something of that magnitude. I imagine the Germans had ample notice from their own agents in England of every mission we flew. I don't remember their ever being asleep when I visited Germany.

So far, I was fine. It was a bright, clear day marred only by the contrails of the bombers ahead of us in formation. I can recall a certain amount of exhilaration and pride. The great battle formations were something to see! As far as the eye could see there were B-17s, some of them olive drab Fs; others, the new silver Gs.

The scene was innocuous enough. Nothing about it even hinted of danger.

A formation of P-38s slanted overhead adding to my feeling of security.

It seemed that we had been flying for hours without incident. We chatted a little on the intercom until Chick told us to shut up.

I heard it before I saw it. Whomp-Whoosh. Simultaneously, the bombardier shouted, 'Flak, 12 o'clock. Christ, look at it!'

By then we were at the IP and turning on the bomb run. A rush of cold air blasted the radio room as the bomb bay doors came open.

The plane began to lurch and reel with the continuous explosions.

Now I could see it. Oily, black bursts with crimson blossoms in the centre. Everywhere. There were literally thousands of bursts as far as the eye could see.

I was throwing chaff out of the chute. Chaff [called 'window' by the British] was shredded tinfoil to confuse the German anti-aircraft radar and aiming devices. I couldn't see that it did any good at all. They had our range perfectly. It did keep me occupied, however.

Just before Bombs Away a moving shadow caused me to look up through the open radio hatch. A bomber had moved directly above us. Horrified, I was looking directly into his bomb bay. I called the pilot, and we slid over in the nick of time.

The bomber lurched as the bombs went away. I stood up in the door of the bomb bay to see if the bombs had all gotten clear. As soon as I did, a jagged piece of shrapnel sliced the command radio set in two and struck me directly in the chest. I was wearing a metal flak vest, which was all that saved my life. It spun me around and stunned me momentarily. I saw that I was bleeding. A piece of spent metal had lodged in my neck, and this was where the blood was coming from. I was not badly hurt and felt no pain at all, but I had had a close shave.

A great column of smoke was coming up as we turned away from the target and headed for home. I felt that the worst was over, but we were in for some more excitement. The group strayed over Braunschweig [Brunswick], which was not on our itinerary and got flakked again. This was not barrage flak. These gunners were really good, and they were shooting at US. It was a chilling sight to see flak bursts directly ahead of us marching toward our bomber. At the last minute Chick would take violent evasive action, and the last burst would explode beneath us. The formation was wallowing all over the sky. Not only were we dodging flak, but also we were trying desperately not to collide with other aircraft. We were finally out of their range and glad to be so.

As a youngster, I had stood on the edge of dove fields at daylight on frosty mornings and watched the doves coming to feed. They came in at great speed, dipping and darting, and were laughingly called 'blue whistlers'. As soon as one was spotted, everyone had a go at him, but sometimes he made it through and flew on out of the field. It was a sad sight when one of those proud, beautiful birds crumpled up and pitched to earth. As the B-17s flew through the maelstrom of flak, I knew exactly how that poor dove must have felt. The guns were larger, and so were the birds, but it was the 'dove field' just the same.

From this first mission on I never again had the feeling that we were out of danger until my feet were solidly placed on terra firma.

Eventually, we crossed the enemy coast and started letting down from altitude. It was a relief to take off the oxygen mask and relax a bit. I ate a Clark bar and felt better at once. We had been on oxygen for about 8 hours.

The hydraulic system was damaged; so we knew we were going to have some problems getting down. Fortunately, we were using the long runway. We touched down; and, after slowing a bit, Chick headed her off the runway onto the grass. We circled to the right, kept circling, slowing gradually; and finally she gave up the ghost and stopped.

We got out and looked her over. It was unbelievable. We had taken a savage mauling, and she was one more lacerated lady. That morning our bomber had been a lovely girl without blemish. The ground crews could do wonders with a shot-up B-17, but they had their work cut out for them with that one. Sometimes when one was shot up too badly, they made her a 'hangar queen' and cannibalised parts off her. I remember the ground crew laid some rueful looks on us.

Lieutenant L. L. Holdcroft's crew [ironically flying *The Road Back*] did not return from the mission, the only casualty from our squadron. The mission would have wound up their tour of operations. We learned later that they were able to parachute safely and were interned as PoWs. Holdcroft wrote me later that they arrived at the *Stalag Luft III* on the same day that the Great Escape took place. The camp was in turmoil as the American and Britisher prisoners were still at large.

The first thing we did after the mission was to go back for debriefing or interrogation. Each of us was given a hefty shot of booze to take the edge off; then the Intelligence Officer interviewed our crew, making inquiry about missing aircraft, whether parachutes were seen, the intensity of flak along the route and at the target, a description of enemy aircraft encountered, and a welter of other subjects.

The alcohol really got to us fast. I got a few extra shots from some of the others who did not drink. We had been on oxygen for a long time and were very susceptible. This caused us to exaggerate greatly, but the Intelligence Officer dutifully wrote down everything we reported. At one of the debriefings later, we reported some striped flak. It was duly noted.

Louis J. Torretta had a very rough ride as they ran into 'a hell of a lot of flak' and fighters and the navigator was hit twice by flak but they all made it back safely, albeit with about twenty holes in the ship. Torretta hoped that he never got to go to the 'Big B' again. His twenty-fourth mission followed on 19 April and the target was Lippstadt.

We were awakened at 0130 and I really expected a long one again but I was surprised to find it was not so bad. We took off at 0630 and landed at 1300. Only 6½ hours. It was a swell mission and the weather could not have been any better. We could see the ground all the way over and back. We saw the town of Dunkirk and Brussels very clear. We had flown over these towns many times before, but this was the first time we could see it so clearly. We were able to see the target clear and we made a direct hit. We encountered no opposition to speak of and no one was hurt but I sure was scared when the lead ship said we had to make another run. I remembered what happened to us one time before when we had to make a second run in the target. We really got shot up.

Mission No. 25 on 20 April was to V-1 rocket sites and our bombing altitude was 12,000 feet. This raid was really a 'lulu'. We were awakened at 0700 and told to go and eat breakfast because we were on the alert. So we ate and reported to the briefing room at 1230. We were briefed and the take-off time was at 1630. We had a very nice trip. We saw some flak but it was not bad. It was really a mixed up affair. They had us all scattered around. We landed at 2100 and it was getting pretty dark. We had to be on the alert until we hit the ground as the Germans had a habit of attacking as we were getting ready to land so being as it was getting dark we had some of our fighters pick us up as we came into our field. We saw a few of them get into a fight with our boys but our group was not hit. A B-24 outfit not far from us was hit pretty bad. The Nazi planes hit and wrecked seven of them as they were making their approach for a landing. I wish they hadn't raised the quota of missions. I would have finished today.

On 21 April I flew my twenty-sixth mission when the target was the marshalling yards at Hamm. We briefed at 1200 and we took off at 1530. It was a very nice trip and we had a very good fighter escort. We encountered some very mean flak. We lost Gilleran[29] and some very good friends of mine. Flak got their ship and they were reported as all having jumped. Then their ship blew up. The bombing was very good and on this raid and we had a pretty fair trip as far as our crew was concerned. We landed at 2140. I decided that each one of five extra missions I would dedicate to someone. This one I gave to my father as I was sure he rode with and watched over me on every mission.

On 22 April the American heavies were late taking off for a raid on the marshalling yards at Hamm. Seven B-17s, including *Thru Hel'en Hiwater* and *Nero*, of the Hell's Angels Group and *Just Nothing* in the 91st and four B-24s were shot down, although fighters claimed twenty-two *Luftwaffe* aircraft for the loss of fifteen of their own. On the homeward trip the *Luftwaffe* was on the look out for stragglers that had been hit and damaged by flak at the target. One was the aptly named B-24 *Flak Magnet* in the 458th, flown by Lieutenant George N. Spaven Jr. At the target an anti-aircraft burst had peeled back a large section of top-fuselage and its skinning now flapped wildly in the slipstream while, inside, fuel spewed from three ruptured main fuel cells. The crew worked feverishly to stem the fuel leaks, jettison the 500 lb bombs still aboard and keep *Flak Magnet* airborne, but they could not prevent the crippled Liberator from dropping out of formation. They were now completely alone and a target for any *Luftwaffe* fighters. Major Heinz 'Pritzel' Bär, CO II./JG1, took off from Stormede in his Fw 190A-7 'Red 23' with

Oberfeldwebel Leo Schumacher, a veteran who had been in action since Heligoland Bight in 1939, flying wingman to intercept the badly damaged Liberator. Bär saw the bombs fall from the bomber and dived on it from 5 o'clock. (He expected return fire from the tail turret but Herman Peacher had baled out when fuel had engulfed his turret and by now none of the guns aboard *Flak Magnet* were manned.) Bär looked through his Revi reflector sight and blasted the bomber with cannon and machine-gun fire and an engine burst into flames. Spaven tried doggedly to keep the plane airborne, but the odds were just too great. From the shattered cockpit, Spaven and his co-pilot Robert L. Zedeker could see Bär's Fw 190 peeling off to the right as he swept round for a frontal attack. Releasing his seat harness, Zedeker hoisted himself clear, yelling at Spaven, 'Let's get the hell outta here!' Bär's next burst shattered the instrument panel, killing Spaven in the process. The back of his armoured seat saved Zedeker and he scrambled out of the doomed bomber. Lieutenant Peter Kowal, the navigator, followed. *Flak Magnet* dived steeply, exploded and crashed near Hoetmar. The victorious Bär landed at Stormede to a rapturous welcome. He climbed out of his Fw 190 and was helped from his flying suit to celebrate his 200th victory.

The eleven B-24 groups were still over the North Sea at the official blackout time of 2138 hours. Unbeknown to the crews, they were being chased by Me 410A-1 *Hornisse* (Hornet) intruders of II./KG 51 *Edelweiss* led by Major Dietrich Puttfarken based at Soesterberg, Holland, who had orders to infiltrate the returning bomber stream.[30] The attackers were aided in their approach by the American formation, which turned on their lights as darkness descended. It was so dark that the Hornet crews incorrectly identified their targets as RAF Halifaxes! There was no mistaking the outcome, however. One of the first victims was *Cee Gee II*, of the 453rd, which was credited to *Leutnant* Nommining of II./KG51, who blasted the Liberator 15 miles off the east coast. Lieutenant James S. Munsey, whose bomber was named in honour of his daughter Carole Geane, and his co-pilot, Robert O. Crall, sacrificed their lives so that their crew and companions might bale out from the flaming torch. As *Cee Gee II* crossed the coast the fuel tanks exploded, blowing three crewmembers out, while five others were able to jump. Since the interphone system was gone, Munsey was unable to determine whether all his crew had jumped. With complete disregard for his own safety, he remained at the controls until he no longer had sufficient height to bale out. Crall, although ordered by Munsey to 'get his butt out of the airplane', said, 'Well I'm staying with it too'. Both pilots died and they share a common headstone at Cambridge Madingley cemetery.[31]

In an instant, a 448th B-24 flown by Lieutenant Cherry C. Pitts fire-balled, plunged into the sea and vanished beneath the waves with all ten crew. In the night's confusion, twelve Liberators crashed or crash-landed in Norfolk and Suffolk as a result of KG51's actions. Thirty-eight American crewmen were killed and another twenty-three injured.[32] Just who shot the two Me 410A-1s down is open to conjecture. One was claimed shot down by Staff Sergeant Raymond G. Chartier, the tail gunner aboard *Peggy Jo* (before the Hornisse shot down the B-24). Staff Sergeant Lewis Brumble, left waist gunner aboard

Last Card Louie of the 458th, flown by Lieutenant H. W. Wells, was credited with the destruction of a Me 410 south-east of Rackheath airfield near Norwich. This Me 410 was reported to have fallen on its right wing and dived straight into the ground on fire followed by a large explosion when he hit the ground. The nose gunner and a waist gunner aboard a 389th Liberator flown by Lieutenant P. T. Wilkerson also claimed the destruction of an Me 410 in the same area. Local eyewitnesses say the Me 410A-1 broke away, racing seawards as Wilkerson's B-24, its engines and fuel tanks riddled, caught fire and spiralled out of formation from about 3,000 feet. Six of the Liberator crew perished. The Me 410 flown by *Oberleutnant* Klaus Kruger and his radio operator, *Feldwebel* Michael Reichardt, crashed and exploded in a field at Ashby St Mary. Uncertainty surrounds the disappearance of Puttfarken and *Oberfeldwebel* Lux's Me 410, because no trace of it has ever been found. Quite possibly, it is the one seen by eyewitnesses and it probably crashed into the North Sea.

For Carlyle J. Hanson in the 388th, 29 April was undoubtedly the worst day in his life to date.

> God answered my prayers for sure. The target was Brandenburg (Berlin!) We got up at 0130 for target 'study'. The assembly was rough because the overcast went up to 12,000 feet. We were the lead ship in the high squadron of the lead group. After a messy wing assembly, the lead pathfinder went out in the middle of the Channel and the second one took over. It seemed like we got flak all the way in. Everything was covered with clouds. After turning on the IP, about 150 enemy fighters struck at us. They looked like a swarm of bees. They made three passes at us, knocking down seven out of our group. Flak was accurate and heavy. King hollered out, 'Flak at 3 o'clock!' We had been flying through flak for half an hour! We didn't even get over Berlin, as the weather was too bad. It would have been twice as bad if we had tried it. We dropped our bombs on a town about 30 miles south-west of Big B. I think we ploughed up a field. Fred and Bob kept the plane going after No. 1 engine was knocked out and another smoking. We got a little flak on the way home. One waist gunner was hit in the head by flak but wasn't too serious. A 20 mm shell hit No. 1 engine. Flak holes were all over the plane (it looked like a sieve), knocking out the radio compass. I had my flak suit off and parachute on once and really thought I would be using it. One of the fellows in our barracks went down and it was his first mission. This was Fred and Tony's thirteenth and my fourteenth. Our group lost more planes than any other day other than their third mission last summer. This was the hundreth mission of the 385th. We made seven trips to Berlin and they were all nasty.

On 29 April Sergeant Louis J. Torretta flew his twenty-eighth mission.

> We were awakened at 0230 and the weather looked very bad, but we flew anyway. Later the weather cleared a little. We thought we were just going to have flak to watch out for which was very heavy but the navigator that

was leading us screwed up and we were 25 miles off course and separated from the rest of the formations. We had an escort at the coast but as we were off course the group that was supposed to relieve them could not find us and the ones that were with us had to leave, as they were getting low on gas. About 5 minutes later the co-pilot called over the interphone and said it looked like a formation of Forts up ahead and Lieutenant Irwin, who was flying as our bombardier, said, 'Hell, those aren't Forts; they are 109s and 190s' and then they came in. We were leading the high squadron (seven ships). In the first attack about eighty of them came from 1 o'clock high. During their first pass at us they got Donahue. He was flying No. 5 in our squadron. His No. 2 engine caught fire and he went down in a steep dive. No chutes were seen. (Every man on that crew would have been finished if they hadn't raised the quota.)[33] Then they made another pass and this one came from 10 and 11 o'clock high and low. This time about ten of them jumped Hughes and knocked him out of the formation and he fell behind. Three were seen to bale out. Then Hughes dived for the clouds. He was under control and that is the last we saw or heard of them.[34] The third attack came from 12 and 6 low and 9 and 3 level. This time they got Dowler.[35]

A 20 mm cannon shell hit and blew up in the tail about 16 inches behind me. I was wearing my flak suit and that saved me. The force of the explosion where it hit, pushed me up against the armour plate in front with such force that it almost knocked me out. I heard the waist gunner call the pilot and say, 'They knocked Torretta out of the tail'.

Then I could hear the pilot cussing. By that time I was getting my senses back and I tried to call the pilot and tell him I was still with them and that I was all right, but my interphone had been hit and I could hear them but I couldn't answer. Finally, the smoke cleared out of the tail and I motioned to the waist gunner that I was all right and that my interphone and oxygen were shot out. I switched over to my emergency supply. The waist gunner kept a check on me and asked if I was hit. By this time I could feel the warm blood running down my back so I motioned to him that I was hit but I did not think it was serious. A few small fragments of the exploding shell had stuck in my back, a little below where the flak suit ended. In all this we got one big hole in the tail (about a yard in diameter). Also, a portion of our left wing was blown off and a number of small holes. I claimed one fighter destroyed as he blew up almost on top of me. (I am pretty sure he was the one that hit me.) Our crew claimed four destroyed. Parachutes from our ships and from the Germans were seen all over the sky. I had given up all hope of getting back because we were the only ship left in our formation, so I reached back and grabbed my parachute only to find it was riddled. Then one lone fighter made another attack on us and I started to shoot and I discovered one of my guns was hit by one of the enemy bullets and it wouldn't work. This fighter fired a couple of times and quit. I guess he ran out of ammunition. Thank God. That is the only thing that saved us. If they had had enough ammunition to make another attack we surely would have gone down. We had quite a bit of trouble with that left wing but good old Moe, our pilot, pulled us through again. Boy what a pilot that guy was. I would fly through anything with him at the controls. Our group put twenty-one ships up in the air and eleven of them came back. I was sure glad to get back alive from this one.

The next day, 30 April, Torretta flew his twenty-ninth mission, to Clermont Ferrand, France, with Lieutenant Bye.

We took off at 0615. It was a very long ride but it was not so bad as it was warm for some reason. We saw some flak but we were able to avoid it. We saw one enemy fighter but he did not attack us. Not that I blame him, I would do just as he did. He followed us for a while and then he pointed his guns away from us and emptied them and went home. There was no flak at the target, but they had a fake that looked just like the real one. We almost bombed it, but at the last minute the navigator said it wasn't time to reach the target. We went a little farther and we found the real one and we made a good hit as it was a very clear day and we could see the target good. We landed at 1420 and as we were taxiing to our parking place we got a flat tyre. We sure were lucky. This raid I dedicated to our families who had been so swell about everything.

In May eighteen Allied air forces began the pre-invasion bombing of France. The invasion was due to take place that same month but General Dwight D. Eisenhower then postponed the date by a month to enable extra landing craft to be built. On 11 May when a range of targets in France were assigned, seventy Liberators of the 486th and 487th Groups, on the last mission before the latter converted to Forts, were briefed to bomb the marshalling yards at Chaumont. The Libs flew into a flak area near Chateaudun and both the lead and deputy lead were shot down and a third was crippled. *Leutnant* Wilhelm Hofmann of JG26 led his *Schwarm* so close to the B-24s in their head-on pass that his wingman, Waldemar Busch, rammed one of the 487th Liberators, causing it to go down.[36] Busch's propeller was knocked off but he was able to force-land his Fw 190 and he suffered only slight wounds. West of Chartres, *Oberleutnant* Waldemar 'Waldi' Radener made a successful attack on another B-24 and then accidentally rammed a second. Radener baled out of his Fw 190 with minor injuries. Among the missing was Colonel Beirne Lay Jr, who had taken command of the 487th on 28 February following a staff appointment and was flying in the lead ship. He recalls:

I find it hard to believe that there were any survivors of my No. 3 man's B-24. I was riding in the co-pilot's seat and witnessed the explosion, busy at the time though I was with our own battle damage. The first burst was right in front of the nose. It was a miracle that the man in the top turret survived. I imagine he would stand the best chance for survival after the ship blew apart. I don't recall anything but the blinding flash and flames where the B-24 had just been. My biggest worry while Walt Duer and I were evading capture for three weeks was falling into the clutches of the *Gestapo*. They were accountable to nobody, and I knew that they would never believe me when I told them that I, a Group Commander, did not know the date of D-Day (which we did not at that level) and that they would give me the works.[37]

'Invasion fever' was never far from everyone's mind. All flight crewmen were ordered to carry their .45s at all times and ground crews were issued carbines. For some weeks the headlines in the London press and *Stars and Stripes* had proclaimed that Operation *Overlord*, the invasion of the continent, was imminent. At Molesworth, Ben Smith in 'Chick' Cecchini's crew in the Hell's Angels Group picked up the *Stars and Stripes* and read that American losses over Europe in the last five months were 1,407 heavy bombers, 673 fighters and 100 medium bombers. These figures did not include those killed or wounded when the planes returned to their home base or crashed in the United Kingdom. Over 14,000 men were lost in the heavies alone. The British, he read, had parallel losses. Their first few short-haul sorties were 'milk runs', which gave the false impression that combat flying was 'a piece of cake'.

I think we went on pass after our fifth mission. We had been decorated with Air Medals. The plumage of a warrior was just as important to us as it was to Caesar's legionnaires. We were inordinately proud of our silver wings, Presidential Unit Citations, and Air Medals. Men will endure much bizarre and varied punishment for the trinkets that declare them valorous. We were no different. Before we parted, there would not be one of us who was not tested to the limits of his endurance, but these trinkets were important to us as though they were the symbols of what we experienced.

We caught the train to London and bivouacked at the Strand Palace Hotel on the famous Strand, near Trafalgar Square. The edifice still endures. All the combat crews stayed at the Strand Palace or the Regent's Palace in Piccadilly. The staid English management took the bawdy Yanks in stride, never lost their cool, and were totally hospitable, although I'm sure they were sorely provoked on occasion.

We dressed up in our ODs and ventured out into the night. Even in the blackout, throngs of people were surging up and down the street. War-time London was a melting pot for the armed services of every nationality, and their uniforms were often picturesque. In the United Kingdom women were drafted into the services; so most decent girls were in uniform. Only prostitutes and elderly ladies were in street dress.

The conviviality of wartime is unimaginable if one hasn't actually experienced it. People who had not seen each other before 5 minutes ago became comrades. Romantic attachments were formed on the spot, sometimes with no more than a searching look. Complete strangers drank out of the same bottle with no thought of disease. Virtuous girls (in another context) quickly availed themselves of the chance of dinner and dancing and a one-night stand with boys who would be dead within the week. Australians, Canadians, and Yanks prowled the city together, denigrating their English cousins and declaring their undying friendship. Language was no barrier. The bottle was the universal language, bestowing upon Pole, Norwegian, Free French, and Yank alike perfect under-standing and instant communication.

The great dance halls of London were fantastic fun palaces. My favourite two were Covent Garden and the Hammersmith Palace. They featured American-style swing bands; damn good ones, too. The peculiar Limeys had strange dance-hall behaviour. There was no freelance move-ment. All the English danced in a circular direction, swooping and dipping with great sweeping strides – exactly like a giant carousel. I got dizzy just watching. It was insane to try to dance upstream. We got clobbered if we did. These orderly people would line up to go into the gates of Hell. To them it made sense for all to dance in the same direction.

It was not unusual to see a sight like two desert rats from Monty's Eighth Army dancing with each other in full battle regalia, including tin hats on their backs, woolly-woolly uniforms, and leggings. The girls would not dance with these heroes; they had a very gamey smell about them. So they danced with each other.

The boys came stag, and the girls did too. Most often it was the girl who broke on the boy. Everyone was very polite about it; there were no scenes. If the girl wanted to dance with a boy, she came up and broke, and the other girl gracefully bowed out for a while, although she would be back in a short time if she liked him. I was much in demand as I could do the shuffling, graceful Lindy-Hop of the Southern Negroes, and the girls loved it. The boys from Brooklyn and the Bronx did a frenetic hopping-about step that was also very popular, but they marvelled at my hang-loose Southern version of the Jitterbug.

I remember vividly a slender English girl who let me take her home. She told me that I was nothing but a baby, which news took me aback. No matter, she was very tender and sweet to the 'baby', and I never forgot her.

We went from one pub to the other drinking gin and Guinness, a standard affectation of the English, but a pretty neat drink withal. One thing sure, it would get the job done. Imagine the improbable combina-tion of gin and beer (Guinness Stout) – boilermakers, English style.

I loved the uproarious good humour of the Cockneys. These people were a breed apart, quite unlike the other English I had met. Hitler had not been able to break these people's spirit. They thrived on adversity. We had a grand time together, but inevitably time would run out on us. Of all sad words of tongue or pen, the saddest were these: 'Time, please, Lideys and Gentuhlmen!' Oh, how we dreaded to hear the familiar closing words.

To awake with splitting head and a full load of remorse – was it worth it? Hell, yes! We were soon at it again. In and out of bars, cafes, theatres, peep shows, and dance halls. Fish and chips, delicious and served in a newspaper right on a street corner!

Piccadilly was all of this. Nude girly shows the English had long before the US. My favourite was the Windmill, which never closed during the entire war, even during the bombings. The star of the revue was named

Dixie. To be legal, there was one odd requirement. Once the girl had peeled down to the buff, she had to remain completely motionless.

At least once or twice each night, the air raid siren would begin its mournful dirge, and the 'ack-ack' would start up. As searchlights plied the sky, we watched from the roof of the hotel, in our drunkenness scornful of shelter or succour. My companions were Australians or Canadians. The English always went dutifully to an air-raid shelter. It was not that they were afraid; they were cool performers under fire. It was just that they always did what they were supposed to do, exactly as they were supposed to.

Something moralistic about my make-up made me eschew the favours of the army of prostitutes that thronged Piccadilly. I never liked the idea of buying sex; they didn't lack for customers, however, simply because I was squeamish. They were ignored by the Bobbies, who wisely knew that this had to go on in a war. These 'ladies of the night' were in every doorway, with a cigarette lighted so you would know they were there. They never left the doorway. When they got a customer, the trick was turned on the spot – in a standing position. They could turn five tricks that way while turning one in a hotel room. Our lads called them Piccadilly Commandos, a name that stuck.

One night Jasper, the navigator, and I took some girls of dubious pedigree (non-commercial) to the ultra-swank Savoy Restaurant, proposing to have dinner with them there. The maitre d' politely but firmly told us that we would have to leave as he had notables. There were plenty in plain sight, we protested. The girls laid him out in Cockney, and we then told him about democracy in the United States and where he could shove his famous restaurant. He was completely unperturbed, merely saying, 'Mind you, sir, I shall have to call the police if you don't leave.'

Somehow I managed to disengage from riotous living for a brief season and went on a walking-riding tour to see the historic sights of London. Our hotel was only a few blocks away from the Nelson Monument at Trafalgar Square. The National Gallery was nearby, but the museums were emptied of their treasures for the duration of the war, something I hadn't counted on. I began to encounter sights and places I had been hearing about all my life – Charing Cross Station, Pall Mall, Leicester Square, Regent Street, Maiden Lane, Berkeley Square, Waterloo Bridge, the Tower of London. All of them were old friends. I had read about them in *Sherlock Holmes*, *Dr Jekyll and Mr Hyde*, *Oliver Twist* and the other novels of my youthful reading.

I took a cab to Parliament and Westminster Abbey. The Abbey was the first Gothic architecture I had ever seen. I took my time and feasted my eyes on this sublime masterpiece of church architecture. I thought to myself: can we really be descended from this race of master-builders and super-artisans? By comparison the best contemporary edifice is trite in the extreme. These people had caught a vision of beauty, which is not given to us to know.

154

Later, as I meandered through the streets, I heard a parade approaching. In the vanguard was a Scottish regimental band, their war drums throbbing. As the kilted veterans passed me, they began to skirl their pipes, the most stirring sound I had ever heard. It got my battle blood up, appealing to some antique strain in me that I was not aware of before. It is said the Scottish regiments marched into battle at El Alamein to the tune of their bagpipes and completely routed the Axis troops. I better understood this after hearing them that day.

After lunch I strolled through St James's Park, a wonderful green place along the Mall in front of Buckingham Palace. I was unprepared for what I saw, a plethora of ruttish couples gambolling and lying about the greensward, quite impervious to the passers-by. They simply spread newspapers over themselves to conceal their tender ministrations to each other. I noticed many of the males were Yanks who had taken to this primal English pastime like ducks to water.

Scattered about the park were the traditional soap box orators; indeed, they could be seen in Kensington Gardens, Hyde Park, and in any of the places where people congregated. I listened to them respectfully as did my British cousins. They could not be styled agitators; no one could agitate the British. Rather, they were minor prophets polishing up their oratory. Many English politicians spent an apprenticeship on the soapbox.

I was bone-weary after my sight-seeing tour, but not so much so that I was incapable of rejuvenation. I soaked in a tub of hot water, dressed and went back to the fleshpots of Piccadilly. It was our last night in London, and I didn't intend to spend it abed.

Next day it was time for the heroes to go back to the shooting war. For a while, we had had a new lease on life, and it was a welcome respite, to be replayed with great relish for days on end.

Chick's crew were not alone in knowing that they would be involved in the long-awaited invasion of *Festung Europa* and they expected all-out opposition. While marshalling yards and airfields in France, Luxembourg and Belgium were hit on a regular basis as part of the pre-invasion Blitz, missions to German targets would continue, as a simultaneous assault on oil and aircraft was in keeping with Eisenhower's strategy of pounding two of Germany's most valuable assets.

Both had to be knocked out or crippled if the invasion of the Continent was to succeed.

Notes

1. Five B-17s and seven B-24s were lost.
2. Heinz 'Pritzel' Bär was a strong personality known for his straight talking, who had arrived at JG1 on 21.1.44 from the fighter training school at Orange in France. At the end of 1940 Bär had been the top-scoring NCO pilot with thirteen victories. His score increased to seventeen before his *Gruppe* was transferred east for *Barbarossa*. Bär shot down ninety-six Soviet aircraft despite being hospitalised with spinal injuries for a time. Then, as *Kommandeur,* he led I./JG 77 from Sicily against Malta and went on to North Africa. After the fall of Tunisia in spring 1943 he was withdrawn from operations with

malaria and a stomach ulcer, his score 158. He returned to combat late that year as *Kommandeur* of II./JG1 on home defence, flying the Fw 190 for the first time against American bombers and claiming at least twenty-one victories.

3. Feist was KIA on 21.2.44, when Steigler was wounded. On 12.5.44 Steigler was one of seven of the unit's pilots killed when he was shot down in combat.

4. At the time the average life of a B-17 in the group was eleven missions. In the less than two years the 100th was in action in Europe, they lost 229 B-17s, 177 listed as MIA and fifty-two from 'other operational losses'. It was the third highest total among 8th Air Force units in WWII. The 100th had the highest loss rate among its sister units for the twenty-two months it was operational.

5. Hanke also arrived at the Odense headquarters where he met Markussen. The American's leather flying jacket with eighteen bombs pictured on the back (he hadn't had time to stencil on the nineteenth nor, now, the twentieth) was taken from him and was later acquired by Hanke. The American crewmembers and German pilots discussed the merits of various aircraft and Hanke gave Markussen a Danish beer. They all shook hands and parted without knowing if they would someday meet again. Markussen was taken by train to Oberursel where he spent about a week in solitary confinement before being moved to *Stalag Luft I* on the Baltic coast in Pommerania. He spent nearly fifteen months in *Stalag Luft I*, which held 9,500 PoWs, including 6,000 AAF officers. Although not mistreated, he lost 50 lb over a three-month period when he subsisted on a daily bowl of dehydrated turnips 'boiled to a gooey mess' and 3 ounces of meat a week. Russians liberated him and the others. Hanke returned to combat and downed four more aircraft to finish with nine confirmed victories and two unconfirmed before he contracted Malta fever in 1943.

6. *Defending the Reich; The History of Jagdgeschwader 1 'Oesau'* by Eric Mombeek.

7. Flecks was KIA on 26.12.44.

8. *I Flew For The Führer*.

9. *Cock o' the Walk* FTR a few days later on 29.2.44.

10. On 9.10.44 *Hauptmann* Heinz Knoke suffered a shattered left knee and right pelvis when his car was blown up by a limpet mine in Czechoslovakia while en route to Anklam and he never returned to combat. He had forty-four victories. He was awarded the *Ritterkreuz* on 27.4.45.

11. *First Over Germany* by Russell A. Strong.

12. The 91st and 384th lost five and four B-17s respectively. Addi Glunz claimed two shot down and a third forced out of formation in the first combat sortie of the day. That same afternoon he claimed two more Fortresses and a Thunderbolt to take his tally to fifty-eight victories. Other victorious pilots included Major Heinz 'Pritzel' Bär and *Hauptmann* Hermann Segatz, who claimed two B-17s. *Oberfeldwebel* Rudolf Hübl also claimed his thirteenth victory, a Fortress. Hübl destroyed two Liberators on 24.2.44 and he scored his nineteenth and last victory with JG1 on 23.6.44. Segatz was KIA on 8.3.44. He had at least thirty-four victories.

13. Both the 445th and 392nd were later awarded Presidential Unit Citations for their part in the raid.

14. *I Flew For the Führer*.

15. Seventy-nine bombers attacked targets of opportunity at Wilhelmshaven. Nine B-17s and two Liberators were lost.

16. *Pegasus, Too* went down with Lloyd L. Wilson's crew on 23.3.44.

17. The First Division lost eighteen Forts.

18. *Nelson King* had been named in honour of the former radio operator on Lauro's crew. On a mission on 29.11.43, having removed his gloves at over 20,000 feet where the temperature was close to –50 degrees below zero, to replace an iced up oxygen mask on

the ball turret gunner, his hands had turned purple and swelled to three times their normal size. King's walk-around oxygen bottle froze and in the efforts to save the ball turret gunner, he lost the tips of several fingers to frostbite and he never flew again.

19. Two of Johnston's crew were KIA. Eight were PoW.

20. Only Lieutenant Clarence A. Gridley and three of the crew of *Duchess of Dixie* survived to be made PoW. The ball turret gunner died later in PoW camp.

21. *Blitzin' Betsy*'s propellers had cut off the leading edge of Job's port wing and had torn a hole in the No. 3 engine's fuel tank on the starboard wing, which erupted in flames. Part of the crew baled out but as the aircraft went into a flat spin. Job and Lieutenant J. P. Lechowski, his co-pilot, were forced on to the roof of the cockpit before the aircraft exploded, throwing Job and Lechowski, who was not wearing his parachute, out of the aircraft to their deaths. J. W. Dupray, navigator and R. T. Gill, bombardier, were believed to have been blown out of the nose. Dupray was killed but Gill survived, as did Captain Paul Brown and Roy Joyce, the top turret gunner, who was also blown out of the aircraft.

22. Ray E. Hess and Harold A. Brassfield, waist gunners, Robert H. Sweeney, ball turret gunner, and Donald Taylor, tail gunner, were found dead in or near the wreckage. The rest of the crew were rounded up and finally sent to PoW camps in the Third Reich.

23. Sixteen Liberators in all FTR. McMahon returned to Berlin in a nose turret on 21.6.44 and saw the same 'terrible flak and fighter attacks with the same results'. Forty-four planes were lost. His ship was hit in the main gas tanks over the target and barely made it to Sweden after fighting off many fighter attacks.

24. *Little Willie* and Dopko's crew went down over Berlin three days later. Eight of the crew were captured. Two evaded. Larry Goldstein recalled that 'we didn't have the heart to do what we had done once before'.

25. US fighters claimed eighty-one enemy planes shot down and the bomber gunners claimed ninety-seven destroyed (the *Luftwaffe* actually lost sixty-four fighters destroyed and two damaged beyond repair).

26. It was for its 'outstanding performance of duty in action against the enemy in connection with the initial series of successful attacks against Berlin, 4, 6, and 8.3.44 ....' that the 100th was awarded its second Presidential Unit Citation, but not until 3.3.45.

27. 5./JG1 was withdrawn from the action for six weeks on 15.3.44. On 28.4.44 Knoke was promoted *hauptmann* and given command of 5./JG5. Specht was shot down and killed by flak on the disastrous Operation *Bodenplatte* on New Year's Day 1945. His score is unknown but he had at least thirty-two victories (including 15 *Viermots*) in the west.

28. *Chick's Crew* by Ben Smith.

29. All ten in Lieutenant Thomas W. Gilleran's crew aboard 42-31724 were taken prisoner.

30. A few days earlier, in the early hours of 12 April, 10 intruders had penetrated airspace over East Anglia and a Me 410A-1 of KG51 had shot down a B-17 flown by Lieutenant Donald M. MacGregor of the 413th BS, 96th BG, while on approach to the 390th BG base at Framlingham

31. Munsey was posthumously awarded the DSC on 13.7.44.

32. Hptm Viner of 4th *Staffel* and Lt Loness of 5th *Staffel* were credited with a B-24 apiece. Fw Zorn of 6./KG51 was credited with a Liberator and a B-17 (sic) and Uffz Leonim, also of 6th *Staffel*, was credited with three B-24s, one of them W of Orfordness. Fw Volg of 6./KG51 shot down a B-24 South of Norwich. Two other victories were credited to Uffz Drongal and Fw Dormsten. KG51 lost two Me 410A-1s and their crews. Oblt Klaus Kruger and Fw Michael Reichardt, his *Bordfunker* (radio operator) gunner, in 9K+HP and Hptm Dietrich Puttfarken and his radio-operator-gunner, Obfw Willi Lux in 9K+MN, were lost.

33. In fact eight men left 42-37866 piloted by Lieutenant Warren D. Donahue and were taken prisoner. Two were KIA.
34. Nine men aboard 42-31144 flown by Lieutenant Hayden T. Hughes were KIA. One PoW.
35. Nine men aboard 42-102421 flown by Lieutenant Charles R. Dowler were KIA. One PoW.
36. *Lazy Lady* piloted by Lieutenant Lorin D. McCleary crashed at Varize, France. Nine were KIA. One PoW. *Peg-O-'My Heart* flown by Lieutenant Frank Vratny, crashed at Bretonelles, France. Four evaded. Seven PoW. 42-52763 *Mean Widdle Kid* flown by Captain Edward J. Brodsky crashed at Orgeres, France. Seven were KIA. Three PoW.
37. Lay successfully evaded.

CHAPTER 5

Brux – Turnstiles to Death

Something plus a terrific wind blinded me. It was blood: a lot of it. I was
covered from head to foot and it went on through the ship painting it red and
freezing. The bomb bays were solid red and slippery .... The blood inside the
ship came from 'Uncle Dudly' Orcutt. The right side of his head was gone.

Dwight N. Miller, *Lady Stardust II*

With double summer time in effect in England, darkness came very late and the nights were much shorter than many Americans were used to. In order to get some sleep before the usual crack-of-dawn (or earlier) briefing for a bombing mission, many found it necessary to close the blackout curtains to darken the room by shutting out the later evening light. During the evening of 11 May, bases across East Anglia received an Advanced Warning notice for a mission and the flurry of activity began. Combat crews scheduled to take part received a Red Alert notice and ground crews began servicing and repairing and refuelling the bombers to ensure that every possible plane was operational. High-octane fumes of bombers running up permeated the cool English breeze and the clanking caterpillar tracks on the seven-ton Cleveland Cletracs towing their General Purpose trailers made sleep even more difficult. At Thorpe Abbotts near Diss, where the Bloody Hundredth were based, Stanley Clark's lead crew waited to be briefed. His lead navigator Fred Robertson and Rheubin L. South, the lead bombardier, knew that their briefing would be sometime between 7 and 9 pm, depending on the time the target came in from Headquarters. Then they could get about 3 or 4 hours' sleep before they were awakened at around 0130 for a 0530 take-off. In between was breakfast, the regular briefing for all crewmembers and then navigation briefing. In the 349th Squadron area nearby, Jack Moore, pilot of *Captain Crow*, received a telegram announcing the birth of his daughter. If he could, he would have liked to send a telegram in reply, but he did not have the time. The mission on the morrow would start like any of their other fourteen missions. Sleep would be shattered by CQs in hobnailed boots stomping in double time up and down the upper halls of the Nissens, banging on doors and bawling loudly. Then it was breakfast and a Mission Briefing before inspecting their aircraft and gear to make sure *Captain Crow* was ready to go. It was no different for aircrews at all the other remote American bases across the length and breadth of the largely featureless East Anglian countryside.

Scattered around every airfield from Bassingbourn to Bungay and Rattlesden to Rackheath, each Nissen hut was small, approximately 20 by 30 feet, with a concrete floor and the typical corrugated steel hemispherical construction, and it usually accommodated twelve officers. Enlisted men's huts with their double decker bunks held more. Huts were lined but not insulated, so they were pretty cold in the wintertime. Rats would get in between the lining and when things got dull some would chase them out to shoot at with their .45s. Adorning the walls, aerodynamically sleek Varga girls, George Petty's sinuous shapely ladies and 'Gil' Elvgren's scantily clad females in negligees and skimpy bikinis torn from the pages of *Yank*, *Esquire* and *Brown & Bigelow* calendars provided the only splash of colour in what was a drab existence. For just a few bucks, artists and cartoonists would copy their images onto the back of an A2 and on the noses of the aircraft. Double entendres like *Miss Manooki*, *Virgin on the Verge*, *Miss Bea Havin'* and *Grin 'n Bare It* and epithets such as *Red Ass* and *Witches Tit* were often added attractions. A potbelly stove in the middle of the room supposedly provided warmth in winter and when it was going the ones near it cooked while the ones at the ends froze – when they had fuel that is. Government Issue fuel consisted of large chunks of coal, actually coke, and occupants quickly found that they could consume the whole weekly allotment of 52 lb of coke in one day if they wanted to keep the hut comfortable. Against strict orders, men often made illegal sorties into local woods and cut off branches that would burn well. Chiefs of Staff, worried about the effect it could have on Anglo-American relations, issued a directive to end the practice. During the really cold weather, everyone requisitioned (stole) extra blankets in an effort to keep warm. One crewmember recalled that at one time he had nine. In order to shave, the men had to use the nearby ablutions building and the bathhouse was anything up to a mile away, which effectively made it necessary for all to acquire bicycles.

At Deopham Green to the east of the forested and heathland area of Norfolk known as Breckland, men of the 452nd tried to get some much needed sleep. A century earlier settlers, including Abe Lincoln's forebears, had set out from Hingham, the nearest village to the airfield, on the start of a long journey to the New World. Airfields are notoriously cold and damp places and it was amazing that any greenery remained at Deopham; during its construction, engineers had ripped out 6 miles of hedges and 1,400 trees and in their place there now stood fifty hardstandings for the Forts and temporary accommodation for almost 3,000 men. Ralph J. Munn, a ball turret gunner in the 731st Squadron, and Lieutenant Cornelius A. Kohlman, bombardier in Lieutenant 'Mike' Maracek's crew of *Lady Stardust II*, were among those who wondered what the target on 12 May would be. Munn often flew as a spare for crews that were short of a ball gunner, but this mission happened to be one of the days that he would fly with his original crew, led by Lieutenant Dick Noble, pilot of *The Lucky Lady*. Sleep was always difficult and if Kohlman, Munn and the others had known then what the target would be, they would probably not have slept at all.

In an old house in the village of Risby, 4 miles from Bury St Edmunds, two Suffolk schoolboys, Brian Tyson and his brother Pat, were asleep. The next morning they would cycle as usual to King Edward VI school in the town and the dawn chorus of the Rougham group would startle the old clock on Moyses Hall into striking 8.30 and silence morning worship. Two members of the 94th were frequent guests in their family home. One called 'Curly' taught young Brian how to play chess. 'Curly' and the other guest would be killed in action before the year was out. Both schoolboys were filled with admiration for the Group that flew from the airbase just across the railway line from their school playing field. Once, Brian had returned from a half-term holiday to find that two Forts had collided over the field and the wreckage was strewn over King Edward's, an engine in the middle of the field and a wing-tip leaning against the headmaster's house. The Forts filled their skies and their hearts and Brian's dreams too. 'In golden August's shadows their wings rippled over ripe wheat fields; in November fogs they stood damp and mute on grey dispersal points. And in bleak January mornings his memory blossomed into red and green flares falling from the planes as they formed up.'

For reasons that are unclear, someone had named the airfield 'Rougham' after a hamlet a little further east of the tiny village of Blackthorpe, which was nearer the base. Bury takes its name from St Edmund, the last East Anglian king, who was executed by the Danes in AD 870 and was once buried in the town's Benedictine Abbey. Ipswich had become the destination for many on 24-hour leaves and the source of many an evening's adventure. Ipswich and Bury St Edmunds were opportunities for rediscovering half-forgotten treasures in the adventures of Dickens's *Pickwick Papers* and his company. In wartime, nowhere could have been further removed from that Dickensian world than Ipswich, which was a dirty, crowded, noisy, evil smelling port and an amusement centre for troops of a dozen Allied nations. Americans thronged it, criticised it and admired it. They changed its life considerably, just as they had in many places throughout the region. On bases, entertainment, official and otherwise, was provided. Rumour once had it that a small group of renegades at Rougham had stashed a blonde and a redhead in one of the Nissens for nearly a week.

Mike Wysocki, a lead bombardier, hit the sack in a hut in one of the many dispersed sites in woodland south of the main road to Ipswich near Blackthorpe. Wysocki and the rest of Fred Koval's crew expected to fly their twenty-sixth mission on 12 May. In another hut slept Lieutenant Victor Bonomo, a navigator in Ralph Brant's crew of *Fortress McHenry*. The plane had been selected by readers of the *Baltimore News Sun* to represent the city and on 6 May Berlin had been its first mission. Since Lieutenant Brant was from Cumberland, Maryland, Colonel Castle, the CO, had decided that it would be appropriate to assign *Fortress McHenry* to his crew. In another hut Lieutenant Abel L. Dolim, a young Hawaiian from Honolulu who three years earlier had stood and watched helplessly as the Japanese bombed his island, waited to fly his ninth mission as navigator in Joe Hamil's crew. Hamil's had been one of thirteen replacement crews assigned a month earlier, but Headquarters had announced that a combat tour was supposedly getting easier and tours therefore were increased, making chances of survival seem even more remote. If he could have got away with it without being court-

161

martialled Dolim would have penned a 'Dear Jimmie', a letter to General James Doolittle. It would have been on the lines of:

The old timers here tell us your HQ jumped the twenty-five-mission tour to thirty missions because 'things are getting better for the bomber crews'. Well sir, we in the 94th have lost twenty-three bombers and crews from April 11th when I joined the group until April 30th .... Six of us navigators were on the rolls but now only John McAllaster and I are left and most of these fellows had less than six missions to their credit. Morale is lousy here. I dread my next mission. Jimmie, if *things* are *getting better*, GOD HELP US ALL.[1]

There were other issues to bitch and gripe about, like the time when word was passed on to clean up the 'bare-assed ladies' on the bombers. 'They would be required to have panties – at least.' Bomber names, too, had to be cleaned up. *Twat's It To You?* had been renamed *?It To You?* And what was worse, rumour had it that hard liquor would no longer be served to the 'boys'. 'Dummies, what do they think we are fighting for' queried Dolim – 'if not for booze and broads.'

Our chest pack situation was a mess. Some high ranking congenital idiot in the Air Materiel Command procurement business had decided that we must have two types of chest packs. One had rings on the harness and snapped on the chute and the other type was just the opposite, an embarrassing situation at bale out time if one was not careful. It was not all bad. The PX tobacco ration for cigarette smokes was seven packs a week. Cigar aficionados were allowed seven cigars a week plus three packs of cigarettes or a block of sliced Edgeworth pipe tobacco. I'd smoked a pipe before trying out the great cigars made in Tampa so I opted for the cigar-pipe tobacco combination. The pipe tobacco was raw stuff but then I had discovered Dunhill's in London, which turned out to be to be a tobacco emporium in a class of its own. The huge sales room sported walls climbing up to 16 feet from the floor, all of them having row upon row of built in drawers containing pipe tobacco blended by the establishment to the personal tastes of their clients. Most of us believed in some sort of luck or chance. Some of us had talismans, lucky charms or a fixed routine, like one of our bombardiers who always urinated on the tailwheel before take-off. Some way or other I *was* lucky. My only nod to superstition was to stand upright facing sideways to 12 o'clock whenever we went through flak, an old habit from my amateur boxing days, of no practical use whatsoever in this new kind of battle.

Superstitious combat crewmen in barrack sites in Billingford and Thorpe woods stretching south and bordering the Diss to Harleston road must have wondered what the fates held for the 'jinxed' Thorpe Abbotts group. Fred Robertson at least knew that after briefing next morning they would be heading for Brux, 42 miles north-west of Prague in western Czechoslovakia, and the longest and most gruelling mission yet flown from East Anglia with return to England. The 45th Combat Wing groups at Snetterton Heath,

Deopham Green and Knettishall near Thetford, home of the 388th, and the 13th Combat Wing groups at Thorpe Abbotts, Framlingham and Horham, all in Suffolk, were to attack the synthetic oil plant at Brux in western Czechoslovakia. Two composite formations would strike at the Fw 190 repair depot at Zwickau, while Forts of the 1st Division and the Liberators of the Second Divison attacked oil refineries and aircraft plants in the Leipzig and Merseburg areas. In all, 886 bombers would be dispatched with 980 escorting fighters to five main plants in central Germany in the first attack on oil production centres.

The morning of 12 May started with clear weather and crews dreading a long flight across France and Germany with the threat of the *Luftwaffe* and flak all the way. At Deopham Green Donald H. Jones, tail gunner in Lieutenant Hugh T. Atkinson's crew heard the CQ enter his crew hut waking everyone a little earlier than usual. It was an ominous sign. Worse, though Jones was not yet aware, he would be flying in the low squadron in Purple Heart Corner with only one B-17 to the left and below them and one Fort to the right and above. It was perhaps best that Jones and Cornelius A. Kohlman would not find out until briefing where they were going. All Kohlman knew was that to be awakened at 0015 then something had to be 'up'. He cycled over to the mess hall. Bedlam greeted combat crewmen as they entered the door and the smoke of burning grease assailed their nostrils and smarted in their eyes as they filed in for real fresh eggs, a slice or two of hard, crisp, salty bacon and dried up toast. Fresh eggs confirmed that a combat mission was in the offing and the first problem was:

> ... could he get them down? Breakfast, prepared to eliminate indigestion and sickness at high altitude was never really tasty and hard enough to stomach before a combat mission. The coffee tasted of rust and the cereal was doused with lumpy reconstituted powdered milk, but sometimes crews ate oatmeal and powdered milk and sometimes hot cakes with syrup that tasted like molasses – not because they liked them but because it was warm and filling. Dehydrated eggs, which came in square boxes, were normally whipped into a great sticky emulsion, then apparently fried in axle grease left over from the needs of the motor pool. The result was a well-vulcanised, plastic lump of lukewarm goo. But they ate! It could be a combat crewman's last meal for quite some time and he might have to walk home. After a drink of lousy grapefruit or tomato juice or coffee it usually became easier, but each mouthful became an additional lump of lead in the pit of the stomach. Why they could even go back for seconds if they could get by the firsts.

Mike Maracek's crew returned to their metal framed Quonset hut in woods on the edge of Deopham airfield to pick up their flight gear. Crews were also permitted to take any small items they wanted to have along and then it was off to the briefing room at 0200 hours. As they entered, they could see that the briefing screen was up in front of the blackboard. Kohlman and Donald H. Jones now fully understood why they had been woken up so early. The feet of the officer posting the information were at the extreme right of the maps, which indicated a long distance mission. The map on the wall was pulled and crews saw the red ribbon to the target; there was a hush over the entire room. Though he was shocked, Ralph J. Munn had been expecting something like this for a week or ten days. He also believed that the condition of the aircraft at Deopham Green was in no way airworthy or mechanically sound to make a trip of this distance. At best, even with extra fuel, he had the feeling of a no return. After briefing, Jones, Munn and Kohlman and all the other aircrew on the mission picked up their parachutes, electrically heated suits, gloves, maps and tried to digest some of details. They carried with them the target information and the fighter escort, flak areas and estimated time for escort changes. Due to the distance, their bomb load was only thirty-eight 100-pounders.

Richard Wynn, a navigator, Jack Moor, and lead navigator Fred Robertson were among those at Thorpe Abbotts who waited for the revealing cloth to be pulled back from the briefing board. Wynn's ship was none other than *Rosie's Riveters*, which was made famous by Robert 'Rosie' Rosenthal, a legendary figure in the Bloody Hundredth. Wynn's crew, captained by Alexander Kinder, inherited the ship from him when his crew had finished their first tour, though really it was either the second or third *Rosie's Riveters*. Moore's assignment would be to lead the Low Squadron in *Captain Crow*, which had a distinctive large black crow with shiny captain's bars as nose art. Get this one out of the way and his crew's next mission would be as Group Leader, as they had been designated as a 'Lead Crew'. This meant they would only fly every fourth mission and only as the Group lead aircraft, just like Fred Robertson, who recalls, 'When the CO, Colonel Thomas S. Jeffery, pulled the curtain back that morning to expose the length of the yarn to all, there were gasps and groans. I don't believe I had seen that piece of red yarn stretched farther. All pilots were advised that we would be at the extreme limits of our range.' Richard Wynn noted that the three divisions of the 8th would fly a common course in trail to the Thuringen area where they would peel off to the five targets. Manningtree was the final assembly point and landfall with the mainland made between Dunkirk and Ostend near the French-Belgian border. To some, probably because of the shuttle mission flown earlier, Brux was considered as just another long mission. Major Marvin 'Red' Bowman of S-2 noted in his diary that, 'Distances mean nothing to this bunch anymore and they would not be surprised at being briefed for Ceylon, Tokyo or Celebes any day.'

At the briefing Stanley Clark's lead crew got a shock. A Squadron Commander, Major Fuller, would be flying his first mission as the Command Pilot, as Fred Robertson recalls.

He had flown about twenty missions but this was to be his first lead and we had the honour of breaking him in. This meant that our co-pilot, Mike Ehorn, flew in the tail gunner's position as the formation control officer. Our *Mickey* (radar) operator in the radio room was George Pendleton, the top turret gunner, Page, the radio operator, Wolfstein, one waist gunner, Scott. Our group was leading the 13th Combat Wing, with the

390th and 95th flying high and low respectively. At the navigation briefing I noticed that our route across southern Germany passed right over Ulm. I had been over it once and near it a few other times on missions to Augsburg and Munich. The flak coming out of that area was thick enough to walk on. I made a mental note to avoid the area to the right or south of Ulm. This was important because the IP (Initial Point – start of bomb run) was not too far ahead. I wanted to make certain we could make our left turn onto the bomb run (north) with plenty of time to be level and on the proper heading as we passed over the IP.

Group chaplains were always at briefings and at Rougham Captain Collins, the Catholic chaplain, held communion service before crews breakfasted and reported for combat briefings. Their presence was certainly welcome on 12 May, when details of the mission had a devastating impact on the combat crewmen. Part of the 94th was going to Brux, the others to Zwickau. Abe Dolim was going to Zwickau in a ship in a composite group in the No. 6 position or Purple Heart Corner. Victor Bonomo was also going to the same target. *Fortress McHenry* would be in the number three position of the composite group. Also Zwickau-bound was Mike Wysocki, who was angered by the thought of the 10½-hour round trip he would be making in *Lucy*, the Koval crew's ship. 'General Doolittle had said missions were now getting shorter and easier!'

At Snetterton Heath 6 miles south-west of the little Norfolk town of Attleborough by the main Norwich to London road, combat crews in the Snetterton Falcons were equally dismayed. When it was revealed that Zwickau was the target, the red acetate leading from Snetterton to the Czechoslovakian target seemed to set a record for length. 'The long trip' wrote Lieutenant Warren Berg, navigator in the crew of *The Reluctant Dragon*, 'seemed to use up all the red ribbon S-2 could find. It was going to be a rough one – we could tell.' The crew were flying their sixteenth mission and had only recently returned from flak leave in the west of England. Three days earlier the new crew in their hut went down, making the second one to be cleaned out since they had been at the base. Charlie Filer's crew of *Stormy Weather* also viewed the target with a jaundiced eye. Only the day before they had lost Baumgartner their co-pilot and little buddy and Lido Mochetti who flew with another crew. Mochetti, the old man at 33 and crew chief, had been the radio operator/gunner Chas E. Williams' closest friend. When Filer's crew had flown their first mission, to Berlin, two months earlier, they had been given *Goering's Nightmare*, complete with skeleton painted on the nose, after their ship blew a tyre while they were revving the mags preparatory to take-off. The 'old crock' had lived up to its name, losing an engine going into the target and running away because it could not be feathered. Williams had thrown everything out that was not bolted down out of the waist windows and they returned to England alone with only two engines still running. Filer landed the ailing bomber at a Spitfire base after dropping through a hole in the thick cloud. Their nightmare was not over, for when the crew returned to Snetterton they found that the ground personnel had gone through their things assuming they had been lost. Williams recalled that:

> ... it was pretty grim because it was obvious that we would be, within three weeks, either dead or prisoners. Most of us did not expect to complete our tour. The attitude of the ground personnel was pretty cynical as well. I heard that one officer who threw in the towel was busted to private and permanent KP. The rest of us soldiered on in quiet desperation.

During the briefing, requests for a twenty-one-plane formation were rejected and the new fourteen-plane formation would be used again and the Group would send up twenty-six Fortresses. Recently, the losses endured by the Snetterton Falcons were such that they made the Bloody Hundredth seem like a lucky outfit. Although there had been no losses on the last three missions, a ten-plane loss on 8 May at Brunswick, coupled with twenty-six plane casualties in April, created an unwanted legend in the 96th. So the Snetterton Falcons' lot was not a happy one of late, especially with the recent increase in a tour of missions from twenty-five to thirty. Fred Huston, a bombardier in the 337th Squadron, whose crew had arrived at Snetterton in the early spring of 1944, 'having done what passed for phase training in Dyersburg, Tennessee' was one who started out to fly twenty-five. 'Every time I flew five, Doolittle added five on the other end, which I still think was rather nasty of the man, although I did admire his taste in WAC drivers ... she was a living breathing doll, reserved obviously for the upper echelons.'

Throughout Norfolk and Suffolk the crews went out to their bombers armed and fuelled up and waiting patiently on their oil-spotted concrete dispersal pans around the airfields. At Deopham Green Dick Noble's crew set off for *The Lucky Lady* while Donald H. Jones and the other nine men in Hugh Atkinson's crew went out to *Hairless Joe*, not the crew's usual plane. They were just borrowing it. Mike Maracek's crew had borrowed two gunners from another crew so Bouchek in the tail and Kemman, the right waist gunner, were flying with the crew of the *Lady Stardust II* for the first time. A less discerning crew had originally called the plane *Kickapoo Joy Juice* but then beauty is in the eye of the beholder!

It was now approximately 0330. Everything was double-checked over and over. Before getting to their post Maracek's crew had their own little briefing by their pilot. There was a lot of joking and kidding, all in good taste, to lessen the pressure and apprehension. The time was coming up to 0745. Maracek instructed his crew to get to their posts when as usual on every mission, an identical, clear, checklist procedure was followed. Escape kits and rations were passed around. Ernest 'Red' Huchinson took up his position as left waist, Sam Fain waited to enter the ball turret and the flight engineer, Sergeant Merle 'Uncle Dudly' Orcutt, took up his engineering station. In the nose, Lieutenant Lawrence DeFeo, navigator, and Cornelius Kohlman took their seats and made their checks, while Harold 'Gabby' Eastman, the co-pilot, who was known as the 'quiet one', assisted Maracek. In the radio room Technical Sergeant Dwight N. Miller checked his radio hatch gun and sat down in front of his radio apparatus. The intercom system was checked.

Maracek waved from the cockpit at the ground crewmen, moved the mixture control and started the 1,200 horsepower Wright Cyclones, first number one, then two and three and four. The prop blades spun slowly then the engines puffed bluish smoke and roared into life. In the cockpit Maracek and Eastman went through their pre-flight check, unlocking the controls, moving the flaps, rudder and elevators through their arcs. After the run-up for about 7 or 8 minutes to check magnetos, oil and manifold pressures and to clear them out and get rid of any 'bugs', the two ground crewmen removed the wheel chocks. Maracek dropped the rpm on the two inboard engines, released the brakes and steered *Lady Stardust II* from her hardstand, joining the queue heading for the runway and taking her place in line on the perimeter track. The squeal of brakes punctuated the roar of the engines as two lines converged at the threshold of the runway and after a pause, began moving, leaving a small cloud of blue smoke. Slowly at first, then gathering speed and tail up, twenty-five tons of bomber roared down the tyre-streaked runway and the needle on the airspeed indicator rolled down past 60, 80, 100 and the *Lady* was airborne. Eastman dabbed the brakes gently and the landing gear eased up into the wings and they slotted into their position in the sky before forming over the English Channel coast.

As they headed out across the Channel, air gunners test fired their .50 calibre guns. At daybreak the bombers crossed over and went into Fortress Europe through Holland. Everything seemed very quiet as the Forts flew easterly into the sun and picked up their first escort team. Cornelius A. Kohlman for one was:

> ... sure glad they made it on time. We were now at about 24,000 feet heading for Germany. After our first escort team, low on fuel, turned back, formations of twenty to thirty Fw 190s and Bf 109s across and stacked up in three to four levels came at us from all directions, going to the front of our group, then turning back to meet us head on. We could see their gun flashes as they approached. Their rate of convergence was so fast that we could not deliver an accurate blast to take them down. Being the lead group, we were hit hard. Then the drone from their engines was gone. The attack was over. I decided that the next assault I would aim as best I could, pick a spot and fire after they passed our group.

For the crew of *Hairless Joe* in the low squadron, the mission was almost over, as Donald H. Jones recalled.

> Suddenly a call over the intercom, 'White flak at 12 o'clock!' And here they come, head-on attack by enemy fighters. As they hit the formation, the air was suddenly full of debris, pieces of aircraft, engine cowlings. Hugh Atkinson was trying evasive action to spoil the fighters' aim. There was oil and smoke streaming from the engines. The intercom was out. My oxygen mask had ceased to function. It was flat against my face. The B-17 flying just to the left of us took a direct hit and exploded. There was nothing left except a ball of fire. Just to the right of us, not more than 50 feet away, a Bf 109 was disintegrating and the pilot was baling out.

167

His dark-coloured chute opened up. Now we were dropping down, out of what was left of the formation. Then, as the pilot was trying to level off, there was much vibration and the only way it would stop was when the pilot put the nose down and picked up airspeed. Then there was a problem of a runaway propeller. The electrical system had failed because the bombs could not be salvoed and they could not be pried out. There was an Fw 190 following us. He was out of range but I fired two or three bursts at him anyway. That alerted the rest of the crew.

Our situation reached the point that Atkinson flipped on the emergency bell and a steady ring meant, 'Abandon ship'. I picked up my chest chute, which had been lying behind me, and carefully snapped each ring onto the harness, then turned and made my way to the tail gunner's emergency escape door, pulled the cable holding the door in place and kicked it out. The door was not big enough to jump out of so I put both legs out, put my head down between my knees and just rolled out headfirst. I was not planning on much of a delay in opening my chute. I estimated that we were at about 10,000 feet (28,000 when we were first hit). As I pulled the ripcord, nothing happened so I bumped the bottom of my chest chute and started pulling it out and then it popped out. What a feeling of relief to see that beautiful white chute blossom out above me. Now wait, here comes that Fw 190. He was flying straight toward me. He did not see me was my first thought. Then I suddenly feared he did see me and was going to shoot me. At the last possible second he banked away and then his prop wash was blowing me and my chute around. I frantically tried to pull my guy lines as hard as I could to stop the swaying. His intentions, I believed, were to collapse my chute. Thank God he did not succeed.

The crew of *Lady Stardust II*, meanwhile, were all extremely busy trying to help one another as Cornelius Kohlman recalls.

Mike Maracek and 'Gabby' Eastman were occupied with trying to keep the plane on course, keep the speed up and the crew safe. Larry's electric suit was not working. He and I shared my suit – one shoe for him, one for me, one glove ... etc. We managed to keep a little warm and comfortable. Under the circumstances we could only perform a limited amount of activity. Once all of us completed whatever immediate safety measures we could, those of us who were able turned to the business at hand. I tried the turret guns and all I could get was about a 15–20 degree sweep. We were having trouble keeping formation. Mike salvoed our bombs to lighten our load. This helped us keep up with the group. We could not get the bomb bay doors closed. We could not locate the crank handle. With only two engines working, we proceeded to our target.

In *Lady Stardust II*'s radio room Dwight Miller heard a terrific roar of guns from his ship and many others.

Our radio room had the old open hatch and I am sure I could hear everything plainly. I saw the sky full of tracers – to the sides of us and above. In the midst of smoke I saw a tail and parts of a fuselage go past.

Some ships to the left were on fire and 846 to the right was flaming from its No. 3. engine The Focke-Wulfs came right over us. Two exploded to the right of us, one to the left and some were on fire. A P-47 to the right was going down burning. Hochstetter's ship was in bad shape. His No. 2 engine was feathered, No. 3 was burning and the right bomb bay door was bent in. Someone baled out from his ship. Immediately his chute opened, right in the midst of everything. A Focke-Wulf exploded by the side of him and his chute folded in rags.[2] I didn't fire a shot because three B-17s were above us. Other than these, the sky around us seemed empty of planes and nacelles, pieces of wings and many smaller obstacles went by. We salvoed our bombs. Some fellows baled out and their chutes opened. Our ship was hit in many places. Left waist window was blown out but the gun was still hanging by one mount. Red was hit by the right eye close to his nose. Kohlman was hit to the side of his right eye and bleeding some also. Sam, in the ball [turret], was hit but said, 'I'm staying in here as long as I can.' The fuselage was covered with slits, some three, some 6 inches long and many smaller holes.

The second pass came, 'Planes coming in at 12 o'clock, let's get them.' We pulled up behind the lead ship, a roar followed and a red streak of tracers followed. Ball said, 'Plane coming in 5 o'clock!' I saw him. The tracers were coming from the front and hitting us hard. The Fws were close at 5 o'clock now, tracers right before my eyes. There was a terrific clanging of metal. The Fw exploded. The left lower side of the radio room was filled with holes. I looked around. Two shells went to the right of me and hit my receiver, leaving only a piece of the receiver on the table and also a large hole to the left in the fuselage. I was pale I know when I saw the bottom of the door leading to the bomb bay gone. One or two shots went between my legs. Two more holes went to my left. They must have hit the right bomb bay rack because it was nearly cut in two. The bomb bay was filled with rips and holes. A good thing the bombs were salvoed on the first pass. Two cables were holding on the left, four being broken.

Suddenly, as they were firing back at the fighters, Cornelius Kohlman saw a shadow coming down from the lead ship above.

It was their tail gunner baling out. Their plane was badly damaged and going down. He fell right into the bombardier's nose section, bounced off and into our right wing. The body was Lieutenant Fred L. Myren from Boris Slanin's crew. Myren was the tail gunner at the time, but was really a formation officer. I could see the harness and lines hanging there. I was hit over my left eye by the gunsight. The bombsight hit my right knee and the pressure from the damage to the plane pushed me back into Larry DeFeo and drove us both back to the stairwell that led to the flight deck where 'Uncle Dudly' Orcutt helped us up and gave us oxygen. It was at this time that he was hit by a 20 mm shell. I covered Merle with an olive drab towel he always used. Plexiglas was blown all over the area (I was picking it out of my scalp for years). With all the bombing and damage we were not aware of how seriously DeFeo was injured. I placed him down behind the pilot's seat for protection.

Back in the radio room, Dwight N. Miller heard 'a sharp snap, something like flak' as the unfortunate Myren bounced off the nose of *Lady Stardust II*.

A parachute went over the right wing and also some stringy stuff was sliding back across my window. I opened the door and looked toward the cockpit. Something, plus a terrific wind, blinded me. It was blood, a lot of it. I was covered from head to foot and it went on through the ship, painting it red and freezing. The bomb bays were solid red and slippery. The nose was gone because of the fellow that baled into it. That was what I saw on my window. The blood inside the ship came from 'Uncle Dudly' Orcutt. The right side of his head was gone.

I heard Red Hutchinson shooting. He was firing at about 7 o'clock. Red quit and looked around with fiery eyes. Later he said, 'I got that plane. I put my sights a little to the left of him and brought them in. He went down smoking.' Sam Fain and Red saw the other Fw turn toward the chutes and fired as he passed through them. 'We saw only burning chutes and that was all,' they said. The lead ship was gone.[3] We were trying to catch the element ahead of us. The guns opened up. I saw the right waist lying on the floor and Red was shooting from both sides. The lower ball was shooting and then the tail guns opened up as the planes passed, throwing tracers everywhere. I knew the 17s were 'putting out' ahead of us for quite a few Fws were smoking. I heard something banging, like a base drummer going mad. It was the landing flap on the right wing. It was hanging down about 6 inches on the inner side and waving in the wind and hitting the wing. We were going down but I didn't know the altitude so I took the extra oxygen bottle and started up the catwalk. There was a hard wind coming from the front. I was holding on to the left rope when it broke. It was weakened from an exploded shell, I guess. I fell on the right rope. It was OK, but I dropped my oxygen bottle and it went tumbling down. I spent some time trying to get the bomb bay doors up with my knife. The crank and extension were gone so I gave the job up. I took some wire from the bomb pins and fixed the rope back. I went on up to the engineer. He didn't look like Dud but from the feeling inside me I had no doubt. He was dead.

I went back to the waist gunners, got some first aid kits and hunted for the powder. There was none. The right waist gunner grabbed a bandage and put it on his head. The expression in his eyes reminded me of a patient taking his first look at the stub of his leg after an amputation. Red was still bleeding and as he would breathe, blood would come out the hole in his eye. I wiped the blood off his face. He returned the act and said, 'I thought you were a walking dead man.' We were away from all planes. Fain came out of the ball, his face covered with blood. I looked at the cut in his head. It was swollen but not bleeding. I only cleaned it up.

We were shocked to learn interphone communication was still OK for our co-pilot, right waist and myself. The left waist could listen. The co-pilot gave us a lift by these words. 'We will go as long as we can. Everything is all right up here.' We flew north, south and west, trying to keep away from flak areas. However, it seemed to be there all the time. The co-pilot gave orders to drop the ball and Fain went to work. We were all nervous but tried not to show it. I guess you could call it past being scared and it was hard to look in your buddy's face. We didn't know the score or chances of getting down. Flak was getting thicker and we knew it was a long way to go if we were trying for the English Channel. Fain was having quite a time with the ball. A shell had hit the ring gear. It was sprung and he had only one small wrench to work with.

Now flak was cracking like sharp thunder. Our suits had been thrown over and I thought of the time my suit was hit about an hour before. Some 2 hours had passed by now. We were alone, flying just above the ground, like a coyote sneaking among bushes in fear of yelping hounds close behind. We passed over a fighter base and could see the Germans shooting at us. We could hear the machine-guns rumble above the rumble and rattle of own plane. Every time I would notice the waist gunners leaning on their guns, I would tell them to keep watching for planes. I knew their heads hurt them, but we all knew a German plane could be on us in an instant. Fain came up sweating and his head was bleeding again. He had lost his bandage and didn't bother to put it on. He said, 'The gears are sprung and the ball won't go out.' I told this to the co-pilot. He said, 'That's OK, just do all you can to make the ship lighter and watch for planes.'

Fain took over the radio gun after I put another bandage on. He never sat down a minute. I was working on my transmitter and over the interphone I heard, 'Plane coming in at 9 o'clock.' Someone had begun to shoot. I looked in the waist and saw Red sprawled out across the waist, bracing against his gun. His face was bleeding again. Fain was standing close by Red, watching the fighter. Red's level aim suddenly dropped as the Fw 190 slid under us almost on the ground. Fain was at the opposite window, trying to get a shot too, I guess. He turned around, nodding his head pointing downward. Red got the Jerry and from the way he was leaning on his gun I knew he was pretty weak from the strain plus the loss of blood.

Fain returned to the radio gun. I began to rig up another antenna. Flak was right on us again. The tail gunner said something about strafing, then he yelled, 'Tail gunner hit!' From the way be said it, I knew there was a lot of pain. I grabbed the first aid kit and ran for him. After lying him down in the waist I began slicing my way to his wound, which was centred in his back. It was a terrible hole and I hurried to get a bandage on so he wouldn't lose too much blood. After getting the bandage on, I gave him a shot of Morphine. He was also in the dark as to what we were going to do, but he lay there ready to take anything.

We were turning away from a church steeple the next time I looked up. We were close to it. I couldn't understand why there were so many people running in the church, but I guess they were scared too.

A flak battery began shooting at us from a slope near a dam to the right of us. The shells were hitting the house directly below us. Quite a few houses were set on fire this way. We were not far from the Channel. The interphone was quiet. Each fellow, some in pain and some not, just wondering, 'Could we make it?'

We seemed to be over a farm area, but anyhow there was always flak. I saw a farmer below in the field. He left his team and began running for cover. It was rather funny but none of us could laugh. Then came a call over the interphone that we loved to hear. 'There is the Channel ahead.'

Yes, there it was, the Channel ahead. Did we actually make it? Well at least we knew we had a chance. I used the command antenna by getting some wire from the bomb bay and stretched it across the radio room to my transmitter. The distress frequency-tuning unit had been hit by flak. I took a chance on a higher frequency. My transmitter tuned up OK. I had no receiver, the IFF was shot up and it wouldn't work. I began sending out a distress call, blind, at the pilot's order.

We were over the Channel, but still getting peppered by some very accurate flak. Later, I learned a German flak boat was after us.

Kohlman and DeFeo came up the catwalk and into the radio room. Nothing was said. They took their ditching positions quietly. Yes, they were wounded too. If there was anyone receiving my message I was giving them a good chance to learn all they could as to our position, wounded, etc.

Things were different now. If it was possible to ditch a B-17, the nose gone, bomb bay doors open, ball turret ready to go the instant we hit the water, we knew our pilot could do it. It wasn't the sort of gamble we had before. Will the next shell get us? Do you think we can get enough altitude to clear these buildings ahead or will we have to turn around and try again? Will this thing blow up before we can find a place to crash-land it? All this in our minds was a shadow that made it impossible to reach the English Channel.

Maracek and Mr Eastman had done the impossible. It wasn't hard to wait now. We ditched. In 1 minute we were all out in our dinghies. All except Mr Eastman. He climbed over the upper turret onto the right wing, grinning. He said, 'Why, aren't you going to wait for me?' We paddled back and got him. From a distant port the RAF were coming out. After our dinghies were tied together, we watched the ship go down. Maracek said, 'I thank God for that.'

'Fain said, "We weren't supposed to come back but we did." The tail of the ship raised as he said, "I wish Dud was with us." The RAF neared us as the two tail guns marked the plane's last appearance.

I've never felt so good and at the same time so bad, in all my life.

Lady Stardust II stayed afloat for 35 minutes before she went under. Cornelius Kohlman concluded that:

It was a sad and joyous time. Those of us who could, gave a salute to our buddy, Merle Orcutt, who was no longer with us and to *Lady Stardust II*, who made sure we were all clear, before she too left us. Merle would never be forgotten. We thanked our lucky stars for the British who picked us up out of the Channel and took good care of us. Our appreciation to the British Hospital staff at the Isle of Sheppey for their conscientiousness in watching over us and caring for our hospital needs.

Mike Wysocki in *Lucy* in the 94th had a ringside seat of the 45th Wing, who were right in front of him. His formation was under constant fighter attack for 4½ hours, but the navigator reasoned that they weren't so badly off as the *Luftwaffe* attacked from the tail position. 'They would sit out of range of our gunners and lob rockets at our formation. B-17s, P-51s, 110s and 109s were going down all over the place. I heard that the 452nd really took a beating.'

They had. *Lucky Lady*, piloted by Dick Noble, was one of fourteen losses in the Deopham Group, as Ralph J. Munn the ball turret gunner recalls.

There was the usual amount of flak, but no fighters until we were quite deep into Germany. As usual, the enemy was reluctant to attack until our P-47s and P-38 escorts made the turn for home base. Until just short of target we had considerable action, mostly high-level attacks down through the squadron. When we reached the IP the flak was a solid carpet. Up to this point we had not had a casualty outside of small to fist-size holes. I had always made it a practice to turn my turret to 12 o'clock when the bomb bay doors opened. Bruce dropped a salvo and at the same time Dick turned into the downwind leg. We were hardly off the target when we took a direct hit in the bomb bay area. In the meantime I had turned around to 6 o'clock to see what was happening. A fraction of a second later, there was another very bad jolt. This one knocked out my source of power, my electrical suit boots and gloves. I was hit in the back and the turret took considerable damage. My guns and intercom were out. It was slippery in the turret. I was then aware that I was isolated and had no control over what was to happen next. The second hit took out the left inboard engine and the ball turret. The engine out was an invitation for the remaining fighters to attack. I think that with the bomb bay doors down, they assumed we were damaged badly enough that they could work on a more active victim. I did not see another fighter until we reached the mountain foothills in eastern Belgium.

By this time Moody and Brush had manually cranked me out of my turret. I was bleeding but did not feel pain. About right here two fighters pulled up on our right wing very close. Dick called everyone to hold their fire and prepare to jump. I later learned we were out of fuel and too much had been damaged to make it back to the Channel. One of the men in the waist pulled the emergency lever for the exit. The door was supposed to break away with the slipstream. Two men at a time took turns and had to beat it off with ammunition boxes. The frame never did give. We managed to beat the skin off enough that we could get through the opening with chutes on. I had made a fast trip up to the bomb bay to see if we could jump from there. No way. In several places the keel girder was torn in in two. I could not see a hole large enough to get through without being hung up. When I arrived back at the waist Moody came over and said, 'Dick just called and said to get ready to bale out.' Within a matter of minutes we all evacuated the 'Not so Lucky Lady'. Surprisingly, it was a very orderly departure, no hesitations either. All of us had had enough for that day.

The fighters stayed with the string of chutes. They flew among us (I cannot bring myself to believe that they were trying to spill the chutes – a close pass and bank creates a vacuum and down like a string.) A couple of the crew were down in a lush meadow. They made a couple of passes at them but did not fire a shot. They stayed with us until all members were on the ground. I was picked up at once by the underground on landing, (The aircraft pancaked in on a hillside at Namur, Belgium. It did not burn.) Eventually, I was taken to Liège where I was issued forged work papers and passport and I stayed with the resistance fighters until I was captured. I had no military proof that I was an American. I was taken to Liège Prison and later turned over to the *Gestapo*. I remained in prison solitary for fourteen weeks. Had my head bashed in, all my teeth knocked out, my toes and fingers broken, beaten to a pulp at least once a day and some days twice or three times. My testicles were the size of indoor baseballs. They kept me with no shoes and naked throughout my stay, a four by six solitary cell with a hand full of straw and a bucket. From Liège I made five more stops. At the sixth stop I was placed in *Stalag Luft IV* at Gross Tychow near Kiefheide, Pomerania, on the Baltic Sea.

Several other crewmen, including Donald H. Jones, from his group joined Munn in the same camp. The tail gunner of *Hairless Joe* had come down by parachute in a ploughed field, which made a good place to land, especially since all he had on his feet were felt electric-heated slippers. He very quickly got out of his chute and Mae West, threw some dirt on top of them and started to run. Several men ran towards him. Jones heard two shots fired and knew he was in enemy territory for sure. As he turned, he saw a German soldier with a swastika on his hat and jacket. His pistol was aimed at the American. He marched Jones toward the road where several people had gathered and the young tail gunner was subjected to a tirade from one of them, who taunted him with names such as '*Luftgangster*', '*Terrorflieger*', 'Al Capone', 'Roosevelt, the Jew', '*Schweinhund*' etc. Then his anger reached the point where he hit Jones on the nose and the soldier pulled him away and got his prisoner away from the mob. He took Jones to a small shed with no windows, opened the door for him to enter and left him there for 2 hours while seven more fliers were rounded up. They joined about twelve more American fliers, some of them officers, and were told to line up. Then a couple of carloads of SS officers drove up. Jones recalls:

> They called us all to attention and proceeded to give us a severe chewing out, tongue lashing and scolding, the worst I had ever been subjected to. Then they got back into their open top touring sedans and left after about 15 minutes. By this time several guards were called in to start marching us away. Jack Covill, our radio operator, could not walk because a German

farmer had beaten him around the legs and knees so they let us use a bicycle for him to sit on and we pushed it. We came to a small village and were locked up in their jail. Some trucks came and we were loaded up and taken to a *Luftwaffe* air base at Longendiabach and locked up in their jail. We were offered black bread and I could not eat it. Nearing midnight they took each man and searched him thoroughly and then we were loaded on trucks and taken to a train station for *Dulag Luft* interrogation centre at Wetzlar. Atkinson was told exactly where he had received all of his training in the US. They had information we thought was confidential. After spending three or four days there we were given clothes and shoes, GI issue. Then we were taken to the train station and put into boxcars and began our journey to a permanent PoW camp. This train ride was very slow, one reason being we stopped so many times and it seemed like every night they left us on a siding near a marshalling yard. We thought their strategy was to present us as a target for the RAF to bomb. After about four days we arrived at *Stalag Luft IV*. This was to be our 'home' for the duration.

In the composite wing, meanwhile, heading for Zwickau was Abe Dolim.

After crossing the enemy coast at Ostend, we received reports that the *Luftwaffe* was up in force. Near Koblenz our escort of P-51s departed to chase bogies. Some minutes later, Lieutenant Burnett Rhett Maybank Jr, our bombardier, spotted a small formation of unidentified fighters at 3 o'clock level. I stood up to be close to my .50s and as I squinted out toward 2 o'clock, I was shocked to see about six jet black Fw 190s fly right through the high squadron, attacking from 12 o'clock level. The group closed up – no one seemed to be hurt. About 10 minutes later, ten more *Rammjäger* Fw 190s attacked the lead squadron from 12 o'clock level. Maybank was the 19-year-old son of a US senator and scion of a family of South Carolina aristocracy, but was taking the same chances as Albert G. Herrera, our American Indian warrior tail gunner from Colorado. BR's favourite expression was 'hubba bubba', which when spoken rapidly is the American equivalent of 'get on with it'. Sergeant George Kelch, Sergeant Howard E. Long and I fired as they went by at 3 o'clock. One of the Fws rammed the No. 6 aircraft in the lead squadron and both exploded.

Two more B-17s dropped out of formation. One began a shallow trailing dive with all ten men baling out. The other maintained speed with the group about 500 feet below the lead squadron and dropped its landing gear to communicate air surrender. After some minutes, it retracted its landing gear and rejoined the group, which was then about 20 miles south-east of Frankfurt. At our altitude of 19,000 feet, there were some stratus layers, ideal for the enemy, and as I scanned at 11 o'clock level, I spotted a large formation of fighters approaching from about 2,000 yards, heading for our low squadron. I got on intercom and notified the crew – Me Bf 109s, about thirty of them in three flights. We opened fire at about 1,000 yards and I picked the far left Me in the lead flight. Two of the Mes were shot out of formation before they approached 500 yards. A string of cannon shells, so close I heard their sharp cracks, exploded just in front of our nose. I fired about sixty rounds at my Me until he passed by our No. 1 engine, forcing me to quit. It was closing fast from about 100 yards when I yelled to Wehrfritz to get him. He poured .50s into the Me at point blank range. Apparently, the enemy pilot was not firing at this point or he would have raked us. His aircraft stalled after passing us and our tail gunner saw it go down and crash – the pilot did not bale out.

Our combined .50s created a tremendous ear-splitting, reverberating racket and the entire bomber seemed to vibrate. The stench of exploded cartridges filled our nose compartment. The 332nd was lucky to be intact, having suffered no losses. The bomb run to the target was a question mark as preceding bomb groups created fires at the target, forcing our lead bombardier to aim through the billowing smoke. Near Weimar, the low group to our right took a pass from 6 o'clock level by ten times by Bf 109s with no apparent effect. The floor of our navigator-bombardier compartment was covered with empty .50 calibre casings and in moving about I felt like I had roller skates on my fur-lined boots.

During the fighter attacks against the composite wing, Victor Bonomo tried to be accurate and deliberate while firing the left cheek gun in the nose of *Fortress McHenry*. Though scared and quite excited, he waited until he was sure that the 109s and 190s were in range before applying the proper lead and firing, but nothing happened. The young navigator cursed the armament people and his weapon as the fighters ripped thorough the Fortress formation. Confusion reigned until static in his earphones revealed that he had been pressing the intercom microphone instead of the gun button. Abe Dolim knew he had flown a long and hazardous mission too.

Fred Robertson in the Bloody Hundredth recalls:

We were the third wing in. Things went routinely most of the way. I don't recall heavy fighter activity. Our cover was doing the job. We were flying off to the right of the second wing to avoid prop-wash and the second wing was to the right of the first. I felt comfortable out there because it kept us a little to the right of Ulm. The problem may come from the first or second wing. When we approached the Ulm area, I warned Stanley that both wings up front were heading over a heavy flak area. If the pilot took his first evasive action to his left, which is normal for all first pilots, he might not have enough airspace remaining to get back on course with enough room left to make a normal 2-minute 90-degree turn onto the bomb run. I was afraid of the congestion near the IP or bomb run. The inevitable happened. The lead wing found itself in the middle of the flak, turned left first, not realising they would have trouble getting to the IP. The same thing happened to the second; evidently neither lead navigator was aware of the flak at Ulm. Both wing commanders had to make a quick decision, whether to do a 360 and try the IP again, or choose a secondary target. One wing chose the latter; I think the second wing and

I think the first wing, made an 8-minute 360 at the limit of their gas consumption and put about ten or twelve B-17s in the Channel. We were sitting off to the right minding our own business. I had put Stanley about 2 degrees off course, avoiding the flak, when suddenly we realised we would be first over the target. Rube told Stanley to have Fuller spread the formation out to cover more area in our bombing pattern. Rube was a great bombardier. If you put him on the IP level and on the proper heading, he never missed. I hit eighteen straight IPs right on and he hit eighteen MPIs. I would love to have been at Eighth Air Force head-quarters. The confusion about strike reports must have been amusing. As the target time passed, there was evidently no strike report from the lead wing, or the second. The brass had to be wondering what in Hell was going on. General LeMay intimated later that they felt the mission had failed. So when our strike report reported the target hit, smoke to 20,000 feet, good results, etc., the big boys realised all was not lost and LeMay was proud as a peacock because he was commander of the Third Division, which always got the long-range jobs.

After the target a number of planes reported that they were running low on gas (on VHF) and were asking for Air-Sea Rescue support when they hit the Channel. None of these were from our wing, however. I ate my Snicker (the co-pilot was always issued ten candy bars and ten packs of gum for every mission). The crux of the Brux story is that if the two lead navigators ahead of me had plotted their flak maps properly, they would have stayed out of trouble; we would have been third over the target and would not have received so much credit. On more than one occasion, I was appalled and ashamed of some of the navigational failures that transpired in 1944 over Europe. My point of view is that of a navigator. Navigational lapses not only put the success of a mission in jeopardy, it caused unnecessary losses and that means PoW and KIA.

For Richard Wynn, navigator in *Rosie's Riveters*, the mission had, for the most part, been uneventful.

Our bomb run was almost due north and we made a hard left at the RP and returned to an intersection with our inbound flight path and followed it home. There was fierce fighter attack on the front end of the formation with heavy counter attack from our fighter cover. We saw it but were not engaged with fighters the entire way to the target, which was an unusual experience for the 100th. Our wing hit the target in three waves. The first wave's target was the centre of the installation and by the time we got there, heavy smoke had risen to well over 10,000 feet. The bombs of the second wave, whose target was the right third of the installation, exploded at the moment the strike photo was taken. Bombing results were 'excellent'.

We encountered light flak over the target but observed some rocket-propelled anti-aircraft fire. We were hit in No. 3 and lost oil pressure before the prop could be feathered. Cockpit procedure was complicated by the fact that a faulty flare from the lead ship deposited a heavy film of 'guck' over the pilot's half of the windshield, putting the co-pilot in control of the ship. His visibility was also limited to some extent. With a windmilling prop and all the drag it created, we were unable to keep up with the formation and became a single straggler on the way home with heavy fuel consumption on a very deep penetration. It is doubtful whether we could have made Britain. I did a fuel consumption problem after a while and had us running out of fuel about the time we would reach the Channel. It would have been interesting to see whether we could have made it or not. We expected fighter attacks and expected to get knocked down soon because, Hollywood notwithstanding, a single B-17 is mismatched against a flurry of fighters usually. We made it alone without any fighter cover all the way to a point a few miles east of the Rhine before six 109s hit us from the rear. We got two of them for sure and had a probable; a third that was streaking for the ground with heavy smoke pouring out. The 109s plastered us good, knocking out the controls and who knows what else. We all got out OK and were buzzed but not fired upon in our chutes by the remaining 109s. Farmers with pitchforks and soldiers were literally waiting beneath for me to land. We were captured immediately a few miles east of St Goarshausen on the Rhine, where we spent our first night in captivity in a civilian jail. Almost all of us were picking flak fragments from our hides for weeks to come. Our tail gunner sustained the only serious injury, a bad laceration of his knee and calf, a really nasty and painful wound. We spent almost a year in *Stalag Luft III* before my pilot and I managed to escape in April 1945.

Luftwaffe fighter commander Adolf Galland recalled that more than 400 fighters were sent up to oppose the American formations on 12 May but:

... only one unit managed to make contact with the enemy in close formation. Good results were attained in the Frankfurt sector. The escorting enemy fighters caught the others while they were still assembling and were soon involved in costly dogfights. Where we managed to break through the fighter escort or found an unaccompanied bomber formation, we were successful. A single wing was attacked head on in a concentrated mass attack and broken up; within a few minutes it lost half its planes. It was only saved from total destruction because fighters from other groups came to their rescue. And again on the way back the bombers were attacked on a second sortie. This action was successful against stragglers and formations, which were not covered at the time by escort fighters. The Americans reported the loss of forty-six bombers.[4] The German record shows a definite bag of seventy-two bombers against a loss of sixty-five of our own aircraft. We had gathered all our strength but we knew that we had neither succeeded in preventing a raid on one of our more vital war industries, nor inflicted such losses on the enemy as to deter them from a repetition of such attacks. The raided works were heavily damaged. The Americans insist that at the Leauna works, a building in which experiments with heavy water for the splitting of the atom were being made, was destroyed.

Twelve of the American bombers, including *Captain Crow* in the Bloody Hundredth formation, were probably shot down by flak. Jack Moore recalls:

> We were attacked by Bf 109s but sustained no damage. Just after successfully bombing the target, a heavy burst of flak hit us between No. 3 and No. 4 engines. This killed both engines and started a fire in the right wing. My co-pilot Robert Blais panicked and ordered the crew to 'bale out' of the aircraft. I immediately countermanded that order, to give me time to evaluate the situation and salvage the aircraft. After a vain attempt to control the plane. I then ordered the crew to 'bale out'. Before I left the cockpit, I called on the intercom to assure myself that there was no one left in the aircraft. I also looked back through the plane to make sure there was no one there. I cannot explain what happened next. All of our training relating to baling out taught us that the pilot, co-pilot and top turret gunner evacuated though the bomb bay. The co-pilot and gunner went that way safely. For some strange reason I chose to go forward to the small hatch which is designated for the navigator and bombardier. By this time the aircraft was in a spin and centrifugal force held me down so that I could not move. Eventually, the spin lessened and I moved forward, only to find my bombardier Monroe T. Whidby stuck in the forward hatch. He had gotten his arms and legs out of the plane, but his backpack parachute was caught in the hatch itself. I simply put my foot on his back and shoved him out. Had I baled out of the plane through the bomb bay, as I should have, he would have died when the aircraft crashed. Shortly after that I left the plane and opened my parachute. Suddenly, there was a loud explosion and parts of the plane came raining down on top of me, catching my parachute on fire. Luckily, I was close to the ground, but I still hit very hard when I struck the ground. I tried to walk, but fell on my face. I then realised my leg was bleeding from a flak wound and I had suffered fractures of my leg. About this time, civilians surrounded me. One of them pointed a pistol at me and asked '*Pistola?*' I said, 'No, I am not armed.' I then asked, 'Czechoslovakian?' The man replied, '*Nein, Deutsche.*'[5]

Back on the bases in East Anglia, the returning crews took stock. When he finally got back, Mike Wysocki went to the officers' club after debriefing and cleaning up and 'proceeded to get gloriously drunk'. After they landed at Bury Abe Dolim and Hamil's crew looked for hits but found none. Dolim recalls:

> At interrogation we learned that our main group force lost two aircraft to Me 210s and 410s using air to air rockets and 40 mm cannons. Wehrfritz was credited with one Bf 109 destroyed and Kelch with one Fw 190 damaged. Our group claimed twenty-one enemy aircraft destroyed, eight probables, and nine damaged for one day's mission. Much unlike the Hollywood version of air combat, I did not hear enemy aircraft engine noise or cannon fire, even though the enemy pressed their attack to within yards of our bomber. It all happened so quickly. I estimated the third firing run at 7 seconds duration with a 550 mph rate of closure. Further,

all members of the crew violently agreed as to enemy aircraft colouring and markings. The *Rammjäger* Fw 190s were believed to be from elite squadrons. Apparently, their tactics were to destroy our group and squadron leaders and to disrupt the cohesion of our formations. The Bf 109 attacks were the dreaded 'company front' formations. The line abreast lead flight were the shooters. The high flight behind the shooters were believed to be high cover to prevent our escort fighters from interfering with the attack. The low flight behind the shooters no doubt were expected to shoot down damaged bombers or stragglers which dropped out of the bomber group. As soon as the bogies showed up, our escort fighters went on 'free hunt'. We were the bait but Jimmie, we got hit four times by Mes and Fw 190s and there wasn't a single 'little friend' around to help us out.

Wysocki and other members of Koval's crew completed their tour just over two weeks later, on 30 May. There would be many more tough missions ahead for Abe Dolim and Victor Bonomo.

At Snetterton, after landing, the crews were served their usual coffee and donuts by the Red Cross girls before heading for debriefing, the navigators going to one place, the bombardiers another and so forth, and intelligence officers asked questions. Debriefing and post-mission huddles were conducted in a furore as crews told the intelligence officers everything they had seen and the debriefing officers offered the standard post-mission shot of whiskey to anyone who wanted it. The mission to Zwickau had cost the group twelve Fortresses, including two that collided over Germany. Among those lost were *Smokey Stover Jr, The 7th Son*, while *Silver Slipper*, which was originally listed as missing, made it back across the Channel to Manston with two engines feathered on the left side. One navigator who survived saw the lead ship pull up into a wing over with half its left wing shot off and then described how the fighters headed back through and started cutting them up. From then on, it was just one long mêlée until finally there just wasn't any Snetterton Falcons to talk about. *Stormy Weather* was also missing. Chas E. Williams was firing his radio gun when a swarm of fighters swept out of the sun and he heard 'popping' sounds coming from the tail proceeding towards the nose.

An Fw 190 had crept up below and was firing point blank. Our 19-year-old tail gunner, Charlie Thornhill of Seymour, Texas, opened both tail .50s until they were shot out of his hands. The whole dorsal fin was shot away. Both waist gunners and Charlie Filer were dead and our co-pilot mortally wounded. The intercom was out. Of the survivors I was injured the most. My blood was all over the radio room floor. A machine-gun slug had gone through my left calf, a shell fragment went through my right knee and numerous shell fragments had hit my hands and back. I baled out and went into free fall for about 7,000 feet. It was as well that I did as the fighter pilots were shooting down airmen in their chutes. I landed in a forest and shortly afterwards I met a short little farmer called Fritz who came at me with a pitchfork. Then he saw what sad shape I was in and put one of my arms around his neck (I am 6 ft 1 in) and half carried me to the nearest house in his village. I was taken to the *Burgomeister*'s office, along with two other downed Americans. They were not hurt but I was slapped and knocked around before being thrown into a dungeon-like jail. (I heard later that an officer was shot in the mouth on the ground and another was bayoneted.) Eventually, I was rescued by Father Hoffmann and put in a little catholic hospital, where they operated on my rapidly swelling knee. They took care of me for two days and then I spent several days in a labour camp with four other Americans and a barracks full of slave labourers kidnapped by the Nazis. It was a wretched, rat-infested hole. Finally, I was sent to PoW camp.

The Reluctant Dragon made it back to Snetterton and Warren Berg wrote up in his diary the day's shattering events.

The carnage was terrific. We were lucky to get back at all. Fw 190s charged through our formations with cannon and machine-guns blazing. B-17s burning, exploding and disappearing on all sides. We were under attack for at least 45 minutes. Plenty of the enemy going down too. A dogfight between ours and enemy fighters swirls by like a windblown tumbleweed. It all happens so swiftly one can't quite grasp the situation. The most heartening sight of the trip was the four P-38s covering us from thirty Fw 190s. They would hang above us and turn to meet the attackers each time they came through. They wouldn't chase but stayed close to us, thereby giving us and themselves maximum protection possible. I'd like to pin medals on those boys. Today we lost the last of the other seven crews that became operational with us. Our crew alone is left. We feel like survivors. We have been most fortunate – so far not one in our crew has been scratched. Again (Graves Registration) are clearing out the effects of the brand new crew in our hut – for the third time. We are all getting calloused. Perhaps we just refuse to take it seriously.

The doors to the 96th Nissens seemed like the turnstiles to death.

Notes

1. *Yesterday's Dragons: A navigator from Hawaii* recalls his fifty-one missions over enemy territory. Abel L. Dolim (2001).
2. All ten men in Lieutenant Herbert C. Hochstetter's crew were made PoW.
3. Three of Boris Slanin's crew were lost. Seven survived to be made PoW.
4. Worst hit was the 45th CBW, the 452nd losing fourteen Forts, the 96th twelve (including two, which collided whilst under attack) and the 388th, one. US fighters claimed sixty-one fighters shot down for the loss of seven of their own. In fact, twenty-eight German pilots perished, twenty-six others being injured.
5. Moore later found out that ball turret gunner, Bill Dishneau, was dead. At *Stalag Luft III* at Sagan, which had a population of 10,000 airmen, most of them officers, he found his navigator, co-pilot and bombardier. The other crewmembers were crew chief and top turret gunner; Henry Heiber; radio operator, John Kidner; waist gunner, John Jedrick; waist gunner, Jim Hunter; tail gunner, Charles Mueller.

CHAPTER 6

'Planes Overhead Will be Ours'[1]

... I'd seen Sharpe in bloody shorts, wrenching his neck to see the wound on his left cheek. I'd seen what a knee looked like with the kneecap clipped away and a waist gunner with his brains all over the Alclad and his legs shot off just below his flak-suit. That guy was just as dead as any of those in the surf today.

'D-Day ....' Serenade to the Big Bird, Bert Stiles

American airmen returning to their bases in East Anglia from 48-hour passes in London – the Mecca of GIs on leave – a little hung over, but dedicated to their *rendezvous* with their duty and their destiny, normally had tales of debauchery or of sightseeing to tell. In Piccadilly, Yanks got propositioned about every 10 feet. The standard question for anyone returning from London was, 'What are the latest quotations?' Two aircrew officers returning to Bury St Edmunds recalled that near Hyde Park they heard a loud unmistakably Yank voice saying, 'Five pounds! Whattayagot a diamond studded snatch?' Now talk of Piccadilly commandos, that army of prostitutes that thronged Leicester Square, of Soho theatres full of English burlesque, pretty corny gags, good looking girls and several naked ones too, had been overtaken by more newsworthy items. Vivid accounts of passenger trains being withdrawn and trucks, jeeps, transports and staff cars jamming the English roads and narrow winding English country lanes and causing vast traffic snarl-ups were being recounted instead. Newspapers announced that in Andover, Hampshire, office workers were being given 15 minutes extra at lunchtime to cross the street! It could all only mean one thing: 'D-Day' was imminent! But where and when? Only General Dwight D. Eisenhower, Supreme Commander at SHAEF (Supreme Headquarters Allied Expeditionary Forces) and a select few knew that a stretch of the Normandy coastline from Quineville to just south of Caen had been selected for the long-awaited second front. On 8 May 'Ike' had selected Monday 5 June as D-Day but though coastal defence installations in the Cherbourg-Caen and Pas de Calais areas were bombed, the day passed without invasion. A local storm front, forming suddenly east of Iceland, forced Eisenhower to postpone the invasion for 24 hours. General Bernard L. Montgomery, C-in-C Land Forces, was prepared to go despite the weather, but ACM Sir Trafford Leigh-Mallory C-in-C AEAF was not in favour, as so much depended upon air superiority.

All convoys at sea had to reverse their courses, but two British midget submarines continued to their positions off the beaches to act as markers for the invasion army when it arrived. Group Captain J. M. Stagg, the Met Officer, predicted 36 hours of relatively clear weather with moderate winds and Eisenhower turned to Montgomery and asked whether he could see any reason for not going on the 6th. Monty replied, I would say 'Go!' The other commanders agreed. 'OK' said Eisenhower, 'We'll go.'

That night at Rougham, Lieutenant Abe Dolim recorded in his diary 'There have been all sorts of rumours about an imminent invasion of the enemy coast.' At Molesworth, Ben Smith saw RAF aircraft and gliders going over 'wave after wave' and he knew that they would be going in the morning. He thought there would be 'hell to pay'. Around midnight Staff Sergeant Frank A. McKee at Watton could hear some of the early airborne invasion force flying overhead as he and his assistant finished getting a photo reconnaissance Mosquito ready for an early D-Day mission. Since early that afternoon they had been painting on black and white invasion stripes, which came as a big surprise to them.

D-Day arrived early at RAF night bomber stations, in the first few hours of the night of 5/6 June, because the British heavies were assigned to softening up targets such as enemy gun positions covering the invasion beaches. D-Day began with an assault behind enemy lines by more than 23,000 airborne troops, 15,500 of them American. On the morning of the 6 June at briefings throughout East Anglia, American aircrews tramped into the briefing rooms to be told what their mission would be. At Rougham, Wilbur Richardson felt, 'this must be it for sure'. Sure enough, at briefing, it was. What a contrast there was. Usually it was groans when they learned of the target. Now, there was animated talk and 'yippee!' it would be off to the shoreline targets at dawn before the landings began about an hour later. At Kimbolton, Franklin L. Betz, a B-17 navigator in the 379th, groped sleepily for his clothes. He knew that to be awakened about 0400 for a mission was 'pretty much routine' but to be 'hauled out of the sack at about 0130 to report to briefing'– well something unusual just had to be 'up'! The atmosphere at briefing was invariably sombre. Sitting quietly on benches dozing or languidly puffing on cigarettes that glowed eerily in the soft light of the starkly furnished rooms, there was very little talk while the fliers, officers and enlisted men, waited for the CO, Colonel Preston, to arrive. 'Tenshun!' someone up front bawled when the CO strode in. Everyone arose, standing erect, eyes straight ahead. 'At ease,' the Colonel said. The men sat down quietly, tensely awaiting roll call and the removal of the cover from the huge map of Europe on which the course to and from the target had been traced. If it showed a deep penetration of Germany that meant dangerous fighter attacks and flak encounters throughout the flight. A groan arose from the dry throats of the airmen that trailed off into excited whispers as briefing continued. But at 0230, when the briefing officer announced, 'This is it – this is D-Day!' it was different; a lusty cheer shattered the quiet of a moment before. Whoops, whispers and yells echoed from the grey walls. It was an unprecedented and ecstatic vocal demonstration by the fliers who had doggedly been carrying the war to Germany for many months

183

with considerable losses of men and planes. It was the day they had waited to share with the ground forces and together they would assault the Nazi war machine, hopefully gaining a foothold on the mainland with the ultimate goal of driving the *Wehrmacht* back to the Fatherland and crushing it.

At Seething, Norfolk Lieutenant Ben C. Isgrig, a bombardier in the 448th, recalled that they were called to the briefing room at 2300 hours on 5 June. Colonel Jerry Mason, the CO, said, 'This is it.' Their target was *Omaha* Beach. The first mission was primarily concerned with the neutralising of enemy coastal defences and front-line troops. Subsequent missions would be directed against lines of communication leading to the bridgehead. At Bassingbourn, home of the B-17s of the 91st, Lieutenant Bert Stiles, co-pilot of a B-17 Fortress crew led by Lieutenant Samuel 'Sam' Newton, was one of the thousands who waited.[2]

We waited for so long it turned into a joke. Each time they woke us up in the night somebody would say, 'It's D-day.' But it never was.

And then on the 6th of June it was.

The squadron waker-upper dragged us out of the sack 29 minutes after the midnight of 5th June. 'Breakfast at one, briefing at two,' he said tiredly.

'Jesusgod,' I said.

'What the hell is this?' Sam said.

We were sick of their war. We'd been in bed a half-hour.

When we went to chow there was a faint glow from the moon, curtained off by a low overcast. The line-men were pre-flighting the Forts, running up engines. There were a lot of RAF planes going over.

All the rank in the group made chow, tables full of majors and colonels and captains.

'Late bridge party,' Bell said.

'Ground-gripping bastards,' somebody else said. 'They go to bed when we get up.'

'Maybe this is D-day,' I said.

Nobody laughed. It wasn't worth a laugh any more. Too many times. I drank a lot of tomato juice and hoped it would be good for the deep weariness in my knees.

Doc Dougherty was there, looking charming. 'I'm going along,' he said. 'Maybe with you.'

'See you in Moscow,' I said.

Maybe it was a shuttle job. It was early enough.

The briefing-map was uncovered when we came in. France again, just south of Cherbourg.

'Good deal,' Sam said. 'Sack-time before lunch.'

Mac, the Public Relations officer, was there in white scarf and flying clothes.

'You think this is D-Day,' I said. He nodded.

The weariness was gone. For the first time I tuned in on the tension in that room. I grabbed the Doc and Bell and Sam in one handful.

'D-day,' I said. 'Honest to God.'

They already knew.

We were in on it. We were flying in the big show.

Colonel Terry (CO), got up. '... This is invasion ...' were the first words I got. There was a lot of noise '... you are in support of ground troops ....'

At Horham, Suffolk, Henry Tarcza, a B-17 bombardier in Matthew McEntee's crew, was awakened some hours before daylight. At first he thought that this was just another routine bombing mission over enemy-occupied Europe. Shortly after 0300 hours he enjoyed a breakfast of bacon and country fresh eggs, a wartime delicacy reserved only for the combat flying personnel. They entered the maximum security briefing room around 0400 hours where the huge map on the wall was covered with yards of thick drapery. After all the noise of shifting chairs had ceased, the briefing officer calmly pulled the covering material towards him and a long moan from all the flying men echoed throughout the room, followed by a hoarse whisper, 'Invasion'.

The red streamers on the map ran from every air base in England and crossed the Channel, converging on one tiny spot near Cherbourg. The briefing Colonel pointed towards that area with what happened to be an old billiard cue and said, 'Yes gentlemen. This is the day you've been waiting for and this is the spot that has been selected'. It was a relatively short briefing because the navigators had already been given separate instructions. Before unlocking the exit doors the briefing officer smiled and said, 'Good luck, gentlemen and give 'em Hell!'

The 8th was required to fly three missions. The first was primarily concerned with neutralising enemy coastal defences and front-line troops. Subsequent missions would be directed against lines of communication leading to the bridgehead. The bombers would be in good company with no fewer than thirty-six squadrons of Mustangs and Thunderbolts patrolling the area. Initially, they would protect the 'big friends', but would later break off and strafe ground targets. It was evident that there could be no lay and that any stragglers would be left to their fate. Any aborts were to drop out of formation before leaving the English coast and then fly back to base at below 14,000 feet. It was a one-way aerial corridor and the traffic flow intense. Aircraft would fly to and fro over the length of England, dropping various coloured flares to denote the aerial corridors. If a Fortress had to be ditched, only those ships returning to England from the bridgehead would stop to pick up crews. Crews were told that if they were shot down they were to wait in uniform until they could join their own troops in France. Finally, an 'inspirational message to the departing troops' from General Eisenhower, the Supreme Allied Commander, was read out. Perhaps it was the tension brought on by the big occasion, but not all crewmen were impressed. Ben Smith thought that Churchill could have done it with a lot more class.

Briefing over, a line of two and a half ton trucks known as 'Deuce and a half' was assembled to take crews to their waiting Fortresses. The pre-dawn calm of the countryside around the farmlands and in the towns and villages near the bomber bases was soon shattered by the roar of thousands of Wright Cyclones and Twin Wasps being pre-flighted at all points of the compass. Overhead the moon shone through a thick black undercast. McEntee's crew said little as they proceeded to their bomber in a canvas-covered truck. Tarcza was sure they all felt as he did. If the Germans shared his secret at that moment it could alter the destiny of mankind. They all did a good job of maintaining composure so that the ground crews might not suspect that D-Day had, in fact, arrived. Their B-17 bore none of the usual fancy paintings. On its nose were the simple words, *El's Bells*, named by McEntee in honour of his girlfriend in New York City and whom he later married. They waited in line on the runway for their turn to take-off. As they left the ground Tarcza had that very comforting feeling that he was coming back safely to England. They circled to gain altitude. It was early daylight and the sight in the vast sky staggered Tarcza's wildest imagination. The air was thick with eastbound aircraft for as many miles as he could see in all directions. *El's Bells* joined in and headed toward France.

Franklin L. Betz in *Old Gappy* lifted off at 0445. A 'fluffy' layer of clouds below hampered visibility, but there were some breaks and he could see the choppy dark waters of the English Channel. Droning steadily toward the continent, he gasped when a huge opening in the clouds revealed ships and boats of all sizes dotting the water as far as he could see. 'Hundreds – no, there must be thousands,' he thought. Although no one type of ship could be identified from nearly 3 miles high, he was to learn later that practically the whole spectrum of powered vessels from battleships to motor launches made up the invasion fleet. Landing ships carrying thousands of troops, tanks, guns, vehicles and ammunition were positioning for the dash to the Normandy beaches. Barrage balloons swayed lazily above the ships to which they were attached by stout cables. More holes appeared in the clouds and the awesome spectacle continued to unfold. Betz rose from his seat in the navigator's cramped work area in the left rear of the B-17G's nose to get a better view from the right waist window. Fascinated, he saw puffs of white smoke from the huge guns of battleships and cruisers aimed toward the mainland and a moment later massive explosions could be seen a short distance inland where the shells landed, kicking up a fountain of dirt and debris. That, he reflected, must be a mixture of 'steel and stones, flesh and bones' when the targets were hit.

Normally, the B-17s and B-24s were up and circling for hours before the fighters took off, but on this particular morning the sky was 'just dark with planes'. As the shadows passed over the airfields, the sky turned sunny then dark, sunny then dark. Eventually, the bombers flew out towards the Channel and the fighters took off. It was just getting light as Ben Isgrig's formation left the English coast and the clouds broke enough for them to see the hundreds of ships in the Channel heading for France. He could plainly see the heavy warships shelling the coast, which was shrouded in smoke. Besides seeing more ships than he had ever seen before, there were also more heavy bombers in the air than he thought possible to put up in one area. The coast itself was covered in clouds and he didn't see their target at all; neither did he see flak or fighters.

(Isgrig and his crew flew three more missions before they were shot down over France on 12 June.)

Claude V. Meconis was co-pilot of a Liberator in the 466th. As they passed over the southern coast of England and headed south over the Channel, he began straining his eyes to see some of the invasion fleet that the briefing at Attlebridge had disclosed. A low undercast in patches obscured most of the water, but whenever open spaces permitted he could see landing craft and large ships moving south and south-east on a fairly rough sea. Also below, just above the clouds, he saw B-26 formations assembling. Meconis did not see a single friendly fighter though thirty-five squadrons were expected as cover. He mused that they were probably at a low altitude, below the clouds, actively aiding the first assault on the coast. Anyway, they did not need them. Meconis knew each man on the crew prayed for the success of whatever those in the landing barges below had to do. He knew that their job was infinitely the more dangerous of the two. His crew were scared a bit because they did not know exactly what kind of air opposition the *Luftwaffe* would throw at them. Frankly, Meconis expected to see a sky 'full of fighters and flak, all confusion', but he knew that the boys in the barges would meet 'steel and concrete and a tough fight!'

Franklin Betz's Fortress, swaying gently, throbbed on. There was still no sign of Bf 109s or Fw 190s, but he could see that their 'little friends' were out in force. The Lightnings, Thunderbolts and Mustangs, their invasion markings – black and white stripes on wings and fuselages – were very prominent, providing an aerial umbrella for the landing forces. Strafing the enemy positions up and down the coast and for some miles inland, they were determined to help the GIs embarking on the great crusade. The white capped wake of hundreds of circling landing craft awaiting the order to head to the shore contributed to the drama of the scene. The cloud cover required a blind bombing technique using radar. According to Franklin Betz's log they were close to the target – gun positions near Arromanches roughly midway between the Cherbourg peninsula and Le Havre. The bombs dropped from the bellies of the bombers, disappearing in the clouds to devastate and disrupt the enemy's fighting capabilities far below. Betz remembered the briefing officer's words, 'There would be meagre flak, if any at all.' he was right. There was none. The German guns were busily exchanging fire with the mighty invasion fleet massed in the Bay of the Seine and stretching for miles into the Channel.

It was daylight, with the sun shining above the clouds in the east, as Meconis's B-24 turned right to head 270 degrees for 90 miles until the formation was west of the Cherbourg peninsula. Several bursts of flak came up. A group to their right passed too close to either Cherbourg or the islands just west of it. A ball of flak, like that he'd seen over Brunswick once, came up at them. Their let down over England was gradual. Clouds broke up and when they arrived back at their base area, only small fair weather cumulus and haze existed. The sky was 'a trifle overloaded', but the group managed to cut their way through the 'snag' and land safely. An S-2 man, Hodges, met the crew at the plane for interrogation. They asked for news but all Hodges could say was, 'The invasion is on.' Meconis was so sleepy on the trip back that he contemplated taking a pill to keep awake. He was glad that he didn't because the crews were allowed to go to bed immediately after landing. They were told that they would be called if they were needed.

At Hethel, Lieutenant Robert A. Jacobs, a DR (Dead Reckoning) navigator in the 564th Squadron, was also having trouble with sleep, or the lack of it. Part of a lead crew, their mission was to lead the 446th from Bungay to bomb the invasion beaches of Normandy immediately prior to the ground assault. The 446th had been selected to be the first American heavy bomb group to cross the French coast on *the* day but Jacobs' B-24 *Liberty Run* would be the first American bomber overhead the beaches. At 0220 *Liberty Run* took off, climbed to 10,000 feet and circled in their prescribed forming area, firing specific flares as the 446th aircraft assembled in formation behind them. The mission went precisely as planned except for an undercast, which necessitated bombing by radar. As *Liberty Run* approached the French coast, the radar navigator called Jacobs over to look at his PPI scope. It clearly showed the vast armada of the invasion fleet standing just off the coast of Normandy. It was a thrilling sight even on radar. Bombs were away at precisely 0600. *Liberty Run* led her aircraft back to Bungay via Portland Bill and returned to Hethel. Much to the crew's surprise, no flak or German fighters were observed and their fighter cover was 'everywhere'. As they started to undress to get some rest, the lead crew was again told to get over to Bungay for another mission. During the course of the briefing the flight surgeon gave each aircrew member a pill with the instruction to take it only 'when you feel you can no longer keep awake'. The crew had been up since 0230, 5 June, and it was now the afternoon of 6 June, some 36 hours later and they were running on reserve energy.

There was little sign of *Luftwaffe* activity. The German pilots had been caught almost cold. In northern France *Leutnant* Wolfgang Fischer of 3./JG2 finally received warning of the invasion in the early hours of 6 June, at about 0500 hours, and his unit was ordered to Criel, just outside Paris. There, in all haste their *Dodels* were prepared and they took off at about 0930 hours for their first low-level attack on the landing fleet in the English sector of Caen-Bayeux where the landing craft provided 'excellent targets'. On board one of the LST landing craft was Gunner Len Woods of the 53rd Medium Regiment Royal Artillery, which arrived off *Sword* beach at 1000 on 6 June. They were unloading by driving onto pontoon rafts, which then ferried them to the beach. After the lower deck had been cleared a German fighter machine-gunned his craft and dropped a bomb, which exploded under the bow doors. This distorted the bow doors and wrecked the lift. To finish unloading they had to pull away from the beach and tie up alongside another LST that had already unloaded and run their vehicles across from one ship to the other by means of wooden planks. Woods remarked, 'It was a quirk of fate that with the thousands of ships in the area, one of the two German planes in the air managed to hit us.'

The only *Luftwaffe* presence over the invasion beaches that morning were two Fw 190s flown by *Oberstleutnant* Josef 'Pips' Priller, *Kommodore* JG26 '*Schlageter*', and his regular *Kacmarek* (wingman), *Unteroffizier* Heinz

Wodarczyk of the Stab flight at Priller's Lille-Nord command post. These were the only two fighters available to JG26.[3] Near Le Havre the pair climbed into the solid cloudbank and emerged to see the invasion fleet spread out before them. Priller, in his usual Fw 190A-8 'Black 13' *Jutta* and Wodarczyk each made a full-throttle (650 km/h – 400 mph) 50 foot low-level strafing run over *Sword* beach just after 0800 hours with cannons and machine-guns before landing at Creil unscathed and honour satisfied.[4]

Abe Dolim, who flew his eighteenth mission bombing a road junction behind the invasion beaches, noted in his diary that there was 'no flak' and 'nothing but bombers and escorting fighters were seen'. Ben Smith did not see a single German fighter or even a burst of flak either. 'Amazing!' he noted, adding that he 'could see a battleship – possibly the *Texas* out in the Channel, firing at shore targets. He saw a solid mass of ships offshore, beached landing crafts and others streaking in with their precious burdens and he knew that a beachhead had been made. Ben Isgrig in the 448th left England just as it was getting light and the clouds broke enough for him to see the hundreds of ships in the Channel heading for France. He could plainly see the heavy warships shelling the coast, which was shrouded in smoke. Besides seeing more ships than he had ever seen before, there were also more heavy bombers in the air than he thought possible to put up in one area. The coast itself was covered in clouds and he didn't see their target at all. Neither did he see flak or fighters.

Bob Shaffer, lead bombardier aboard B-24 Liberator *Naughty Nan* piloted by Lieutenant Sneddon, in the 93rd, noted that the flak was light and the mission successful. There was a full moon and he had never seen as many ships of all descriptions as there were crossing the Channel. Shaffer saw battleships firing at gun emplacements and recalled 'It was quite a sight – quite a show. The flak was light and the mission successful.' A fellow crewman, Ed 'Cotton' Appleman, engineer-gunner aboard *Duration Baby*, who was flying his fourteenth mission, saw the Channel filled with Allied ships of all kinds and he could see them just off the French coast making their landings. Though they had good fighter cover and the B-24s none, he imagined they needed it. He saw no flak and no fighters. The group made two runs on the target but *Duration Baby* did not get the bomb bay doors open in time. Appleman hoped that the 'boys on the ground' had it as easy as they did. He still had sixteen missions to go.

The 493rd from Debach near Ipswich, who were flying their first combat mission and were led by the CO, Colonel Elbert Helton, set out for Lisieux but 10/10ths cloud cover prevented Helton's Hellcats from bombing their target and all thirty-six Liberators returned with their bomb loads intact. Lieutenant Francis S. Milligan recalls, 'I guess we were too green to appreciate a "milk run".' Then at 11,000 feet *No Love – No Nothin* piloted by Captain Jack Cooper struck the tail of *Moby Dick*, which was being flown by Lieutenant Donald L. Russell. *No Love – No Nothin* disintegrated and both Liberators disappeared into the overcast. Milligan adds, 'The sight sobered most of us.' There was only one survivor from Cooper's ship and none from Russell's. The death toll could have been higher – a piece of flak went through the steel helmet worn by Sam Hale, the 861st Squadron commander, through the cloth helmet and lodged on top of his head. Two inches taller and he would not have gone on to finish the twenty-six missions he flew. Lieutenant Joe Gualano, a pilot in the 860th Squadron, adds, 'It was said that "Lord Haw-Haw" that evening, announced that Germany had nothing to fear from the new Group with the "X" tail markings as they were killing themselves.'

All told, four B-24 Liberators were lost on D-Day. One was shot down and *Shoot, Fritz, You've Had It* in the Sky Scorpions crashed and exploded at Northrepps near Cromer during assembly killing all ten men in the crew. It was a sad blow for 11-year-old Norfolk schoolboy, Fred Squires, who often walked the 2 miles from his home to the Hethel runway, creeping through the hedges and climbing into the aircraft. He did not like the olive green ones, so he picked *Shoot, Fritz, You've Had It*, a silver bomber and he got in through the open bomb bays. He thought the smell incredible. He didn't know then that it was from the aviation fuel and cordite. All he could see were what he thought were bombs but were actually oxygen bottles and he took it into his head it was going to blow up, so he got out as fast as he could and ran. The Flying Eightballs almost lost a Liberator in a mid-air collision. John W. McClane, a navigator who on D-Day flew two missions with two different crews, recalled that all was going well and they were climbing on course through very dense clouds. Visibility was at best only 50–100 feet. Suddenly, a loud and confusing shout of voices filled his earphones and about the same time he felt the tail of his aircraft go down sharply, perhaps as much as 30 degrees, then almost as quickly level out again. The babble of voices continued until the pilot calmed them down enough to find out what had happened. The men in the rear were almost in shock. A British bomber had hit the right twin rudder of their B-24! McClane marked it up to the SNAFU[5] that went with the best of planning.

Henry Tarcza aboard B-17G *El's Bells* 'gazed with awe' at the hundreds of ships and boats off Omaha Beach. All were headed towards the beach and it appeared from his altitude that one could almost step from one vessel to another and walk between England and France. His group of about forty B-17s in close formation began to ease its way into the narrow corridor for the bomb run. At this time the bombardier instructed Tarcza to activate the bombs. He climbed out onto the catwalk and after cautiously removing the safety pins from each bomb, notified him that they were now 'live'. For the first time since take-off he now experienced a sense of fear. This was mostly for the unknown because he began to wonder what the Germans had in store for them in that critical area. As they reached *Omaha* Beach the lead plane released a smoke bomb, which was a signal for all forty aircraft to drop their bombs simultaneously. Thus, more than 100 tons of bombs exploded in a matter of a few seconds. This was the only mission over Europe when Tarcza actually felt the concussion of his own bombs. The explosions caused *El's Bells* to bounce and vibrate. He thought that, obviously, the long-planned invasion had remained a well-guarded secret. 'We encountered no German aircraft in the target area and enemy gunfire was very light and inaccurate.'

Five squadrons of Lightnings were given the job of covering the ships in the Channel because not even the most trigger-happy ack-ack gunner on the ships could mistake the twin-tailed P-38. The coast was 'black' with ships and landing craft and one fighter pilot thought it looked like 'the jam at Piccadilly Circus on a Saturday afternoon'. German fighters were in short supply. On the evening of D-Day 3./JG2 had just three serviceable Fw 190s but *Hauptmann* Herbert Huppertz landed at about 2000 hours with eight Fw 190s of his III *Gruppe*. Together with *Leutnant* Eickhoff, *Oberfähnrich* Heinz 'Pritzel' Bär and *Leutnant* Wolfgang Fischer, he was going to lead an attack on the beachhead and upon freight-carrying gliders. They took off shortly after 2030 hours and approached at low level the great road-bridge over Risle, west of Bernay, where they saw twelve Mustangs shooting-up a German supply column. The Fw 190s were too late to help so Huppertz led them away in a left turn at about 1,200 metres. They headed for a light evening haze. It was then that they saw the other 'Indians'. The Fw 190s dodged away from eight Mustangs, then caught four more. Fischer got his in a high reverse turn as he approached the bridge. The P-51 fell on fire into a wooded bank on the Risle and set a tree on fire. He then observed Huppertz and his *Katchmarek* attack another aircraft. The fire was 'devastating' and the Mustang disintegrated. Eickhoff and Bär each scored an *Abschuss* (victory). After landing at Senlis, two reporters sent in confirmation of their victories, for they had seen the whole battle.[6]

When Bert Stiles got back to Bassingbourn the truck didn't come for a while, so he went back behind the tailwheel and lay down in the grass. He mused that it had been the 'milk run of all milk runs, no flak, no fighters, no weaving around for position on the bomb-run ... just straight in, turn right and straight home again, alone in our blue-white world of sunshine.' After the truck came Stiles and the crew got dressed quickly so that they could get to a radio.

> We spent an empty day waiting around the radio in Fletch's room, thinking about that long shot through the clouds and the curve of landing-craft.
>
> One look was all I got.
>
> I looked out the window, south toward France and tried to imagine what it was like.
>
> I'd been to Paris, Avord, Metz, Nancy, Le Havre, St Dizier, Cherbourg, Calais and all the places between. I could tell how green the fields look in Normandy. I could see no sign of a maid when we went over Orleans. I know about the sun patterns on the Seine and the flowers in the fields, the way the Alps grow up out of the mist, east of Chalon.
>
> I could tell, too, about the diseased sky over Paris, the flak-blotches over all the towns and all the ports.
>
> ... I'd seen Sharpe in bloody shorts, wrenching his neck to see the wound on his left cheek. I'd seen what a knee looked like with the knee-cap clipped away and a waist-gunner with his brains all over the Alclad and his legs shot off just below his flak-suit. That guy was just as dead as any of those in the surf today. A dead one lies just as still in the sky as in a mud-hole.

But most of the time you don't live with death in a Fort the way they must in a ditch. The smells don't get to you and neither do the sounds and every night as long as the luck holds out, your sack is in the same place, ready and waiting, soft and dry.

I thought about those guys in the grass, moving down the roads, crawling through the brush, ready and waiting and I hoped they made it okay ....[7]

Wilbur Richardson flew two missions on D-Day, as did everyone else in the 94th. The few that didn't go on the early missions made theirs toward evening just after the others returned. Wilbur and his fellow crewmen stayed on the ramp between flights as their B-17s were refuelled and rearmed. The press interviewed the young Californian as they waited. By the second sortie, the cloud cover was broken up and he could see even more of the action and the hundreds of vessels in the Channel. He saw the *Texas* firing her big guns and watched the three 1,400 lb shells travel to the target. He told the pressman that the view from the ball turret was 'an awe-inspiring sight'. The crews were very tired with the loss of sleep and so much time (15 hours total) in the air but the events of the day left them keyed up and talkative.

At Horham, Henry Tarcza returning in B-17 *El's Bells* was also interviewed by the press. He and his crew were a little apprehensive on their return to Horham because of a diminishing fuel supply. *El's Bells* landed at a RAF base in southern England, refuelled and flew on to Horham, where they gave an Associated Press reporter their views on the historic mission. Emotions varied. Many of their thoughts, feelings and opinions they kept to themselves. Tarcza's pilot Mathew McEntee said, 'Thank you men for your fine co-operation as a combat crew. It is doubtful if any of us will ever in our lifetime, participate in a [more] historic undertaking of this magnitude.' So far nobody has.

Old Gappy touched down at Kimbolton at 0926 hours and Betz could sense an air of excitement on the base when he dropped to the ground from the Fortress after the pilot parked it in the dispersal area. 'How was it Lieutenant?' asked the crew chief in charge of keeping the Fortress flying, an intense look on his leathery face weathered by the winds of his native Texas.

'What I saw through the breaks in clouds was an unforgettable sight,' Betz replied. There was no time to say anything more. A truck pulled up to take the crew to interrogation, after which they had to get ready for the afternoon flight, his thirtieth mission. B-17s continued to peel off from the formation and land as the sun shone brightly through the cloud covering that was breaking up. Betz thought it a 'good omen'.

That night in England US ground crews worked throughout the night of 6 June and all day on the 7th so that two missions could be flown. At the American bases throughout East Anglia crews rightly felt pleased with their contribution. However, as Allan Healy in the Rackheath 'Aggies' near Norwich, Norfolk, says.

The D-Day missions were disappointing. No results of our action could be seen and we had not been able to do what we had in our potentiality to do to further the great undertaking. Nevertheless, the presence of nearly every flyable plane in England, the gigantic and continual roar of their engines and the bombs hurtling down through the overcast, must have given the Germans pause, aware of the destruction capable of being sent to him from on high and it must have given our own men a sense of security in the airpower overhead.

A message from Lieutenant General Doolittle was sent to all bomber bases.

Today the greatest effective strength in the history of the 8th Air Force was reached; an overall effectiveness of approximately 75 per cent of all crews and airplanes assigned. Please extend my congratulations to all members ... for their untiring effort in achieving this impressive strength.[8]

The intensity of D-Day and for a long while after sapped the strength, but replacements were on the way. Lieutenant Eugene Fletcher, who would pilot *Government Issue* at Horham, arrived at Valley. Aware that the invasion was in progress, walked over to a Welsh farmer not far from the runway and asked if there was any news from the Continent. 'Aye, 'tis a great contest going on over there. 'Tis a great contest.' Lieutenant Edmund A. Wanner, another replacement pilot earmarked for *Asbestos Alice* in the Tibenham Group, was somewhat bemused. Wanner noted that here they were in a 'foreign land' where they drove on the 'wrong' side of the road, where 'knocked up' meant they were busy that night and where the great Normandy Invasion was happening. Larry Goldstein was one of many GIs at Chorley waiting to go home on D-Day. Immediately, the rumour started that all men on the base would be sent back to fly more missions. But by dinnertime it was announced that all officers and enlisted would return to the USA as scheduled. When they sailed from Liverpool on the troopship HMS *Pasteur* on 9 June it was at least two days out before the Americans realised that they were 'really' on the way home. They were never told that losses were so heavy that they were needed as instructors to train new crews. On the ship were German PoWs from the *Afrika Korps*. They were not let out of confinement until the ship was three days out. When they saw the Americans' A2 jackets they realised that they were bomber men. One asked Larry Goldstein if they had bombed their home cities? He says, 'We were quick to say no but of course we probably did.'

Abe Dolim made an entry in his diary on Wednesday 7 June.

We crossed the invasion coast on the way to bomb a railway bridge over the Loire River at Nantes. The English Channel was positively jammed with ships and boats of all descriptions. Several landing craft were burning on the beaches. The fields near the coast were littered with Horsa and CG-4 gliders, all painted with the same black and white invasion striping we carried on our fuselage and wings. We took flak at Tours and then began our bomb run from the south of Nantes. Halfway down the bomb run, it became apparent we were on a collision course with a B-24 group. The enemy was beginning to pound us with 88s so we elected to do a '360' and came up behind another B-24 group. The second bomb run was good. We hit the target just at the southern approach to the bridge and there was a very large ball of flame in the marshalling yard – gasoline! We took more flak on the way out at Rennes and at Guernsey Island, where we were clobbered at only 11,000 feet.

On 8 June 1,135 bombers were despatched to communication targets in France. Bad weather prevented 400 heavies from bombing and next day postponed any bomber strikes at all. It also severely curtailed operations on 10 June. Of the 873 bombers airborne, over 200 were forced to abort because of cloud conditions. Some 589 bombers, including thirty-one Pathfinders, attacked eight airfields in France and nine coastal installations in the Pas de Calais. Field Marshal Wilhelm Keitel, head of Armed Forces High Command, rang Field Marshal Gerd von Rundstedt, Commander-in-Chief West from Paris in a panic. 'What shall we do?' he asked.

Von Rundstedt replied, 'Make peace you fool.'

Notes

1. Quote by General Dwight D. Eisenhower SHAEF, in a message to troops preparing for the invasion.
2. He wrote these words about D-Day in his classic work, *Serenade to The Big Bird*, which he penned while he was flying a thirty-five-mission tour, 19 April to 20 July 1944.
3. The First *Gruppe* was heading for Reims while the Third was en route to Nancy-Essey in SE France. *Hauptmann* Naumann's Second *Gruppe* at Mont de Marsan and Biarritz had taken off at 0700 and flew as far as Vrox, where they waited for further orders. The Third *Gruppe* reached the JG2 airfields at Creil and Cormeilles by 0930, but did not begin flying sorties until noon, while the Second *Gruppe* flew from Vrox to Guyancourt near Paris and took no further part in the momentous day's events
4. Priller scored his 100th victory on 15 June when he shot down a B-24 Liberator of the 492nd Bomb Group. Wodarczyk was KIA on 1 January 1945. *Oberst* Priller survived the war with 101 victories.
5. Situation Normal All Fucked Up
6. Fischer's combat career ended abruptly on 7 June, when his Fw 190 was shot down by AA gunfire while attacking shipping off the British beaches. He survived to become a prisoner. His commander, Herbert Huppertz was credited with five Mustangs destroyed on 6 June.
7. Staff Sergeant Edward L. Sharpe was the 21-year-old tail gunner from Hot Springs, Arkansas.
8. Some 2,362 American bomber sorties involving 1,729 B-17s and B-24s were flown on D-Day, dropping 3,596 tons of bombs. Fighter Command flew 1,880 sorties and claimed twenty-eight enemy fighters shot down.

CHAPTER 7

The Lady Named Death is a Whore

There was death all over that sky, the quiet threat of death, the anesthesia of cold sunlight filled the cockpit.

The lady named death is a whore . . .

Luck is a lady . . . and so is death . . . I don't know why.

And there's no telling who they'll go for. Sometimes it's a quiet, gentle, intelligent guy. The lady of the luck strings along with him for a while, and then she hands him over to the lady named death.

'Leipzig', Serenade to The Big Bird, Bert Stiles[1]

In France in June 1944 all German soldiers and airmen were ordered by their *Führer* to stand and fight it out where they stood. There would be no German surrender as far as Adolf Hitler was concerned, which was bad news for young conscripts like Helmut Schade, an 18-year-old born in Düsseldorf, who was a member of a six-gun battery of flak guns defending an airfield in north-eastern France. In spite of the continual loss of young men to the fronts, Germany found it possible to double the numbers of flak personnel, principally by decreasing the personnel per battery and using the *Reichsarbeitsdienst* and approximately 75,000 *Luftwaffenhelfer* (schoolboys) from higher school. After the German disaster at Stalingrad when thousands of soldiers within the borders of the Fatherland were needed for front-line duties, all schoolboys in Germany at age 16 had to enter the flak school in their neighbourhood. Schade's hometown was often the target for RAF night bombers and the Americans by day. One night in 1943 a British Blockbuster bomb fell across the street from Schade's home, destroying ten houses and filling the street with at least 10 feet of debris. The aunt of one of his friends was killed when she refused to go to the bomb shelter. Helmut had been conscripted into the German Army and in the winter of 1943 he was sent into the Taunus Mountains to train as a cannoneer. Supplies were so short that the conscripts did not even have coats to protect them from the brutal alpine cold, but by the spring of 1944 Schade was manning flak guns at Juvincourt airfield south of Reims, the capital of the Champagne-Ardenne region.

On 28 June Juvincourt airfield was a target for the Forts in the Hell's Angels group when just over 670 B-17s and B-24s visited airfield and bridge targets in France and marshalling yards at Saarbrücken. Theodore R. Beiser and his co-pilot Richard 'Dick' Johnson were flying their twenty-third mission, in *Buzz Blond*. Johnson recalls:

Finally, our bombs were away from 24,400 feet, right on target. Four minutes later, a flak battery at Laon scored a direct hit near the right wing root of *Old Crow* flown by my recent friend Lieutenant P. S. Wardowski. The plane immediately became a ball of fire and rolled over in a 180 degree turn to the left. I soon lost sight of it but Charlie Lana in the ball and Carroll Brackey in the tail counted six parachutes. After diving 3,000 or 4,000 feet, the airplane exceeded its limit and disintegrated into thousands of pieces. Wardowski was not able to get out. Neither was the navigator, W. C. Birnbaum, or the tail gunner, D. G. Wagner. This was their fifth or sixth mission.[2] Of our twenty-six B-17s, only six escaped damage. Since the German gunners were aiming visually, the chaff that we dropped to jam their radar did little good. After all this action, the mission was still not over. The weather had turned sour over England while we were away, and as we started across the English Channel we received word that we should land at alternate bases. Our group got under the clouds and headed for the nearest base, being driven below 300 feet at times by the overcast. At times we flew over a rise in the ground losing sight of our wingman for a few moments in the cloud, but still able to see the ground. This happened three or four times, until one time as we descended into the clear we met another B-17 going in the opposite direction at our altitude and only about 300 feet to our left. A very close call. When we found Debach, a B-24 base, we were flying so low to avoid clouds that we had to make shallow turns to avoid hitting trees with our left wing-tip. Amazingly, all our group landed safely and after a little red tape for landing away from base, we all returned to Molesworth before dark. Nine of us landed at Debach, ten at Hardwick, two at Seething and one at Lavenham. One made it to Bradwell Bay on three engines after flak had destroyed an engine, which fell from the plane.'Al' Lehmann landed *Old 99* at Downham Market with two wounded crewmen aboard. *Bet Jane* was the only one that managed to land at Molesworth. It was a bad day for me, having lost several new friends who had slept near my bunk in the 427th officers' barracks.

When the war ended Helmut Schade emigrated to America to see his future wife, whom he had met earlier in Germany. Virginia had arrived in the United States in 1949 as a refugee from Estonia where she was classified as a political refugee, or 'Displaced Person'. Helmut owned a furniture finishing business in Georgetown in the District of Columbia until he retired to a waterfront home near Solomons and my home was nearby. I got to know Helmut and his wife and I asked him if his battery ever shot down a B-17. 'Well, we damaged several,' he said rather evasively. 'One time we hit a B-17 and set his number two engine ablaze. The fire reached back past the end of the tail. We all started jumping up and down, celebrating our good marksmanship. We were certain that we had shot him down. However, in a little while the fire went out and then the smoke stopped and the B-17 never left the formation. As they disappeared into the distance, our celebration turned into glum disappointment. I couldn't believe it. The guy never got out of formation.'

'But,' I insisted, 'did you guys ever shoot down a B-17?'

'We did manage to shoot down a couple of B-24s during the course of the war,' he said, still being evasive. 'They were much easier to shoot down than a B-17. One B-24 was out of formation and we fired at it, but the crew baled out before the flak got there. The plane flew on with its autopilot for about 50 miles before it crashed.'

After I got to know Helmut better, I again asked him the same question, 'Helmut, did your crew ever shoot down a B-17?'

'Well, yes,' he replied, 'they were hard to shoot down but we did manage to shoot down a couple of them. One that we shot down came all to pieces with engines still turning, making the eeriest noises, and several parachutes came out. I'm glad that it wasn't the one you were flying.'

'Not nearly as glad as I am,' I replied. 'But I think it must have been your battery that shot down a friend of mine, Lieutenant Wardowski on 28 June 1944. He and his navigator from my barracks were killed along with their tail gunner. It's strange how we could be sworn enemies at one time and then develop a friendship at another time.' 'It's a different time and place.' He said, 'We were both doing our job and your job was to break things, while mine was to try to stop you from breaking things in my area.'

On this particular day, our bombs missed the airfield at Juvincourt and almost hit the flak battery, which would have been a lucky accident for us but not so lucky for Helmut and the others. The last bombs in the pattern hit the ground a bare 300 feet short of the guns. Helmut said the roar of the explosion was a mighty thud that felt like a minor earthquake!

Despite Hitler's edict, *Soldaten* like Helmut Schade were forced to retreat towards the Fatherland as the Allies swept across France, Belgium and Holland. In July a second shuttle mission was flown from England to Russia by the Fortresses. In the east by mid-September the Russian offensive had reached the outskirts of Warsaw where the Polish Home Army was encouraged to rise up against the Nazi occupiers, but since Josef Stalin the Soviet Dictator wanted a Soviet-dominated Poland no assistance was offered in return. B-17s were finally allowed to drop supplies to the Poles but by then it was too late. Meanwhile, RAF Bomber Command heavies and the American day bombers continued to pound Berlin and other cities and the oil refineries and aircraft factories in the Reich. German production of fighter aircraft actually increased in 1944 and it peaked in September when an astonishing 2,876 single-engined fighters were completed. That same month, an average of three German fighters and two pilots KIA were lost for every bomber shot down. The dispersed manufacturing plants were beyond the power of the 8th Air Force to damage seriously. Therefore, some post-war surveys concluded that the bombing offensive was a failure, but the bombing was just good enough that the *Luftwaffe* fighters had to keep rising to attack and then the P-51s and P-47s mostly destroyed them. The USAAF was clearly winning the battle of attrition, as trained fighter pilots at this stage of the war were impossible to replace.

The *Luftwaffe* then was hard pressed to stem the tide, but on occasion when fate took a hand it could still inflict heavy losses. It was also a matter of luck where the axe fell. On 27 September it fell squarely on the 445th at Tibenham when the B-17s headed for oil targets and engineering centres at Cologne and Ludwigshafen and Mainz and 315 B-24s for the Henschel engine and vehicle assembly plants at Kassel in central Germany.

At Tibenham, the day began like many other days in England and the omens were not good. Solid cloud overhead in the morning showed signs of probable rainfall but Lieutenant George M. Collar, a bombardier who had finished twenty-eight missions, did not care because he had a three-day pass in his pocket. However, when a young bombardier failed to return from leave, Collar was informed that he would be taking his place aboard one of thirty-nine Liberators, piloted by Lieutenant James W. Schaen. Everyone had gone to briefing when members of the Lindenberg crew arrived on the base. They were one of several crews at Halesworth who were surplus to requirements now that the 489th was returning to the ZOI. William K. Koch and the enlisted men reported to the First Sergeant who told them to go to the flight crew barracks and pick out their bunks. They did, but they could not find any empty bunks so they reported back. The First Sergeant told them to go back to the barracks and wait. 'There will be empty bunks,' he said ominously.

Crews sat impatiently in their cramped Liberators on the runway at Tibenham, waiting for a long time for better weather before they got the green light. Then, at 30-second intervals, each roared down the runway, lights on, slowly climbing into the pre-dawn darkness. Lieutenant Rene J. Schneider ran off the perimeter track and cut a tyre and his crew took no further part in the mission. At 15,000 feet the sun was shining brightly in the blue sky. Flares of red-green, at regular intervals, were fired from the Zebra ship, the gaudily painted, stripped-down old war-weary used as an assembly ship, as it continually circled to allow the group to form up on its tail. In the distance, other Zebras were firing green-green, green-red or red-red flares, as they, too, circled in their patch of the sky. The 445th formed up, took its place at the head of the 2nd Combat Wing and joined the divisional assembly line stretching for 60 miles heading for Kassel. *Tahelenbak* and *Heavenly Body* aborted with various mechanical problems and returned early, but the rest flew on and made landfall at the Dutch coast before proceeding uneventfully towards Kassel. Aboard *Patches* Lieutenant Raphael E. Carrow's crew were old hands on their twenty-first mission and they did not talk much on the intercom. Another four missions and their tour would be finished. Then the lieutenants in the crew could let their hair down in the officers' club and the gunners could celebrate in the Rocker Club where non-coms had to be at least a sergeant with a rocker under his chevrons – staff and up. Most of the crew were anticipating the leave, which would be due to them before returning to the States for reassignment.

As the IP approached, George M. Collar saw flak coming up in a blanket and bursting at their altitude. Suddenly, the lead plane in the lead squadron flown by Captain John H. Chilton with Major Donald W. McCoy aboard made a left turn and the whole group followed. Corman Bean the navigator aboard Schaen's ship said over the intercom, 'That Mickey man in the lead ship has screwed up. We shouldn't have turned yet.' But it was too late to turn back on course, as all the other groups following were in the way as they proceeded to the correct IP. In Collar's judgement they would have still been okay if the lead pilot had circled 360 degrees and followed the last group in, but he made a snap judgement to continue on an easterly course and bomb the town of Göttingen about 20 miles north-east. The group dropped their bombs through solid cloud cover using PFF, but they fell in open fields half a mile short of the town. Collar recalls:

> Unfortunately, we lost our fighter escort. At this point our leader, in my opinion, made another error in judgement. Instead of getting out of there and making a beeline for England, his army-trained mind followed the original plan for Kassel and he turned us south from Göttingen with the intention of flying to a line, which would bring us back towards Koblenz. By this time we were 100 miles behind everyone else, with no fighter escort.

The Tibenham outfit had flown into an area a few miles from Eisenach where three elite *Sturmgruppen*, each with a strength of around thirty Fw 190s, were forming for an attack.[3] Known as *Rammbock* (Rammer) or *Sturmbock* (Battering Ram) the storm groups had been formed using volunteers to look for a fight only with four-engine bombers and whenever possible to avoid engagement with a fighter. They were not to open fire on the bombers until they were at a range of 150 to 200 metres, when the four engines appeared in the target circle of the reflex gun sight. If the fighter's guns failed or the gunfire was ineffective, they were expected to ram the bomber. In addition, three 'cover' groups equipped with Bf 109s waited to pick off any badly damaged stragglers that were left. Ernst Schroeder, a 22-year-old Focke-Wulf 190 pilot in II.JG/Sturm 300 at Finsterwalde, flying 'Red 19' with the designation '*Kolle-alaaf!*' (*Cologne-aloft*) because he was born in Cologne, recalls:

> We had an overcast sky and had to climb through a relatively thin cloud layer at about 1,500–2,000 metres (4,920–6,560 feet) altitude in order to get to the Americans, flying at about 7,500–8,000 metres (24,600–26,240 feet). We were led to the bombers by the Y-Command of the fighter division. Because we were flying over the clouds, we could not see the ground. The orders often changed our course direction, so we never knew where we really were. Normally, a pilot would look on his maps for locations, which were radioed to us. But a pilot of a single-seater fighter could not do that; he had to concentrate on the flight of the group and the steering of the plane. Around 11.00 am we were flying farther and farther west. The ground commander became more and more agitated and said we now had to see the enemy planes in front of us. Indeed we did. After a

short time we saw a large group of B-24 Liberator bombers at our altitude like a swarm of mosquitoes, flying right in front of us, going in the same direction. The silhouettes very soon became bigger and bigger because of our great speed.

The B-24 pilots put out frantic calls for help on the Fighter Channel. Leo Pouliot, co-pilot in Lieutenant Jackson C. Mercer's B-24, which was flying low left, saw the tail gunner of *Patty Girl* to their right fire at something. Then he noticed that small white puffs were appearing throughout the formation and realised that enemy fighters were jumping them. Pouliot started to call for some of the escort and he was answered immediately. He told them they were having trouble. They asked their position and Pouliot switched the jackbox to interphone to get their position from Milton Fandler the navigator. Then their B-24 got several hits in the waist and the radio was knocked out. Immediately, two Mustang groups covering the 3rd Division, 75 miles away near Frankfurt and the 361st Fighter Group, escorting the 1st Division 100 miles distant, were speeding to the rescue. However, a precious 6 minutes were to elapse before the 361st Fighter Group could reach the beleaguered 445th and the other two P-51 groups would arrive too late. The *Sturmgruppen* attacked in three waves, each wave with fighters in line abreast from the rear and with cannon and machine-guns blazing. Werner Vorberga, a young *Rammbock Staffelkapitän* in II.Sturm JG4 at Welzow, south of Berlin, recalls:

> After repeated course changes and arriving undisturbed by enemy fighters the unit reached the Liberators and flew from behind into the stream of bombers. We divided up and flew toward individual ships. Whoever was not shot down had to be rammed. Flying from the back of the formation to the front we shot down ships and crews from *Viermots* flying further ahead, were baling out. Ten or twelve bombers exploded in the air, although they had already dropped their bombs. We had collision losses due to the closeness when opening fire. After the march through the entire stream of bombers, we distanced ourselves quickly in order not to be caught by enemy fighters. Our losses included ten machines, one *Staffelkapitän* and six other pilots. Three pilots, one of whom rammed a bomber, were wounded.[4]

The *Sturmgruppen* ripped through the four squadrons in the 445th with ease and the sky was filled with exploding shells and burning and exploding aircraft. Crews later estimated that there were between 100 and 150 attacking fighters. William R. Dewey, pilot of *Wallet A-Abel*, felt the entire plane shudder and shake with the guns in the rear of the plane firing simultaneously and from the impact of 20 mm and 30 mm enemy shells. His co-pilot, Bill Boykin, pointed out of his side window at B-24s in the other squadrons going down on fire and enemy fighters exploding. Then the intercom went out to the waist and tail within seconds and the top turret gunner, Charley Craig, reported that there were five enemy fighters on their tail. Dewey saw the tail gunner in the element lead motioning for him to tuck in closer so he could get

better shots at the 109s and 190s. 'Then as suddenly as it started, it was all over
– maybe 3 to 5 minutes in all.' *Heavenly Body* and *Ole Baldy* were shot out of
the sky and *Little Audrey* was badly shot up and crash-landed south-west of
Koblenz, while Lieutenant Edgar N. Walther's ship exploded in the air.
Walther, who was wearing a backpack, was thrown clear and awoke in a
German prison hospital suffering from leg and arm wounds, concussion and
amnesia. He was the only survivor. *Sweetest Rose of Texas* and another ship,
flown by Lieutenant D. W. Smith, made it back to Tibenham. Dewey and his
co-pilot Boykin, a tough ex-football player and former cavalryman, nursed
Wallet A-Abel to Manston and landed safely. Both waist gunners and the tail
gunner were wounded and bloody. There was a huge hole in the right waist
ahead of the window and the left waist window was shattered. Control cables
to the tail were partially damaged, the twin vertical rudders were frayed and
disintegrating and there was a 3-foot hole in the upper surface of the wing
behind the No. 3 engine where 100-octane gasoline splashed out. A hydraulic
fluid fire in the tail turret was quickly extinguished. There was no oxygen and
the electric flying suits were inoperative at the waist positions.

Leo Pouliot, looking to the right, saw 'just plain Hell'. Planes were going
down in flames, others just exploding. The air was full of 20 mm shells. He
thought the whole German Air Force was in the air at the same time. 'The first
pass that they made took most of the squadron with them'. Six ships,
including *Fridget Bridget* and *Hot Rock* were shot down. Only Frank T. Plesa,
tail gunner, who was also badly wounded and burned, and Theodore J. Myers,
the top turret gunner, survived after the plane exploded. Myers was wounded
in the right foot and both legs and then he saw a blinding flash and was on fire
from head to foot. He felt his face burning and thought he was dying. Myers
regained consciousness to find himself hanging in his parachute. Mercer's
crew and Isom's ship *Patty Girl* made it back to England, *Patty Girl* landing at
Tibenham and Mercer making it to Manston. Lieutenant William S. Bruce,
pilot of *Bonnie Vee*, found it just unbelievable how many enemy fighters came
at them in large groups. 'They sat at the back and below and shot the living
Hell out of us' he said later. 'They had their wheels down, stayed in formation
and raked us steadily with machine-gun fire and 30 mm cannon. It was just a
hopeless situation – there were just too many of them. I saw at least seven
ships go down in flames. Our fighters were nowhere in sight. I could not
understand where the Hell they could be.' *Bonnie Vee* was hit several times,
two engines were on fire and the interior of the plane was in a shambles. The
gunners kept firing, but finally they were all wounded or dead. Bruce gave the
bale-out order and asked his co-pilot to unbuckle his seat belt before he baled
out. Just as he stood up to do so a 30 mm cannon shell cut him in half. *Bonnie
Vee*'s right wing had been rammed by a German fighter, tearing it off and the
crippled Liberator blew up at 19,000 feet, hurling Bruce out. The next thing he
knew he was clear of the plane and 'hurting very, very much'.[5]

Sergeant Tom G. Spera, photo-observer aboard *Terrible Terry's Terror*,
piloted by Lieutenant William F. Hunter, saw one Liberator on fire from nose
to tail.

It came swinging towards us like a severely wounded animal, then peeled away as if to pick a spot away from us to die. The next bomber moved up in its place. One Liberator with two engines on fire on the left wing came up from below us to explode when it had reached our level. A human form fell out of the orange-coloured ball of fire. As he fell through space without parachute or harness, he reached up as if to grasp at something.

Then it was their turn.

A 20 mm shell tore through the bomb bay, ripping off the doors and severing fuel lines. Two fires started simultaneously in the bay. What strange mystery of fate kept us from exploding, I'll never, never be able to fathom. The engineer, Robert Ratchford, threw off his parachute, grabbed a fire extinguisher and put both fires out before the 100-octane gas had been ignited. Then we attended to the gas leaks from which fuel was pouring out like water from a fire hydrant. Gasoline had saturated the three of us in the ship's waist and we all had a difficult time moving about. The two waist gunners were slipping and sliding as they sighted their guns. A large puddle of gasoline accumulated on the camera hatch, blown in by the slipstream outside. A bullet from a Focke-Wulf probably saved my life. My oxygen mask had become disconnected and before I realised it I was losing consciousness. A 20 mm shell came through the waist above the head of waist gunner Joseph K. Selser and caused Robert J. Cannon to look around from his position at the right waist gun, notice my trouble and connect the oxygen line again. I gained consciousness to find the battle continuing. One wave of enemy fighters followed another until after 6 minutes the attacks ceased as suddenly as they had started. In spite of the loss of one engine, our ship managed to keep in contact with the others for a while. When navigator Robert M. Kaems informed us that we had reached friendly lines, the sickening feeling relaxed its hold in the pit of my stomach, but a dry muddy taste remained in my mouth. It proved impossible to stay with the other bombers for long and an escort of P-51 Mustangs picked us up in answer to a call from the radio operator. We were approaching a landing field in northern France when the second engine on our left wing cut out and a third engine spat and sputtered. Those of us in the waist rushed to crash-landing positions in the nick of time. Hunter cleared a clump of trees by inches, clipped a set of high-tension wires and brought the ship down on a potato patch, skillfully jumping several ditches, only to have one wheel catch in a hole, buckle and dig the right wing into the ground. We all took a severe bouncing but our only casualty was a cut hand for the bombardier, George E. Smith.[6]

Patches, flown by Lieutenant Raphael E. Carrow, was not as fortunate. Carrow explains.

I noticed an unusual red glow in the sky around us. As I turned my head to the right through my co-pilot's window, I saw a parachute floating down. Then the plane in front of us burst into flames. Other parachutes appeared on all sides. Suddenly, an Fw 190 swooped in front of us from underneath and behind. At the same time my co-pilot, Newell Brainard, was pounding my arm. One engine was on fire; while working to feather the prop, other German fighters came into view. All around us was on fire ... black smoke ..., planes going down ..., more parachutes ..., machine-guns firing ..., the shudder of 20 mm shells hitting ..., another engine gone ..., intercom out ..., plane out of control ..., a gripping fear ..., near panic ..., then, fire! The bomb bay was a roaring inferno. Our route of escape was blocked. On the flight deck behind me the radio operator stood petrified, fascinated, staring into the flames. Brainard quickly got out of his seat. I never saw either again.[7] Now I had to find a way out but I was frozen to the seat! The simple task of unbuckling the seat belt, removing my flak vest and Mae West became major problems. The plane was now completely out of control. All possible means of escape raced through my head. Each one presented an alternative death. There seemed to be no way out. Finally, free, I arose from my seat in the falling plane and as I faced the rear, instead of the expected inferno, I saw the blue sky. The plane had broken in two and the other half had taken the fire with it.

Carrow baled out and landed in a field near a group of buildings surrounded by a high fence. A German soldier who apprehended him, pointed a rifle at the American and asked, 'Jude?' Carrow had landed near a slave labour camp.

Staffelkapitän Oskar Romm leading *Sturm* IV/JG 3 'Udet' recalls:

I attacked a flight of three bombers. Just like during my first downing of a *Viermot* over Oschersleben on 7 July 1944, my approach for the attack was divided into three actions, going off really quickly. First to fire into the fuselage to hit the machine-gun positions, then hit the pilot's compartment and finally to hit and set fire to two engines on one side of the aircraft. If two engines on one side were on fire, control was almost immediately put out of action. I first attacked the bomber on the left position of the flight, then the one on the right and lastly the leading B-24 of the flight. I then pulled up in a steep turn and while flying over them, observed them going down, spinning, burning, and the breaking off of wings in the area of the burning engines. The film from my gun cameras showed the downing, demonstrating in an appalling way the location of the hits and the effect of the shots on the three aircraft. The two MK 108 39 mm guns did the most devastating damage. I opened up aerial combat by first firing the two 13 mm machine-guns, then the two 20 mm guns and between less than 400 metres and ramming distance with all six guns firing off short bursts.[8]

Ernst Schroeder continues.

Suddenly, several of these big ships began to burn and to plunge down with fire and smoke – even before we had fired a single shot. A fighter unit flying ahead of us had begun the attack. Immediately the sky was full of parachutes and wreckage and we were flying right into it. My

Staffelkapitän and I had installed a new aiming device that included very rapid running gyros, which automatically calculated the necessary aiming allowances. Therefore, one could shoot rather precisely and effectively from a greater distance than otherwise. The result was impressive in my case. Even before I had covered the remaining distance to my bomber, it already stood in flame as a result of my six machine-guns. Both left engines of the bomber were burning. The airplane turned on its side and plunged. The neighbouring machine was already smoking from a previous attack and I only needed to change aim to shoot again. Then this one stood in bright flames. The new aiming device was functioning astonishingly. I was so surprised and fascinated that I flew alongside my victim and stared at the metre-high flames, which were pouring out of this Liberator all the way back beyond the tail. Then this great machine clumsily laid itself over on its back and went down. Although these four-engine airplanes were equipped with up to twelve heavy 12.7-cm weapons, they had no chance alone against attacking fighter aircraft. The explosive effects of our shells in the poorly armoured bomber fuselages were horrible.

I naturally wanted to know where my two opponents would fall, because a double shoot down of two *Viermots* (they were my only ones) was something exceptional. I circled my two crashing adversaries in large downward running spirals but my intention was hindered in a most horrible way. The sky was filled with fliers in parachutes and small and large chunks of airplane debris, which suddenly appeared in front of my windshield as I dived at 600–700 km/h. I had to close my eyes often because I believed I would run into something. Underneath was a cloud layer through which, here and there, the ground was shimmering as I drew closer and closer. Through this cloud cover rose ten to fifteen columns of smoke from the explosions of the crashing aircraft. I flew through the relatively thin cloud layer, which now spread itself out at about 1,000 metres (3,280 feet) above the ground. Below me lay a valley with forest-covered mountainsides. Through the valley ran a stretch of double railroad tracks and on it stood a long train with the smoke of the locomotive climbing vertically. Where had the two bombers fallen? Everywhere there was burning wreckage. The fields were covered with white parachutes, where American and German fliers had come down. I could clearly see crewmen who had baled out running through the fields. When I flew over they stood and raised their hands high. Soldiers and policemen were running toward them to take them captive.

Aboard the PFF lead ship, Frank J. Bertram, the lead navigator, sitting just behind Captain Reginald R. Miner, the pilot, and facing the rear of the aircraft, could see the battle through a small side window. Bertram saw 'little puffs of black about the size of basketballs' and thought it was a new kind of flak. Fw 190s then 'rained destruction upon all our ships practically at once'. Stanley F. Krivik's B-24 made it back and crash-landed in Norfolk but the rest of the lead squadron, including *Roughhouse Kate*, *Our Gal*, *Eileen*, *Fort Worth*

Maid and *King Kong*, flown by Lieutenant James C. Baynham, were shot down in fierce fighter attacks. German civilians murdered three members of Baynham's crew. Bertram's ship was hit badly, but why it did not blow up was a mystery too him. Shells ripped through the ship followed by explosions, fire and direct hits on vital parts. Virgil China, the co-pilot, and Joseph H. Guilfoil, the radio operator, were killed. The rest baled out. As he floated down, there were so many parachutes that Bertram thought that the sky looked like a 'paratroop invasion'.

George M. Collar saw the fighters attacking the lead squadron 'like a swarm of bees' and saw Miner's ship go down. At this time he heard the bale-out bell ringing, so he got out of the turret and found Corman Bean putting on his chute.

> The whole nose compartment looked like a sieve. Those exploding 20 mm shells had blown up right between us, but neither of us was hit. By this time we were nosing down and the whole left wing was on fire. We opened the nose wheel door and baled out. In the meantime, Eppley was still firing from the Martin turret and failed to hear the bale-out bell. He happened to look down and saw the pilot coming out of the cockpit and starting across the flight deck, so he decided it was time to leave. He followed the pilot down into the bomb bay. Imagine his surprise when he found the bomb bay doors closed. Schaen was going up the tunnel towards the nose, following the radioman and the co-pilot. Eppley automatically reached for the bomb door handle and to his surprise the doors opened, so he went out there. He was no sooner out than the ship blew up. We learned later that the radioman, Sergeant Collins, and the co-pilot, Bobby McGough, got out, but were wounded. Unfortunately, Jim Schaen never made it. He left a wife and baby. We never found out why the men didn't go out of the bomb bay as they were supposed to. Perhaps the first one down pulled the handle the wrong way and thought the doors were stuck.[9]

Even the intervention of the 361st Fighter Group's P-51 Mustangs was not enough to prevent the destruction of the 445th, although, in a brief battle they did manage to shoot down a few enemy fighters. Lieutenant Leo H. Lamb died when he collided with an Fw 190. Another Mustang pilot intercepted Ernst Schroeder at low altitude but after flying towards one another 'like jousting knights of the Middle Ages' for five or six times the Fw 190 pilot finally 'hugged' the ground and escaped. Schroeder concludes:

> I must say that I never experienced such a bomber massacre in any of the numerous air battles in which I participated. This event made very clear that the Americans in 1944 had their air superiority thanks only to the fact that their fighter escorts were very effective and most often successful in protecting the bomber squadrons against attacks of the German intercept fighters.

No fewer than twenty-five Liberators were shot down and five more, including *Mairzy Boats* and *Bugs Bunnie*, had crashed in Belgium, France and England.

Only five made it back to England. It proved the highest group loss in 8th Air Force history. Altogether, 117 men were killed and forty-five officers and thirty-six enlisted men had been made prisoners-of-war. Some, like George Collar, who landed close to the village of Lauchroeden near Eisenach, were ordered by the Germans to collect the burnt and charred remains of their colleagues from the crashed aircraft. Collar had been forced to run the gauntlet of a mob determined to beat the '*Americanishe Terrorflieger*' to death. An irate farmer broke Collar's nose and blackened both his eyes and a younger man kicked him before the village *Burgomeister* and a policeman finally rescued him. In an orchard lying on the ground, Collar saw the body of one of their fliers. The victim had obviously been blown out of the plane as he landed without a chute. Every bone in his body was broken. Collar and other crewmembers travelled up and down the hills and forests all day, picking up approximately a dozen bodies, some of them horribly mangled. In the middle of an open field they came across a radioman lying in a pool of blood who was dead. One of the bodies he picked up was that of Lieutenant Martin Geiszler. After the war, Collar had the painful duty of confirming his death to his parents. Back at Tibenham, Thomas J. Campana, returning from a 72-hour pass in London, saw three planes landing. He and the rest of the crew joked about that being all that was left of the group. Little did they know how right they were. Rows of empty seats in the mess halls that evening were almost as soul destroying.

Edmund A. Wanner's crew had not had a mission for some time and had 'fussed with Operations' until they put them on standby for the Kassel mission. Wanner recalled that the standby crews felt bad about not getting mission credit until the bad reports of fighter attacks started coming in. 'The shock stunned us all. The fellows in the next hut that we joked with the night before were gone. The next morning there were trucks backed up to many huts, loading personal belongings. My crew learned never to volunteer for missions again.'

A plan to bring in twenty-eight crews from other groups was considered, but by nightfall it had been shelved and the decision taken that all new replacement crews coming into the division would be diverted to the 445th. Ten crews, including Wanner's, were scraped together for the mission the following day, ironically to Kassel again. *Patty Girl*, flown by another crew, was the only Liberator from the earlier debacle to fly. All ten crews returned safely to Tibenham on this occasion.

Just over a month later, on 2 November, the *Sturmgruppen*, part of an overall fighter force totalling between 400 and 500 aircraft, struck again in similar circumstances, except that this time it was the B-17 groups that were on the receiving end. Over 1,100 bombers were scheduled to bomb one of the deadliest targets in Western Europe, the I. G. Farbenindustrie's synthetic oil refinery complex at Leuna 3 miles south of Merseburg. Not only was the location deep into Germany, but the ground defences there were at least 500 heavy flak guns of 88 mm, 105 mm and 120 mm calibre. Merseburg was rated the number one priority and was estimated to be producing 10 per cent of all Germany's synthetic oil and a third of its ammonia and other chemicals.

Despite mounting losses, there was increasing evidence that the offensive against oil targets was reaping results. During August German oil production had fallen to only 16,000 tons, compared with 195,000 tons in May that same year, and during September it plummeted to only 7,000 tons. *Reichsminister* Albert Speer was given 7,000 engineers from the army and an unlimited number of slave labourers to reconstruct the synthetic oil-producing plants. Hundreds of additional flak guns were erected around the '*Hydriesfestubngen*', as the plants became known and workers, who now came under the direct supervision of the SS, built deep shelters in which to take cover during air raids. Plants quickly demonstrated a remarkable ability to regain full production quotas and between bombing raids were able to produce 19,000 tons during October and 39,000 tons in November.

In October, refineries like Merseburg and Politz were hit and losses were high. That month the 457th at Glatton, ironically nicknamed the Fireball Outfit, lost ten Forts, four of them on the 7 October raid on Merseburg, when one of them carried their CO, Colonel James R. Luper, a graduate of West Point. On 1 November the Fireballs attended a lecture by Squadron Leader Barron in the Main Briefing Room entitled, 'Our Mission – How it looks to the German Controllers'. For the cookhouse it was the Feast of All Saints and a Holy Day of Obligation. The movie theatre on base was showing *Marriage is a Private Affair*, starring Lana Turner. At 0230 hours the next day Orderly Room personnel began waking thirty-five combat crews for their briefing at 0500. At briefing, crews were warned that German fuel and replacement pilots were in such short supply that Hermann Goering, the *Luftwaffe* chief, was massing his forces to strike a telling blow on a single mission. All they needed was the opportunity. Merseburg was always the main topic of conversation among the old-timers and at briefing there was usually an audible groan that went up from crews when they learned that it was their target for the day. Herman Hager, a radio operator in Lieutenant Fred Wismer's crew of *Zoomeriago* in the 398th at Nuthampstead, had been there before and knew what to expect. 'To say the least, shivers always ran up and down our spines when we saw this mission on the map. Like Schweinfurt and others, this was one mission on which you could count your blessings if you returned unharmed.'[10]

At Bassingbourn, when Wayne 'Tex' Frye, navigator in Jack O'Neil's crew of *The Witch*, was awakened that morning, he felt that the day's mission would be a 'rough one'. In the barracks the night before, Norman Passeger, his best friend and a fellow navigator, had won the lottery to guess the next day's target when he had drawn 'Merseburg' – the 'lucky devil'. Frye had given the engineer on the crew money to get a ring in town. He had it in his locker and Frye told him that he didn't think that he would be coming back from this one, so he wanted him to get the ring and send it home to his wife. This was the third time that the navigator felt that he wouldn't make it and when he got to briefing he was positive of it. 'This was one for the books! The target was Merseburg; 473 flak guns and all of them big ones. Flying time 7:45. Time on oxygen 4:30. Bomb load – 18,250 lb. Flight altitude – 26,200 feet where the temperature was 38 degrees below zero. We were to be the last group in the Eighth Air Force over the target. That is really being "Tail End Charley".' It was usually a superstition among crews that a change of aircraft also meant a change of luck and O'Neil's crew had a change of ships right at the last moment and would fly *General Ike*, an old timer named after Eisenhower.

At Rattlesden, Lieutenant Emile 'Tim' Tetreault, flying *The Bonnie Baby*, led one of the crews in the 447th. At the dispersal the gunners carried out their mandatory checks as the ground crew finished their exhaustive checks. *The Bonnie Baby*'s bomb bay contained a maximum internal load of 6,000 lb of general-purpose explosive. As Tetreault dismounted from the truck, he was met by Sergeant Willie Stacy, tail gunner, who said, 'Tim, I don't think I should fly today. I have a feeling it is not going to be lucky for me. I will fly if you say so but please take me off the mission.' Tetreault hesitated, since this was a serious matter, but sensing the sincerity in his voice he finally agreed to the tail gunner's request and he called for a replacement. Sergeant Urban Florin, a gunnery instructor with several missions to his credit came forward. He could now 'practise what he preached', but he would pay a physical price in doing so. Just over forty Flying Forts approached the main runway from either side of the perimeter track, took off individually at alternate intervals of 30 seconds and began the laborious but necessary procedure of forming up. The heavy cloud cover fortunately did not persist beyond 2,500 feet and *The Bonnie Baby* soon slotted into the 'Secondary Lead' role at the head of the Lead Squadron. Fully 2 hours passed before the Rattlesden bombers pointed their noses towards Holland and climbed to cruising altitude. The strain of holding a fully loaded B-17 in formation was shared equally by Tetreault and his co-pilot Jack Stanich at intervals of 20 minutes as the formations bore on towards the Merseburg refinery.

The Fireball Outfit meanwhile, had been blown off course and away from the target by a 50-knot wind. They flew on alone and sought the secondary target at Bernberg, 35 miles to the north of Merseburg. After bombing, the group turned right to the south-west to link up with other returning aircraft. Some 15 minutes after the turn, they had still not joined the rest of the divisional bomber stream when out on a limb and at the mercy of more than 400 fighters, about forty *Sturmgruppen* Fw 190s attacked the low squadron from 6 to 8 o'clock. *Lady Margaret*, which had its wing severed by the wing of a passing Fw 190, went down in flames and exploded with only six men baling out in time. *Prop Wash* followed her down with the loss of all nine of Gordon Gallagher's crew and another seven Forts, including *Paper Doll*, *Patches n' Prayers* and *Delores*, exploded or crashed with twenty-one men killed and forty-three taken prisoner. Nine more bombers were badly damaged in fighter attacks and only the timely intervention by Mustangs saved the Fireball Outfit from total annihilation.

As the 91st neared the target the flak guns really opened up. Tex Frye heard later that some said there was some 200 mm flak and he did not doubt it at all.

It was sure big. We could see enemy fighters ahead of us on the other side of the target and were afraid that we were going to get it from them. After we turned off the target we could see them preparing for attack. Bobbie, in the tail, was keeping us informed on their activities. About 400 Me 109s and Fw 190s hit us. No words can describe how terrible this was. The 20 mm started bursting all around us. Robbie and Bill and Mac were calling out the fighters all around the clock. I sure admired Robinson; he was back there shooting like mad and calling out every plane close to us. I heard him call up that he blew up one. An Fw 190 came in and Bill really poured the lead to him. The pilot was either hurt or out of control or maybe neither, but he tried to ram into our right wing, just missing it as he was going down. Jack had to pull up the wing for him to miss it. A Bf 109 did a slow half roll right over our plane and I called to Bill to get him. The top turret in *General Ike* was so small that Bill couldn't sight straight up so he didn't get a shot at this one. Just then, an Fw 190 stalled out right in front of where my left cheek gun should have been, but there was no such gun in my ship. I could have shot the pilot with a .45 pistol. I could see his face as easy as if in the same plane with him. Bill called up and said he just knocked down another fighter. An Fw 190 came diving down in front of our nose and I started letting him have it with my right cheek gun. I could see the bullets going from his right wing tip right on into the cowling. Pieces of cowling starting flying off, his engine caught fire and he started spiralling down. Before I was through shooting my gun jammed and I had to try to fix it while watching everything and writing down observations in my log. Paul, the toggileer, damaged a fighter at this time. I kept wondering where the damned P-51s were.

The two ships in our element were shot up and left the formation. Jack was really doing some wonderful evasive action. There were four jet-propelled fighters around and one of the tail gunners in our squadron shot one down. The fighters kept coming back and attacking again. They were coming in with flaps down and their throttles back, just sitting back of us at 6 o'clock staggered, shooting at us. Bombers were going down all around us. Jim was riding in another ship and I did a lot of worrying about him. We had sixteen separate attacks on our ship. After 8 minutes of fighter attack, they finally stopped. I had seen one B-17 go down, apparently under control, and two fighters followed him down and chopped him right in two.

Our fighters finally showed up – two of them. I saw one '51 shoot down five German fighters in one sweep. It was a pretty sight but why in the hell weren't they there all the time? Bobbie called up and told us that we just had six planes in our squadron left out of twelve that started with us. Norman Passeger had gone down. I kept looking for the ship that Jim was in. Finally, it scooted up to join the rest of us. I was so thankful that he didn't go down that I shed a few tears right there and then. The flak was still coming up intense and accurate. It was really a pleasure to have flak instead of fighters. In the 8 minutes of having fighter attacks, I had made six entries in my log. I don't have any recollection of making any. The navigators were all messed up and did not quite know just where we were, I know I didn't. We did not come back the way we were supposed to, but we were on the way home, even if the flak was still coming up.

We finally got out over the North Sea but we could not relax, having been on such a nervous strain. I was still having a little trouble with my machine-gun; it would shoot a few bursts and then jam but I finally got it fixed. When we got to the coast of England, Bobbie came on the interphone and said, 'This is the first time I ever thought that I would be glad to see this damned country.' We all felt the same way. I smoked two packages of cigarettes after we could take off our oxygen masks. We had been under fighter attack for 8 minutes and in flak for 45 minutes. We had been in the largest air battle ever since the war started. Bombers claimed fifty-three enemy aircraft and our fighters, 155. The German fighters were Hermann Goering's famed yellow-nosed boys. We had 7.6 mm machine-gun holes all over the ship and a hole in the tail big enough to put a washtub through from a 20 mm cannon burst. When we got out of the ship everybody was there waiting for us, asking questions about everything. I was so sick at heart I just sat down on my equipment bag and couldn't say anything. I realised then that 'O'Neil and Company' were very lucky boys. I couldn't get over Passeger going down. There were sure lots of empty bunks in my room that night. Our group had lost thirteen bombers. Mullins, pilot of the lead ship in our element, got back on two engines after we had counted him as number fourteen. The next day we had to help sort out the fellows' clothes. They were to be packed and sent to their families. This was one job that I did not like.

In total, the raid on Merseburg had cost thirty-eight Forts. The 447th had lost five, four of them over the target where the bomb run had taken 8 minutes, an eternity. The losses could have been higher still but for the bravery of men like navigator Lieutenant Robert Feymoyer, whose B-17 was rocked by three flak bursts, which showered the plane with shrapnel. Feymoyer was hit in the back and the side of his body, but refused all aid despite his terrible wounds so that he might navigate the Fortress back. He was propped up in his seat to enable him to read his charts and the crew did what they could for him. It was not until they reached the North Sea that Feymoyer agreed to an injection of morphia. He died shortly after the aircraft landed at Rattlesden and was posthumously awarded the Medal of Honor. One of the losses was *The Bonnie Baby*, which Tim Tetreault flew back across the North Sea with two engines shut down, the propellers 'feathered' and the oxygen system out before he was forced to ditch. All nine men, including Urban Florin, who had been struck in the left arm by a shell fragment, survived. But once in the water, they had only a single life raft built to hold no more than five to cling to. Turns were taken for 53 minutes before an RAF Air-Sea Rescue launch turned up and night had fallen by the time the vessel gained its mooring point in the harbour at Great Yarmouth. Florin was given immediate temporary treatment before dispatch to a hospital. His eight companions returned to Rattlesden the next day, from where they were subsequently sent on seven days' R and R to the Palace Hotel in Southport, Lancashire. The flak fragment, which had penetrated Florin's arm on the inside of the elbow, was located up by the shoulder. By great fortune, it had missed bones and veins and was extracted with minimal difficulty. The number seven could be seen clearly stamped on the fragment.[11]

Merseburg became synonymous with flak and crews hated all missions to the city. On 21 November the Forts returned and lost fourteen B-17s while four Liberators went missing from a raid on another refinery at Hamburg. An oil plant at Gelsenkirchen-Nordstern was bombed without loss on 23 November and two days later, on Saturday 25 November, over 700 Forts returned to Merseburg yet again. Eight B-17s were shot down and almost 200 more were damaged by flak, but at least over 270 Liberators were able to bomb marshalling yards at Bingen and return without losing a single bomber. However, this was a situation that did not exist for long in the ETO (European Theatre of Operations) and everything would change once the Liberators were assigned an oil target. The first steps were being taken as the bombers were hitting Merseburg and Bingen. At 1516 hours at the daily operations conference in the War Room at Daws Hill Lodge at High Wycombe, staff were already planning the next day's mission and they reached the moment of decision. The Commanding General studied the wall map with targets for 26 November marked with red ribbon. He turned to the Weather Officer. 'You say 1/10 to 5/10 cloud cover with ground haze at Bielefeld. Can you do any better at Misburg?'

'Yes Sir, 1/10 to 2/10 cloud cover.'

'Well, let's go.'

It was 0430 hours on the morning of Sunday 26 November when Master Sergeant John T. Keene, crew chief of *Ark Angel*, in the 491st at North Pickenham, Norfolk, swung out of bed. This was no time to get up but like a hundred other mornings, he dressed and was off to the mess hall. At 0150 hours a chill wind blew across the base. The Teletype at Operations began to clatter, just as it did at every other base that morning, where out on the hardstands ground crews busily prepared the Liberators and Fortresses for the day's mission. Thirty Liberators were loaded with 500 lb bombs and 2,780 gallons of fuel. *Ark Angel* had survived a tour in the hands of Lieutenant Box's crew and now Lieutenant David N. Bennett was working on his. He would fly the *Ark Angel* to the synthetic oil refineries at Misburg near Hanover, a target that had been partially destroyed three weeks before. Lieutenant Don F. Ferguson, navigator in Lieutenant James K. Wenzel's crew, recalled that it was 'a beautiful, clear flying day and the stage was set for a great sky battle. Our crew was flying deputy lead and the usual nine men were aboard. We'd flown a mission just the day before to Bingen, west of Frankfurt on the Rhine. Misburg would be our fifteenth mission and the crew had become rather "flak happy" at this stage of combat.'

Late in the morning the Liberators took off from North Pickenham and rendezvoused above East Anglia at the usual 7,000 to 10,000 feet level for group assembly before joining the wing formation. The lead plane, *Ragged But Right*, piloted by Captain Joseph R. Metcalf, had Lieutenant Colonel Charles C. Parmele flying as air commander. Close behind flew a stream of B-24s, all jockeying their controls to remain in a tight, defensive formation.

Formed up, the bombers left the British Isles behind and climbed to their bombing altitudes of 20,000 feet and above. Just over 1,130 bombers escorted by over 660 fighters headed for several marshalling yards and oil targets in Germany, but aborts reduced the numbers. One of them was a Liberator from North Pickenham, which encountered trouble and had to leave the group. Crossing the Dutch coast, word was received that bandits were in the area and the group was in for a rough time. It was then that a second B-24 announced that it was aborting the mission. This left twenty-eight Libs to fly on into Germany and face the inevitable flak and fighters. Timing began to go awry and ultimately it affected the outcome of the mission for the 491st, which was flying 'Tail-end-Charlie' or last group in the divisional bomber stream. Over the North Sea two groups turned late, which placed them a few minutes' behind schedule when they crossed the enemy coast. More time was lost en route to the target by both the Liberators and Forts. This increased the time spread between divisions and assisted the enemy in intercepting the B-24s. The B-17 formation became spread over 40 miles instead of 20 as briefed, and the three escorting fighter groups could not hope to protect all the Forts. Three groups of P-51s battled with the enemy for about 20 minutes, but forty slipped through and shot down four B-17s.

The Liberators flew the remaining 30 minutes to the target alone. As the 491st approached the IP, between 150 and 200 fighters were spotted high above the bombers, but they made no attempt to attack the Liberators. Instead, the escorts were lured away to dogfight with the enemy at 30,000 feet and half a mile to the south-east. The *Luftwaffe*, in anticipation of a deeper penetration, had prepared another striking force at the Muritz Sea. By the time the bombers had reached Steinhuder Lake, this concentration was in the process of assembling. However, as the Fortresses swung west to bomb Misburg, the 'out-foxed' enemy hurried his forces west. More than 350 fighters converged on the IP for Misburg at about the same time that the Liberators reached that point. In scenes reminiscent of the battles of Kassel and Merseburg, up to eighty German fighters attacked the tightly packed boxes of bombers on a wide front between Uelzen and Perleberg. At this point the Liberators, now over Wittenberge, changed direction and headed south. Then they flew west past Stendal to cross the high ground at Gardelegen and headed for the target from the east. About 150 German fighters converged on the bombers, just as the leading elements were approaching Hanover, and made mass attacks on the Liberators out of the sun in waves of three and five. Mustang pilots and the B-24 gunners replied to the onslaught with heavy machine-gun fire. Three Fw190s were shot down and their pilots killed. Over Rethen, *Oberleutnant* Vollert, 5./JG301 CO, was intercepted by two Mustangs while hard on the tail of a Liberator and was downed after a tense dogfight.

Don Ferguson saw flak bursts, a B-24 on fire and losing altitude, and many parachutes opening up and floating to earth. By this time they were approaching the south-eastward turn towards Magdeburg and the IP. Over the intercom, talk of their 'little friends' coming was welcome, as more and more enemy fighters were being seen. As the Liberators arrived at the IP and made the turn for Misburg, dense, heavy, black flak was seen straight ahead and the intercom was full of comments from the entire crew. Ferguson was taking notes 'like mad' and trying to log 'anything of importance'. Without fighter escort the 491st, which was the last over the target, was extremely vulnerable. The German anti-aircraft guns ceased firing and over a hundred fighters bore in for the kill.

> Our squadron began taking a beating from the Fw 190s, with some starting to shoot down our stragglers. Gunners fired at the enemy fighters coming from 4 and 5 o'clock low as the intercom chatter stated. It was bedlam with planes in and out of formation, taking evasive action. Charles Parmele decided to miss the flak ridden target area and ordered a sudden left turn to the south and thence to the west to reach the original Rally Point with the rest of the bombers in formation. This may have been a mistake, as the fighter attacks from the south and east appeared to be on the increase. Parmele's decision effectively split the group and placed one squadron about 1,500 yards behind the leading Squadron and off to the left by itself. Two minutes after bombs away approximately seventy-five single-engined enemy fighters attacked over the Teutoburger Wald and the Ems. The Fw 190s dived through the B-24 formation flying low-left and attacking again, alone, or in pairs. They singled out stragglers and made their attack from 5 to 7 o'clock, a little high.

Staff Sergeant Al Oliveira, armourer-right waist gunner in Lieutenant Hal Fandell's crew, recalls:

> I had a remarkable view of B-24s exploding, with engines falling in flames as well as bombers angling downward trailing smoke and flames. During this action I saw only three parachutes. An Fw 190 pilot appeared to be looking straight at me as I returned fire. On the left side of the 190 there was painted on the fuselage below the canopy, five American flag symbols reflecting his record of 'kills'. I continued firing and I saw the 190 spiral downward trailing smoke. There was no parachute. Being excited, I fired through our own vertical stabiliser. Just about this time, a cannon shell exploded by the left waist window and Bill Meerdo, left waist gunner, fell against my machine-gun and disengaged the .50 calibre from its mount. Bill had taken shrapnel in the neck and I applied first aid and morphine but he had been killed instantly. Tail gunner Arzie Richardson could do nothing but watch as cannon fire hit his turret armour plate. His guns had frozen. Bomb bay doors were buckled and torn from flak. Control cables were severed and hanging in the waist section. Hal Fandell, pilot, did an outstanding job of flying the plane back to England with the use of trim tabs.

Lieutenant Charles W. Stevens was flying his first mission since bringing his B-24 back to England on 20 June with the nose shot off and his navigator and bombardier dead in the mangled front section. He could have gone home after this but elected to stay and fight because 'that's what I'd joined for'. The decision cost him his life. Stevens' engineer, Joe Boyer, was hit by a 20 mm shell and fell through the open bomb bay doors before the Liberator went down. *Firebird* followed. *The Moose* and *Idiot's Delight*, whose crew were on their thirtieth mission, were hit but managed to make it over the target before falling out of the formation. *Problem Child* went down and *Dorty Treek* and *Ark Angel*, which was badly damaged with a large hole in the right wing and its upper turret missing, tried in vain to tack onto the lead squadron. Gradually, they lost altitude and finally disappeared from view. Lieutenant John S. Warczak's B-24 was hit by fighters and exploded. Warczak was thrown clear, the second time in two months that this had happened to him. Wave after wave of fighters tore through the formation, coming directly out of the sun, at 10 o'clock high, attacking in waves of up to eight abreast, breaking away below the bombers. These were followed by simultaneous attacks from 3 and 9 o'clock by fighters four-abreast or in echelon. *Scarface* went down. Three of the ten-man crew were killed in the aircraft and German civilians murdered six more after they touched down. Kenneth M. Peiffer, the tail gunner and only survivor, was saved by a Frenchman who talked a farmer out of killing him. Matthew Vukovich's Liberator fell off in a deadly spin from which it never recovered. There were no survivors. *Grease Ball* was brought down by 20 mm cannon fire, which set the bomb bay on fire. Only three of the crew managed to bale out before it exploded. *Hare Power* and *House of Rumor* were also set on fire. Three gunners ignored the bale-out bell and went down with *House of Rumor*, firing their guns to the end. The rest of the crew survived and were taken prisoner.

The Reluctant Dragon, piloted by Harold F. Lanning, was also in trouble. On the bomb run it did not have its bomb-bay doors open in time and the bombs fell through the doors, leaving them flapping in the breeze and causing the plane to fall behind. The bombardier, Henry J. Latimore, recalls:

> Our aircraft was severely damaged with both right engines dead and we were losing altitude and unable to keep up with the remainder of the group. Our two waist gunners had been hit by enemy fire. I had no further duties in the nose and went to the rear compartment to help the tail gunner give first aid to them. Taylor had received a bullet in his stomach and another in his buttocks and was in a bad condition. Carbone was wounded in the shoulder but was complaining about hurting in the groin area (the bullet passed from his shoulder to his groin). I inspected it but could not see any wound. We placed bandages over the wounds to try to slow the loss of blood. Meanwhile, Lanning was able to maintain control of the plane by gradually losing altitude, and as Taylor would not survive the opening shock of the parachute, we decided to try and reach friendly territory and land at an airfield in Belgium. We were at about 10,000 feet when we crossed the front lines, as there was a barrage of enemy fire in the area. Lanning decided we would have to bale out because he did not have sufficient control to make a safe landing. The tail gunner and I got the injured men out of the rear compartment lower escape hatch and followed them. By the time I made my exit the aircraft was at about 8,000 feet.[12]

No fewer than sixteen Liberators had been blasted out of the sky – all in the space of just 15 minutes. Only one Squadron had reached the target without being attacked. Further bomber losses were prevented by the timely arrival over the Minden Canal of eight P-51 Weather Scouts led by Bob Whitlow, which held the Fw 190s at bay until reinforcements could arrive to save the dozen remaining B-24s. Then an orderly retreat back to England began by regrouping the bombers into one formation. In East Anglia, pensive and worried ground crews waited for their return. At the end of the runway at North Pickenham, ambulances stood by, the wreckers near the tower waiting for accidents. The sky remained empty. At 1550 the long wait was almost over. All eyes turned. Someone called, 'There they are!' At 1600 a squadron and a half came over the field. One aircraft touched down and when the crew got out his replacement waist gunner hit the ground and kissed it. His missions were over. John Keene, waiting forlornly at *Ark Angel*'s revetment waited patiently, praying that the *Angel* would come home as she always had. He began to think that maybe she had landed somewhere else. The crew chief wandered aimlessly over the oil stained concrete where he had worked on her so many days. 'Yeah, Bennett was a good guy ... the *Angel* was a good ship ... I bet she gave those damn Germans a run for their money. Damn! Damn! Damn!' Keene picked up his toolbox and put it in his shack (bomb crate box) by the hardstand. He then rode his bicycle back to the 853rd. Forty years were to elapse before he discovered that the *Angel* had crashed and burned 20 km south of Misburg. Villagers ran to the Liberator and found all the crew-members still strapped into their seats, but they had burned to death.

Command acted quickly to replace the losses. The control tower log entries for that day said: 'Sixteen replacement B-24s arrived from Stansted, Shades of Dawn Patrol.'

Replacement crews were needed in great numbers throughout the rest of 1944. November and December became a constant battleground as missions to oil targets, especially to Merseburg, and marshalling yards, remained the order of the day. In an effort to maintain the flow of experienced combat crewmen to the bomb groups, some crews had been persuaded to 'volunteer' for a second combat tour by the offer of a thirty-day rest and recuperation leave in the States first. Abe Dolim in Joe Hamil's crew at Bury St Edmunds had flown his twenty-seventh mission on 7 July when the primary was the oil refinery at Merseburg-Leuna. A combat tour was officially thirty-five missions and to refuse would have meant flying eight more missions. Dolim had had his 'fill'.

> My affair with the B-17 was like an infatuation with a comely young wench. How was I to know that she would eventually lead me down the primrose path to perdition? She was lover, mother comforter ... all that a young swain hopes for in his loved one. Then alas, as in all earthly relationships, reality intruded and destroyed my dreams. I began to see her faults, her aberrations, and all the petty deceits that marred her beauty. I tried to come to terms but the advantages were all on her side because of her great power over me ... it was a true power of life and

death ... and it became in time a love-killing death blow from which I never recovered. Love turned sour, I began to watch her every move. My nerves took a beating. She developed suicidal tendencies ... I had the feeling she wanted me to share in her death wish. I was terrified and fiercely resolved to escape her clutches the very instant she made any attempt to involve me in her wild schemes. The strain eventually got to me and I longed for an end to our deadly relationship ....

Dolim's home was in Honolulu so he calculated that what with slow convoys and Patton on his way to Paris, the war in Europe might be over before he had to return. The Hawaiian gambled and lost. He was given an A-4 air travel priority and Patton slowed down after he got to Paris. It was good, however, to be back among his comrades. 'People at home did not seem to comprehend air warfare.'[13]

Experience was sorely needed. On 27 November fifty-six bombers were shot down and on 30 November, when Merseburg was bombed, the headlines in *Stars and Stripes* said: 'Terrific Flak Costs 56 Heavies. 30 Fighters Also lost.' The report revealed that it had been necessary to make a course correction near the target and this had brought the formation within range of 750 guns. Flak had actually claimed forty-eight of the bombers over the target. Merseburg soon became the main topic of conversation among the old-timers. When Ken Blakeborough,[14] a replacement pilot, arrived at Glatton on Christmas Eve, he was quick to notice it. Blakeborough threw his baggage on an empty bunk and was told by one of the old-timers in the Fireball Outfit that the bed he had chosen had belonged to Gordon Gallagher, who had gone down at Merseburg on 2 November. Blakeborough observed that combat losses were rather hushed up; he did not know whether by intent or not. 'Unless you knew someone who'd gone down you didn't ever hear about losses.'

December 1944 brought the worst weather in England for fifty-four years. Water froze in the pipes and a thin film of ice coated runways at bases throughout eastern England. The temperature dropped to as low as minus 18 degrees Centigrade. One of the worst features of the weather was lack of visibility during missions. On Christmas Eve it finally relented and allowed a record 2,534 Allied bombers to make the largest single strike ever flown. Their targets were airfields and lines of communication leading to the 'Bulge'. Crews were told that their route was planned on purpose to go over the long-suffering ground pounders' positions for morale purposes. Navigator Lieutenant Lawrence W. Rasmussen in the 493rd had never seen so many aircraft in all his life. 'Everything from heavies, mediums, lights and pursuits.'

Brigadier General Fred Castle led the 3rd Division on his thirtieth mission in a Fort called *Treble Four* named after the last four digits of its serial number, with Lieutenant Robert W. Harriman's crew from Lavenham. All went well until 23,000 feet over Belgium, about 35 miles from Liège, his right outboard engine burst into flames and the propeller had to be feathered. The deputy lead ship took over and Castle dropped down to 20,000 feet. But at this height the aircraft began to vibrate badly and he was forced to take it down another 3,000 feet before levelling out. The Fortress was now down to 180 mph indicated airspeed and being pursued by seven Bf 109s who attacked, wounding the tail gunner and leaving the radar navigator nursing bad wounds in his neck and shoulders. Castle could not carry out any evasive manoeuvres with the full bomb load still aboard and he could not salvo them for fear of hitting Allied troops on the ground. Successive attacks by the fighters put another two engines out of action and *Treble Four* lost altitude. To reduce airspeed the wheels of the Fortress were lowered and the crew ordered to bale out with the terse intercom message, 'This is it boys'. Castle managed to level out, long enough for six of the crew to bale out. However, at 12,000 feet the bomber was hit in the right wing fuel tank, which exploded, sending the B-17 into a plunging final spiral to the ground. Brigadier General Castle was posthumously awarded the Medal of Honor, the highest ranking officer to receive the award. Harriman and Castle were buried in the American cemetery at Henri-Chattel.

Overall, the Christmas Eve raids were effective and severely hampered von Rundstedt's lines of communication. The cost in aircraft though, was high. Many crashed during their return over England as drizzle and overcast played havoc with landing patterns. Tired crews put down where they could. Meanwhile, the bases hosted parties and at Old Buckenham the 453rd entertained more than 1,250 children from the neighbouring villages and towns, ranging in age from 4 to 14. Many were orphans from the London Blitz. As night fell the Aero Club was thrown open to all, regardless of rank. The next morning a Liberator took off from the base with gifts for 300 French children and delivered them to the American Red Cross Club at Rainbow Corner in Paris. On Christmas Day over 350 bombers hit eighteen targets, mostly rail bridges and communications centres in the tactical area west of the Rhine. Nine escorting fighter groups encountered over 300 fighters and claimed more than forty shot down. Only 150 aircraft were available for another strike on 26 December and the next day the wintry conditions were responsible for a succession of crashes during early morning take-offs. On 30 December, lines of communication were attacked again.

At dawn on New Year's Eve, while the Battle of the Bulge raged, groups returned to oil production centres in a 'maximum effort' over Germany. When Roland L. Douglas, a tail gunner in Lieutenant Clifton Williams' crew at Thorpe Abbotts, heard that their target was Hamburg with its oil refineries and other heavy industrial plants, he was relieved. 'I had bombed this target on 4 August with a different crew and it hadn't been rough so I figured it wouldn't be to bad on my twenty-sixth mission. The only difference was that on 4 August there were 170 anti-aircraft guns at the target area and now there were reported to be 490!' Lieutenant Glenn H. Rojohn, pilot of *The Little Skipper*, and his co-pilot, Lieutenant William O. Leek Jr, had been scheduled for leave after flying several missions in a row, but their plans were interrupted at 0400 hours when they were awakened for the 'maximum effort'. The navigator, Lieutenant Robert Washington, flying his twenty-seventh mission, recalled that 'Take-off was delayed due to fog and when we assembled in the air and departed the English coast we learned that our fighter escort had

217

been delayed due to the weather'. In all, thirty-seven B-17s of the Bloody Hundredth took off.

The Bloody Hundredth formation was flying over the North Sea at around 22,000-feet when successive waves of enemy fighters were encountered. Some came so close that the faces of the pilots could be clearly seen, as they shot by. Fighters came from directly ahead and behind and from both the bottom and top. One sergeant's body became cold and numb with fright when he realised that only $1/16$ inch of aluminium stood between him and this battery of firepower. Ten B-17s were quickly lost and *The Little Skipper* and the B-17 flown by Lieutenant William O. McNab were involved in a mid-air collision that joined the B-17s together 'like breeding dragonflies' and the two planes became one before they impacted at Tettens near Wilhelmshaven.[15] German soldiers on Wangerooge Island watching the inter-twined B-17s could not believe their eyes. The Bloody Hundredth's loss of twelve Forts was half the total lost by the 3rd Division.

Meanwhile, raids on lines of communication continued for several days, until the position in the Ardennes gradually swung in the Allies' favour. The final great offensive of the *Wehrmacht* under von Rundstedt ground to a halt and Germany had no reserves left. The big gamble had turned into a disastrous defeat. The Allies' overwhelming air superiority led to German plans to try to destroy simultaneously the RAF and American aircraft on the ground in Holland, Belgium and Northern France in a single, decisive, blow. *Unternehmen Bodenplatte* began early on New Years Day 1945 using 875 single-engined fighter aircraft, primarily in support of von Rundstedt's Ardennes offensive. But the German losses were catastrophic. Although Allied aircraft losses amounted to 424 destroyed or heavily damaged, German losses were 300 aircraft lost, 235 pilots killed and 65 pilots taken prisoner.

The *Luftwaffe*, though, was still far from defeated.

Notes

1. Stiles, from Sioux City, Iowa, completed his bomber tour, but instead of returning to America on leave due to him, he asked to be transferred to fighters and he moved to the 339th FG and to P-51 Mustangs. At age 23 he was shot down and killed on 26.11.44, gaining his only victory as a fighter pilot while escorting bombers to Hanover.

2. Remarkably, the co-pilot, N. E. Hainlin, was able to team up with the two waist gunners, Sergeant A. Willard and Sergeant J. I. Snede, and they all evaded capture with the help of the French underground. The bombardier, Lieutenant C. F. Eisel, became a PoW, as did the engineer, Sergeant R. J. Kowatch, and the ball turret gunner, Sergeant B. L. Hope.

3. The Fw 190A 8/R2 fighters were specially equipped with an armoured oil cooler, bullet-proof windshield, 6 mm fire-proof plates and cabin sides and 9 mm armour plate behind the pilot's seat, which could deflect the American .50 calibre bullets with ease. Power was provided by a fourteen-cylinder double star BMW 801 engine capable of 2400 hp. Standard weaponry was two heavy MG131 30 mm cannon and four MG 151/20 20 mm machine-guns. All this extra weight doubled then fuel consumption so to guarantee 3 hours of flight time, the fuel load was raised to 960 litres with the help of a 300-litre ejectable auxiliary tank and a 110-litre auxiliary tank behind the pilot's seat. A tanked up and fully armed Fw 190 A8/R2 reached a flight weight of seven to eight tons.

4. Werner Vorberg could not confirm his unit's kills as the gun camera films were confiscated after the war and at the time he wrote these words they were reported to be in the Imperial War Museum in London. The storm group continued attacks on *Viermots* units until the end of 1944. After that they were called to action in defence of Germany.

5. Bruce (only one other member of his crew survived) had broken his neck and his right pelvis and badly damaged his right shoulder. After capture, German officers fractured his jaw with a pistol butt. Almost totally paralysed and black and blue all over, Bruce spent three days on a train, which took captured airmen to Frankfurt interrogation centre, and then another week on a train, before a German doctor at last treated his severe injuries. Bruce was finally sent to *Stalag Luft III*, Sagan.

6. Hunter's crew, which had come down at Willems, near Lille, returned to England. The majority of them were KIA on 9 March 1945.

7. It is possible Brainard was one of at least nine airmen who landed in or near the village of Nentershausen who were murdered or executed by German civilians and, in one case, by a German soldier home on leave.

8. The next day, Romm claimed two more B-17 kills, which took his tally to eighty-five. Subsequent aerial combat with Lockheed Lightning P-38 fighters was without result.

9. Schaen's B-24 went down 800 metres South of Forstgut Berlitzgrube, and Collar was among five of the crew who were captured.

10. Three crews in the 398th were lost on 2.11.44. Wisner's crew were not among them, but they went down over Merseburg on 21.11.44. One KIA. Eight PoW.

11. Tim Tetreault, who was awarded the DFC, and his crew, completed their thirty-five-mission tour of duty.

12. All but Lee Taylor (who landed on a roof and was killed) in Lanning's crew were picked up by a British patrol and taken to Brussels, where Carbone was treated at a British field hospital.

13. Victor Bonomo, who also returned to the Group, finished his second combat tour, a total of fifty missions, in March 1945 and was possibly the first in his group to be twice nominated for the 'Lucky Bastard Club'. Abe Dolim was the second 'two times winner', having amassed a total of 410.25 combat hours on fifty-one combat missions. 'The last weeks and days were an agony. [When] finally it was all over, I was FREE, home safe and I didn't give a damn if I ever laid eyes on the old whore [B-17] again.'

14. Author of *The Fireball Outfit*. By VE Day he had flown thirty-two missions, was awarded an Air Medal and four clusters and was sent home. His stay in England was a brief seven months but he recalled that they were indelibly part of his life.

15. Of the six men in Rojohn's crew who baled out, four survived. Staff Sergeants Little and Chase were KIA. Four of the McNab crew also survived.

CHAPTER 8

Visions of Victory

... We finally got a ship of our own. The name is Dozy Doats. *Don't ask me why 'cause we didn't name it. It has 36 missions without any trouble .... I guess my worries are over. The Germans have already sent up the flak with my number on it and it failed. It tore thru the skin of the ship behind me and hit me in the back, but by the time it got to me it was too spent to do any damage. It stuck in my flying suit. It wasn't as big as the hole in the ship so there must have been another part that broke off when it came through. I have the piece with me and I'm going to bring it home and show it to you .... I saw in Stars and Stripes that they are getting ready to ring the Victory bells in the US pretty soon. They must be crazy. I agree with Ernie Pyle. The war will probably go into the winter and early spring.*

Letters home. On 9.2.45 a report received from the German government through the International Red Cross stated that Staff Sergeant William Y. Ligon Jr, had been KIA on 6.10.44 when Lieutenant Everett l. 'Ike' Isaacson's crew was one of 11 in the 385th BG that were shot down.

On the freezing cold night of 4 January, Lieutenant Sylvester P. Bergman and the crew of *Delectable Doris* in the Sky Scorpions at Hethel, just outside Norwich, studied the bulletin board in the operations room to see if they were to fly their twenty-fourth mission the next day. Fog and rain had threatened to ground the bombers but Bergman saw his name and the crew went back to the barracks to shave and clean up. This was done to ensure that the oxygen mask fitted properly the next morning. The crew spent a restless night before the CQ came to wake the pilot for the mission. Bergman had to sign a wake-up sheet so that the CQ had proof that he had awakened the pilot. Bergman then had to wake his crew. The first question the pilot asked the CQ was, 'What is the gas load?' This gave him an idea of just how deep he would be going into Germany. The answer on the morning of 5 January was '2,700 gallons' so they knew they had a long mission. Then it was a short walk through icy puddles to the mess hall for their mission breakfast of fresh eggs and bacon, hot coffee and powdered milk. Crews boarded the open top two and a half-ton trucks and motored through the snow-covered canopy of Hethel Wood, where in spring bluebells grew, to take them to briefing.

The Bergman crew met in the briefing room, which had a map on the wall with a curtain covering it. When all had assembled, the curtain was rolled back to display the mission of the day. The target was a railroad junction located in Neustadt. Many thoughts went through crews' minds. The Sky Scorpions were briefed by the CO, Colonel John B. Herboth Jr, who had been in command for less than a month. The CO would die two months later when a *Rammjäger* hit his lead ship, *The Palace of Dallas*. Next came the weatherman and intelligence officer. The map indicated all the mission fly-over points. It also showed all possible enemy fighter bases and flak batteries, which had been reported, from previous missions. In the base chapel Father Gerald Beck, the Catholic Group Chaplain distributed communion to the combat crews. It was not uncommon to see a protestant boy also receive, as a feeling of more spiritual insurance. Father Beck quite often drove his jeep at top speed from plane to plane, making sure that no one was denied communion before take-off. One time in North Africa, he was inside a Liberator administering the sacrament at take-off time and was an observer for that mission. He loved it. Father Beck often played poker with his boys, officers and enlisted men alike. Shooting craps was his meat. He would shout as he threw the dice: 'For the Chaplain!' He played baseball with GIs 20 years his junior. He would drink beer with them in town, after first removing his Chaplain's cross and replacing it with a Field Artillery insignia.

After the briefing the crew dressed in their one-piece flight suits under the electrically heated suit under a leather flight suit. On their hands they wore a nylon liner, then the electrically heated gloves topped with the leather fleece lined gloves. After dressing, the crew checked out their parachutes and saw the Chaplain before going to the plane. Meanwhile, the gunners were briefed and installed their guns. The flight crew went to *Delectable Doris*'s hardstand to conduct pre-flight on the Liberator, which had been named in honour of Doris Falconer, pilot Bill Graf's English fiancée, whom Graf married in August 1944 after his last mission. Sergeant Michael Otis Harris had painted a beautiful nude, artistically posed, on the nose for free and in record time. On entering the bomber, the crew helped the pilot and co-pilot, Flight Officer O. Laws, get into their flak suits, which were draped over their seats. Then there was a steel helmet that went over their flight caps. They always carried with them an extra pair of boots and a musette bag filled with trading goods such as chocolate and cigarettes in case they were shot down.

It was now time to start engines and taxi. On this flight the Bergman crew was deputy lead crew and this meant that they would take off first. The weather that morning was sleet and snow so heavy that crews could not see their hands in front of their faces. The severe wintry weather over England was responsible for several fatal accidents during take-off and at Hethel the runway was covered with 3 inches of snow and slush. Bergman put *Delectable Doris* on the runway on a heading of 06. He had to do an instrument take-off with Laws watching out of the window to help him stay on the runway. Halfway down the runway, the B-24 had not reached take-off speed because of the runway's condition. At this point, Laws pointed out that they had reached the point of commitment. Bergman then asked for emergency power. This still didn't give them enough speed to take off and the end of the runway was fast approaching. They were still 15–20 mph too slow. Bergman then jerked the column back into his stomach as hard as he could. This raised *Delectable Doris* about 3 feet off the ground before it set back down, but it did give them 5 mph more airspeed. After four jumps, she stayed up just in time because there was no more runway. *Delectable Doris* carried ten 500 lb general-purpose bombs. The plane went right into the clouds and headed south to home on radio beacons to get into formation. When all the B-24s were in position, they headed for the target. Everything went according to plan on the way to the target. *Delectable Doris* flew at an altitude of 23,300 feet. On the bomb run, the lead ship had a malfunction and the Bergman crew, as deputy lead, took over the lead. They hit the target, which led to a lead crew commendation. On the return trip, the trim tabs froze and the cables broke. This made the handling of the B-24 difficult. It had to be controlled strictly by brawn. On returning to Hethel, they shot an emergency red flare to indicate trouble and the need to land first. *Unstable Mabel* and *Gallopin' Kate* failed to return to Hethel, but their crews were safe after crash-landings away from base.[1]

A period of fine weather, beginning on 6 January, enabled the heavies to fly missions in support of the ground troops once more. These were mostly against lines of communication, airfields and marshalling yards. Finally, the German advance in the Ardennes came to a halt and ultimately petered out. Hitler's last chance now lay in his so-called 'wonder weapons' – the V-1 and V-2. Missions were flown to tactical targets throughout the remaining days of January but when the weather intervened, the 8th Air Force mounted shallow penetration raids on *Noball* targets in France. The 8th also attempted several tactical missions but the weather was so bad, morale sagged as mission after mission was scrubbed, often just after take-off. But at least each mission flown was a 'another day closer to home'. At least that is how Norman K. Andrew, navigator in Jack Stanley's crew in the 487th viewed his twentieth mission on 7 January. The crew was awakened at 0400 to lead the group. The primary target was a railroad viaduct, but it could only be bombed visually. If it was obscured then the crews were told to head for the secondary target, the Paderborn marshalling yards, and bomb using PFF. It was 10/10ths and the bombers hit the secondary target. Andrew recalls: 'We went right over Bielefeld and there was no flak. The only flak we saw was for groups ahead who crowded the Dutch corridor on the southern side. A three-gun battery put up about 40–50 rounds. We had to come all the way home at 20,000 [feet] because of clouds.'

Despite adverse weather conditions, missions continued to be flown as the Allied forces moved triumphantly eastwards toward the River Rhine on the western border of central Germany, and marshalling yards and railway bridges were important bombing targets. Very dense fog was common at this time of the year and hampered operations considerably. At each base hundreds of men were detailed to clean the runways of snow in the early hours before take-off times so that the surface was safe enough to use. Some crews could not see the star on the top of their left wing until the ice had melted at about 20,000 feet. On their return, bomber crews just beat snowstorms that reduced visibility to a dangerous point and got down as best they could. The weather played havoc with practice missions as well as combat missions as Quintin R. Wedgeworth, a navigator in the 392nd at Wendling, recalls:

On the 18th the Colonel ordered a practice mission, in complete disregard for the weather. Lieutenant J. C. Decker and four crew of *Little Lulu* disappeared during the snowstorm and were never heard from again. More victims of the North Sea, no doubt! The only mission that could be launched during this period was assigned to the marshalling yards in Heilbron on Sunday 21 January. It was another blind drop with un-observed results. There was no enemy reaction. The weather really wasn't all that much better on the 28th either when we went to Dortmund in the dreaded Ruhr Valley, or flak alley, as it was more normally referred to, in *Rebel Gal'*. We were still having snow squalls but it was a double anniversary and tradition must be served. First of all, it marked the third birthday of the Eighth, having been activated at Savannah, Georgia, on 28 January 1942. There were seventy-four officers, eighty-one enlisted men and no airplanes! Now, personnel and machines were numbered in the thousands and not many were questioning its mission any more. It was also the second anniversary of the first full-scale attack on the Reich; 806 bombers, together with 634 fighters for escort, bombed Frankfurt. We couldn't celebrate any anniversaries of our own but we sure had a lot of 'firsts' going: first trip to the Ruhr Valley, first oil target and our first mission since baling out. Specifically, we were briefed to attack the Kaiserstuhl and Gneisenau benzol plants, 3 miles NE of Dortmund. The Germans were mixing it with their gasoline to stretch their dwindling fuel supplies. The price we were paying to deny the Germans any oil was high, but it did not deter the High Command's determination for pressing home this campaign. The enemy, of course, was just as determined to protect their dwindling supplies. We would test their resolve. The *Luftwaffe* conserved its fighters until it was certain that we would once again attack, then it would come up in force. Some 12,000 AA guns were moved into the areas ringing the targets. Even so, the Germans were losing this battle. Had our High Command realised the real significance of their losses, we probably would have hit them even more.

By Saturday 3 February Marshal Zhukov's Red Army was only 35 miles from Berlin and the capital was jammed with refugees fleeing from the advancing Russians. Accompanied by 900 fighters, 1,200 bombers dropped over 2,000 tons of bombs on the centre of Berlin, killing an estimated 25,000 inhabitants and destroying 360 industrial firms and heavily damaging another 170. An area 1½ miles square, stretching across the southern half of the *Mitte* or city centre, had been devastated. Twenty-one bombers were shot down, ninety-three suffered flak damage, and another six crash-landed inside the Russian lines.

Further German disruption in the face of the Russian advance occurred on Tuesday 6 February when 1,300 heavies, escorted by fifteen groups of P-51 Mustangs, bombed Chemnitz and Magdeburg and the synthetic oil refineries at Lutzkendorf and Merseburg. At Wendling, Norman K Andrew, who had been awakened at 0200, wondered if there was any weather in which the bombers did not fly in the ETO. When he found out that his twenty-fifth mission would be the Bohlen synthetic oil refinery, he exclaimed, 'Hold your hat!' The bombers took off in the dark, as usual, and hit Chemnitz and Magdeburg.[2] At Wendling the base had no ceiling and Andrew's crew 'sort of felt their way in'. 'After landing we watched the boys come in. They liked to scare us to death! Finally one went off the end of the runway'. Three crews landed on the Continent and one crew baled out by Beachy Head. Altogether, twenty-two bombers were lost in crash-landings in England and three exploded in mid-air collisions over Suffolk. On 9 February when the heavies returned to the oil refineries in the ever-diminishing *Reich*, now seriously threatened by the Russian armies converging from the east, there was another incident, this time over Norfolk, as Edward D. Cronnelly, navigator on *Spirit of Notre Dame* in the 453rd Group, recalls.

> The pilot was Lieutenant John P. Glass of Louisville, Kentucky. It was a rule that during take-off and landing the navigator, bombardier and nose gunner would be on the flight deck. I would always stand between and just behind the pilots, which gave me a higher point of view than either of them. On this particular day we were returning from a mission to Magdeburg, Germany. Near the target we had lost an engine, but were able to 'filter' back below the bomber stream though we could not match their speed. We had flown from just inside Germany to England alone. As we neared Old Buckenham, Glass was given clearance to make a straight in approach. We made a higher than usual approach because of being on only three engines. We were only a few hundred feet off the ground when I suddenly saw another B-24 just a bit to the right and slightly ahead and below us. I immediately pounded the pilot on the shoulder and literally screamed about the other plane. He pushed the throttles forward and pulled back on the 'stick', but the planes crashed together. As you can see from the photograph, the left rudder assembly of the other plane was cut off. Fortunately, Glass was a big, strong man and he was able to get our plane under control despite the fact that another engine was knocked out and we sustained other damage. Thanks be to God, we were to land safely. The other plane, piloted by Lieutenant Rollins, crashed and all aboard were killed instantly. To compound the tragedy, Rollins and his crew were flying their thirty-fifth mission, which would have ended their tour. I know that an investigation was held and that Glass was held blameless. We completed our tour of missions the following month.

At the Yalta Conference early in February 1945, Josef Stalin, the Russian leader, and his army chiefs asked that the RAF and 8th Air Force paralyse Berlin and Leipzig and prevent troops moving from the west to the eastern front. British Prime Minister Winston Churchill and American President, Franklin D. Roosevelt, agreed on a policy of massive air attacks on the German capital and other cities such as Dresden and Chemnitz. These cities were not only administrative centres controlling military and civilian movements, but were also the main communication centres through which the bulk of the enemy's war traffic flowed. Spaatz had set the wheels in motion with a raid on Berlin on 3 February. Magdeburg and Chemnitz were bombed three days later, but the most devastating raids of all fell upon the old city of Dresden in eastern Germany, starting with an 800-bomber raid by the RAF on the night of 13 February. Two waves of heavy bombers produced firestorms and horrendous casualties among the civilian population. The next day, 400 bombers attempted to stoke up the fires created by RAF Bomber Command while 900 more bombers attacked Chemnitz, Magdeburg and other targets. Crews were to return to the Pottery City of Dresden again in March and April on similar raids, but the Allied air forces' top priority remained the oil-producing centres.

On 14 February Jule Berndt, navigator in Lieutenant Rolland B. Peacock Jr's crew in the 850th Squadron, completed his thirty-fifth and final mission in his 'loveable' B-17 *Maggie*.

When *Maggie* finally came to rest in her stand we all joyfully jumped from the plane and crowded about her. We all tried to express our gratitude to this magnificent plane that had brought us back so many times. The ground crew chief and his assistants also shared our joy with us, not only inwardly but also by a few more tangible signs – namely a bottle of Scotch and a box of cigars. It was a glorious feeling. Years of anxiety and care just dropped from my shoulders. Before the ship had stopped rolling I offered my thanks to my God, who had so mercifully protected us during our months of flying. Later, as I thought back over all the missions, the realisation of what I have been through reinforced my belief that God looked favourably upon me. There were so many instances when our ship could have been one of those mentioned in the daily communiqué – 'Fifteen of our bombers failed to return'. Also, when I thought of those boys who sadly lost their lives, I recalled the number of close calls we had and from which we emerged unscathed. A few weeks it almost seemed like a bad dream to me. I just could not visualise having gone through a complete tour of missions in Europe, of having been in England, over Germany, of having flown the ocean and of having crossed it by liner. The memories of those anxious moments over targets, of seeing the face of our wounded ball turret gunner, of the time over Duisburg and Merseburg when there just didn't seem to be a plausible excuse for emerging unscathed from the clouds of flak that we entered. All those seemed like parts of one of those bad nightmares that are hard to reconstruct after you wake up. The long hours of thinking before falling asleep on the night before a mission and the anxious moments spent contemplating the thought of dying so young – worrying about such things not just for yourself but also for your parents, who you knew were praying for your safety back home. All this had become just a part of the past and here today I was whole, alive and writing about it. It was almost too good to be true.

On 22 February *Clarion*, the systematic destruction of the German communications network, was launched. More than 6,000 Allied aircraft from seven different commands were airborne and they struck at transportation targets throughout western Germany and northern Holland. All targets were selected with the object of preventing troops being transported to the Russian front, now only a few miles from Berlin. Despite the low altitudes flown, seven bombers only were lost, including two B-17s to a Me 262 jet fighter. The next day only four bombers were lost from the 1,274 despatched.

Sunday 25 February was, for Norman K. Andrew, his thirtieth mission and Graduation Day! It was so easy that he was 'almost ashamed to finish up on this one'. For others it was not easy at all. A piece of flak hit a B-17 co-pilot in the neck, killing him, and the engineer had to spend 10 minutes getting him off the flight controls. The Fort was finally landed at a P-51 base in France. For George Rubin in Lieutenant William C. Wiley's crew in the 486th, 25 February was their eighteenth mission.

> Clarence Baugh was added to our crew as a 'toggelier-gunner'. He replaced our regular bombardier George Stiftinger, who was removed before the mission because we now dropped our bombs on a flare signal from the lead plane in each element, rather than having a bombardier in each plane. We were flying in a spare plane, a new B-17G, as our *Oh Miss Agnes* was out for engine overhaul. Our primary target was Memmingen, the second Munich. There was an abort before take-off and we moved up and were the low squadron lead. It was a cold day and the flak was intense and heavy over the target. Overcast at the primary made us shift to the second target and a run over Munich. We were badly hit by intense flak. Oxygen and C-1 (Automatic Pilot) shot out, three of the 1,000 lb bombs failed to salvo and had to be dropped manually. Four of the crewmembers were wounded. Our navigator's eyes were filled with Plexiglas. Our co-pilot was hit in the right leg. Our radio operator was hit by glass over the eyes. Two engines and our control system were badly damaged. Flak also hit the tail section, luckily missing our tail gunner. We lost altitude and our formation. We flew south, trying to find Switzerland. We were too low in the Alps to fly on and control of the ship was getting more precarious. We tried to get rid of all extra weight. I toggled the bombs out of the plane manually and we even tried getting rid of the ball turret.
>
> Wiley made a beautiful wheels-up landing in a field outside the town of Sonthofen. We were all safe and tried to destroy papers and other material on board. A German Youth group captured us and for a time it looked as if they would execute our officers. This was stopped by a German Alpine troop, which took over our capture and marched us back into Sonthofen. We were beaten by the townspeople as we were marched through the town to the local jail. We found out much later that the hostility was due to a bombing of the town by the Royal Air Force the night before. Our wounds were treated at the jail and officers were separated from enlisted men. We were fed bread and water and some potatoes and meat and we slept on the cell floor all night. Late the next afternoon we were moved by truck to Kaufburen. I think the move was

partly out of fear that the townspeople would attack the jail. At Kaufburen we were put in solitary confinement and individually questioned for the first time. We were fed bread and soup. We met another crew here and on the second day we were taken from our cells and given enough rations for three days – one loaf of bread, butter and some meat for two men. With a German sergeant and seven other guards, our two crews started a trip by train to Oberusel, our interrogation centre near Frankfurt-Am-Main.

After interrogation, Rubin and his fellow crewmembers were incarcerated in a PoW camp.

On 26 February, only three bombers were shot down over Berlin. If there was a good time to be flying bombing missions or even beginning a tour, this might be that time. It was on 2 March, a Friday, that Quintin R. Wedgeworth in the 392nd flew his thirteenth mission.

It was an ominous day for all who were overly superstitious. It was Friday, our 13th mission and we would be flying *Wabash Canon Ball*! And, can you believe, back to Magdeburg? During the first part of February the Group went there five times out of six missions. We wound up with eighteen casualties and four ships destroyed. The briefing outlined the usual strategy employed for this target. The primary objective was the synthetic oil refinery north of the city, but it was stipulated that it must be a visual attack. Otherwise, the secondary was to be the marshalling yards in the centre of the city. Only two squadrons from the 392nd were committed to this effort. Our squadron would fly high-right off the 44th and the 576th would fly high-right off the 491st. The launch got underway on schedule. The wheels on our ship swung up and out at 0710 hours, just 5 minutes behind the lead ship. We climbed out over the Wash as usual and then circled back over Beacon 21 to form up. The assembly had been planned for 12,000 feet, but we were forced up another 2,000 feet in order to get on top. Departing the English coast near Happisburgh, we made landfall on the coast of the Netherlands just north of Bergen Aan Zee at 0922 hours. Our climb continued over Enkhuizen, the Zuider Zee, Meppel and the German frontier, where we were supposed to level out at 22,500 feet while rendezvousing with the P-51 fighter escort. However, we continued to push upward, reaching 23,000 feet. We had been discharging chaff for the last 14 miles but the Dummer Lake flak defences were strangely quiet! Near Celle, Lieutenant Down's ship broke away from the formation and headed back, but apparently under control.[3]

We finally levelled off at 24,000 feet at the IP over Wittingen. The chaff screen was dispersed immediately and continued all the way into the target. We didn't have long to wait before the first bursts of flak began to appear, mostly below us. I pulled my helmet down (already had the vest on) around my chest and dragged the chute a little closer! Taylor was soon reporting that the lethal black puffs were climbing higher! Ahead of us, and uncomfortably close, it was sure enough bursting at our level.

227

Suddenly it was on all sides, the whole ship shuddered and bounced. Inevitably a loud metallic 'clang' told us that we had been hit. The question was, where? It wasn't visible from any of our stations. I toggled the ten 500 lb bombs loose in unison with the lead ship. As we circled left to withdraw, we (unknowingly) came close to becoming involved in a major air battle. Anticipating an attack against their dwindling oil supplies, the *Luftwaffe* had assembled a large force of Bf 109s and Fw 190s. However, Fighter Groups intercepted them near Wittenburg and downed thirty of the e/a while losing eight of their own.

The return trip was not the usual uneventful story either. As before, we commenced discharging a screen of chaff prior to reaching Dummer Lake. During this operation someone accidentally fired their guns and raked Lieutenant Blakeley's ship with heavy .50 calibre ammo at close range. It tumbled from the formation and was last seen spiralling down with only two chutes being observed. The flight back across The Netherlands was a sombre one. Because of some deep-rooted human emotion, accidental fatalities were always much harder to swallow than those which were the direct result of some enemy action. We arrived at the Dutch Coast at 1313 hours and commenced the letdown immediately. Our intended landfall was at Great Yarmouth, the usual point, but we turned north-eastward and came ashore over Happisburgh. We had made a similar deviation earlier this morning over the same area! Maybe the lead had a girl in Happisburgh? As we neared the base, I collected my briefcase and went aft to the flight deck, my normal station during landing. We touched down and piled out as soon as Adsit had her parked. Except for one squadron, the effectiveness of this day's effort was poor. Although the target was partially obscured by clouds, our squadron bombardier got a visual sighting and put 74 per cent within 2,000 feet of the MPI at the oil refinery. The other element bombed the marshalling yards and wound up with poor results from the H2X. Amazingly enough, our ship was the lone recipient of all that flak!

By March the systematic destruction of German oil production plants, airfields and communications centres, had virtually driven the *Luftwaffe* from German skies. But despite fuel and pilot shortages, Me 262 jet fighters could still be expected to put in rare attacks and almost all enemy fighter interceptions of American heavy bombers were made by the jets. On 4 March two Liberator groups bombed Swiss territory by mistake. The US Ambassador had only recently attended a memorial service and visited reconstruction projects of the previous bombing in September 1944. General Marshall urged General Spaatz to visit Switzerland secretly and reparations involving many millions of dollars were made to the Swiss Government. On 15 March, 1,353 bombers escorted by 833 fighters hit the German Army HQ at Zossen near Berlin and a marshalling yard at Orienburg. Two days later, 1,328 bombers escorted by 820 fighters bombed targets in west and north central Germany. Bomber losses were minimal, but accidents could always occur. Around this time a new hazard materialised when due to some error, a formation of B-26

Marauders arrived over the target at the same time as the Forts, but headed in the opposite direction. Both formations flew right through each other 'like cards being shuffled'. Incredibly, there were no collisions, but it did nothing for crews' nerves. Bad weather brought danger while forming up over England and while flying over the Continent. While flying through contrails so thick that he could not see the wing tips of his own aircraft, Sergeant Harry E. Thatcher, ball turret gunner in Lieutenant Harry Waggoner's crew in the 490th, witnessed *Big Poison* flown by Lieutenant Robert H. Tennenberg and Lieutenant Arthur Stern's B-17 (none of whose crew survived) collide on the starboard side of the formation.

> They blew the whole formation apart. The most frightening thing was the voice of the pilot in one of them coming over the intercom, shouting 'Every man for himself!' Fortunately, no other aircraft were involved and the rest of us returned safely to base.

Tennenberg recalls.

> We encountered no flak and proceeded to the target without incident. After bombs-away on target we headed home for England, flying back down our own contrails. We were about 5 minutes away from the German border (I was leading the third element) when the plane leading the fourth element pulled up in front of me and we collided in mid-air. The other plane just broke in two and went down; none of its crew got out and they were all lost. My plane had two gaping holes in the fuselage next to Nos 2 and 3 engines, the Plexiglas nose had gone and so had the pitot tube. My toggelier had been flung up to the ceiling, wrenching his back and cutting his head. He had to be carried to the radio room and was there administered to by some of the crew. The navigator was hanging out of one of the gaping holes in the fuselage by his table next to the engine; despite a badly gashed elbow he somehow managed to pull himself back in. In the confusion the radio operator inadvertently opened his parachute in the radio room. Although two engines were out I still had control of the plane so I told all the crew not to bale out.
>
> We flew in the general direction of the Group and decided to let down to a more bearable altitude because at 29,000 feet the freezing air coming in through the open nose was too much to bear. In doing so we passed through two layers of cloud and to our surprise we were picked up by a friendly P-47 fighter who led us to his base at St Trond in Belgium. As we approached the airfield I told the engineer to shoot off flares and we made our landing. When we had completed our landing roll and I had shut down the engines, my navigator told me that there was a body on his table. It had no head, no arms and no legs. None of them felt like moving it. From a laundry tag on the under-shirt, we later found out that it was the radio operator from the other aircraft. When his plane broke in half our props had pulled him into our aircraft, decapitating him in the process. The ground medics removed the remains and then the base CO came out to us in his staff car. When I had explained what had happened,

he said we were all very lucky. The crew, including myself, went on to Brussels, which was near the base, and that night we all got drunk. After a few days we were picked up and returned to our base at Eye. When we got back to our barracks we found that all our bags had been packed as though we also had been lost on that raid; apparently nobody had been informed that we had, in fact, survived.

On Sunday 18 March a record 1,329 bombers bombed Berlin again. Twelve bombers were shot down, all claimed by Me 262 pilots who also claimed six more shot out of formation. The jet menace became such a problem that beginning on Wednesday 21 March, a series of raids were flown against airfields used by the Me 262s. The raids also coincided with the build up for the impending crossing of the Rhine by Allied troops. For four days the heavies bombed jet airfields and military installations. On 22 March 1,301 B-17s and B-24s bombed targets east of Frankfurt and ten military encampments in the Ruhr in preparation for the Allied amphibious crossing of the lower Rhine on 23/24 March. Twenty-seven Me 262s attacked the bomber formations and claimed thirteen B-17s shot down, but only one Fortress was actually lost. The next day 1,244 heavies bombed rail targets as part of the rail interdiction programme to isolate the Ruhr and cut off coal shipping. Since the loss of the Saar basin, the Ruhr was the only remaining source of supply for the German war machine. On 23/24 March, under a 66-mile long smoke screen and aided by 1,749 bombers, Field Marshal Bernard Montgomery's 21st Army Group crossed the Rhine in the north, while further south simultaneous crossings were made by General Patton's Third Army. Groups flew two missions on Saturday 24 March, hitting jet aircraft bases in Holland and Germany, while 240 B-24s, each loaded with 600 tons of medical supplies, food and weapons, dropped vital supplies to the armies in the field. Flying as low as 50 feet, the Liberators droned over the dropping zone at Wesel at 145 mph, using 10–15 degrees of flap to aid accuracy in the drop. Spasmodic and highly accurate small arms fire and 20 mm cannon fire brought down fourteen Liberators and 103 more returned with battle damage.

During March there were mixed fortunes for two pilots in Helton's Hellcats at Little Walden, where the group was based temporarily while the runways at Debach were being repaired. Lieutenant Donald J. Schmitt was reaching the end of his tour and on 27 March his son David was born. As soon as he heard of the birth he named his plane *SON OF A BLITZ*. On 30 March, the day Schmitt flew his twenty-seventh mission, Lieutenant Russell A. Goodspeed's crew taxied out for their first. After months of classes in gunnery school, weather prediction, aerodynamics and flight training, they hoped they were ready to do their part to help win the war, none more so than Lieutenant Roger D. Laib, the co-pilot.

Our crew sat together in the ready room with the other flight crews to be briefed on the day's mission. We heard the moans from everyone when the cover was removed from the map of the target – the submarine docks in Hamburg with 271 flak guns protecting the city. After take-off word was flashed to us to level out at 24,000 feet because of clouds over the target. When we turned at the IP I saw another squadron headed in the same direction to follow us over the target. On closer inspection, I noticed black smoke appearing beneath the planes. It must be the flak bursts I had seen in the newsreels. We felt our plane start to bounce around and knew flak was bursting beneath us. A big explosion shocked me into the realisation that we were hit. I saw the windshield crack and, looking to our wing, saw the prop of No. 4 engine slow to a halt and saw oil oozing from a hole in the wing. I switched my headphones from monitoring England to the intercom and heard lots of yelling. Goodspeed was trying to have me check for planes beneath us to salvo the bombs while he tried to feather the No. 4 propeller to reduce drag on the plane. The bombs were dropped but we were too late on the feathering procedure. The hydraulic oil had already frozen. Just then, the crankshaft broke and the propeller cocked at an angle and started rotating slowly. We hoped it would not cartwheel across the flight deck. As we looked around, our squadron was not in sight. We tried to maintain our altitude while Harold G. Teters, the navigator, plotted our way back to England – alone. As we flew over the island of Heligoland in the North Sea, we wondered whether fighters from the five German airfields there would come to shoot us down. Fortunately, our friendly P-47s and P-51s flew up to check us out periodically so we felt safer. Passing by Holland on our left, we saw the other planes headed back but well below us. Apparently, we were fighting a strong head wind. I walked through the empty bomb bay to the radio room to check the condition of the crew. They were all smiles and excitedly told me how lucky we were to have flown through the barrage and were able to fly home. Several had holes in their flight suits but none were hit by the shrapnel.

Debating whether or not to land at the emergency field at Woodbridge, the decision was made to try for our base at Little Walden. With the field in sight and all fuel warning lights blazing, Sergeant Harry N. Davis, the engineer, fired the rocket to inform the tower that the plane was damaged but no one was injured. Being so low on gas, we waited until well on the final approach before lowering the flaps. All the gunners were in the radio room in crash position so no one was up to check the flaps during extension. When the switch was activated, the right wing dropped and we thought that No. 3 engine had run out of gas but, in reality, the left flap moved into position and the right flap didn't. The wing-tip touched the ground and the plane broke in half at the trailing edge of the wing. The tail section remained upright and the front half of the plane skidded to a halt in the farmer's field upside down. Later investigation found that the flak explosion had cut the right flap cable. The four airmen in the radio room and the toggelier in the nose were killed instantly.[4]

Bomber crews were now hard pressed to find worthwhile targets and the planners switched attacks from inland targets to coastal areas. Beginning on 5 April, the weather over the continent improved dramatically and the Forts were despatched to U-boat pens on the Baltic coast. Everywhere, the Allies were victorious, but while the Germans kept on fighting, missions continued almost daily. Such was the Allied superiority, the bombers assembled over France on 5 April before flying in formation for an attack on the marshalling yards at Nürnburg. In Germany, the now frantic situation called for desperate measures to be taken against the all-powerful bomber streams and last ditch attempts were made by the *Luftwaffe* to try to stem the tide. One concept was to bring down American bombers by deliberately ramming them with converted Bf 109 fighters, called *Rammjäger*. Some 2,000 Germans volunteered for *Rammjäger* duty, but by the end of March only about 150 Bf 109s and 150–250 pilots were available for ramming. Such small numbers could never strike a crushing blow against the four-engined bomber force, but the ramming operation went ahead on 7 April with about 130 young and inexperienced pilots. The main targets for over 1,200 bombers were underground oil storage at Buchen, a munitions factory at Geesthacht near Hamburg and an Army depot at Gustrow. Many ramming pilots were intercepted and shot down by the American fighter screen and some others had technical problems and returned early to their bases. Even so, about twenty-five Bf 109s and a few Me 262s managed to break through the American fighter screen and twenty-two bombers were rammed. At least eight bombers were lost to *Rammkommando* Elbe fighters and another fifteen suffered damage from ramming Bf 109s, but were able to regain Allied occupied territory. The desperate ramming mission on 7 April was the *Luftwaffe*'s piston-engined swan song.

The end of the *Reich* was nigh. On 16 April General Spaatz ended strategic missions and only some tactical missions remained. On 17 April Dresden was bombed by almost a thousand bombers. Eight Forts, including six shot down by Me 262 jet fighters, and seventeen fighters were lost. On 25 April almost 600 Flying Forts and Liberators bombed the Skoda armaments factory at Pilsen in Czechoslovakia and four rail complexes surrounding Hitler's mountain retreat at Berchtesgarden respectively. Ten Me 262 jet fighters, fighting to the last, claimed seven Forts shot down. *Generalmajor* Adolf Galland, commanding one of the jet fighter wings said:

> We were convinced that nothing could be changed about the outcome of the war. The war was completely lost . . . we knew it could only last a few more days. On the other hand, we had the most advanced, far superior [jet] aircraft . . . having the best fighters in the world . . . we couldn't tell the people no . . . we won't take off any more because the war is lost. It was a moral question for us. We had to go into combat.

During the first week of May the German armies surrendered one by one to Montgomery at Lüneberg Heath, to Devers at Munich and to Alexander at Casserta and finally to Eisenhower at Rheims in the early hours of 7 May. Starting on 1 May, Fortress crews flew mercy missions, called *Chowhound*, to starving Dutch civilians in Holland,[5] until the end of hostilities, carrying food. During the winter of 1944–45 15,000 Dutch civilians had died of starvation. Some of the deaths had been caused by the Germans in revenge for the help Dutch railway workers had given the Allies at the time of the Arnhem operation. Agricultural land had been flooded as an anti-invasion measure and the invasion of Germany from the west had also left three and a half million Dutch in western Holland living in a virtual island fortress. Sergeant Harry E. Thatcher, in Lieutenant Harry Waggoner's crew in the 490th, whose last mission on Thursday 3 May was a food drop, recalled:

> We came in at 600 feet, low enough to see that the roofs of the buildings were jammed with people waving what seemed to be hundreds of flags. One man waved an American flag so big that I'm surprised it did not take him off the roof. Two German soldiers were riding down the street in a horse-drawn wagon; startled by the planes, the horse reared up and I can still see the fright on those soldiers' faces.

The sixth and final *Chowhound* mission was flown on 7 May, the day before VE (Victory in Europe) Day, when the 493rd dropped their last consignment of British rations over the airfield at Schiphol.

VE Day took place on 8 May. At Debach, Robert 'Gus' Gaustad, navigator in the Munday crew, recalls that on VE Day, '... in front of a neat and flower-bordered farmhouse not far from my hut, a small American flag was displayed, along with a large sign which read, "Thank You America!" I was moved to tears'.

Five days later a Victory Flypast was made over 'Widewing', the 8th Air Force headquarters at Bushy Park, where Lieutenant General James H. Doolittle and his staff were housed. About 1,400 bombers and fighters were scheduled to take part, but while the heavies were on course to Teddington, clouds moved in. Bad weather, the bane of American operations in England for the past four years, forced the formation of B-24s and B-17s down under the cloud layer and they followed the usual formation landing procedure to get back on the ground. Final honours, therefore, went to more than 700 American fighters, which flew over in wave after wave.

By the spring of 1945 the more than 300,000 men and women who served in the 8th Air Force from August 1942 vanished and only 30,000 remained by late October. Even they had their bags packed. Most of the American bomber airbases punctuating the British landscape had emptied. Some bases once had 250 dogs on base, but after the boys went home the dogs were either destroyed or adopted by English families. All that remained was a ghostly atmosphere; building doors left open, curtains blowing in the wind, forgotten ashes in the pot-bellied stoves, tattered *Yank* and *Esquire* magazines on the floor and once colourful pin-ups on walls without an appreciative audience anymore. Beneath a torn map of the United States with the signatures of fliers scrawled over their home states, a rickety chair and against another wall, an iron cot and a foot locker, which once had a water bucket on top of it for shaving. Roadways were deserted and hospitals empty; control towers and fire stations were vacant and runways where thousands of take-offs and landings had been made, disused. Nothing remained alive. There were massive 'graves' where motorcycles and bicycles had been flattened by a bulldozer and then buried. Schoolboys still visited old haunts where a few weeks earlier they had enjoyed coffee and eggs, but all was silent. There were no more songs from the theatre or over the intercom, no more oaths from crews, tired, disgusted and many times ill from the cold and high-altitude flying. Gone too, the sounds of engines warming up, the roar of take-offs, the squeal of landing wheels as they hit the runway after a long mission and that peculiar squeaking sound and the whisper as the engines were cut off and the bomber came to rest. The 'Yanks' would eventually return to kick over the traces of the places where many left their youth behind and hundreds of their companions never returned.

But for the time being, it was the end of a perfect friendship.

Notes

1. *Delectable Doris* and Lieutenant Robert W. Bonnar's crew FTR 3.2.45. Seven KIA. Two PoW.
2. Bad weather forced all except one 1st AD Fortress to return to England while over the North Sea.
3. 'We learned later that Down's crew had bombed a target of opportunity and then were subsequently hit by AA fire while attempting to leave the French coast near Calais. One of the waist gunners was injured and died before they could reach Manston.' Q. R. Wedgeworth.
4. Only the flight engineer, the navigator and Roger Laib survived. Goodspeed died 6 hours later. Donald Schmitt flew his thirty-fifth and final mission on 16.4.45.
5. Together with operation *Manna* by the RAF, which had begun on 29 April.

CHAPTER 9

The Ties That Bind
by Ben Smith

Clear warm sunshine flooded the silent field. Here, where thousands of take-offs and landings had been made, we found our reason for coming. Silent tribute was paid to hundreds of our companions who never returned. We were remembering the heavily loaded ships that crashed at the end of the runway on take-off, the exploding bombs, the clouds of black smoke; the crippled B-24s that had found their way home only to crash-land and burn. We remembered seeing our friends shot out of the sky over Germany – of the empty beds in those cold Nissen huts after a rough mission. Yes, we trembled inside. Grown men with hot tears burning our eyes. All those memories were fresh now.

Milton R. Stokes, pilot

During the war, the phrase 'The Yanks are overpaid, oversexed and over here' was current. It was such a neat phrase that unfortunately it gained much credence as a general complaint of the English people. I personally attest that, from my vantage point, Anglo-American relations were excellent. Despite the great inundation of men and machines, the extremely civilised English took it all in stride with great good nature. I was quite at home with these people. They were friendly, literate, and had beautiful manners, true even of the poorest folk. Everywhere I went I was treated with unflagging courtesy and respect. Over 25,000 English girls took American husbands during the war.

At the Red Cross in Cambridge, the lovely old university town, I got the name of an English family that entertained American fliers on weekends. Their name was Newman, and they lived in Royston, a town nearby. I was to spend many happy hours with them. Their home was a fine old Georgian mansion with lawn tennis courts, orchards, formal gardens, and beautiful groves of trees. These people were very kind to me. Each night my bed would be turned down. A glass of milk and a bowl of fruit were on the nightstand by my bed. Sometimes there would be a book of poetry or a magazine, too. They treated me like a son and I shall never forget them.

It was near the end of my tour that I obtained a three-day pass and first visited Cambridge. It was only about 20 miles from Molesworth. I fell in love with the place. Its fine old Gothic buildings, many of them dating from the thirteenth and fourteenth centuries, were deeply satisfying to me. I could not get enough of roaming its medieval streets. Everyone walked or rode bicycles; the streets were almost too winding and narrow for automobiles. Here the timbered veneers of Tudor England were very much in evidence. Some of the houses and inns were many centuries old. The University owned all the land thereabouts, and they did not countenance any of the tomfoolery called progress. They wanted Cambridge left just as it was, a decision I would have to applaud wholeheartedly.

The University was made up of a number of colleges, thirty-five to be exact; each had its own identity, such as Queen's College, Trinity College, St John's College, and the like.

I learned that in ancient times Cambridge had been a monastic establishment built in the fens of East Anglia. Eventually, it began to be a centre of learning. It was already a great university when it was visited by the great Erasmus, the foremost prophet of the Reformation. He came to Cambridge in 1500 and remained there at Queen's College for three years.

The finest of the medieval edifices was King's College Chapel, begun in 1446. With its inspired fan vaulting, it was the supreme example of the perpendicular Gothic. I had only a rather general understanding of the decorative vocabulary in those days, but there were many knowledgeable people about who were glad to explain these things to me.

The loveliest area of all was that part of the University called The Backs, where the tree-shaded lawns and gardens ran from the backs of the colleges down to the picturesque River Cam from which the town derived its name. I strolled along the grassy banks of the green river with its weeping willows and ancient stone bridges and thought to myself, 'This is the loveliest spot in the world'.

I happened upon a cricket match and was fascinated. The players were immaculate; it seemed a very antiseptic sport to me, but as I watched I could see that a lot of co-ordination and agility were being displayed. I never did fathom what was going on, despite a friendly bystander's attempts to tell me.

The Backs had once been marshes, but in the seventeenth century had been filled in by one of the distinguished alumni, Oliver Cromwell, the Great Protector, to become the beautiful garden spot that one now sees. I was told that a great summer fair had been held annually on the Commons in olden times. The Commons was a great grassy expanse near the River. Here, the stout English yeomen had come from every part of the Midlands and East Anglia to socialise, carouse, shoot their longbows in competition and vie with each other in feats of strength. Farmers, merchants, and artisans hawked their wares on all sides, drinking and wenching betimes. It was said that the fair was the model for Vanity Fair in Bunyan's *Pilgrim's Progress*. It was a lusty, brawling time. Now a hearty new breed had invaded the Commons. The Yanks were to be seen everywhere, intruding a jarring note upon the timeless, pastoral scene.

I wandered again along the banks of the Cam and saw an apple-cheeked underclassman [working class] poling a punt down the meandering stream. His passenger, an upperclassman, was eating an apple and reading a book. Being an American, I did not understand why the boatman was not rebelling at the supine role he was forced to play. This custom, which to me seemed an anachronism, had wide acceptance, going unchallenged by the underclassmen. But who knows what noble concepts had germinated in these verdant surroundings. Here, the young Tennyson might have dreamed dreams, which became *The Idylls of the King*, or the youthful Charles Darwin might have explored broad vistas of the intellect, which eventuated in the *Origin of Species*.

Since the Middle Ages, Cambridge had been a market town. Farmers from the surrounding country brought their vegetables and produce to the great open market place behind St Mary's Church. A lively place, it held great fascination for me, as I had never seen an open air market before.

What a delight to rest in an ancient inn, drinking the excellent light brown ale! While chatting convivially with the other customers, I exulted in a milieu of Jacobean tables and chairs, mullioned windows, exposed ceiling beams, rich dark oak wainscoting, an open-hearth stone fireplace, and, finally, church warden pipes on the wall, not added as a decorator's touch, but centuries old and once used by the patrons of the inn – a jewel of a setting for one who needed no such encouragement to drink. Had this genteel place once been the favourite haunt of Edmund Spenser or John Milton? Had the youthful Wordsworth and his friend Coleridge sat in these very chairs quenching their thirsts from the lovely old pewter tankards? I did not know, but I did not doubt it, for this was a place of poets.

The next morning I resumed my exploration of the old medieval town. In the narrow streets I saw the handsomest shops I had ever seen. I had a thing about bookstores and here was the oldest one in England, Bowes and Bowes, founded in 1581. Bookbinding had been a major craft in Cambridge for centuries, and the shop was a treasure-trove of handsome and rare volumes. Moving along, I was delighted to find a shop that had an amazing collection of jazz records. The proprietor told me that the college students and many of the professors not only loved jazz, but there were many connoisseurs of the idiom at the University. These were collector's items, some of which could not be found at home. I bought an album of a recording session by Louis Armstrong and Earl 'Father' Hines, featuring the venerable 'West End Blues' and 'Tight Like That'. This was really vintage jazz, and I was amazed to find it in this place. It only increased my esteem for the kind of people to be found hereabouts.

I had seen the genius of Sir Christopher Wren at St Paul's and St Mary-le-Bow's in London. I hadn't realised he was here also. The outstanding examples of his art in Cambridge were the magnificent Wren Library at Trinity College and the Emmanuel College Chapel. There were many quaint churches in the city. I was fond of poking and prowling about the graveyards. I was no necrophile, but the epitaphs on the tombstones were an unending source of delight to me. I sought out these places. They did not depress me. On the contrary, I rather fancied the idea of resting in one of these lovely old churchyards one day, for they did not seem like places of death to me, but rather fitting ambiences for departed spirits.

And now I began to understand why Cambridge held such fascination for me. I had been looking for a place like this all my life. I felt that I was part and parcel of this greatest outcropping of the human spirit. In those days I only dimly understood the great thirst of the spirit that was growing in me, but I sensed that, somehow, in this place was the repository of every value that I held near and dear. My very soul sped across the centuries to unite with the antique refrain of the old medieval town.

In desperation, I began to think of ways that I could manage to stay here. It seemed logical that every human being should be in a place where he was contented and happy and safe. I was in such a place. Here in this green Eden, was peace and sanctuary. About 20 miles away the apparatus of death and terror was in ceaseless operation, but now it seemed to have nothing to do with me. I did not want to be wasted just as I had begun to catch a vision. I knew that I belonged here. The other Americans did not care about this place, but I did. So my mind raced – was there a way? In the end I knew it was no good – I had to go back to Molesworth and finish the other business, one way or the other. It would have been better had I never come to Cambridge. Sadly, I turned my back on the place and boarded the bus.

The villagers near the air bases quickly adopted the American fliers as their own. The Yanks visited their homes, shops and churches and became a part of village life. Each day the villagers anxiously awaited the return of the mission in the afternoons, counting the planes in the formation just as we did.

While we were recuperating I visited a lot of nearby towns and villages. Kimbolton was nearby and Thrapston, too. These picturesque villages with thatch-roofed cottages were a delight to me. I was fond of the dignified, sturdy villagers, who were friendly and hospitable once I learned a few 'ice breakers'.

Our base was in a lovely section of England on the perimeter of what is usually referred to as the Midlands. The countryside was unbelievably green and rolling. Many stately groves of trees ringed the base, and I was fond of taking long walks and bicycle rides in the countryside. I loved this verdant country. Somehow, I had the feeling that I had been here in another life. I knew that my roots were here – that my people had all come from England in earlier times. Anyone with a passion for literature could not help being in love with this lovely pastoral land. Beginning with *Mother Goose*, this land had shaped my life from childhood on. I knew it intimately from my books. So I bicycled constantly over hill and down dale, rejoicing in the lush greenery of Huntingdonshire. The war seemed far away.

The English had been cultivating the same farms for thousands of years, but they were still fertile and productive. These people had a deep reverence for the land; they did not exploit it. The farmhouses were quaint and attractive with flower beds and rose gardens in profusion. One never saw a bad piece of landscaping. It had been going on for centuries, just getting better and better. A cottage would be set down in the perfect place, every tree and every shrub in proper place and scale. Yet it was not a studied effect at all, but completely artless and charming.

I could almost believe someone was arranging these things for my personal delight. Bicycling around a bend, I would see a chuckling brook spanned by an arched stone bridge, then a hedgerow with a stile over it, then a little farther an antique haywain parked in an orchard. Every foot of this land was steeped in history. Near our base there was an old Saxon church, St Swithin's. It was a thousand years old and still being used for worship. There were many such churches scattered throughout this part of England. The parish church in Kimbolton was registered in the Domesday Book, the census ordered by William the Conqueror in 1085. Catherine of Aragon spent the final years of her exile in nearby Kimbolton Castle. This was the country of John Bunyan, the great Puritan preacher. He had preached in all the glades and hamlets hereabouts and had written his great allegory *Pilgrim's Progress* in Bedford Gaol only a few miles away.

At that time I had a passion for the English landscape painter, John Constable. Constable has been able to capture the beauty of the English landscape as no other artist has. His paintings do not exaggerate. There are still many areas in England where these lush landscapes may be seen. Curiously enough, I never felt depression here. As soon as I was away from the base and out in the countryside, I was transported to another realm.

I was quite taken with the country inns and pubs and never intentionally passed one by. These were venerable institutions, nothing like saloons. They were homey places, family-oriented. Misbehaviour was not tolerated in them. I eventually learned to appreciate the English ale and beer, served unchilled, and came to prefer them to the American, probably because they were much more potent. Their lager was phenomenally good. All of it had much more of a malt taste than our own.

There was always a plink-plank piano and the Limeys and Yanks liked to gather around it and sing the old First World War songs: 'Long, Long Trail', 'Tipperary' and 'Pack Up Your Troubles'. 'Roll Out the Barrel' was a standard, but the most popular of all was 'Roll Me Over in the Clover'. At least three or four times an evening there would be bawdy renditions of it. The Yanks were as fond of it as the British. There were at least a hundred verses, each describing more graphically a new violation of the unfortunate lassie, the heroine of the song.

These were the best times of all to me. I loved to sing and I loved to drink. I remember the blazing logs and the hearty camaraderie of these places. It was not difficult to believe that I was set down in the time of Dickens, for these places had in no way changed from those times. Many of them were hundreds of years old.

Many of my friends felt that the English were a backward people, slow to accept changes and new ideas. This was precisely what I liked about them. I was a traditionalist; so were they. They held on tenaciously to their enduring monuments. The British had a sense of history and were fully aware of the greatness of their past. They did not demolish old churches and other historic landmarks to make way for junk food places, gas stations, and other forms of visual pollution. This was all to the good as far as I was concerned. They did not compromise with the quality of life in this respect and I hoped they never would.

Some of our people were quite vocal in their criticism of English institutions; and I for one, was greatly embarrassed when it occurred in my presence. I was quick to apologise for the rudeness of my countrymen. The English merely ignored these few loudmouths. They never attempted to defend their customs and way of life; indeed, they had no need to as far as I was concerned. I think it is significant that in our own country when we want to give something a touch of class, we give it an English name.

In the parish church at Kimbolton, there is a touching tribute to the American visitors. At the altar there is a leather-bound volume, dedicated to the memory of the American airmen stationed at Kimbolton who lost their lives during the war. In careful script the name and rank of each dead airman is entered on the pages of the book. Sad to say, the entries were many. These were the men of the 91st and 379th Heavy Bombardment Groups.

At the old Saxon church at Quidenham in Norfolk, there is a magnificent stained glass window, which was dedicated as a memorial to the airmen of the 96th Bomb Group, stationed at nearby Snetterton-Heath. It depicts an American airman in flight uniform looking at the ascended Christ, a glorious and appropriate tribute to our comrades who fell.

The following incident shows the bond that bound the English and Americans together. In the summer of 1944, a young man named Staff Sergeant Bill Brockmeyer was flight engineer on a B-17 crew of the 92nd Bomb Group, stationed at Podington. On their first mission as they became airborne, they suddenly lost altitude and crashed into a wood at the end of the runway. A young farmer named Walter Nottage was working in the wood and ran to the crash site. There, he saw Brockmeyer, the only survivor, walking around in the wreckage, dazed, his clothes on fire. Nottage dashed into the flames, scooped up the young American flier and ran with him. He kept going until he was some distance from the crash, and luckily so; the bombs began to explode.

In August 1977, through English friends in an association called Friends of the Eighth, we located Nottage! A group of us, Brockmeyer included, went over to see him. He had no idea what we wanted with him. Bill introduced himself, related the incident, and told the now middle-aged Englishman that he was the living proof of this heroic feat. The two men, overcome with emotion, embraced and stood in silence for a long moment thinking of that fateful day in the long ago.

These poignant instances underscore the nature of the Anglo-American relations far better than the trite phrase 'Overpaid, oversexed, and over here'.

Glossary

A Bag	barracks bag
a/c	aircraft
AA	anti-aircraft
AAA	anti-aircraft artillery
Abschuss	claim for a victory in air combat
Abschussbeteiligung	contribution to a claim for a victory in air-combat
Abschusse	claims for victories in air combat
AF	Air Force
AFCE	Automatic Flight Control Equipment
AI	Airborne Interception (radar)
Alarmstart	'Scramble'
Anerkannter Abschuss	officially confirmed air-combat victory claim
ASR	Air-Sea Rescue
BBC	British Broadcasting Corporation
BG	Bomb Group
Big friend	bomber
Big-B	Berlin
Bird Colonel	full colonel
bitch	to complain
BM	*Bordmechaniker* (flight engineer) (German)
bogey	unidentified aircraft
Bordfunker or *Funker*	German radar/radio operator
BS	Bomb Squadron
buzz job	'attack' base, etc., at very low level
CAVU	ceiling and visibility unlimited
chaff	window
chow hound	GI who likes to eat
chow line	mess queue
chug-a-lug	drink vast quantities of beer
CO	commanding officer
CoG	centre of gravity
cr.	crashed
Dear John	a letter from a girl back home saying she's found someone else
Deutsches Kreuz (DK)	German Cross
'Dicke Autos'	'Fat Cars' (four-engined heavy bombers)
DFC	Distinguished Flying Cross
dogface	infantry soldier
e/a	enemy aircraft
Eichenlaub (El)	(Knight's Cross with) Oak Leaves

241

Einsatz	operational flight
Eisernes Kreuz I, II (EK I, EK II)	Iron Cross (1st and 2nd Class)
ETA	Estimated time of arrival
ETO	European Theatre of Operations
Experte(n)	expert, an ace/aces (five or more confirmed victories)
Express-Express	German R/T code for 'hurry up'
Fähnrich (Fhr)	Flight Sergeant
feather merchant	loafer, lazy individual
Feindberührung	contact with an enemy aircraft
Feldwebel (Fw)	German rank equivalent to sergeant
First John	first lieutenant
flak (*Flieger Abwehr Kanone(n)*)	anti-aircraft artillery
flak alley	heavily defended bomb run
flak happy	state of victim of combat fatigue
flak house	rest home
flak shack	rest home
FTR	Failed to return
Führer	Leader
funny money	pounds sterling
furlough	leave
Gee	British navigational device
General der Flieger	German rank equivalent to Air Marshal
Generalfeldmarschall	German rank equivalent to Marshal of the Air Force
Generalleutnant	German rank equivalent to Air Vice-Marshal
Generalmajor	German rank equivalent to Air Commodore
Generaloberst	German rank equivalent to Air Chief Marshal
Geschwader	Roughly equivalent to three RAF wings. Comprises three or four *Gruppen Gruppe* containing three or four *Staffeln*, eg: IV./NJG1 (the fourth *Gruppe* in *Nachtjagd Geschwader* 1), 12./NJG1 (the 12th *Staffel* (in the fourth *Gruppe*) of *Nachtjagd Geschwader* 1)
GI	Government Issue, American fighting man
GIs	diarrhoea
GP	General Purpose bomb
greenhorn	inexperienced flyer
Gruppenkommandeur	Commander or Captain, a *Gruppe* command position rather than a rank
'heavies'	four-engined bombers
H_2S	British 10 cm experimental airborne radar navigational and target location aid
Happy Valley	Ruhr Valley
Hauptmann (Hptm)	German rank equivalent to Flight Lieutenant

242

HE	High Explosive (bomb)
HEI	High Explosive Incendiary
Herausschuss	claim for a bomber shot out of formation
Holy Joe	chaplain
Horrido!	German for 'Tallyho'
hot crock	garbage, nonsense, untruth
IAS	Indicated air speed
IFF	Identification friend or foe
IO	Intelligence Officer
IP	Initial point at the start of the bomb run
iron ass	hard, demanding, tough officer
Jagdbomber (Jabo)	fighter-bomber
Jagdgeschwader (JO)	fighter wing, includes three or four *Gruppen*
Jagdwaffe	fighter arm or fighter force
Jager	fighter
Jägerleitoffizier	JLO or GCI-controller
Jug	short for Juggernaut, P-47 Thunderbolt
Junior Birdman	inexperienced pilot
Kampfgeschwader (KG)	Bomber Group
KIA	Killed in action
Kommandeur	Commanding Officer of a *Gruppe*
Kommodore	Commodore or Captain, a *Geschwader* command position rather than a rank
Kurier	R/T code for 'Allied heavy bomber'
latrine rumour	unfounded rumour
Leutnant (Lt)	German rank equivalent to Pilot Officer
liberty run	night off into town
Lichtenstein	early form of German AI radar
light colonel	lieutenant colonel
little friend	fighter aircraft
looie	lieutenant
LORAN	Long-range navigation
lucky bastard	one who has completed his tour of missions (and given a certificate for The Lucky Bastards Club)
Lufberry	fighter manoeuvre
Luftflotte	Air Fleet (German)
Luftwaffe (LW)	Air Force
Major	(German) rank equivalent to Squadron Leader
Maschinen Gewehr (MG)	machine-gun
Maschinen Kanone (MK)	machine cannon
milk run	easy mission
Nachtjagdgeschwader (NJG)	Night fighter Group
Nachtjäger	nightfighter
NCO	Non-Commissioned Officer
NFS	Night Fighter Squadron

Noball	Flying bomb (V-1) or rocket (V-2) site
Non-com	NCO
Oberfähnrich (Ofhr)	German rank equivalent to Warrant Officer
Oberfeldwebel (Ofw)	German rank equivalent to Flight Sergeant
Oberleutnant (Oblt)	German rank equivalent to Flying Officer
Oberst (Obst)	Group Captain
Oberstleutnant (Obstlt)	German rank equivalent to Wing Commander
over the hill	absent without leave
Pauke! Pauke!	'Kettledrum! Kettledrum!' (R/T code for 'Going into attack!')
PFC	poor fucking civilian or private first class
Piccadilly commando	prostitute
pill roller	medic
POM	Preparation for overseas movement
poop	information
PoW	Prisoner of war
PR	Photographic reconnaissance
prop wash	air disturbed by preceding planes
pubbing mission	pub crawl
PX	Post exchange – military shop
R/T	Radio telephony
RCM	Radio counter measures
red-lined	cancelled
Reflex Visier (Revi)	gun sight
Reichs(luft)verteidigung	Air Defence of Germany
Reichsluftfahrtministerium (RLM)	German Air Ministry
re-tread	old officer recalled to active service
Ritterkreuz (träger) (RK/RKT)	Knight's Cross (holder)
Rotte	tactical element of two aircraft
Rottenflieger	wingman, the second man in the *Rotte*
RP	rocket projectile
sack time	bedtime, sleep
sack	bed
Schlachtgeschwader (SG)	ground attack group
Schwarm	flight of four aircraft
Schwarmführer	flight leader
Schwerten (S)	(Knight's Cross with Oak Leaves and) Swords
scrubbed	cancelled
second John	second lieutenant
Section Eight	discharge given for mental breakdown, insantity etc.
shack job	easy woman
shack up	sleep with woman
short snorter	a bill of currency autographed to prove one had been in that country

shortarm	VD inspection
shuttle	long bombing mission via stop en route
sky pilot	chaplain
SNAFU	Situation normal all fucked up
snowdrop	military policeman, so-called because of his white helmet
Stab	Staff flight
Staffel	roughly equivalent to a squadron, designated sequentially within the *Geschwader* by Arabic figures, e.g. 4./NJG1
Staffelkapitän (St.Kpt)	Captain, a *Staffel* command position rather than a rank
tour	series of missions
TS	Tough Slit
UEA	Unidentified enemy aircraft
UHF	Ultra-high frequency
Unteroffizier (Uffz)	Corporal
USAAF	United States Army Air Force
VHF	Very-high frequency
Viermot (4-mot)	four-engined bomber abbreviation of *viermotorig* – four engined
V-Mail	a letter greeting card written on a special form; they were photographed on microfilm, flown to the States and delivered
WAAF	Women's Auxiliary Air Force
WIA	Wounded in action
Window	metal foil strips dropped by bombers to confuse German radar
Wolfpack	fighter outfit
Y-Service	*Ypsilon, Y-Verfahren, Ypsilonverfahren*: *Luftwaffe* ground-controlled navigation by means of VHF
Zerstörer	'Destroyer', heavy twin-engined fighter-bomber aircraft (Bf 110/210/410)
ZI	Zone of the Interior (USA)
zoot suit	flying suit
Zweimot	twin-engined aircraft

Index